LABOR RELATIONS AND PUBLIC POLICY SERIES

No. 30

CONFLICTS BETWEEN LABOR LEGISLATION AND BANKRUPTCY LAW

by

THOMAS R. HAGGARD
and
MARK S. PULLIAM

INDUSTRIAL RESEARCH UNIT

The Wharton School, Vance Hall
University of Pennsylvania
Philadelphia, Pennsylvania 19104-6358

Library of Congress Catalog Card Number 86–083223
Manufactured in the United States of America

ISBN: 0-89546-064-5
ISSN: 0075-7470

Foreword

In 1968, the Industrial Research Unit inaugurated its Labor Relations and Public Policy Series as a means of examining issues and stimulating discussions in the complex and controversial areas of collective bargaining and the regulation of labor-management disputes. Thus far, twenty-nine monographs have been published in this series. Eleven of these deal with various policies and procedures of the National Labor Relations Board. The other eighteen cover such significant issues as collective bargaining in the 1970s; welfare and strikes; opening the skilled construction trades to blacks; the Davis-Bacon Act; the labor-management situation in urban school systems; old age, handicapped, and Vietnam-era antidiscrimination legislation; the impact of the Occupational Safety and Health Act; the Landrum-Griffin Act; the effects of the AT&T–EEO consent decree; unions' rights to company information; employee relations and regulation; operating during strikes; union violence and the law; the impact of antitrust legislation on employee relations; prevailing wage legislation; and comparable worth theory and practice.

This study, *Conflicts Between Labor Legislation and Bankruptcy Law,* No. 30 in the Labor Relations and Public Policy Series, is the first thorough analysis of the relationship of these two sets of legislation. The study had its genesis as it became apparent during the severe recession of the early 1980s that bankruptcies were becoming more common, and that high labor costs institutionalized in union agreements were under great pressure. Litigation was then underway to determine both the rights of parties and the power of bankruptcy courts to modify or to abrogate union agreements in bankruptcy situations. Later, of course, Congress enacted legislation on the subject. The authors examine the law as it has developed and consider the relationship to bankruptcy legislation of the Norris-La Guardia Act, the National Labor Relations (Taft-Hartley) Act, the Employee Retirement Income Security Act (ERISA), and various other laws and labor relations activities. This comprehensive treatment ensures that anyone seeking information concerning the relationship or conflict between bankruptcy law and labor legislation must consult this book.

The study was begun by Professor Thomas R. Haggard, University of South Carolina Law School. Professor Haggard, who received both his undergraduate and law degrees from the University of Texas, is the distinguished author of numerous law journal articles as well as author of *Compulsory Unionism, the NLRB and the Courts,* (1977), No. 15 in the Labor Relations and Public Policy Series, and co-author of *Union Violence: The Record and the Response of the Courts, Legislation, and the NLRB* (1985), No. 25 in this same series. As Professor Haggard progressed with the research, he became convinced that a co-author more versed in bankruptcy as well as labor law was required. Fortunately, Mark S. Pulliam, Esq., a principal in the San Diego, California, office of Latham & Watkins, who also received his law degree from the University of Texas, offered his services and the law firm generously contributed his not inconsiderable time. Mr. Pulliam had previously authored several articles on aspects of the bankruptcy issue, and was therefore already well versed on the subject.

As the study progressed, several articles were published. We are grateful to the journals listed on the page following the Foreword for the privilege of reprinting materials from these articles which are copyrighted by the authors. Mr. Pulliam wishes to thank his colleague John S. Welch for helpful comments and the patience and cooperation of Latham & Watkins for allowing him to pursue the project.

The manuscript was edited by Kathryn Pearcy, Chief Editor of the Wharton Industrial Research Unit; she also constructed the case index. Mrs. Marthenia Perrin, the Unit's Business Manager, supervised the administrative aspects of the project.

The initial research was funded by the generous grant of the J. Howard Pew Freedom Trust in support of the Labor Relations and Public Policy Series. The interest in our work by Fred H. Billups, Jr., Vice President and Executive Director, the Pew Trusts, Dr. John W. Gould, Vice-President, James McGann, Senior Program Associate, and Robert G. Dunlop, Member, Board of Directors, as well as the staff of the Glenmede Trust Company, which administers the Pew Foundations, is most heartening and much appreciated. Later research and publication were funded by the unrestricted membership fees of the Wharton Industrial Research Unit's industry Research Advisory Group.

As in all works published by the Wharton Industrial Research Unit, the authors are solely responsible for the research and for all opinions expressed, none of which should be attributed to the grantors or to the University of Pennsylvania.

HERBERT R. NORTHRUP, *Director*
Industrial Research Unit
The Wharton School
University of Pennsylvania

Philadelphia
April 1987

Acknowledgements

Material from the following published articles has been utilized in this book by permission.

By Thomas R. Haggard:

"The Appointment of Union Representatives to Creditors' Committees Under Chapter 11 of the Bankruptcy Code," *South Carolina Law Review,* Vol. 35, No. 4 (Summer 1984), pp. 517–539.

"The Power of Bankruptcy Courts to Enjoin Strikes Resolving the Apparent Conflict Between the Bankruptcy Code and the Anti-Injunction Provisions of the Norris-La Guardia Act," *The George Washington Law Review,* Vol. 53, No. 5 (August 1985), pp. 703–740.

"Labor Arbitration and Bankruptcy: A Trek into the Serbonian Bog," *Loyola University of Chicago Law Journal,* Vol. 17 (Winter 1986), pp. 171–202.

"The Continuing Conflict Between Bankruptcy and Labor Law—The Issues that *Bildisco* and the 1984 Bankruptcy Amendment Did Not Resolve," *Brigham Young University Law Review,* Vol. 1986 (No. 1, 1986), pp. 1–54.

By Mark S. Pulliam:

"The Collision of Labor and Bankruptcy Law: *Bildisco* and the Legislative Response," *Labor Law Journal,* Vol. 36 (July 1985), pp. 390–401.

"Bankruptcy Status of Employee Compensation and Benefits Claims," *Employee Relations Law Journal,* Vol. 12, No. 2 (Fall 1986), pp. 221–240.

TABLE OF CONTENTS

PART ONE

Introduction

CHAPTER I

Introduction

Labor law and bankruptcy law have in common only that they are comprehensive bodies of federal law. Labor law, or more specifically the system of collective bargaining between employers and labor unions, consists of a relatively short, general, and stable federal statute,[1] supplemented by a larger, more specific, and ever-changing backdrop of decisions by the National Labor Relations Board (NLRB),[2] the federal courts of appeals, and the United States Supreme Court.[3] The published decisions of arbitrators interpreting particular collective bargaining agreements comprise yet another layer of federally sanctioned authority in the field of labor law.[4] Collective bargaining is a comparatively recent phenomenon in the United States, having been created by Congress in 1935[5] pursuant to its authority to regulate interstate commerce.[6]

Bankruptcy law, in contrast, consists of a complex and comprehensive scheme of federal legislation[7] that has existed, in widely varying forms, since 1800.[8] The Constitution expressly authorizes Congress to enact "uniform Laws on the subject of Bankruptcies throughout the United States."[9] Federal courts, including specialized bankruptcy courts, interpret these statutes as necessary in the

---

[1] The National Labor Relations Act (NLRA), enacted as the Wagner Act in 1935 and amended by the Taft-Hartley Act in 1947 and the Landrum-Griffin Act in 1957, is codified at 29 U.S.C. §§ 151 *et seq.*

[2] The National Labor Relations Board was created by the NLRA. *See* 29 U.S.C. § 153.

[3] The NLRA grants the federal courts of appeals jurisdiction to review the NLRB's final orders. *See* 29 U.S.C. § 160(f). The Supreme Court may review decisions of the courts of appeals. *See* 28 U.S.C. § 1254.

[4] *See* Textile Workers Union v. Lincoln Mills of Alabama, 353 U.S. 448 (1957); United Steelworkers of America v. American Mfg. Co., 363 U.S. 564 (1960); United Steelworkers of America v. Warrior & Gulf Navigation Co., 363 U.S. 574 (1960); United Steelworkers of America v. Enterprise Wheel & Car Corp., 363 U.S. 593 (1960).

[5] 49 Stat. 449 (1935).

[6] NLRB v. Jones & Laughlin Steel Corp., 301 U.S. 1 (1937).

[7] The Bankruptcy Reform Act of 1978, as amended, is codified at 11 U.S.C. §§ 101 *et seq.*

[8] *See* Act of April 4, 1800, ch. 19, 2 Stat. 19, *repealed by* Act of Dec. 19, 1803, ch. 6, 2 Stat. 248.

[9] U.S. Const., art. I, § 8, cl. 4.

adjudication of bankruptcy cases, but in most instances the courts simply apply statutory provisions to disputed facts. The Bankruptcy Reform Act of 1978 (Code), unlike the National Labor Relations Act (NLRA), is not a statement of general concepts to be filled in by an administrative agency. The Code is, rather, an enormously specific and technical statute with abundant legislative history. Perhaps because of its specificity and historical background, bankruptcy law has undergone a number of significant revisions.[10]

Both labor and bankruptcy law seek uniformity of application. For this reason they are creatures of federal law, which overrides the potentially conflicting laws of the 50 states. Moreover, the NLRB has *exclusive* jurisdiction over cases involving unfair labor practices,[11] subject only to appellate review by the courts of appeals. The bankruptcy law seeks uniformity through its comprehensive scheme of legislation, which treats all persons within a particular classification alike. The goal of uniformity is also served by having bankruptcy cases decided, in the first instance, by specialized federal courts which handle only such cases and which have plenary authority over all claims against the debtor's estate.

The principal goals of labor law, in short, are to protect employees' rights to engage in (or refrain from) union activities,[12] including the majority's right to select a union as the exclusive bargaining representative[13] of an appropriate unit of employees;[14] to require employers to bargain in good faith with (but not to agree with) the authorized representative of its employees before acting unilaterally on many (but not all) subjects affecting employees;[15] to enforce agreements between employers and unions reached as a result of collective bargaining negotiations,[16] including the private arbitration of disputes pertaining to the contract, if the parties have so agreed; to prohibit and remedy unfair labor practices by employers

---

[10] "Congress enacted comprehensive bankruptcy laws in 1800, 1841, 1867, 1898, and 1938 to grant relief to debtors and to provide for adjustment of creditors' rights in the wake of severe economic depressions. The first two statutes lasted less than four years." Kennedy, *Creative Bankruptcy? Use and Abuse of the Bankruptcy Law—Reflections on Some Recent Cases,* 71 Iowa L. Rev. 199, 199 (1985) (footnotes omitted).

[11] 29 U.S.C. § 160(b).

[12] 29 U.S.C. § 157.

[13] 29 U.S.C. §§ 158(d), 159(a).

[14] 29 U.S.C. § 159(b); *see* J. Abodeely, R. Hammer & A. Sandler, The NLRB and the Appropriate Bargaining Unit (1981).

[15] 29 U.S.C. §§ 158(a)(5), 158(d); *see* P. Miscimarra, The NLRB and Managerial Discretion: Plant Closings, Relocations, Subcontracting, and Automation (1983).

[16] *See* 29 U.S.C. § 185.

and unions;[17] and generally to disfavor strikes and favor negotiation as a means of resolving labor disputes.[18] The primacy of the NLRB is subject to the qualification that Congress has vested the federal district courts with jurisdiction over suits for violation of a collective bargaining agreement.[19] Congress has also sharply limited the federal courts' jurisdiction to issue injunctions in labor disputes.[20]

The goals of bankruptcy law are two-fold. "The original and still significant objective of bankruptcy laws is to provide for the orderly liquidation of a financially distressed debtor's estate and the equitable distribution of the proceeds. A second, and for most debtors the dominant objective of the country's bankruptcy laws, is to provide the debtor a fresh start by relieving the debtor of the burden of oppressive debt and facilitating rehabilitation."[21] An essential element in the rehabilitation or reorganization of a debtor is the ability to discharge existing obligations, both accrued debts and executory contracts, so that the reorganized debtor can attract customers and credit.[22] The bankruptcy goal of reorganization, as opposed to liquidation, has existed since 1933[23] and is now contained in Chapter 11 of the Code.[24] "The premise of a business reorganization is that assets that are used for production in the industry for which they were designed are more valuable than those same assets sold for scrap."[25] To this end, a Chapter 11 debtor is entitled to reject (with certain exceptions) any executory contract or unexpired lease to which it is a party,[26] and is automatically shielded from all acts or proceedings to collect, assess, or recover any claims that arose before the debtor's Chapter 11 petition was filed.[27]

The interaction between labor and bankruptcy law has developed almost exclusively in the context of unionized employers undergoing reorganization in Chapter 11. When a company which is a party to a collective bargaining agreement files a petition for reorganization under Chapter 11, the goals and policies of labor and bankruptcy law seem to collide. Labor law generally favors stability of the

---

[17] *See* J. Hunsicker, J. Kane & P. Walther, NLRB Remedies for Unfair Labor Practices (revised edition, 1986).

[18] 29 U.S.C. § 141.

[19] 29 U.S.C. § 185.

[20] 29 U.S.C. §§ 101–115.

[21] Kennedy, *supra* note 10, at 210 (footnotes omitted).

[22] *Id.*

[23] *Id.*

[24] 11 U.S.C. §§ 1101 *et seq.*

[25] H. R. Rep. 595, 95th Cong., 1st Sess., 220 (1977), *reprinted in* 1978 U.S. Code Cong. & Admin. News 5963, 6179.

[26] 11 U.S.C. § 365(a).

[27] 11 U.S.C. § 362(a).

collective-bargaining relationship and generally disfavors unilateral actions by employers. Bankruptcy law, on the other hand, often contemplates a radical alteration of existing business relationships and permits changes whether other affected parties consent or not. Whereas labor law attempts to strike a somewhat neutral balance between the rights of employers and the rights of employees, bankruptcy unquestionably favors debtors over creditors. And although labor law affords unions certain privileges and immunities that are not enjoyed by others in the business community, bankruptcy law generally disfavors the special or unequal treatment of creditors.

It is not surprising that these apparently conflicting viewpoints have engendered a myriad of specific bankruptcy / labor law issues: Under what circumstances can a debtor-employer reject a collective bargaining agreement? What bargaining obligations, if any, does a Chapter 11 debtor continue to have under the labor statute? Is a purchaser of the assets of a bankrupt estate bound by the labor law obligations of the debtor-employer? If both the bankruptcy court and the NLRB claim jurisdiction over a particular dispute, how is that to be resolved? What authority does a labor arbitrator have to resolve contract claims against a debtor-employer? Can the bankruptcy court enjoin strikes? And in general, what rights do employees and unions have as creditors in bankruptcy proceedings?

Some bankruptcy / labor law conflicts are more apparent than real, for these can be satisfactorily resolved by reference to the underlying and, indeed, often complementary policies of the two statutes. This is not to say that the courts and the NLRB have always resolved them in that fashion; it is merely to say that they could have, and this study will demonstrate how.

Other bankruptcy / labor law conflicts do not yield so easily. It is the thesis of this study, however, that in order to promote the overriding goal of facilitating the reorganization of financially distressed companies and thus serve the long-term interests of debtor-employers, employees, unions, creditors, and society alike, the comprehensive system of bankruptcy law should generally prevail over any conflicting provisions of labor law.

PART TWO

CHAPTER II

Rejection of Collective Bargaining Attempts[1]

The primary purpose of the Bankruptcy Amendments and Federal Judgeship Act of 1984 (BAFJA),[2] signed into law by President Reagan on July 10, 1984, was to resolve the jurisdictional crisis created by *Northern Pipeline Construction Co. v. Marathon Pipe Line Co.*[3] In *Marathon Pipe Line,* decided on June 28, 1982, the Supreme Court had declared unconstitutional Congress's broad grant of jurisdiction to Article I bankruptcy judges in the Bankruptcy Reform Act of 1978 (Code)[4] because Congress failed to confer on bankruptcy judges the life tenure and salary guarantees of Article III judges.[5] In apparent recognition of the chaos its decision could create, the Supreme Court applied its holding prospectively only and twice stayed its judgment pending congressional enactment of remedial legislation.[6]

After *Marathon Pipe Line,* the bankruptcy courts functioned under interim Judicial Conference rules until June 27, 1984, when the deadline for reform legislation finally expired, despite four extensions.[7] During the ensuing two-week hiatus, the bankruptcy

[1] Portions of this chapter originally appeared in Pulliam, *The Collision of Labor and Bankruptcy Law: Bildisco and the Legislative Response,* 36 Labor L. J. 390 (1985); Haggard, *The Continuing Conflict Between Bankruptcy and Labor Law—The Issues that Bildisco and the 1984 Bankruptcy Amendments Did Not Resolve,* 1986 Brigham Young L. Rev. 1; Pulliam, *The Rejection of Collective Bargaining Agreements Under Section 365 of the Bankruptcy Code,* 58 Am. Bankr. L. J. 1 (1984).

[2] Pub. L. No. 98-352, 98 Stat. 333 (1984).

[3] 458 U.S. 50 (1982).

[4] Pub. L. No. 95-598, 92 Stat. 2549 (1978). The Code became effective October 1, 1979.

[5] *See generally In re* Benney, 44 Bankr. 581, 584–86 (Bankr. N. D. Cal. 1984); R. DeMascio, W. Norton & R. Lieb, Fourteen Years or Life: The Bankruptcy Court in Dilemma (1983).

[6] *See* Marathon Pipe Line, *supra,* 458 U.S. at 88 (staying judgment until October 4, 1982 to "afford Congress an opportunity to reconstitute the bankruptcy courts or to adopt other valid means of adjudication, without impairing the interim administration of the bankruptcy laws."); Northern Pipeline Construction Co. v. Marathon Pipe Line Co., 459 U.S. 813 (1982) (extending the stay of judgment until "to and including December 24, 1982").

[7] See chapter IV, *infra.*

courts suspended operations while Congress hurriedly hammered out new legislation. "When Congress was working on the changes, it was pressured by many different lobbying groups," according to the *American Bar Association Journal.*[8] Bankruptcy expert Professor Lawrence King observed that "The consumer credit industry, shopping center owners, farmers, fishermen, unions, the securities industry, and trial lawyers all put in their two cents."[9] The resulting legislation, Professor King stated, was "one of the sloppiest jobs Congress has ever done enacting a law," and the BAFJA was "not a matter of public policy but of who had the loudest voice and the greatest pull."[10]

Title I of the BAFJA resolved the *Marathon Pipe Line* problem by conferring on the federal district courts original and exclusive jurisdiction of all bankruptcy cases. The bankruptcy courts now serve as a unit of the district courts, and bankruptcy judges are now appointed by the courts of appeals to fourteen-year terms. This aspect of the 1984 BAFJA legislation, however, is but a small part of the package Congress enacted. "The Title III amendments significantly revised many of the substantive provisions of the 1978 Bankruptcy Reform Act."[11]

One of the most significant changes was Congress's addition of section 1113, which altered the existing provisions of the Code dealing with rejection of collective bargaining agreements by an employer undergoing a Chapter 11 reorganization. Section 1113 was motivated by the Supreme Court's interpretation of section 365 of the Code in *NLRB v. Bildisco & Bildisco.*[12]

In order to put section 1113 in perspective, this chapter will analyze the judicial authorities prior to the *Bildisco* decision. Chapter III will review the majority and dissenting opinions in *Bildisco.* Chapter IV will evaluate the impact of section 1113 on existing law by analyzing its legislative history and the judicial decisions applying it.

THE LAW PRIOR TO BILDISCO

Under section 8(a)(5)[13] of the National Labor Relations Act[14] (NLRA), an employer[15] covered by a collective bargaining agreement must ordinarily bargain to "impasse" with the union(s) rep-

---

[8] *Bad Law?,* 70 A.B.A. J. 28, 28 (Dec. 1984).

[9] *Id.*

[10] *Id.*

[11] Waxman & Drake, *The New Practice Under the Amended Bankruptcy Code,* 71 A.B.A. J. 55, 55 (Feb. 1985).

[12] 465 U.S. 513 (1984).

[13] 29 U.S.C. § 158(a)(5) provides that "[i]t shall be an unfair labor practice for an

resenting its employees before implementing a change in the terms and conditions of their employment.[16] Moreover, section 8(d) of the NLRA forbids such an employer to terminate or modify the terms of the collective bargaining agreement prior to its expiration without the union's consent.[17]

In contrast, Chapter 11 of the Bankruptcy Code[18] permits financially troubled businesses to avoid liquidation by reorganizing their affairs under the supervision of the bankruptcy court.[19] Under section 365(a) of the Code,[20] a debtor-in-possession formerly could, with the court's approval, reject or assume any executory contract or unexpired lease[21] of the debtor.

Although virtually all courts addressing the issue had concluded that collective bargaining agreements under the jurisdiction of the

---

employer to refuse to bargain collectively with the representatives of his employees, subject to the provisions of section 9(a)."

[14] 29 U.S.C. §§ 151 *et seq.*

[15] 29 U.S.C. § 152(2) defines employer broadly (albeit circularly) as "any person acting as an agent of an employer, directly or indirectly," with the exception of governmental entities an "any person subject to the Railway Labor Act," 45 U.S.C. §§ 151 *et seq.*

[16] Section 8(d) of the NLRA, 29 U.S.C. § 158(d), states in pertinent part that

> to bargain collectively is the performance of the mutual obligation of the employer and the representative of the employees to meet at reasonable times and confer in good faith with respect to wages, hours, and other terms and conditions of employment, or the negotiation of an agreement, or any question arising thereunder, ... but such obligation does not compel either party to agree to a proposal or require the making of a concession.

See generally NLRB v. Katz, 369 U.S. 736 (1962).

[17] 29 U.S.C. § 158(d) provides further that:

> where there is in effect a collective bargaining contract covering employees in an industry affecting commerce, the duty to bargain collectively shall also mean that no party to such contract shall terminate or modify such contract, unless the party desiring such termination or modification ...
>
> (4) continues in full force and effect, without resorting to strike or lockout, all the terms and conditions of the existing contract ... until the expiration date of such contract....

[18] 11 U.S.C. §§ 1101–1174, enacted as the Bankruptcy Reform Act of 1978, Pub. L. No. 95–598, 92 Stat. 2549, 11 U.S.C. §§ 101–1330. President Carter signed the Code into law on November 6, 1978. The Code took effect on October 1, 1979. The previous bankruptcy law was the Bankruptcy Act of 1898, ch. 541, 30 Stat. 544, as amended by the Chandler Act, ch. 575, 52 Stat. 840 (1938) (codified at 11 U.S.C. §§ 1–1103 (1976) (repealed 1978).

[19] The Code combined Chapters VII, X, XI, and XIII of the 1898 Act into a single chapter, Chapter 11, whose purpose was to facilitate the rehabilitation of bankrupt businesses through reorganization rather than through liquidation. *See* Hughes, "*Wavering Between the Profit and the Loss*": *Operating a Business During Reorganization Under Chapter 11 of the New Bankruptcy Code,* 54 AM. BANKR. L. J. 45 (1980).

[20] 11 U.S.C. § 365(a).

[21] *See* Simpson, *Leases and the Bankruptcy Code: Tempering the Rigors of Strict Performance,* 38 BUS. LAW. 61 (1982).

NLRA[22] are "executory contracts" within the meaning of section 365(a),[23] some courts prior to the Supreme Court's decision in *Bildisco* had—without any express statutory authorization—devised a special standard for debtors' rejection of collective bargaining agreements.[24] In *Bildisco*[25] the Supreme Court resolved the propriety of this more exacting treatment, which some courts had reasoned was necessary to accommodate the provisions of the NLRA, in particular section 8(d). This section will examine the interface between the Code and the NLRA and the development of the courts' "accommodation" of the two statutes prior to *Bildisco.*

History and Meaning of Section 8(d)

The Wagner Act, passed by the 74th Congress in 1935,[26] contained no section 8(d) or similar provisions. Congress added section 8(d) to the NLRA in 1947 with the Taft-Hartley amendments.[27] In section 8(d), the 80th Congress provided for the first time a statutory definition of collective bargaining.[28] Moreover, the new section 8(d) addressed mid-term modifications of a collective bargaining agreement.

> Taft-Hartley added a proviso related to the extension or renewal of an agreement, and provided that such an agreement could not be terminated or changed during its term without mutual consent.... This provision, making contracts in effect binding and laying down procedural rules, was intended to make for stability.[29]

---

[22] Section 1167 of the Code States in pertinent part that: "[n]otwithstanding section 365 ..., neither the court nor the trustee may change the wages or working conditions of employees of the debtor established by a collective bargaining agreement that is subject to the Railway Labor Act (45 U.S.C. § 151 *et seq.*) except in accordance with section 6 of such Act (45 U.S.C. 156)." Section 6 of the RLA forbids mid-term modifications of contractual working conditions absent compliance with certain notice and mediation procedures.

[23] *E.g., In re* Brada Miller Freight System, Inc., 702 F.2d 890, 894 (11th Cir. 1983); Borman's, Inc. v. Allied Supermarkets, Inc., 706 F.2d 187, 189–90 (6th Cir. 1983); Local Joint Executive Bd. v. Hotel Circle, 613 F.2d 210, 214 (9th Cir. 1980).

[24] *See* Truck Drivers Local Union No. 807 v. Bohack Corp., 541 F.2d 312 (2d Cir. 1976) (Bankruptcy Act case); Brotherhood of Railway, Airline and Steamship Clerks v. REA Express, Inc., 523 F.2d 164 (2d Cir.), *cert. denied,* 423 U.S. 1017 (1975) (Bankruptcy Act/RLA case); Shopmen's Local Union No. 455 v. Kevin Steel Products, 519 F.2d 698 (2d Cir. 1975) (Bankruptcy Act case).

[25] 104 S. Ct. 1188 (1984), *aff'g,* 682 F.2d 72 (3d Cir. 1982).

[26] 49 Stat. 449 (1935), codified as amended at 29 U.S.C. §§ 151 *et seq.* For a basic overview of the origins of the Wagner Act, *see* H. MILLIS & E. BROWN, FROM THE WAGNER ACT TO TAFT-HARTLEY, ch. 1 (1950).

[27] The Labor-Management Relations Act of 1947 (LMRA), 61 Stat. 136 (1947). *See generally* H. Millis & E. Brown, *supra* note 26, ch. 8.

[28] *See* note 16 *supra;* H. MILLIS & E. BROWN, *supra* note 26, at 448, 452.

[29] H. MILLIS & E. BROWN, *supra* note 26, at 452–53.

The legislative history of section 8(d) is quite clear. Senate Bill 1126, unlike its House companion, H.R. 3020, contain a section 8(d) which was in every relevant respect identical to the provision ultimately enacted. Senate Report No. 105 stated that

> [u]nder this section, parties to collective agreements ... would be required to give 60 days' notice in advance of the terminal date [of the expiring contract], if they desire to terminate or amend ... Should the notice not be given on time ..., it becomes an unfair labor practice for an employer to change any of the *terms or conditions specified in the contract* for 60 days. ...[30]

It is evident, therefore, that Congress intended section 8(d) to restrict only modification of working conditions "specified in the contract."[31]

The National Labor Relations Board (NLRB), and the courts have understood the mid-term modification language of section 8(d) to limit only the alteration of a term or condition of employment directly controlled by the collective bargaining agreement. An employer's modification of working conditions not explicitly governed by the contract (so-called mandatory subjects of bargaining) is subject only to the duty to bargain with the union in good faith prior to implementation.[32] Management rights not expressly waived by the contract are presumed to have been retained. Section 8(d) deals only with modifications of the *contract.*

---

[30] 1 Legislative History of the Labor Management Relations Act, 1947, at 430 (1948) (emphasis added).

[31] In Allied Chemical & Alkali Workers of America v. Pittsburgh Plate Glass Co., 404 U.S. 157 (1971), the Supreme Court interpreted section 8(d) to mean that an employer commits an unfair labor practice when it unilaterally modifies a labor contract mid-term only when the change involves a mandatory subject of bargaining. The reason section 8(d) was added in 1947, the Court stated, "was to stabilize collective-bargaining agreements." 404 U.S. at 186. Congress rejected proposed unfair labor practice liability for contract violations because

> "[o]nce parties have made a collective bargaining contract the enforcement of that contract should be left to the usual processes of the law and not to the National Labor Relations Board."

404 U.S. at 186–87 (*quoting* H.R. Conf. Rep. No. 510, 80th Cong., 1st Sess. at p. 42). In light of the Court's holding that an employer does not violate section 8(d) when it modifies mid-term a permissive subject of bargaining, it did not need to define what constitutes a "modification."

[32] *See, e.g.,* Fibreboard Paper Products Corp. v. NLRB, 379 U.S. 203 (1964) (employer must bargain with union over decision to subcontract bargaining unit work); University of Chicago v. NLRB, 514 F.2d 942, 949 (7th Cir. 1975) ("unless [work] transfers are specifically prohibited by the bargaining agreement, an employer is free to transfer work out of the bargaining unit if ... the employer complies with *Fibreboard* ... by bargaining in good faith to impasse"); NLRB v. Massachusetts Machine & Stamping, Inc., 578 F.2d 15 (1st Cir. 1978).

Thus, the major distinction between sections 8(a)(5) and 8(d) is that whereas section 8(a)(5) requires bargaining with the union on a fairly broad scope of topics prior to employer action, section 8(d) requires union consent as to a more constricted number of topics. "Before [a section 8(d)] violation can occur, ... an employer obviously must be found to have modified some term or condition that actually appears in or is a part of the contract."[33]

As one commentator stated, "[m]ost of the cases in which section 8(d) has been invoked against an employer, because of an alleged 'modification,' have involved midterm changes made by the employer in the general wage scale or in the manner of computing compensation."[34] Significantly, the NLRB has held some employer actions, including partial sales of the business[35] and an employer/debtor-in-possession's decision to institute bankruptcy proceedings,[36] to be free of the *decision-bargaining* duty of section 8(a)(5). Axiomatically, these decisions cannot be subject to the more restricted scope of section 8(d). Otherwise, unions would possess veto power over virtually all employer conduct affecting employees during the term of a collective bargaining agreement.[37]

In the recent *Milwaukee Spring Division of Illinois Coil Spring Co.*[38] case however, the NLRB initially adopted precisely this position. Although the contract in *Illinois Coil* did not expressly prohibit work transfers or plant relocations during the term of the agreement—indeed, the contract contained a broad management rights clause granting the employer the exclusive right "to determine the operations or services to be performed in or at the plant"—the NLRB reasoned that such a prohibition should be presumed in the absence of a "clear and unmistakable waiver" by the union. Thereby transforming existing law almost completely, the NLRB held that section 8(d) gives the union veto power over all employer

---

[33] Baskin, *NLRB Restricts Plant Relocations During Term of Union Agreement,* NAT'L L. J., Jan. 31, 1983, at 32.

[34] R. GORMAN, BASIC TEXT ON LABOR LAW 421 (1976).

[35] *See* General Motors Corp., 191 N.L.R.B. 951 (1971), *aff'd,* 470 F.2d 422 (D.C. Cir. 1972).

[36] *See* Airport Limousine Service, Inc., 231 N.L.R.B. 932, 935 (1977) ("[W]hile we have some reservations concerning the power of a bankruptcy court to permit a receiver lawfully to disavow a collective-bargaining agreement, we do not find a violation of the Act simply in the receiver's procedurally valid attempt to have the [bankruptcy] court allow this.").

[37] This, of course, would contravene the Supreme Court's statement in First National Maintenance Corp. v. NLRB, 452 U.S. 666, 676 (1981) that "Congress had no expectation that the elected union representative would become an equal partner in the running of the business enterprise...." *See* Irving, *Plant Relocations and Transfers of Work,* DAILY LABOR REPORT (BNA) No. 90, at D-3 (May 9, 1983).

[38] 265 N.L.R.B. No. 28, 111 L.R.R.M. 1486 (1982).

conduct not expressly *permitted* by the contract, instead of merely requiring union approval of modifications to working conditions *specified* by the agreement.[39]

Upon reconsideration, the NLRB in *Illinois Coil* reversed its original position and held that section 8(d) forbids an employer to modify, without the union's consent, only those working conditions *expressly set forth in the contract.*[40] All other mid-term modifications are governed, if at all, by the bargaining duty of section 8(a)(5), the breach of contract remedy provided by section 301 of the LMRA,[41] and/or the contractual arbitration procedure.

That the legal consequences of an employer's instituting bankruptcy proceedings may be a modification of employees' working conditions, even those (such as wages) specified in the collective bargaining agreement, does not necessarily alter this conclusion. The Supreme Court has held, for example, that an employer has no duty to bargain with the union over fundamental business decisions such as the partial or total termination of operations.[42] If an employer has no duty to bargain over a decision under section 8(a)(5), he is necessarily free of the restrictions of section 8(d).[43] "Congress had no expectation that the elected union representative would become an equal partner in the running of the business enterprise in which the union's members are employed."[44] Further,

---

[39] The NLRB cited as precedent for its decision the following cases: Oak Cliff-Golman Baking Co., 207 N.L.R.B. 1063, 1064 (1973), *enf'd,* 505 F.2d 1302 (5th Cir. 1974), *cert. denied,* 423 U.S. 826 (1975) which dealt with an employer's unilateral midterm reduction of *wages* specified by the contract; C & S Industries, Inc., 158 N.L.R.B. 454, 457 (1966), which involved an employer's midterm implementation of a *wage incentive system* prohibited by the contract; and Los Angeles Marine Hardware Co., 235 N.L.R.B. 720, 735 (1978), *enf'd,* 602 F.2d 1302, 1306–07 (9th Cir. 1979), where a confused Ninth Circuit panel cursorily affirmed an ALJ's erroneous dictum concerning the meaning of section 8(d) in a relocation situation.

[40] 268 N.L.R.B. No. 87 (1984).

[41] 29 U.S.C. § 185.

[42] *See* First National Maintenance Corp. v. NLRB, 452 U.S. 666 (1981); Textile Workers of America v. Darlington Mfg. Co., 380 U.S. 263 (1965). *See generally* P. Miscimarra, The NLRB and Managerial Discretion: Plant Closings, Relocations, Subcontracting, and Automation (1983).

[43] *See* note 31 *supra.* In *Bildisco,* the Supreme Court held that sections 8(a)(5) and 8(d) do not restrict a debtor's right to reject a collective-bargaining agreement because "from its filing of a petition in bankruptcy until formal acceptance, the collective-bargaining agreement is not an enforceable contract within the meaning of NLRA § 8(d)." NLRB v. Bildisco & Bildisco, 465 U.S. 513, 532 (1984). Moreover, "[i]n a Chapter 11 case, ... the 'modification' in the agreement has been accomplished not by the employer's unilateral action, but rather by operation of law." *Id.* at 1200. *Cf.* George, *Collective Bargaining in Chapter 11 and Beyond,* 95 Yale L. J. 300, 306 n. 33 (1985) ("The types of alterations generally at issue during Chapter 11 proceedings, i.e., wage and benefit reductions, unquestionably qualify as 'modifications' [within the meaning of § 8(d)]").

[44] First National Maintenance Corp. v. NLRB, 452 U.S. at 676.

many employer decisions affecting its employees' working conditions, such as choice of advertising and promotion, product type and design, financing arrangements, and other decisions at the "core of entrepreneurial control," are not subject to the constraints of the NLRA.[45] "Decisions concerning the commitment of investment capital and the basic scope of the enterprise are not in themselves primarily about conditions of employment, though the effect of the decision may be necessarily to terminate employment."[46] "[T]hose management decisions which are fundamental to the basic direction of a corporate enterprise ... should be excluded from [section 8(d)]."[47]

History and Meaning of Section 365(a)

In contrast to section 8(d) of the NLRA, section 365(a) of the Code has a complex origin. Prior to recodification of the federal bankruptcy laws in 1978, the Bankruptcy Act of 1898[48] as amended (Act), governed the rights and liabilities of debtors-in-possession. Section 313(1) of the Act[49] stated that

> [u]pon the filing of a petition [for reorganization under Chapter 11[50]], the court may, in addition to the jurisdiction, powers, and duties

---

[45] *See* Fibreboard Paper Products Corp. v. NLRB, 379 U.S. 203, 223 (1964) (Stewart, J. concurring).

[46] *Id.*

[47] *Id.* Economic necessity, however, will not justify noncompliance with section 8(d) if the mid-term modification involves a mandatory subject of bargaining, such as wages. Thus, in NLRB v. Manley Truck Line, Inc., 779 F.2d 1327 (7th Cir. 1985), the court enforced the NLRB's determination that a financially distressed employer had committed an unfair labor practice when it unilaterally reduced employees' wages in order to avoid bankruptcy. The employer had not filed a Chapter 11 petition. The court stated that Congress' enactment of 11 U.S.C. § 1113 in response to the Supreme Court's decision in *Bildisco* "suggests the inference that [Congress] disfavors unilateral mid-term modifications by an employer absent the economic hardship which warrants a filing for bankruptcy, and then, only under the meticulous procedural safeguards provided by § 1113." *Id.* at 1331 n.7. *Cf.* note 75 *infra* (economic necessity may justify post-petition noncompliance with section 6 of the RLA).

[48] Bankruptcy Act of July 1, 1898, ch. 541, 30 Stat. 544, codified as amended at 11 U.S.C. §§ 1–1200 (repealed).

[49] 11 U.S.C. § 713(1) (repealed 1978). *See also* 11 U.S.C. § 757(2) (repealed 1978). Section 313 of the Act governed all bankruptcies filed prior to October 1, 1979, the effective date of the Code.

[50] Parallel provisions for rejection of executory contracts under the Act were sections 70(b), 11 U.S.C. § 110(b) (repealed) for Chapter VII straight bankruptcies, and section 116(1), 11 U.S.C. § 516(1) (repealed) for Chapter X corporate reorganizations. *See generally* 6 COLLIER ON BANKRUPTCY ¶ 3.23 (14th ed. 1978) (§ 116(1)); 8 COLLIER ON BANKRUPTCY ¶ 3.15 (14th ed. 1978) (§ 313(1)). These provisions of the 1938 Chandler Act, ch. 575, 52 Stat. 840 (1938), restated the authority previously conferred by 77B(c)(5) of the 1934 Amendments, 48 Stat. 912 (1934). *See* Senate Report No. 1916 on H.R. 8046, 75th Cong., 3d Sess. p. 24 (1938). *See also In re* Cheney Bros., 12 F. Supp. 605 (D. Conn. 1935).

> conferred and imposed upon it by this chapter . . . permit the rejection of the executory contracts of the debtor, upon notice to the parties to such contracts and to such other parties in interest as the court may designate.

Under the Act, a person injured by such a rejection was "deemed" to be a creditor for bankruptcy purposes.[51] So long as the damages arising from the debtor-in-possession's rejection of the contract were reasonably subject to quantification, the creditor had a claim (albeit unsecured) that it could assert in the bankruptcy proceedings.[52]

Significantly, unlike the claims of other creditors, the damages to union employees arising from the debtor's rejection of the collective bargaining agreement were regarded as too speculative for recovery. As a result, the claims of union employees were effectively subordinated to the claims of other contract creditors under pre-Code practice. As one court stated:

> [I]n relieving a debtor from its obligations under a collective bargaining agreement, [the Bankruptcy Court] may be depriving the employees affected of their seniority, welfare and pension rights, as well as other valuable benefits which are incapable of forming the basis of a provable claim for money damages.[53]

This feature of contract rejection has been corrected under the Code.[54] As one leading bankruptcy authority has observed:

> Under Section 57d of the Act the claim of the employees arising from the breach caused by the rejection might not have been allowable on the grounds that it was too speculative to be capable of estimation. Now, under Section 502(c) of the Code such claims must be estimated.[55]

---

[51] *See* section 353 of the Act, 11 U.S.C. § 753 (repealed) (Chapter XI). *See also* section 202 of the Act, 11 U.S.C. § 602 (repealed) (Chapter X).

[52] *See* sections 57(d) and 63(d) of the Act, 11 U.S.C. § 93(d), 103(d) (repealed).

[53] *In re* Overseas National Airways, Inc., 238 F. Supp. 359, 361–62 (E.D.N.Y. 1965). The court expressly noted that this disparity of contract remedy would enable the debtor "at the expense of the employees, to consummate what may be a more favorable plan of arrangement with its other creditors." *Id.* at 362.

[54] *See* section 365(g)(1) of the Code: "[T]he rejection of any executory contract or unexpired lease of the debtor constitutes a breach of such contract or lease—(1) if such contract or lease has not been assumed under this section or under a plan confirmed under chapter 9, 11, or 13 of this title, immediately before the date of the filing of the petition. . . ."

[55] 2 Collier on Bankruptcy ¶ 365.03 at 365–17 (15th ed. 1983). 11 U.S.C. § 502(c) provides in its entirety as follows:

> There shall be estimated for purpose of allowance under this section—
>
> (1) any contingent or unliquidated claim, fixing or liquidation of which, as the case may be, would unduly delay the closing of the case; or
>
> (2) any right to an equitable remedy for breach of performance if

Commentators have noted that "[t]he power of rejection is an anomaly to contract or property law. Instead of getting what he bargained for, the disappointed obligee has only a right to file a claim for damages for breach and to share in such dividend as there may be after payment of administrative expense. . . ."[56] This "anomaly," a long-standing feature of our Anglo-American legal tradition,[57] is justified primarily by Chapter 11's policies favoring rejuvenation of moribund enterprises, relieving financially troubled businesses from burdensome obligations, and the equitable adjustment of the bankrupt's debts to its unsecured creditors.[58]

The principal purpose of reorganization under Chapter 11 is "rehabilitation and continued operation of the debtor,"[59] which can be achieved only if the debtor is able to extricate itself from burdensome or disadvantageous contractual obligations. As the legislative history of the Code states,

> [t]he purpose of a business reorganization case, unlike a liquidation case, is to restructure a business's finances to that it may continue to operate, provide its employees with jobs, pay its creditors, and produce a return for its shareholders. The premise of a business reorganization is that assets that are used for production in the industry for which they were designed are more valuable than those same assets sold for scrap. . . . If the business can extend or reduce its debts, it often can be returned to a viable state. It is more economically efficient to reorganize than to liquidate, because it preserves jobs and assets.[60]

A bankrupt's ability to reject burdensome contracts in effect "force[s] all creditors doing business under executory contracts with

---

such breach gives rise to a right of payment.

The legislative history of section 502(c) makes clear that "[t]his subsection requires that all claims against the debtor be converted into dollar amounts." S. Rep. No. 989, 95th Cong., 2d Sess., p. 65 (1978) (emphasis added), *reprinted in* 1978 U.S. Code Cong. & Admin. News 5787, 5851. Further, section 502(c) "requires estimation of any right to an equitable remedy for breach of performance if such breach gives rise to a right to payment." 124 Cong. Rec. H11089 (1978) (statement by Rep. Don Edwards), *reprinted in* 1978 U.S. Code Cong. & Admin. News 6436, 6449. Thus, Congress intended to treat all contract creditors in the rejection context on an identical basis. *See* 11 U.S.C. § 101(a)(A) (defining "creditor" to include all entities having a claim against the debtor).

[56] Silverstein, *Rejection of Executory Contracts in Bankruptcy and Reorganization,* 31 U. Chi. L. Rev. 467, 468 (1964).

[57] *See* Bourdillon v. Dalton, 1 Esp. 233, 170 Eng. Rep. 340 (1794) (Mansfield, J.); Silverstein, *supra* note 56, at 468–72.

[58] *See* Jackson, *Bankruptcy, Non-Bankruptcy Entitlements, and the Creditors' Bargain,* 91 Yale L. J. 857, 857–58 (1982).

[59] Silverstein, *supra* note 56, at 480.

[60] H.R. Rep. 595, 95th Cong., 1st Sess., p. 220 (1977), *reprinted in* 1978 U.S. Code Cong. & Admin. News 5963, 6179.

the debtor in economic distress to renegotiate their mutual rights, relinquishing some in order to maintain the enterprise as a going concern so that they can at least realize a substantial percentage of what they would otherwise receive."[61]

The operation of section 365(a) is straightforward: a debtor-in-possession may, with the approval of the bankruptcy court, reject executory contracts if the debtor in good faith deems rejection to be in the best interests of the debtor's estate and its creditors.[62] Under this so-called "business judgment test," a debtor need only show that the rejection of an executory contract "will benefit the estate," whether or not the contract is otherwise burdensome or its rejection otherwise economically justified.[63]

Injury to other parties is irrelevant. One court has held that a debtor's request to reject an executory contract should be granted unless there are extraordinary countervailing circumstances, such as fraud.[64] The Code does not define "executory contract." The legislative history of section 365 states that "[t]hough there is no precise definition of what contracts are executory, it generally includes contracts on which performance remains due to some extent on both sides."[65]

By filing a petition for reorganization under Chapter 11, a debtor invokes the "automatic stay" provisions of the Code. Under section 362(a) of the Code,[66] a debtor's filing of a petition with the bankruptcy court operates automatically to halt all acts or proceedings to collect, assess, or recover a claim against a debtor that arose before the petition was filed. The legislative history of section 362 explains the purpose of the automatic stay:

> The automatic stay is one of the fundamental debtor protections provided by the bankruptcy laws. It gives the debtor a breathing spell from his creditors. It stops all collection efforts, all harassment, and all foreclosure actions. It permits the debtor to attempt a repayment

---

[61] Brotherhood of Railway, Airline and Steamship Clerks v. REA Express, Inc., 523 F.2d 164, 169 (2d Cir.), *cert. denied,* 423 U.S. 1017 (1975).

[62] Section 365 of the Code governed all bankruptcies filed from October 1, 1979 to July 10, 1984, the effective date of the Bankruptcy Amendments and Federal Judgeship Act of 1984, Pub. L. No. 98-353, 98 Stat. 333 (1984).

[63] *See* In re Lafayette Radio Electronics Corp., 8 Bankr. 528, 533 (Bankr. E.D.N.Y. 1981). *See also* Group of Institutional Investors v. Chicago, Milwaukee, St. Paul & Pacific R. Co., 318 U.S. 523 (1943); *In re* Minges, 602 F.2d 38 (2d Cir. 1979).

[64] *See In re* Summit Land Co., 13 Bankr. 310, 315 (Bankr. D. Utah 1981).

[65] S. Rep. No. 989, 95th Cong., 2d Sess., p. 58 (1978), *reprinted in* 1978 U.S. Code Cong. & Admin. News 5787, 5844. *See* Jenson v. Continental Finance Corp., 591 F.2d 477, 481 (8th Cir. 1979); Countryman, *Executory Contracts in Bankruptcy* (pt. 1), 57 Minn. L. Rev. 439, 460 (1973).

[66] 11 U.S.C. § 362(a).

> or reorganization plan, or simply to be relieved of the financial pressures that drove him into bankruptcy.
>
> The automatic stay also provides creditor protection. Without it, certain creditors would be able to pursue their own remedies against the debtor's property. Those who acted first would obtain payment of the claims in preference to and to the detriment of other creditors. *Bankruptcy is designed to provide an orderly liquidation procedure under which all creditors are treated equally.... All proceedings are stayed, including arbitration, license revocation, administrative, and judicial proceedings.*[67]

If the debtor-in-possession or trustee in bankruptcy elects to reject an executory contract pursuant to section 365(a), sections(g)(1) and 502(g) deem the contract to have been breached prior to the filing of the petition for purposes of pursuing an unsecured contract claim against the estate.[68]

In a liquidation proceeding under Chapter 7 of the Code, the trustee must assume or reject an executory contract or unexpired lease within 60 days after the order for relief, or else the contract or lease is deemed rejected by operation of law.[69] In a reorganization proceeding under Chapter 11 (and actions under Chapters 9 and 13), the debtor may assume or reject an executory contract at any time prior to the bankruptcy court's confirmation of the plan of reorganization.[70] Under section 1123(b)(2), a Chapter 11 plan may provide for the assumption or rejection of any executory contract or unexpired lease. The estate must reject or assume executory contracts in their entirety.[71] If the debtor or trustee elects to assume a contract, it must do so *cum onere,* meaning "subject to all its provisions and conditions."[72]

An important exception to the various rejection provisions of the Act was section 77(n), which stated that "[n]o judge or trustee

---

[67] H.R. Rep. 595, 95th Cong., 1st Sess., p. 340 (1977) (emphasis added), *reprinted in* 1978 U.S. Code Cong. & Admin. News 5963, 6296–97. *See also* Johnson v. England, 356 F.2d 44, 51 (9th Cir.) *cert. denied,* 384 U.S. 961 (1966).

[68] 11 U.S.C. §§ 365(g)(1), 502(g).

[69] *See* 11 U.S.C. § 365(d)(1).

[70] *See* 11 U.S.C. § 365(d)(2). "Assumption or adoption of the contract can only be effected through an express order by the court." 2 COLLIER ON BANKRUPTCY ¶ 365.03 at 365–25 (15th ed. 1985). However, "[a]s long as rejection is not ordered the contract continues in existence.... [I]f the contract is not affected by the plan, it rides through the proceedings having neither been assumed nor rejected and will thereafter be binding on the debtor." *Id.* at 365–25 to –26. Under section 365(d)(2), in a Chapter 11 reorganization a party to an executory contract or lease may move the court for an order requiring the debtor to reject or assume within a specified period prior to confirmation.

[71] *See In re* Handy Andy, Inc., 109 LRRM 3298, 3306 (Bankr. W.D. Tex. 1982); *In re* David A. Rosow, Inc., 9 Bankr. 190, 193 (Bankr. D. Conn. 1981).

[72] 2 COLLIER ON BANKRUPTCY ¶ 365.01 at 365–7 (15th ed. 1983).

acting under this Title shall change the wages or working conditions of railroad employees except in the manner prescribed in sections 151 to 163 of Title 45. . . ."[73] This exception for Railway Labor Act (RLA) contracts was preserved under the Code. Section 1167 of the Code[74] states that

> [n]otwithstanding section 365 of this title, neither the court nor the trustee may change the wages or working conditions of employees of the debtor established by a collective bargaining agreement that is subject to the Railway Labor Act (45 U.S.C. 151 et seq.) except in accordance with section 6 of such Act (45 U.S.C. 156).

Section 6 of the RLA provides for 30 days' written notice of "an intended change in agreements affecting rates of pay, rules, or working conditions," as well as conferences between the parties and, upon request, mediation by the National Mediation Board. Section 6 prohibits the alteration of contractual working conditions until exhaustion of the specified conference and mediation procedures.[75] Congress made no such exception for collective bargaining agreements between parties subject to the NLRA in either the Act or the Code.

The legislative history of section 1167 states that

> notwithstanding the general section governing the rejection of executory contracts (section 365), neither the court nor the trustee may change the wages or working conditions of employees of the debtor established by a collective bargaining agreement that is subject to the Railway Labor Act, except in accordance with section 6 of that Act.[76]

Whether section 1167 governs only railroad employees is uncertain. By its terms, section 1167 applies to all collective bargaining agreements subject to the RLA. The language of its predecessor,

---

[73] 11 U.S.C. § 205(n) (repealed 1978). Section 77(n) of the Act dates to as early as 1933, when the operative language was added by Pub. L. No. 420, ch. 204, 47 Stat. 1467 (1933), as section 77(o). The section was re-numbered section 77(n) by the Act of August 27, 1935, ch. 774, 49 Stat. 911 (1935).

[74] 11 U.S.C. § 1167.

[75] *See* 45 U.S.C. §§ 155–56. These requirements are not absolute. In Brotherhood of Railway & Steamship Clerks v. Florida East Coast Railway Co., 384 U.S. 238 (1966), the Supreme Court held that a carrier need not comply with section 6 prior to implementing unilateral changes in working conditions during a lawful economic strike, so long as the changes are "reasonably necessary" to continue operating. Some courts have extended this reasoning to excuse a bankrupt air carrier from complying with section 6 in order to implement post-petition modifications. *See In re* Continental Airlines Corp., No. 83-04019-H2-5 (Bankr. S.D. Tex. 1984) (*quoted in* McDonald, *Bankruptcy Reorganization: Labor Considerations for the Debtor-Employer,* 11 Employee Relations L.J. 7, 13 (1985)).

[76] H.R. Rep. No. 595, 95th Cong., 1st Sess., p. 423 (1977) (emphasis added), *reprinted in* 1978 U.S. Code Cong. & Admin. News 5963, 6379.

section 77(n) of the Act, was narrower, speaking in terms of "the wages or working conditions of railroad employees." Since 1936, the RLA has also applied to air carriers.[77] The legislative history of section 1167 states that "[s]ection 1167 is derived from present section 77(n)."[78] However, the legislative history is confusing because Congress significantly broadened the language of section 1167 without any indication that it intended to alter the meaning: "The subject of railway labor is too delicate and has too long a history for this code to upset established relationships. *This provision continues that balance unchanged.*"[79] Moreover, the term "railway labor" can be interpreted to refer to all employment relationships subject to the RLA.

The location of section 1167 within the Code suggests that it is limited to railroad employers. Section 1167 appears in Subchapter IV of Chapter 11, dealing with "railroad reorganization." Section 103(g) of the Code states that "Subchapter IV . . . applies only in a case . . . concerning a railroad."[80] However, the express language of section 1167 suggests a broader application.[81]

The few reported judicial authorities hold that section 1167 is limited to railroad employers. Commentators report that "[n]o cases have discussed the implications of rejecting a collective bargaining agreement in the railroad context."[82] There are cases dealing with rejection of labor contracts by non-railroad employers subject to the

---

[77] *See* Act of April 10, 1936, ch. 166, 49 Stat. 1189, *codified at* 45 U.S.C. §§ 181–82. Consequently, air carriers are subject to the RLA, including section 6, rather than the provisions of the NLRA. *See generally In re* Continental Airlines Corp., 50 Bankr. 342, 347–48, 119 L.R.R.M. 2752, 2753–54 (S.D. Tex. 1985) (airline subject to National Mediation Board jurisdiction over representation disputes involving its employees).

[78] H.R. Rep. No. 595, 95th Cong., 1st Sess., p. 423 (1977), *reprinted in* 1978 U.S. Code Cong. & Admin. News 5962, 6379.

[79] *Id.* (emphasis added).

[80] 11 U.S.C. § 103(g). At least one commentator has concluded from section 1167's placement in Subchapter IV that "[t]his provision does not cover airlines." McDonald, *Bankruptcy Reorganization: Labor Considerations for the Debtor-Employer,* 11 Employee Relations L.J. 7, 30 (1985). *See also In re* Funding Systems Railcars, Inc., 15 Bankr. 611, 616 (Bankr. N.D. Ill. 1981) ("§ 1168 is applicable only to cases proceeding under Subchapter IV of Chapter 11," *i.e.,* those "concerning a railroad"). 11 U.S.C. § 101(36) defines "railroad" as a "common carrier by railroad engaged in the transportation of individuals or property, or owner of trackage facilities leased by such a common carrier."

[81] In *Bildisco,* the Supreme Court described section 1167 as an exemption for "collective-bargaining agreements subject to the Railway Labor Act," but also noted that "[t]his provision was derived from former § 77(n) of the Bankruptcy Act." NLRB v. Bildisco & Bildisco, 465 U.S. 513, 522–23 & n. 8 (1984).

[82] 5 Collier on Bankruptcy ¶ 1167.01 at 1167-2 (15th ed. 1985). *But see* In re Michigan Interstate Railway Co., 34 Bankr. 220, 227 (Bankr. E.D. Mich. 1983) (dictum).

RLA, but these decisions contain little or no analysis of the distinction between sections 365 and 1167 of the Code. Some decisions, like the Second Circuit opinion in *REA Express* and the bankruptcy court opinion in *In re Braniff Airways, Inc.,*[83] simply fail to distinguish between sections 365 and 1167 in the RLA context, at least when non-railroad employers are concerned. In *In re Braniff Airways,* the court specifically rejected the union's argument that section 1167 is broader than its predecessor, section 77(n):

> Section 77(n) was limited to railroad employees and by § 103(g) the Bankruptcy Code limits § 1167 to cases concerning a railroad. The change was merely in statutory organization and there is no indication Congress intended a change in the law.... [T]he restriction on the right to affect [*sic*] collective bargaining agreements applies only to employees of debtor railroads.[84]

This analysis, however, operates in both directions. It is equally possible that Congress intended section 77(n) to cover all RLA employees, and altered the language of section 1167 to reflect the expanded coverage of the RLA. In light of the inclusion of air carriers in the RLA in 1936 and the express language of section 1167, it is difficult to discern a basis for treating air carriers differently from railroads for bankruptcy purposes.[85] Until a court of appeal or Supreme Court decision on this point, the scope of section 1167 remains an open question.

Another relevant provision of the Code, which has the effect of an exception to section 365, is the priority accorded to

> unsecured claims for wages, salaries, or commissions, including vacation, severance and sick leave pay—
>
> (A) earned by an individual within 90 days before the date of the filing of the petition or the date of the cessation of the debtor's business, whichever occurs first; but only
>
> (B) to the extent of $2,000 for each such individual.[86]

This provision, although not technically an exception because it essentially tracks other sections of the Code that prohibit the discharge of accrued obligations via the rejection mechanism,[87] is sig-

---

[83] 25 Bankr. 216 (Bankr. N.D. Texas 1982).

[84] 25 Bankr. at 217. *Accord, In re* Air Florida System, Inc., 48 Bankr. 440, 443 (Bankr. S.D. Fla. 1985) ("Section 1167 ... applies only to railroad reorganizations").

[85] *See* IAM v. Central Airlines, Inc., 372 U.S. 682, 685 (1963) (the aim of the 1936 legislation "was to extend to air carriers and their employees the same benefits and obligations available and applicable in the railroad industry").

[86] 11 U.S.C. § 507(a)(3). *See generally* Comment, *The Priority of a Severance Pay Claim in Bankruptcy,* 27 UCLA L. Rev. 722 (1980); Chapter VII, *infra.*

[87] *See In re* Public Ledger, Inc., 161 F.2d 762, 767–69 (3d Cir. 1947); 11 U.S.C. § 365(b); 2 Collier on Bankruptcy ¶ 365.04 (15th ed. 1983).

nificant because it evinces Congress' intent to treat separately specific aspects of the employment relationship. In light of sections 1167 and 507(a)(3), it is plain that Congress knew how to distinguish between contracts for the sale of labor and ordinary commercial contracts. Other than the exceptions noted above, Congress authorized debtors to reject *all* executory contracts under section 365(a).

Judicial Development of Conflict Between Section 365 and the NLRA: The Path to Bildisco

Early on, courts held that debtors-in-possession are "responsible for the unfair labor practices which occur during a [bankruptcy] reorganization."[88] There was never a dispute that debtors or trustees of a bankrupt company are subject to the provisions of the NLRA and capable of committing unfair labor practices as an employer.[89] Likewise, just as with ordinary commercial contracts, a debtor's lack of good faith could disqualify its attempt to reject a collective bargaining agreement[90]; when the employer's motivation is simply to avoid an improvident contract rather than to consummate a plan of reorganization, the bankruptcy court will deny its attempt to reject executory contracts.[91]

These, however, are propositions quite distinct from the question of what conduct by a debtor constitutes an unfair labor practice, in particular whether the rejection of an executory collective bargaining agreement violates the NLRA. Further, these questions are distinct from whether, and to what extent, the NLRA impliedly restricts the debtor's ability to reject executory contracts under the bankruptcy laws. Authorities bearing on this discrete issue—the doctrinal course leading to *Bildisco*—bear a recent and diverse pedigree.

The starting point of analysis is *In re Klaber Bros., Inc.*[92] In *Klaber Bros.,* an employer filed a petition with the referee in bankruptcy for reorganization under Chapter XI of the Act. As part of its re-

---

[88] NLRB v. Baldwin Locomotive Works, 128 F.2d 39, 43 (3d Cir. 1942).

[89] *Id.*

[90] *See generally In re* Victory Constr. Co., 9 Bankr. 549 (Bankr. C.D. Cal. 1981); Ordin, *The Good Faith Principle in the Bankruptcy Code: A Case Study,* 38 Bus. Law. 1795 (1983).

[91] *See In re* Mamie Conti Gowns, Inc., 12 F. Supp. 478 (S.D.N.Y. 1935).

[92] 173 F. Supp. 83 (S.D.N.Y. 1959). *See also In re* Public Ledger, Inc., 63 F. Supp. 1008, 1013 (E.D. Pa. 1945) (trustee's right to reject executory labor contract in proceeding under Chapter X of the Act not questioned; regarding severance pay issue, court opines that "[t]he instant case demonstrates the difficulties which are likely to arise when Trustees in bankruptcy fail to expressly adopt or reject executory contracts as expediently as possible"), *rev'd in part on other grounds,* 161 F.2d 726 (3d Cir. 1947).

organization, and pursuant to section 313(1) of the Act, the employer moved to reject an executory collective bargaining agreement with the union. After a hearing, the referee ruled that "the contract is a burden on the estate. The motion, therefore, for leave to reject it is granted."[93] The union appealed that (1) the NLRA preempted section 313(1) of the Act, (2) the NLRB has exclusive subject matter jurisdiction over the rejection of collective bargaining agreements governed by the NLRA, and (3) the referee abused his authority in allowing rejection. The district court rejected all three contentions.

On the issue of preemption or implied limitation of section 313(1) of the Act, the court ruled that "[i]t is clear that there is no intent to limit the application of the authority and power granted to the [bankruptcy] court in [section 313(1) of the Act,] Title 11 U.S.C.A. § 713 to reject executory contracts."[94] Quoting the pertinent language of section 313(1), the court noted:

> As the Referee stated in passing upon this issue: "The Bankruptcy Act makes no distinction among classes of executory contracts. The power to permit rejection of an executory contract should be exercised where rejection is to the advantage of the estate. . . ." I likewise conclude that there should be no differentiation in the treatment of executory employment or collective bargaining contracts as to termination under the circumstances of this case.[95]

The court also rejected the union's argument of exclusive NLRB jurisdiction:

> The fact that the Union filed with the National Labor Relations Board on March 18, 1959 a charge of unfair labor practice based upon the application for the rejection of the contract and refusal to bargain, is immaterial. The National Labor Relations Board, in my opinion, has no jurisdiction here to interfere with the rejection of an executory contract, as provided for by Section 713 of Title 11 U.S.C.A. It has not attempted to do so.[96]

Finally, the district court in *Klaber Bros.* gave short shrift to the union's contention that the bankruptcy referee had abused his discretion:

> The Referee in Bankruptcy did not abuse his power in making the order of rejection. . . . [At the hearing a union witness] recognized the injury to the estate if the contract were to be continued, and offered, it is true, certain concessions. However, as stated in Collier on Bankruptcy, 14th Ed., Vol. 8, p. 163: "An executory contract cannot be

---

[93] 173 F. Supp. at 85.
[94] *Id.* at 84.
[95] *Id.* at 85.
[96] *Id.*

> rejected in part, and assumed in part.... The contract must be rejected in its entirety, or not at all."
>
> The Referee, after hearing the testimony and arguments of the parties, said: "It appears from the testimony of the union representative that the contract is a burden on the estate. The motion, therefore, for leave to reject is granted." In my opinion, the Referee's determination was fully justified under the circumstances here involved.[97]

For present purposes, the notable features of the court's decision in *Klaber Bros.* are that (1) the court perceived no difference between executory collective bargaining agreements between parties governed by the NLRA (as opposed to the RLA) and ordinary commercial contracts; (2) the court discerned no conflict between the clear language of the Act and the (to some extent inconsistent) provisions of the NLRA, and therefore felt no need to "accommodate" or reconcile the two statutes by limiting the debtor's nearly plenary power of rejection; (3) both the court and the NLRB regarded the application of section 313(1) of the Act as a function over which the Board had "no jurisdiction," notwithstanding sections 8(a)(5) and 8(d) of the NLRA; and (4) the court applied a standard for rejection that, although employing the "burdensome" contract rubric, was essentially a "business judgment" test.

With these key points in mind, the doctrinal evolution that emerges from subsequent decisions is quite pronounced. The next significant ruling, nearly six years later, involved the rejection of a collective bargaining agreement between parties in the airline industry, who were therefore subject to the RLA.

In *In re Overseas National Airways, Inc.*,[98] the referee in bankruptcy had permitted an employer-air carrier to reject two executory collective bargaining agreements pursuant to section 313(1) of the Act on the ground that they were "onerous and burdensome." The union, the Air Line Pilots Association, petitioned the district court for review of the referee's order on the grounds that (1) the referee had no authority to permit rejection because, unlike *Klaber Bros.*, rejection of labor contracts subject to the RLA is expressly limited by the Act, (2) in the alternative, the referee's finding that the contracts were "onerous and burdensome" was clearly erroneous, and (3) labor agreements were not "executory contracts" within the meaning of section 313(1).[99]

---

[97] *Id.*
[98] 238 F. Supp. 359 (E.D.N.Y. 1965).
[99] *See id.* at 359–61.

The court found the union's first argument to be persuasive. Section 77(n) of the Act[100] contained an exception to section 313(1), which was retained in the Code, that restricts a debtor's ability to reject a labor contract subject to the RLA except in the exclusive manner prescribed by section 6 of the RLA.[101] Section 6, in turn, requires elaborate procedures prior to mid-term modification of contractual working conditions. In the face of the union's argument along these lines, the court in *Overseas National Airways* was forced to concluded that "[t]he collective bargaining agreements in question, governed, as I believe they are, by the provisions of the Railway Labor Act, can be changed or cancelled only in conformity with that Act."[102] The court evidently felt the need to distinguish the leading authority permitting plenary rejection of NLRA labor contracts, *Klaber Bros.:*

> The case of *In re Klaber Bros. Inc.* . . ., cited by the debtor as authority for an arrangement under Chapter XI of the Bankruptcy Act, has the power to permit the rejection of a collective bargaining agreement if the rejection is to the advantage of the debtor's estate is clearly distinguishable from the case at bar. In the *Klaber* case Judge Levet found . . . that that case involved "no conflict [between the Act and the NLRA]." In the case at bar, on the other hand, the debtor's employees are covered by the Railway Labor Act which by the terms of the Bankruptcy Act itself . . . prescribes the only method by which collective bargaining agreements of the kind here involved may be disaffirmed.[103]

Even though this holding was sufficient to resolve the case, the court addressed, in dicta, the union's other arguments. Reviewing the transcript of testimony the Referee heard at the rejection hearing, the court concluded that "[i]t is my opinion that the testimony of [the debtor's two witnesses] is inadequate to support the Referee's finding that the agreements in question were onerous and burdensome and the Referee's finding to that effect is, therefore, clearly erroneous."[104]

Finally, the court addressed the union's last position:

> The petitioner has argued that collective bargaining agreements are not "Executory Contracts" within the meaning of Section 313(1) of the Bankruptcy Act . . ., and cites as authority therefor the case of *United Steelworkers of America v. Warrior & Gulf Navigation Co.,* 363 U.S. 543 [(1960)], and the case of *John Wiley & Sons, Inc. v. Livingston,* 376 U.S. 543 [(1964)]. I disagree. Both of the above-cited

[100] 11 U.S.C. § 205(n) (repealed 1978).
[101] 45 U.S.C. § 156.
[102] 238 F. Supp. at 360.
[103] *Id.* at 360–61.
[104] *Id.* at 361.

> cases involved the right to arbitrate a dispute, and the implementation of Congressional policy favoring the settlement of industrial disputes through the machinery of arbitration.[105]

Then, continuing in dictum, the court remarked without explanation or citation of authority that

> the Bankruptcy Court, when it *has* the power to reject a collective bargaining agreement, should do so only after thorough scrutiny, and a careful balancing of the equities on both sides, for in relieving a debtor from its [contractual] obligations . . ., it may be depriving the employees affected of their seniority, welfare and pension rights, as well as other valuable benefits *which are incapable of forming the basis of a provable claim for money damages. That would leave the employees without compensation for their losses, at the same time enabling the debtor, at the expense of the employees, to consummate what may be a more favorable plan of arrangement with its other creditors.*[106]

Whether this statement was premised on the Act's failure to allow unsecured claims for damages resulting from debtors' breaches of labor agreements, or whether it was nothing more than a barb directed at "the learned Referee"[107] is unknown because Judge Rayfiel did not elaborate or explain his cryptic statement.

The only thing certain about *Overseas National Airways* is its holding that contracts under the RLA cannot be rejected in the same manner as those under the NLRA. The court's discussion of the standard for rejection was merely *obiter dictum.* To the extent this dictum was attributable to prevailing practice under the Act, or to the exception under both the Act and the Code for RLA-covered contracts, it had no application to rejections of NLRA-covered labor agreements pursuant to section 365 of the Code.

The next decision of note followed several years later. In *Carpenters Local Union No. 2746 v. Turney Wood Prods., Inc.,*[108] an employer in "straight" or liquidation bankruptcy proceedings under section 70(b) of the Act[109] sought to reject an executory collective bargaining agreement. The union sued the trustee in bankruptcy for specific performance of the agreement, which was subject to the NLRA. The trustee moved to dismiss the union's complaint; the district court treated the motion as one for summary judgment.

Following the employer's filing of a voluntary petition in bankruptcy, the referee appointed a trustee, who resumed operations.[110]

---

[105] *Id.*
[106] *Id.* at 361–62 (emphasis added).
[107] *Id.* at 359.
[108] 289 F. Supp. 143 (W.D. Ark. 1968).
[109] 11 U.S.C. § 110(b).
[110] 289 F. Supp. at 145.

The referee authorized the trustee to reject the collective bargaining agreement with the union. As the court reports, "[w]hen the plant was reopened, the receiver repudiated the contract without notice to or prior consultation with the Union. Employees were laid off without regard to seniority, and wages were reduced."[111] Aside from a number of procedural and jurisdictional issues not germane here, the court was faced with a single issue: "the *power* of the Bankruptcy Court to deal under section 70b with a collective bargaining agreement."[112] The court did not address the standard for rejection or the propriety of the particular rejection before it based its decision on that standard.[113] The court's treatment of the "power" issue is instructive:

> There is no question that during the life of a collective bargaining agreement it is an "executory contract" and falls within the literal language of section 70b. The Union does not contend otherwise, nor does the Union question the proposition that in general a trustee in bankruptcy may at his option adopt or reject an executory contract. The position of the Union is that federal legislation in the field of labor relations has so preempted the field as to take collective bargaining agreements out of the scope of section 70b. To put it another way, the Union contends that if a bankruptcy receiver is to operate the business of a bankrupt at all, he must do so subject to the terms and provisions of any existing collective bargaining agreement entered into by the bankrupt prior to adjudication.[114]

The court, however, eschewed the notion of "implied restrictions" on the trustee's power of rejection under the Act:

> It is clear that to uphold the contentions of the Union would imply a conflict between federal legislation in the labor relations field, on the one hand, and the Bankruptcy Act, on the other hand. The Court does not believe that any such conflict exists if the two bodies of legislation are read together and properly construed.
>
> The National Labor Relations Act was adopted in 1935. The Chandler Bankruptcy Act was passed in 1938.... The Taft-Hartley Act was adopted in 1947....
>
> Neither the labor legislation of the Congress nor the Bankruptcy Act contains any language which would generally exclude collective bargaining agreements from the operation of section 70b. *Had Congress desired that there be such general exclusion, it surely would have said so.*[115]

Noting the exception in section 77(n) for rejection of RLA contracts, Judge Henley concluded that "section 70b is applicable to a collec-

[111] *Id.* at 146.
[112] *Id.* at 147 (footnote omitted).
[113] *Id.*
[114] *Id.*
[115] *Id.* at 148–49 (emphasis added).

tive bargaining agreement, and that the trustee has a right to reject such an agreement just as he has a right to reject any other executory contract."[116] The court recognized the authority of *Klaber Bros.* in the Chapter XI reorganization context and reasoned that there is "no reason why [a collective bargaining] agreement cannot be rejected under section 70b in a straight bankruptcy proceeding. . . ."[117] Therefore, the court dismissed the union's complaint with prejudice.

The doctrinal approach of this line of cases was soon to be altered. In *Shopmen's Local Union No. 455 v. Kevin Steel Prods., Inc.*,[118] the Second Circuit consolidated two related cases—the debtor's appeal from a district court order forbidding rejection of an NLRA labor contract and the NLRB's petition for enforcement of an unfair labor practice determination. The bankruptcy court had permitted rejection under *Klaber Bros.* because the contract was a "burdensome and onerous obligation" and because the debtor filed a petition under Chapter 11 and sought rejection in good faith.

The district court reversed the bankruptcy court on the ground that section 313(1) does not permit rejection of collective bargaining agreements because "Congress intended to distinguish collective bargaining agreements as a class from all other contracts," even if the labor contract is, as it had found in *Kevin Steel*, "burdensome and onerous."[119] Judge Feinberg's opinion for the Second Circuit panel framed the issue in stark terms: "This case squarely presents to an appellate court, apparently for the first time, the question whether section 313(1) of the Bankruptcy Act allows rejection of a collective bargaining agreement as an executory contract. We conclude that the answer is yes. . . ."[120]

Yet this was not an unequivocal "yes," as the court considered the parties' competing arguments at length.[121] The union and Board argued that the NLRA and Act were in conflict and could be reconciled or accommodated only by restricting the debtor's power of rejection under section 313(1)[122]; the lower court authorities were "few," "not controlling," and "wrongly decided"[123]; and in section 77(n) Congress recognized the special status of labor contracts.[124]

[116] *Id.* at 149.
[117] *Id.*
[118] 519 F.2d 698 (2d Cir. 1975), *rev'g* 381 F. Supp. 336 (S.D.N.Y. 1974).
[119] *See* 381 F. Supp. at 338.
[120] 519 F.2d at 700.
[121] *See* 519 F.2d at 701–06.
[122] *Id.* at 702.
[123] *Id.*
[124] *Id.* at 703. The NLRB—with Peter Nash as General Counsel and John Irving

The debtor countered that section 313(1) is broad and plain in its terms[125]; the lower court authorities are unanimous and correctly decided[126]; and section 77(n) evinces a congressional distinction between RLA and NLRA contracts.[127] Despite its acknowledgement that "the debtor has the better of it in these volleys back and forth,"[128] and that the language of section 313(1) is "obviously broad in its literal scope,"[129] the court declined to permit rejection under the business judgment standard. The court's "new entity" analysis and analogies to successorship liability[130] indicate an unwillingness to rest its decision solely on bankruptcy law principles or section 313(1).

The court's ultimate conclusion that "section 313(1) of the Bankruptcy Act does permit rejection of a labor agreement"[131] was based on a holding that the NLRA did not conflict with, and therefore did not impliedly restrict, the rejection provisions of the Act:

> We do not see any irreconcilable conflict here between the Bankruptcy Act and the National Labor Relations Act. We recognize, of course, that the policies animating the two statutes are different.... Should Congress prefer to alter the present balance between these policies, it can do so.[132]

However, the court then ruled, without any doctrinal support or express statutory authority, that even though labor contracts are identical to ordinary commercial contracts for purposes of the debtor's *power* of rejection, the bankruptcy courts must nonetheless treat labor contracts differently. The court stated, in the absence of any

---

as Deputy General Counsel—took the position that sections 8(a)(5) and 8(d) of the NLRA precluded rejection under section 313(1) of the Act. The Board defended its position that "bankruptcy courts do not possess the power to set aside collective bargaining agreements" *under any circumstances* on the assumption that "if collective bargaining agreements are not set aside in bankruptcy, unions have an interest in agreeing to the modification of burdensome contract terms to prevent employers from going out of business, thereby preserving jobs for their members." Brief for the National Labor Relations Board at pp. 12, 23. One obvious defect of this argument is that it would treat union employees in preference to all other categories of contract creditors. As Justice Douglas once remarked: "The theme of the Bankruptcy Act is 'equality of distribution'; and if one claimant is to be preferred over others, the purpose would be clear from the statute." Nathanson v. NLRB, 344 U.S. 25, 29 (1952) (*quoting* Sampsell v. Imperial Paper & Color Corp., 313 U.S. 215, 219 (1941)).

[125] 519 F.2d at 701.

[126] *Id.* at 701–02.

[127] *Id.* at 702.

[128] *Id.* at 703.

[129] *Id.*

[130] *Id.* at 704.

[131] *Id.* at 706 (footnote omitted).

[132] *Id.*

legislative direction, that "bankruptcy courts must scrutinize with particular care petitions to reject collective bargaining agreements."[133] What does "particular care" mean and how did the court justify this standard in the face of the absolute language of section 313(1)?

One possible explanation is a concern for the "loss of intangible employee rights" resulting, as we saw earlier, from the speculative damages arising from rejection of labor contracts under the Act (but *not* under the Code).[134] *Kevin Steel*'s quotation from *Overseas National Airways* supports this view.[135] Another possible basis for the court's concern is the possibility that employers would exercise the power of rejection in bad faith. The court warned, for instance, that "[t]he decision to allow rejection should not be based solely on whether it will improve the financial status of the debtor. Such a narrow approach totally ignores the policies of the Labor Act and makes no attempt to accommodate to them."[136]

This reasoning is subject to criticism on at least two grounds. First, there was ample doctrinal basis under the Act for testing the bona fides of a petitioning debtor, without the need for resort to "implied restrictions" derived from the NLRA and notions that labor contracts are "unique." If, as the court in *Kevin Steel* necessarily ruled in order to reverse the district court, labor contracts are the same as ordinary executory contracts, the good faith of the debtor arguably should be tested by the same standard, not a judicially-devised hybrid. Second, to the extent that the policies of the NLRA, passed in 1935, conflicted with the policies of the Act, the relevant provisions of which were adopted in 1938, Congress itself seems to have "accommodated to" this supposed conflict by *creating* it.[137]

---

[133] *Id.*

[134] *See* 519 F.2d at 707.

[135] *See id.* The NLRB had argued on appeal, without any citation of authority, that the rejection of collective bargaining agreements "occurs at the expense of employees who have no means of recouping their losses and whose only remedy is utilization of the right to strike. . . ." Brief for the National Labor Relations Board at p. 23.

[136] 519 F.2d at 707.

[137] The cardinal principle of statutory construction is that "the meaning of the statute must, in the first instance, be sought in the language in which the act is framed, and if that is plain . . . , the sole function of the courts is to enforce it according to its terms." Caminetti v. United States, 242 U.S. 470, 485 (1917). Phrased another way, "[w]here the language is plain and admits of no more than one meaning the duty of interpretation does not arise and the rules which are to aid doubtful meanings need no discussion." *Id.* Even assuming that textual ambiguity existed between the NLRA and the rejection provisions of the Act, or that ambiguity currently exists between the NLRA and the Code, the duty of interpretation is to discover the controlling legislative intent. *See generally* 2A C. SANDS, SUTHERLAND ON STAT-

If, as the court conceded, the language of the subsequently-enacted section 313(1) is unqualified, and if, as the court admitted, holding that the Act "excludes by indirection the power to reject labor contracts ... would, in effect, be amending the statute,"[138] what basis is there for judicially "correcting" a conflict? The *Kevin Steel* court purported to resolve the conflict by ruling that section 313(1) meant what it said. Imposing a more exacting standard for the rejection of labor contracts seems inconsistent with the court's earlier statement that "[t]he remedy for any such 'oversight,' affecting two very important statutes, rests with the legislature."[139]

In sum, the holding of *Kevin Steel* on the issue of *power* to reject labor contracts was undoubtedly correct. The court's prolonged discussion of the *standard* for rejection—"the bankruptcy court must move cautiously in allowing rejection of a collective bargaining agreement"[140]—injected a good deal of uncertainty into the law. The standard, and not the power, was now up for grabs.

Only a month after *Kevin Steel* was decided, another panel of the Second Circuit issued its decision in *Brotherhood of Railway, Airline and Steamship Clerks v. REA Express, Inc.*[141] *REA Express* was two unions' appeal from a district court order allowing a Chapter 11 debtor's rejection of two RLA labor contracts pursuant to section 313(1) of the Act.

The *REA Express* case is significant for a number of reasons. First, the debtor's labor contracts contained drastic "supplementary unemployment benefit" provisions and restrictions on the consolidation of the debtor's operations, both of which would impede reorganization under Chapter 11.[142] Second, the appellate court evidently wanted to permit rejection at any cost, even though section 77(n) of the Act and the holding of *In re Overseas National Airways* presented substantial legal obstacles to rejection. Finally, the *REA Express* court overcame this difficulty by finessing the critical distinction between RLA and NLRA contracts. The result was an

UTES AND STATUTORY CONSTRUCTION § 45.09 (4th ed. 1973). When two statues are in direct conflict, the subsequently enacted provision controls: "if there is an irreconcilable conflict between the new provision and the prior statues relating to the same subject matter, the new provision will control as it is the later expression of the legislature." *Id.* § 51.02 at 290. "The whole doctrine applicable to the subject [of statutory construction] may be summed up in the single observation that prior acts may be resorted to, to *solve,* but not to *create* an ambiguity." Hamilton v. Rathbone, 175 U.S. 414, 421 (1899).

[138] 519 F. 2d at 705.

[139] *Id.*

[140] *Id.* at 707.

[141] 523 F. 2d 164 (2d Cir.), *cert. denied,* 423 U.S. 1017 (1975).

[142] *See* 523 F.2d at 166–67, 172.

"interpretation" of *Kevin Steel* that treated section 8(d) of the NLRA as the virtual equivalent of section 6 of the RLA. In order to make *REA Express* look like *Kevin Steel,* and hence to justify the debtor's rejection of RLA contracts in *REA Express* despite the explicit statutory restrictions in section 77(n) of the Act, the court in *REA Express* rewrote *Kevin Steel* as resting on the "different entity theory."[143]

The *REA Express* court overcame section 77(n) by analogizing section 6 of the RLA to section 8(d) of the NLRA. The court stated that

> [t]he purpose of [section 6 and related] provisions of the RLA, *like that of § 8(d) of the National Labor Relations Act, 29 U.S.C. § 158(d), which was before us in Kevin Steel,* is to avoid disruptions of commerce by forcing the parties to exhaust collective bargaining procedures and, where the RLA applies, to encourage use of arbitration and mediation before engaging in self-help strikes or other forms of unilateral action.[144]

Having drawn an analogy between the rejection of RLA and NLRA contracts that ignored section 77(n), the court boot-strapped *Kevin Steel* into an all-purpose balancing standard. The effect of this gloss on *Kevin Steel,* of course, was to make the standard for rejecting NLRA contracts more difficult and to permit rejection of RLA contracts under this more difficult standard, despite the explicit exception of section 77(n).[145] Observe the *REA Express* court's use of *Kevin Steel* as a means to circumvent section 77(n):

> Faced with this apparent conflict in the language and purposes of [section 6 of] the RLA and [section 313(1) of] the Bankruptcy Act *we must give effect to both statutes to the extent that they are not mutually repugnant.* In the present case we are persuaded, *as we were in Kevin Steel, that this can be accomplished by holding that where, after careful weighing of all the factors and equities involved, including*

---

[143] *Id.* at 167.

[144] *Id.* at 168 (emphasis added). This theme was suggested by the district court in *Kevin Steel,* which characterized section 77(n) of the Act as a "seemingly irrelevant distinction[] between different kinds of labor agreements." 381 F. Supp. at 338. Accordingly, the district court determined that "it seems more logical to assume that the Congress intended [with section 77(n)] to distinguish collective bargaining agreements as a class from all other contracts. . . ." *Id.* The very existence of *two* distinct statutory schemes of collective bargaining, the RLA and the NLRA, provides an adequate basis for distinguishing between RLA and NLRA labor contracts. *See In re* Brada Miller Freight System, Inc., 702 F.2d 890, 897 (11th Cir. 1983); note 76 *supra* and accompanying text.

[145] The court's desire to permit rejection of the labor contracts in REA, despite the explicit language of section 77(n), is transparent. The court stated, for instance, that "[n]o reason is shown why the unions and the employees represented by them should [in a Chapter 11 reorganization] be permitted to insist upon strict compliance with their executory agreements with REA." 523 F.2d at 169-170. *Cf.* note 146 *infra.*

> *the interests sought to be protected by the RLA, a district court concludes that an onerous and burdensome executory collective bargaining agreement will thwart efforts to save a failing carrier in bankruptcy from collapse, the court may under § 313(1) authorize rejection or disaffirmance of the agreement.*[146]

The *REA Express* court's focus on permitting rejection, even in the face of section 77(n), is evident from its repeated references to the debtor's financial distress and the egregious nature of the RLA labor contracts it sought to reject:

> To hold that the RLA precludes rejection under such circumstances would ultimately be to defeat the purpose of the RLA itself.... If REA's collective bargaining agreements with the unions, for instance, are too onerous and burdensome to permit it to survive, no purpose would be served by obligating it to resort to RLA negotiating procedures....[147]

The *REA Express* court later opined that "[u]nless the debtor-in-possession is permitted to act promptly, albeit unilaterally, in avoiding onerous employment terms that will prevent it from continuing as a going concern, the enterprise, and with it the employment of its workers, may fail."[148]

In addition to its reliance on *Kevin Steel* for the questionable analogy between section 8(d) of the NLRA and section 6 of the RLA that purported to justify the avoidance of section 77(n), the *REA Express* court also placed a great deal of importance on *Kevin Steel*'s brief reference to the debtor as a "successor employer" under the doctrine of *NLRB v. Burns International Security Services, Inc.*[149] *Kevin Steel*'s off-handed reference to debtors as "new entities" which have the status of successor employers emerged in *REA Express* as a full-blown legal theory. Even though *Kevin Steel* did not rest on this rationale, and notwithstanding that the *Burns* doctrine relates to non-bankruptcy situations of corporate mergers, sales, and transfers of operations, and that in any event the notion of successorship is a product of the NLRA and not the RLA, the

---

[146] 523 F.2d at 169 (emphasis added). *But see* Countryman, Executory Contracts in Bankruptcy (part 2), 58 Minn. L. Rev. 479, 498 (1974) ("[T]he RLA seems also to preclude any interim relief from the onerous collective bargaining contract of a railroad or an airline in bankruptcy proceedings.").

[147] 523 F.2d at 169. The REA Express court divined that the procedures Congress prescribed in section 77(n) of the Act and section 6 of RLA could be ignored because they "assume that the carrier involved is viable and will be able to meet its payroll and contractual obligations to employees and other creditors." 523 F.2d at 169 (footnote omitted). When this "assumption" is not applicable, the court stated that "§ 313(1) must govern." *Id.*

[148] 523 F.2d at 170–71.

[149] 406 U.S. 272, 281–91 (1972). *See* Kevin Steel, 519 F.2d at 704.

court in *REA Express* stated that "[w]hen REA, after going into Chapter XI proceedings, was authorized to operate as the debtor-in-possession, it acted as a new juridical entity. It was not a party to and was not bound by the terms of the collective bargaining agreement entered into by REA as debtor. . . ."[150]

The *REA Express* court concluded that the judicially-devised new entity theory justified departure from the statutory provisions of section 313(1):

> For these reasons, we are persuaded that REA, as the debtor-in-possession in bankruptcy, is a new employer which, while obligated as a carrier to negotiate with its employees' collective bargaining representative, is not bound to follow the elaborate and protracted procedures of § 6 of the RLA before putting into effect its proposed terms of employment.[151]

If the *REA Express* court was serious about the new entity theory, of course, a debtor would have the plenary power to reject its "predecessor's" contract because, after all, the debtor was not a party to the contract. But the court in *REA Express* did not go this far. Citing the intangible contract damages resulting from the debtor's rejection, which were not recoverable against the estate under the Act (a fact having little relevance if the debtor were, in fact, a "new juridical entity"), the court concluded that

> in view of the serious effects which rejection has on the carrier's employees, it should be authorized only where it clearly appears to be the lesser of two evils and that, unless the agreement is rejected, the carrier will collapse and the employees will no longer have their jobs.[152]

In light of the tenuous reasoning of Judge Mansfield's opinion in *REA Express,* it is surprising that these words would become a common standard for rejection of all labor agreements, even those between parties subject to the NLRA.[153]

In *Truck Drivers Local Union No. 807 v. Bohack Corp.,*[154] which involved a reorganization under Chapter 11 of the Act, the Second Circuit refined its approach in *Kevin Steel* and *REA Express.* Although *Bohack* dealt mainly with complex procedural and jurisdictional issues beyond the scope of this chapter and not directly

---

[150] 523 F.2d at 170, *citing* Kevin Steel, 519 F.2d at 704.

[151] 523 F.2d at 171.

[152] *Id.* at 172.

[153] *See, e.g., In re* David A. Rosow, Inc., 9 Bankr. 190, 191 (Bankr. Conn. 1981); *In re* Allied Technology, Inc., 8 Bankr. 366 (Bankr. S.D. Ohio 1980); *In re* Alan Wood Steel Co., 449 F. Supp. 165, 169 (E. D. Pa. 1978), *appeal dismissed,* 595 F.2d 1211 (3d Cir. 1979); notes 236 & 237, *infra.*

[154] 541 F.2d 312 (2d Cir. 1976).

relevant to the issue of rejection[155]—such as the power of bankruptcy and district courts to enjoin strikes by a union against a debtor-in-possession—the court did address the standard for rejection of NLRA labor contracts and the "new entity theory." The *Bohack* court adopted *REA Express'* section 8(d) gloss on *Kevin Steel* but rehabilitated *REA Express'* reliance on the successor employer doctrine:

> We have recently held ... that upon the filing of a chapter XI petition, statutory requirements precedent to the termination of a collective bargaining agreement by the employer under Section 8(d) of the National Labor Relations Act ... do not prevent its rejection by the bankruptcy court under Section 313(1) of the Bankruptcy Act. [*Citing Kevin Steel* and *REA Express.*] We reasoned that the status of the debtor-employer is, in some respects, analogous to that of a successor employer so far as an existing collective bargaining agreement is concerned, insofar as the debtor is a "new juridical entity."[156]

The court retracted a good deal of its new entity rhetoric, however, because the successorship argument obviously proved too much; if the debtor was a "new entity," why did it have to reject a contract to which it was not a party, and why should *any* restrictions be placed on rejection? The *Bohack* explained: "Of course, the statement that the debtor is not a 'party,' and the analogy to the successor employer, cannot be taken literally, since neither affirmance nor rejection of the collective bargaining agreement would be possible by one not a party to it."[157] Where does this leave *Kevin Steel* and *REA Express,* if the successorship analogy is not to be taken "literally"?

Close reading of *Bohack* reveals other analytical weaknesses in the "implied restriction" theory. The court stated, for example, that "if the contract is rejected, the [bargaining unit] employees become creditors of the estate and may have a claim for damages against the estate...."[158] This statement is inconsistent with the "speculative damage" language in *In re Overseas National Airways*[159] that the Second Circuit had expressly relied on in *Kevin Steel* and *REA Express.*[160]

---

[155] *See* chapter VI, *infra.*

[156] 541 F.2d at 320. Note the court's facile equation of the NLRA and the RLA; section 77(n) of the Act is virtually ignored.

[157] *Id.*

[158] *Id.* at 321.

[159] 238 F. Supp. 359, 361–62 (E.D.N.Y. 1965).

[160] *See* Kevin Steel, 519 F.2d at 707; REA Express, 523 F.2d at 172.

Two-thirds of the *Bohack* panel (Judges Hays and Gurfein) cautioned in *In re Unishops, Inc.*[161] that the "new entity" language in *Kevin Steel*

> should not be extended as a generalization in cases other than those involving labor collective bargaining agreements where the claim is that Section 8(d) . . . precludes disaffirmance of the labor agreement in a Chapter XI proceeding without taking the steps required under Section 8(a) [*sic*] of the Labor Act; or under the Railway Labor Act. . . .[162]

Once again the court failed to distinguish between RLA and NLRA contracts, rendering section 77(n) meaningless.

The Ninth Circuit, to its credit, avoided the *REA Express* muddle when it first confronted the issue of a Chapter 11 debtor's ability to reject NLRA labor contracts in *Local Joint Executive Board, AFL-CIO v. Hotel Circle, Inc.*[163] After considering what had become the standard arguments by unions and employers in labor contract rejection cases, the Ninth Circuit simply concluded that

> the unique features of labor agreements do not overcome the plain language of the Bankruptcy Act and the policies embodied in Chapter XI proceedings. While we recognize that important employee interests are at stake when rejection of a labor agreement is considered, the policies of the Bankruptcy Act are designed to assist failing businesses, a goal in which employees ultimately have a stake as well.[164]

The court pointedly avoided the thicket of dicta created by *Kevin Steel* and *REA Express:* "We also do not need to address the question whether the bankruptcy court should apply a stricter standard for authorizing the rejection of collective bargaining agreements as a means of reconciling the policies of the labor and bankruptcy laws."[165]

The first U.S. Court of Appeals case interpreting section 365 of the Code in the context of the rejection of collective bargaining agreements was the Third Circuit's decision in *In re Bildisco.*[166] *Bildisco* was consolidated action involving a union's appeal from a bankruptcy court order permitting the rejection of a NLRA collective bargaining agreement by a Chapter 11 debtor-in-possession and the NLRB's application of enforcement of its determination that

---

[161] 543 F.2d at 1017 (2d Cir. 1976) (per curiam).

[162] *Id.* at 1019 (emphasis added).

[163] 613 F.2d 210 (9th Cir. 1980).

[164] *Id.* at 214.

[165] *Id.* at 213–214 n.2. *Cf. In re* Pacific Far East Lines, Inc., 654 F.2d 664, 668 (9th Cir. 1981) (relying on new entity theory and quoting *Kevin Steel* with approval).

[166] 682 F.2d 72 (3d Cir. 1982), *cert. granted,* 103 S. Ct. 784 (1983), *aff'd,* 104 S. Ct. 1188 (1984).

the debtor committed an unfair labor practice by unilaterally changing the terms of the agreement.

The labor agreement was between Bildisco, a partnership engaged in the sale and distribution of building supplies, and Teamsters Local 408. Bildisco filed a voluntary petition for reorganization under Chapter 11 on April 14, 1980 and moved to reject the Teamsters contract pursuant to section 365(a) of the Code in December 1980. When Bildisco entered bankruptcy, the bargaining unit consisted of eighteen employees. By January 5, 1981, the date of the hearing on the debtor's motion to reject, the bargaining unit had shrunk to three employees.

The only witness at the hearing, one of Bildisco's partners, testified that rejection of the Teamsters contract would save approximately $100,000 in 1981. The union cross-examined the witness, "but it did not offer any other evidence concerning the effect of rejection on Bildisco's employees."[167] The Third Circuit summarized the remaining facts as follows:

> The bankruptcy judge, without expressly articulating the standard that he applied, granted permission to reject on January 15, 1981. . . . The union appealed to the district court, which on May 4, 1981, issued a bench opinion affirming that order of the bankruptcy court. Noting that the bankruptcy judge had not identified the test he had used, the district court held that the permission to reject was proper in any event.[168]

The bankruptcy court appears to have employed the "business judgment test." The bankruptcy judge stated, for example, that "I don't know under the Code what power the court has to disapprove an application to reject a contract, unless it can be shown it was a promiscuous act on the part of the debtor, and it was really a beneficial contract. . . . Under Section 365 I have to grant the motion to reject."[169] The district court affirmed the bankruptcy court on the ground that rejection was appropriate under either the *REA Express* or the business judgment standard.[170]

Meanwhile, the union filed unfair labor practice charges with the NLRB, which issued a complaint on July 31, 1980. The debtor failed to answer the complaint and, after several warnings by the General Counsel that it would seek summary judgment, on April 23, 1981 the Board granted summary judgment against Bildisco. Notwithstanding the bankruptcy court's order granting rejection on Jan-

---

[167] 682 F.2d at 75.
[168] *Id.*
[169] *Id.* n.3.
[170] *Id.* at 81 n.14.

uary 15, 1981, the NLRB essentially ordered specific performance of the Teamsters contract.

From the outset of its opinion, the Third Circuit described the rejection of collective bargaining agreements under the Code as an issue "which implicates a significant confrontation of labor and bankruptcy policies" and which "is a matter of first impression in the courts of appeals."[171] Perhaps mindful of the union's and NLRB's arguments that the NLRA conflicts with section 365(a) of the Code,[172] the court remarked that "[t]his case places the statutory policies underlying Chapter 11 in tension with our national labor policy, as expressed in the National Labor Relations Act."[173] "Our task," the court said, "is to reconcile the apparent conflict between the NLRA and the Bankruptcy Code and the policies they represent."[174] The court analyzed the key components of this "conflict," section 365(a) of the Code and section 8(d) of the NLRA, in isolation.

The court observed that Congress had enacted in the Code detailed provisions excluding various types of executory contracts from the rejection mechanism of section 365(a): shopping center leases;[175] commodities futures contracts;[176] and collective bargaining agreements under the RLA.[177] Section 1167, therefore, "permits an inference that, with this one exception, Congress did not intend to distinguish collective bargaining agreements from executory contracts in general."[178] As in *Kevin Steel,* however, the court was reluctant to decide the case based on the literal language of the statute.

Thus, while section 365(a) "authorizes the bankruptcy court to permit the rejection of [NLRA] collective bargaining agreements,"[179] the appropriate *standard* for rejection is a separate is-

---

[171] *Id.* at 76.

[172] It is interesting to note that the Board did not rely so much on section 8(d) as on more generalized "policy considerations supporting the *Kevin Steel* standard" and congressional approval—*through silence*—of the Kevin Steel and REA Express decisions. *See* Brief for the National Labor Relations Board, *In re* Bildisco, 682 F.2d 72 (3d Cir. 1982) at pp. 16–23. The union relied almost exclusively on the "approval by silence" argument, buttressed by numerous citations to cases applying the Kevin Steel/REA Express standard for rejection. *See* Brief of Appellant Local 408, *In re* Bildisco, 682 F.2d 72 (3d Cir. 1982) at pp. 10–19; Reply Brief of Appellant Local 408 at pp. 2–4.

[173] 682 at 77–78.

[174] *Id.* at 78.

[175] 11 U.S.C. § 365(b)(3).

[176] 11 U.S.C. §§ 765, 766.

[177] 11 U.S.C. § 1167.

[178] 682 F.2d at 78.

[179] *Id.*

sue.[180] Further, the court invoked the "new entity theory" to avoid section 8(d).

Judge Aldisert's opinion in *Bildisco* acknowledged that the "usual test" for rejection of an executory contract is the "business judgment test."[181] Even though it had previously held that, with the exception of RLA labor contracts, "Congress did not intend to distinguish collective bargaining agreements from executory contracts in general,"[182] the court rejected the "usual test" for rejection: "The impact of rejection of a collective bargaining agreement on the rights of workers and the favored status those rights have been accorded by Congress ... require a more stringent examination of the evidence offered to justify rejection of such a contract."[183]

One may wonder why a particular class of contract creditors should be treated differently from others absent some indication of congressional intent; the Third Circuit in *Bildisco* had already reviewed the Code and concluded that "Congress afforded collective bargaining agreements no special treatment."[184] How, then, could the court deem workers to possess a "favored status" for purposes of bankruptcy law? Judge Aldisert offered no explanation except to note that *Kevin Steel*

> accommodated the interests of the workers by holding that rejection of a collective bargaining agreement requires "thorough scrutiny, and a careful balancing of the equities on both sides."
>
> We accept this formulation of the appropriate relationship between the competing statutory policies.... It plots a middle course between the possible extremes....[185]

The *Bildisco* court, however, emphatically rejected the gloss *REA Express* had placed on *Kevin Steel:* "According to *REA Express,* rejection should be permitted 'only where it clearly appears to be the lesser of two evils and that, unless the agreement is rejected, the carrier will collapse and the employees will no longer have their jobs.' "[186] Judge Aldisert rebuked *REA Express* and its progeny as decisions "which purport to follow the rule of *Kevin Steel* but instead replace its 'balancing of the equities' with" a substantially more

---

[180] The dichotomy between power to reject and the standard for rejection is subject to criticism. If, indeed, the NLRA conflicts with the Code, rejection of labor contracts is forbidden. In the absence of conflict, however, debtors should logically be able to reject labor agreements on the same basis as any other contract, if they can reject labor contracts at all.

[181] 682 F.2d at 79.

[182] *Id.* at 78.

[183] *Id.* at 79.

[184] *Id.* at 78.

[185] *Id.* at 79 (*quoting* Kevin Steel, 519 F.2d at 707 (citations omitted)).

[186] *Id.* (*quoting* REA Express, 523 F.2d at 172).

stringent standard for rejection.[187] These decisions, the *Bildisco* court scathingly admonished, "reflect a phenomenon ... called 'trampling upon graves': adding a substantial gloss to a previously stated holding but improperly citing the former case as the authority for the new formulation."[188] The gloss on *Kevin Steel* added by *REA Express* "disguise[d] an expansion of the law by pretending that the court [was] simply applying a previously stated rule of law."[189]

The court explained its rejection of the *REA Express* standard at length, citing both "pragmatic" and "prudential" reasons. The pragmatic basis for *Bildisco*' disagreement with *REA Express* was that "it may be impossible to predict the success *vel non* of a reorganization until very late in the arrangement proceedings"[190]; the prudential considerations were that the "lesser of two evils" test "could work to the detriment of the workers it seeks to protect" by forcing marginal companies into liquidation rather than reorganization.[191]

The *Bildisco* court concluded the first aspect of its bifurcated analysis of the rejection of labor contracts by summarizing the reasons for its adoption of the *Kevin Steel* standard:

> We are satisfied that *Kevin Steel*, isolated from its illegitimate progeny, provides the appropriate framework for an intelligent and equitable approach to the problem because it gives collective bargaining agreements a measure of protection beyond that available under the business judgment test *without unduly advancing the interests served by the Labor Act over the other interests of the employees and those of the debtor's other creditors.*[192]

The Third Circuit remanded the case to the bankruptcy court "for reconsideration in light of the precepts we announce today"[193] because the trial court's "woefully inadequate treatment of a sophisticated subject"[194] did not address the "hitherto unsettled area"

---

[187] *Id.*

[188] *Id.* n.11

[189] *Id.*

[190] *Id.* at 80.

[191] *Id.* The court seemed to assume that an employer in liquidation could reject a labor contract under section 365(a), although the absolute reading of section 8(d) urged by the NLRB in *Kevin Steel* and the unions in *Bildisco* would seem to preclude *any* termination or modification of the contract during its term.

[192] 682 F.2d at 81 (emphasis added). The court at least recognized that it *was* advancing the interests of union employees over the interests of other contract creditors. Query how it determined this unauthorized preference was not "undue." Significantly, the court clarified a point of confusion under the Act by observing that "under [11 U.S.C.] § 365(g) rejection constitutes a breach of contract, the employees may assert a claim for the value of the benefits lost." *Id.* at 80.

[193] *Id.* at 82.

[194] *Id.* at 81.

of the standard for rejection.[195] The *Bildisco* court mentioned, but (unlike its treatment of the union's and Board's *REA Express* argument) never specifically refuted, the employer's argument that "collective bargaining agreements are to be treated like all other executory contracts and that rejection should be permitted whenever it would benefit the debtor."[196] Apparently the court felt its assertion of conflicting policies between the NLRA and the Code was sufficient to foreclose this "extreme" position.[197]

This is ironic, because *Bildisco*'s sharp criticisms of *REA Express* and that decision's unwarranted extension of *Kevin Steel* is arguably applicable to *Kevin Steel*'s departure from the *Klaber Bros.* reasoning. In fact with the single exception of *In re Overseas National Airways, Bildisco*'s discussion of or reference to pre-*Kevin Steel* authorities is notable only by its absence.[198] The doctrinal transition from the *Klaber Bros.-Turney Wood Products* line of cases to *Kevin Steel* was far more significant and lacking in statutory support than the shift from *Kevin Steel* to *REA Express,* with which the court in *Bildisco* took such umbrage. In fact, *Kevin Steel*'s reliance on an RLA case such as *In re Overseas National Airways* to derive the "balancing of equities" alternative to the then-prevailing business judgment standard for rejection of NLRA labor contracts is similar to the "illegitimate" "trampling upon graves" in *REA Express* that the court deplored.[199]

To its credit, however, the *Bildisco* court drew a line regarding the development of a progressively noninterpretive approach to the standard for rejection of collective bargaining agreements. At the same time, the court in *Bildisco* ignored—without discussion or analysis—a whole range of pre-*Kevin Steel* authorities arguably more consonant with the language and structure of the statutory bankruptcy scheme.

The first part of the *Bildisco* opinion is even more inexplicable in light of its separate treatment of the unfair labor practice issues. The Board was seeking enforcement of its determination that *Bildisco* had committed an unfair labor practice by unilaterally changing the terms and conditions of union employees' employment, *i.e.,* rejecting the collective bargaining agreement under the auspices of Chapter 11 reorganization. The *Bildisco* court denied enforcement

[195] *Id.* at 82.
[196] *Id.* at 81.
[197] *See id* at 79.
[198] *See id.*
[199] *See* 682 F.2d at 79 n.11, 81.

on the now-familiar theory that the debtor-in-possession is a new entity:

> The Board's theory depends upon its contention that the debtor-in-possession is an alter ego of the debtor and thereby a party to the collective bargaining agreement. The Board's argument fails, however, because, as a matter of law, a debtor-in-possession is "[a] new entity . . . created with its own rights and duties, subject to the supervision of the bankruptcy court."[200]

In light of the Second Circuit's retreat from the new entity theory and the confused analysis of the rejection cases, the Board's position was at least doctrinally (if not statutorily)[201] plausible. The *Bildisco* court, however, chastised the Board even more severely than it had the Second Circuit's decision in *REA Express*:

> The debtor-in-possession's position is analogous to that of a successor employer: it may be required to recognize and bargain with the union, but it is not a party to its predecessor's collective bargaining agreement unless it assumes that agreement. *Because Bildisco as debtor-in-possession is not a party to the agreement with Local 408, it had the ability to reject the agreement without following the procedures outlined in § 8(d).* We suggest to the NLRB that, at least in matters within this judicial circuit, it cease operating under such a fundamental misconception of the law. *Indeed, we believe that persisting in such a misconception—one that goes to the difference between the pre-bankruptcy company which was the signatory to the collective bargaining agreement and the succeeding debtor-in-possession—is so fundamental that this error in and of itself is sufficient reason to refuse to enforce a summary judgment so predicated.*[202]

The *Bildisco* court's discussion of the section 8(d) issue proves too much. If the debtor is truly a different entity from the pre-bankruptcy employer, why is the debtor required to reject the contract at all? If the debtor "is not a party to its predecessor's . . . agreement," it logically should be bound to comply with neither section 8(d) *nor* section 365(a). If the "conflict" between the NLRA and the Code on the unfair labor practice issues could be resolved by the "new entity theory," why did the court feel compelled to "balance" the equities and "accommodate" the policies in the rejection context, where the statutory language and legislative history are so clear? How could the court assert the new entity doctrine to avoid section 8(d) and at the same time impose a more stringent standard for the debtor's rejection of contracts to which it is *not* a

---

[200] *Id.* at 82 (*quoting* Kevin Steel, 519 F.2d at 704.).
[201] *See* notes 26–47 *supra* and accompanying text.
[202] 682 F.2d at 83 (emphasis added).

party than for rejection of ordinary commercial contracts to which it *is* a party?[203]

The *Bildisco* decision contains a number of defects. Bifurcating its analysis into separate components required the court to treat the issues of rejection under section 365(a) and rejection under section 8(d) in isolation. This allowed the court to make some interesting arguments regarding the standard for rejection under section 365(a) and to criticize the reasoning of *REA Express.* However, section 8(d) provides the basis for the alleged conflict with section 365(a). Divorcing the analysis of section 8(d), and then resolving the section 8(d) issue by reliance on the new entity theory articulated most prominently by *REA Express,* resulted in an internally inconsistent opinion. Both components of *Bildisco*'s analysis are incomplete: the standard for rejection under section 365(a) overlooks the plain language of the statute and the reasoning of the pre-*Kevin Steel* authorities; the section 8(d) discussion relies on a question-begging and inapt analogy to the successorship doctrine. Taken together, the two components of the Third Circuit's opinion in *Bildisco* are inconsistent and contradictory, thus compounding and magnifying the defects in each part.

The Third Circuit ultimately fell prey to the same mirage of complexity that led the Second Circuit astray in *Kevin Steel* and *REA Express.* Why apply the literal language of a statute and follow lower court authorities in a pedestrian fashion when a court can contrive "policies in conflict" that can be resolved only with elaborate judicial balancing? Boredom with the passive nature of the judicial function or dissatisfaction with the policy choice made by the legislature is often the motivation for judicial activism. The "balancing of equities" test the court adopted in *Bildisco* is judicial legislation—adopting by fiat the exception to section 365(a) that Congress could have enacted, but did not.

Following the Third Circuit's decision in *Bildisco,* but before the Supreme Court issued its decision on February 22, 1984, other appellate courts faced the question of rejection of collective bargaining agreements under the Code. In *In re Brada Miller Freight System, Inc.,*[204] several Teamsters Locals appealed a district court order affirming the bankruptcy court's holding that a Chapter 11 debtor-

[203] Presumably, the *Burns* successorship doctrine is limited to an employer's obligations under the NLRA, and is not applicable to changes of control in commercial law generally. *See* NLRB v. Burns International Security Services, Inc., 406 U.S. 272, 281–91 (1972)

[204] 702 F.2d 890 (11th Cir. 1983).

in-possession could reject its NLRA collective bargaining agreements under section 365(a) of the Code.

The scenario in *Brada Miller* was a familiar one:[205] The trucking company suffered chronic operating losses, curtailed operations and laid off personnel, eventually filed a voluntary petition for reorganization under Chapter 11, and then moved to reject its collective bargaining agreements with the Teamsters. The union filed unfair labor practice charges with the NLRB.[206] The bankruptcy court found that "[a] large portion of the Company's costs were its obligations under the collective bargaining agreements. The bankruptcy court found that these obligations ... cost the Company approximately $32,000 per day. The Company's remaining operating expenses equaled $70,000 per day in 1980."[207] Accordingly, without articulating the legal standard it employed, the bankruptcy court granted the debtor's motion to reject the labor contracts under section 365(a). The district court affirmed this aspect of the bankruptcy court's order because the facts supported rejection under either the *Kevin Steel* or *REA Express* standard.[208]

In a scholarly opinion the Eleventh Circuit rejected the unions' principal argument that section 8(d) forbids rejection of labor agreements under section 365(a), ruling instead that "Congress intended collective bargaining agreements to be subject to unilateral rejection by the bankruptcy trustee (with the approval of the court) under § 365."[209] More significantly, the court rejected as unsound the "new entity theory" as a means of accommodating the two statutes: "The most obvious problem with the new entity theory is the statutory requirement that a debtor-in-possession, purportedly not a party to contracts executed by the pre-bankruptcy corporation, apply to a bankruptcy court for approval of its rejection of a collective bargaining agreement."[210]

Rather, having concluded that section 365(a) permits rejection, the court "accommodated" the NLRA and the Code by devising a more rigorous standard for rejection. The business judgment stan-

---

[205] *See Wilson Foods: Nine Days to Chapter 11,* Bus. Wk. (May 30, 1983) at p. 68; *Chapter 11 Filing by Wilson Foods Roils Workers' Lives, Tests Laws,* Wall St. J. (May 23, 1983) at p. 29; *Bankruptcy Filed to Erase Contract,* L. A. Times (April 23, 1983) at p. I-28; *Firms Using Bankruptcy to Fight Labor,* Wall St. J. (March 30, 1983) at p. 25; *A Louder Union Voice in Settling Bankruptcies,* Bus. Wk. (Dec. 8, 1980) at p. 87.

[206] 702 F.2d at 892.

[207] *Id.* at 893.

[209] *Id.* The district court reversed the bankruptcy court on a number of points not relevant here. *See id.* nn. 5–6.

[209] *Id.* at 894.

[210] *Id.* at 895.

dard for rejection of "ordinary commercial contracts" is "insufficient to protect the special rights accruing to employees under the federal labor laws."[211] The *Brada Miller* court then surveyed the development of *Kevin Steel* and *REA Express* and, like the Third Circuit in *Bildisco,* concluded that "the *Kevin Steel* balancing of the equities test provides a more satisfactory accommodation of the conflicting interests at stake in a rejection proceeding."[212]

The *Brada Miller* court identified the factors that the bankruptcy court should balance before authorizing rejection of labor contracts: the probability of liquidation; harm to employees resulting from breach of the agreement; the cost-spreading abilities of the parties; the degree of cooperation of the parties; and the good faith of the employer in seeking rejection.[213] The court stated that "[w]e stop short of requiring that the parties commence the bargaining process prior to the granting of a motion to reject, but we leave it to the discretion of the bankruptcy court to require such bargaining. . . ."[214]

In light of the Supreme Court's granting of certiorari in *Bildisco,* the *Brada Miller* court remanded the case to the bankruptcy court "for reconsideration in light of the foregoing and in light of the disposition of the Supreme Court of *Bildisco.*"[215]

The *Brada Miller* opinion is essentially identical to *Bildisco* except that it rejected the problematical new entity theory. Otherwise, it conformed to the *Bildisco* analysis: section 8(d) does not preclude rejection under section 365(a), but the "accommodation" of the policies of the NLRA and the Code require a more stringent standard for rejection than the business judgment test. Both courts adopted the balancing approach of *Kevin Steel.*

In *Borman's Inc. v. Allied Supermarkets, Inc.,*[216] the Sixth Circuit addressed a variant of the typical rejection contest. A member of a multi-employer bargaining group filed for reorganization under Chapter 11 and moved to reject its labor contracts. Unlike the usual situation, the *union* approved but the debtor's *competitors* objected on the ground that the remaining members of the multi-employer group would be adversely affected. The bankruptcy court permitted rejection, and the district court affirmed.

On appeal, the Sixth Circuit rejected the competitors' argument that *their* interests had to be considered in the *Kevin Steel* balancing approach: "Whatever the merits of the 'rule' that the courts must

[211] *Id.* at 897.
[212] *Id.* at 899.
[213] *Id.* at 899–900.
[214] *Id.* at 900 (footnote omitted).
[215] *Id.* at 901 (footnote omitted).
[216] 706 F.2d 187 (6th Cir. 1983).

judge applications to reject labor contracts by a more stringent standard than applications to reject other executory contracts, that rule is inapplicable here."[217]

The court traced the evolution of the *Kevin Steel* standard from *Klaber Bros.* and observed that "[o]nly the *Kevin Steel* and *REA Express* decisions ... suggest that applications to reject executory labor contracts must be more strictly scrutinized than applications to reject other executory contracts."[218] The court also noted that the Ninth Circuit reserved the issue in the *Hotel Circle* case and stated itself that "[s]ince here the unions have not opposed [the debtor's] application, we similarly need not pass upon this question."[219]

Finally, in *Yorke v. NLRB.*[220] the Seventh Circuit considered the related issue of a Chapter 11 debtor's duty to bargain with the union over the *effects* of rejection under section 8(a)(5) of the NLRA. The divided panel in *Yorke* held that the debtor had a duty to bargain about the effects of a plant closure upon the union's request, even though the debtor had no antecedent duty to inform the union of its impending action.[221] Judge Coffey dissented because, *inter alia,* a debtor's commencement of effects bargaining might be viewed as an assumption of the contract, the imposition of a duty to bargain over effects invites conflict between the bankruptcy court and the NLRB, and "the majority's decision foists an unreasonable burden on business enterprises involved in Chapter XI bankruptcy proceedings."[222]

Objections to the "Accomodation" or "Implied Restriction" Rationale: A Critique of the Kevin Steel *Balancing Approach*

The major decisions from *Klaber Bros.* in 1959 to more recent cases, *In re Bildisco* (1982) and *In re Brada Miller Freight System* (1983), took different, sometimes conflicting, and frequently internally inconsistent approaches to the rejection of collective bargaining agreements.

---

[217] *Id.* at 190 (footnote omitted).
[218] *Id.* n.8.
[219] *Id.*
[220] 709 F.2d 1138 (7th Cir. 1983).
[221] *Id.* at 1144.
[222] *Id.* at 1151 (Coffey, J., dissenting). Judge Coffey added that:

> It is the height of absurdity for the NLRB to exert a fatal chokehold on Congress's specific intent to allow mortally wounded businesses a chance to make a financial comeback at a time when our basic industries are struggling to survive.

Id.

Some commentators have argued that the courts improperly departed from the literal mode of analysis exemplified by the *Klaber Bros.* case.[223] According to these commentators, the plain language of section 365(a) leaves little room for consideration of conflicting policies and implied restrictions: "[T]he trustee, subject to the court's approval, may assume or reject *any* executory contract . . . of the debtor."[224] In the face of this language, the "power" to reject and "standard" for rejection are identical issues. If a collective bargaining agreement constitutes "any executory contract," and is therefore subject to rejection, there is no legitimate basis for holding a labor agreement to a more stringent standard for rejection. Courts may like to balance,[225] and in some contexts are forced to balance—when, for instance, the relevant statute calls for balancing or there is a genuine statutory or doctrinal conflict to be resolved. With section 365(a), however, one must presume that Congress did all the balancing it wished to be done when it enacted the broad and absolute language of the statute.

The only honest and fair conclusion to be drawn from section 1167 and its legislative history is that Congress intended to exclude certain types of labor agreements from the rejection mechanism, but not others. This may seem arbitrary or imprudent, but this objection applies with equal force to Congress' decision to enact two distinct and very different schemes of collective bargaining, the

[223] *See* Pulliam, *The Rejection of Collective Bargaining Agreements Under Section 365 of the Bankruptcy Code,* 58 AM. BANKR. L.J. 1, 36–42 (1984).

[224] 11 U.S.C. § 365(a) (emphasis added). Under 11 U.S.C. § 1107(a), a debtor-in-possession has all of the rights and powers of a trustee appointed under Chapter 11.

[225] Nobody, however, likes to balance as much as law students. *See, e.g.,* Note, *The Bankruptcy Law's Effect on Collective Bargaining Agreements,* 81 COLUM. L. REV. 391, 399–404 (1981) (proposing "partial rejection" approach and a "synthesis" of *Kevin Steel* and *REA Express* to "accommodate" the "conflicting policies" of the NLRA and the Code); Note, *The Labor-Bankruptcy Conflict: Rejection of a Debtor's Collective Bargaining Agreement,* 80 MICH. L. REV. 134, 148 (1981) ("courts should recognize the conflict between the bankruptcy and labor laws, and exercise their discretion to approve or disapprove rejection requests in a way that will strike a sound balance between the competing policies"); Note, *Bankruptcy and the Rejection of Collective Bargaining Agreements,* 51 NOTRE DAME LAW. 819, 822 (1976) (in *Kevin Steel* and *REA Express,* "the Second Circuit attempted to reach an equitable compromise" between the Act and the NLRA); Comment, *Collective Bargaining and Bankruptcy,* 42 S. CAL. L. REV. 477, 491 (1969) ("Where bankruptcy and labor law conflict, the former should not preempt the latter where some suitable accommodation can be found."); Note, *The Automatic Stay of the 1978 Bankruptcy Code Versus the Norris-LaGuardia Act: A Bankruptcy Court's Dilemma,* 61 TEX. L. REV. 321, 335 (1982) ("courts should weigh the contrasting bankruptcy and labor policies involved, . . . and attempt to reconcile the effects of the conflicting statutory provisions as much as possible"); Note, 27 WAYNE L. REV. 1601, 1608 (1981) (strict standard for rejection accommodates competing policies of NLRA and the Act); Note, 22 WAYNE L. REV. 165, 176 (1975) (the "major shortcoming" of *Kevin Steel* is that it did not articulate adequate guidelines for balancing).

RLA for railroads and airlines, and the NLRA for most other industries affecting commerce.[226]

The primary policy of the Bankruptcy Code is equality of treatment within the classes of creditors prescribed by Congress. The rejection mechanism, while permitting a debtor to escape burdensome financial obligations that impede profitable operations and successful reorganization, protects the interests of contract creditors by regarding rejection as a pre-petition breach and allowing an unsecured claim for damages against the estate. Allowing a debtor to reject non-labor executory contracts subject only to a minimal "business judgment test," but imposing a more stringent standard on the rejection of labor contracts, has the obvious practical effect of making rejection of labor contracts more difficult.

Thus, while commercial contract creditors are compelled to pursue an unsecured claim for damages against the estate, in some cases labor unions are entitled to specific performance of their collective bargaining agreement with the debtor.[227] Moreover, while the favored treatment of collective bargaining agreements may have been justified under the Act due to the difficulty of computing, and therefore recovering, intangible damages resulting from rejection,[228] this is no longer the case under section 502(c) of the Code. In fact, some commentators suggest the inapplicability of the *Kevin Steel* standard under the Code. The leading bankruptcy authority states that

> one of the possible grounds for [the *Kevin Steel* standard] has been removed.... [U]nder Section 502(c) of the Code such claims [by employees arising from the breach caused by rejection] must be estimated.... Although a mere showing that rejection would improve the financial condition of the debtor did not suffice under the Act, the result may be different under the Code due to the failure of Congress to incorporate a requirement of burdensomeness into section 365.[229]

Another commentator notes that

---

[226] Yet, in the face of this distinction, commentators have made the absurd argument that "[c]ertainly, it is doubtful that Congress would create a distinction between the treatment of labor contracts under the RLA and labor agreements under the NLRA." Note, *Bankruptcy and the Rejection of Collective Bargaining Agreements,* 51 NOTRE DAME LAW. 819, 827 (1976.)

[227] *See* Johnson v. England, 356 F.2d 44, 51 (9th Cir.) *cert. denied,* 384 U.S. 961 (1966); *see also* Nathanson v. NLRB, 344 U.S. 25, 28 (1952) (question of priority of wage claim against a bankrupt employer "is a legislative decision").

[228] *See* La Penna, *Bankruptcy and the Collective Bargaining Agreement,* Proceedings of the 29th N.Y.U. Conf. on Lab. 169, 180 (1976).

[229] 2 COLLIER ON BANKRUPTCY ¶ 365.03 at 365-17 to 365-18 (15th ed. 1983) (footnote omitted).

> [i]n the Code, Congress did not choose to treat collective bargaining agreements differently than other executory contracts, which are governed by section 365.... With the exception of section 1167, the Code does not give special treatment to labor contracts and offers no definite guide to whether labor contracts are more or less vulnerable to the section 365 power to assume or reject than other executory contracts....[230]

After observing that under the Act courts resolved the conflict between the policies of the Act and the NLRA by permitting rejection under the more stringent *Kevin Steel / REA Express* standard, this commentator concludes that

> [i]n view of the lack of special treatment given labor contracts in § 365 and the failure by Congress legislatively to overrule cases under the Bankruptcy Act giving bankruptcy policy more weight than labor law policy, such a holding under § 365 has a less solid basis than such a holding under the Bankruptcy Act.[231]

Now that all executory contracts are on the same footing insofar as recovery of damages is concerned, this potential justification for treating collective bargaining agreements differently no longer applies.

In addition, impediments to rejection contravene Congress' intent that debtors be given a "breathing spell" from the collection efforts and harassment of their creditors and be relieved of "the financial pressures that drove [them] into bankruptcy."[232] The policies of Chapter 11 *encourage* reorganization over the alternative of liquidation.[233] Authorizing Chapter 11 debtors freely to reject collective bargaining agreements would make reorganization far more likely to succeed. Many economists believe that permitting the free market to operate in the field of labor relations would increase productivity, make employers more competitive, and greatly increase the efficient utilization of resources.[234] To the extent the Code conflicts with the NLRA, these compelling factors alone justify the primacy of the Code. In the rejection context more than any other, employers have

---

[230] Hughes, *"Wavering Between the Profit and the Loss": Operating a Business During Reorganization Under Chapter 11 of the New Bankruptcy Code,* 54 AM. BANKR. L. J. 45, 84–85 (1980).

[231] *Id.* at 86 n.286.

[232] S. Rep. No.989, 95th Cong., 2d Sess., pp.54–55 (1978), *reprinted in* 1978 U.S. Code Cong. & Admin. News 5787, 5840–41; 11 U.S.C. § 362(a)(6).

[233] As the Supreme Court has noted in an analogous context, "[s]addling [a new or successor] employer with the terms and conditions of employment contained in the old collective-bargaining contract may make [corporate and operational] changes impossible and may discourage and inhibit the transfer of capital." NLRB v. Burns International Security Services, Inc., 406 U.S. 277, 288 (1972).

[234] *See* D. HELDMAN, J. BENNETT & M. JOHNSON, DEREGULATING LABOR RELATIONS 133 (1981). *See also* R. POSNER, ECONOMIC ANALYSIS OF LAW, ch. 11 (2d ed. 1977).

an overriding need for speed, flexibility, and predictability, factors the Supreme Court found determinative in *First National Maintenance.*[235] The *Kevin Steel* balancing approach arguably hampers each of these considerations.

The Practical Consequences of the Kevin Steel *Standard*

Despite these criticisms of the *Kevin Steel* standard, or any other departure from the business judgment test, the ultimate criterion for analysis is the practical consequence of the more stringent standard(s) for rejection. The "bottom line" is federal courts' application of the *Kevin Steel* and other standards in reported cases. From this standpoint, the semantic distinction between the business judgment test and *Kevin Steel* standard does not amount to a substantial legal difference; both before and after the Third Circuit's decision in *Bildisco,* courts typically authorized rejection under the *Kevin Steel* standard or variants thereof.[236] The *REA Express* standard posed a more substantial obstacle to rejection, but even under the more rigorous test rejection was granted more often than it was denied, at least in the reported cases.[237]

---

[235] First National Maintenance Corp. v. NLRB, 452 U.S. 666, 679, 682–83 (1981).

[236] *In re* Southern Electronics Co., 23 Bankr. 348 (Bankr. E.D. Tenn. 1982) (rejection granted in NLRA case decided under Code); *In re* Overseas National Airways, 238 F. Supp. 359 (E.D.N.Y. 1965) (rejection denied in RLA case decided under the Act); *In re* Handy Andy, Inc., 112 L.R.R.M. 2657 (W.D. Tex. 1983) (rejection granted in NLRA case decided under the Code); *In re* Braniff Airways, Inc., 25 Bankr. 216 (Bankr. N.D. Tex. 1982) (rejection granted in RLA case decided under the Code); Local Joint Executive Board, AFL-CIO v. Hotel Circle, Inc., 613 F.2d 210 (9th Cir. 1980) (rejection granted in NLRA case decided under the Act); *In re* Price Chopper Supermarkets, Inc., 19 Bankr. 462 (Bankr. S.D. Cal. 1982) (rejection granted in NLRA case decided under the Act after debtor converted Chapter 11 reorganization to Chapter 7 liquidation); *In re* Reserve Roofing Florida, Inc., 9 B.C.D. 202 (Bankr. M.D. Fla. 1982) (rejection granted in NLRA case decided under the Code); *In re* Allied Technology, Inc., 7 B.C.D. 233 (Bankr. S.D. Ohio 1980) (rejection granted in NLRA case decided under the Code); *In re* Yellow Limousine Service, Inc., 22 Bankr. 807, 9 B.C.D. 725 (Bankr. E.D. Pa 1982) (rejection granted in NLRA case decided under the Code); *In re* Briggs Transportation Co., 39 Bankr. 343 (Bankr. D. Minn. 1984) (rejection granted in NLRA case decided under the Code); *In re* Ryan Co., 4 B.C.D. 64 (Bankr. D. Conn. 1978) (rejection granted in NLRA case decided under the Code); *In re* Blue Ribbon Transportation Co., 113 L.R.R.M. 3505 (Bankr. D.R.I. 1983) (rejection conditionally granted in NLRA case decided under the Code); *In re* Penn Fruit Co., 92 L.R.R.M. 3548 (E.D. Pa. 1976) (rejection granted in NLRA case decided under the Act); *In re* Parrot Packing Co., 115 L.R.R.M. 2607 (N.D. Ind. 1983) (rejection granted in NLRA case decided under the Code, provided that non-union personnel of debtor made proportionate economic concessions); *In re* Maverick Mining Corp., 36 Bankr. 837 (Bankr. W.D. Va. 1984) (rejection denied in NLRA case decided under the Code); *In re* Gray Truck Line Co., 34 Bankr. 174, 99 Lab. Cas. (CCH) ¶ 10534 (Bankr. M.D. Fla. 1983) (rejection granted in NLRA case decided under the Code).

[237] *In re* Alan Wood Steel Co., 449 F. Supp. 165 (E.D. Pa. 1978), *appeal dismissed,* 595 F.2d 1211 (3d Cir. 1979) (rejection granted in NLRA case decided under the

The procedure set forth in section 365(a) is limited to rejection of pre-petition contracts that are executory in nature. The significance of these basic requirements is best illustrated by cases where rejection was denied, notwithstanding the debtor's compliance with the other prerequisites for rejection. In *In re IML Freight, Inc.,*[238] and *In re Schuld Mfg. Co.,*[239] the bankruptcy court denied the debtors' motions to reject collective bargaining agreements entered into *after* the petition was filed.

In *IML Freight,* the company filed under Chapter 11 on July 15, 1983 and simultaneously moved to reject certain labor contracts, which the court authorized on August 11, 1983. Shortly thereafter, however, a trustee replaced the debtor-in-possession and on November 11, 1983 the trustee entered into new collective bargaining agreements subject to bankruptcy court approval, which was granted on December 10, 1983. On February 2, 1984, the trustee moved to reject these post-petition labor contracts. The bankruptcy court denied the motion to reject because:

(1) Section 365(a) by its literal terms authorizes rejection of "any executory contract ... of the debtor"; "it does not apply to post-petition contracts negotiated by a trustee or a debtor-in-possession on behalf of the bankruptcy estate";[240]

Act); *In re* David A. Rosow, Inc., 9 Bankr. 190 (Bankr. D. Conn. 1981) (rejection denied in NLRA case decided under the Code); Shopmen's Local Union No. 455 v. Kevin Steel Prods. Inc., 381 F. Supp. 336 (S.D.N.Y. 1974) (rejection denied in NLRA case decided under the Act), *rev'd,* 519 F.2d 698 (2d Cir. 1975); *In re* Brada Miller Freight Systems, Inc., 16 Bankr. 1002 (N.D. Ala. 1981) (rejection granted in NLRA case decided under the Code), *rev'd,* 702 F.2d 890 (11th Cir. 1983); *In re* U.S. Truck Co., 24 Bankr. 853 (Bankr. E.D. Mich. 1982) (rejection granted on motion for reconsideration in NLRA case decided under the Code); *In re* Allied Supermarkets, Inc., 6 Bankr. 968 (Bankr. E.D. Mich. 1980) (rejection granted in NLRA case decided under the Code), *aff'd sub nom.* Borman's, Inc. v. Allied Supermarkets, Inc., 706 F.2d 187 (6th Cir. 1983); *In re* Studio Eight Lighting, Inc., 91 L.R.R.M. 2429 (E.D.N.Y. 1976) (rejection denied in NLRA case decided under Act).

According to testimony at joint hearings on H.R. 5174 before the Senate Judiciary Committee and the Senate Human Resources Committee on April 10, 1984, debtors succeeded in rejecting collective bargaining agreements in 19 of 22 cases reported during the period 1982 through 1984 in which such requests were made. *See* Daily Labor Report (BNA) No. 70, at F-9 (April 11, 1984) (statement of Robert F. Thompson, Chairman of the U. S. Chamber of Commerce Labor Relations Committee). Professor James J. White calculated in 1984 that "courts have ruled on thirty-three proposals to reject collective-bargaining agreements since January 1, 1975. Management has won an outright victory in twenty-two of those cases, and a victory tempered by a remand in three. In only eight has the union been successful in arguing that its contract should not be rejected." White, *The* Bildisco *Case and the Congressional Response,* 30 Wayne L. Rev. 1169, 1184–85 (1984). Professor White believes that "few if any cases would have been changed even if the *REA Express* test had been adopted." *Id.* at 1182.

[238] 37 Bankr. 556 (Bankr. D. Utah 1984).

[239] 43 Bankr. 535 (Bankr. W.D. Wis. 1984).

[240] 37 Bankr. at 556.

(2) If section 365(a) were applied to post-petition contracts, the debtor (or trustee) would be required to seek court approval prior to entering into all contracts; "[s]uch decisions fall within the trustee's or debtor-in-possession's discretion to make decisions in the ordinary course of business";[241] and

(3) "[A]pplying section 365 to post-petition contracts would . . . discourage creditors and others from dealing with Chapter 11 trustees" because if the debtor were able to reject contracts under section 365(a), the creditors' damages arising from breach would be treated as pre-petition claims pursuant to section 365(g) rather than as administrative expenses under section 503(b).[242]

The court in *IML Freight* declined to follow *In re Reserve Roofing*,[243] where the debtor moved to reject pre-petition labor contracts that were renewed during reorganization.[244] The *Reserve Roofing* court held that it had "power to authorize rejection of an executory contract of the debtor regardless of whether entered into or renewed following filing of the Chapter 11 petition."[245] The court in *IML Freight* distinguished *In re Sombrero Reef Club, Inc.*,[246] where the court authorized rejection of pre-petition contracts that the debtor had previously assumed. The *IML Freight* court pointed out that the debtor *sub judice* had rejected the pre-petition labor contracts and then entered into new and wholly different labor contracts, a situation distinct from renewal of pre-petition contracts.[247]

In *In re Schuld Mfg. Co.*,[248] the debtor filed its Chapter 11 petition on April 30, 1982, entered into a collective bargaining agreement on August 2, 1982, and subsequently moved to reject the agreement under section 365(a). The court denied the motion because "the power to accept or reject executory contracts applie[s] only to contracts in effect at the time the bankruptcy proceedings commenced."[249]

The same rule pertains to *expired* contracts, on the ground that they are no longer executory. Thus, in *Gloria Mfg. Corp. v. Inter-*

---

[241] *Id.*

[242] *Id.*

[243] 21 Bankr. 96 (Bankr. M.D. Fla. 1982).

[244] 37 Bankr. at 558.

[245] 21 Bankr. at 100.

[246] 18 Bankr. 612, 615 (Bankr. S.D. Fla. 1982).

[247] 37 Bankr. at 559. The bankruptcy court's unreported August 11, 1983 order authorizing rejection of the original contracts, which was affirmed by the district court on June 25, 1984, was reversed by the U.S. Court of Appeals for the Tenth Circuit in International Brotherhood of Teamsters v. IML Freight. Inc., 789 F.2d 1460 (10th Cir. 1986).

[248] 43 Bankr. 535 (Bankr. W.D. Wis. 1984).

[249] *Id.* at 536.

national Ladies' Garment Workers' Union,[250] the court of appeals affirmed the district court and bankruptcy court, which had denied the debtor's motion to reject an expired collective bargaining agreement that had been entered into pre-petition. The court of appeals reasoned that Congress intended section 365(a) to extend to contracts " 'on which performance remains due to some extent on both sides.' "[251] Because the union had fully performed its contractual obligations under the expired agreement, it was no longer executory and "there was nothing left for the trustee to reject or assume."[252] The court of appeals rejected the debtor's argument that the relation-back feature of section 365(g)(1) authorizes rejection of expired contracts because that statute only prescribed the priority status of damage claims for post-petition breach of a pre-petition executory contract.[253]

The apparent basis for the debtor's desire to reject the expired labor contract in *Gloria Mfg. Corp.* was pending unfair labor practice charges against the debtor and successor Chapter 7 trustee based on the debtor's failure to make wage and benefit payments required by the labor contract.[254] Hence, obtaining court approval of rejection would convert the employees' claims from first priority administrative expenses under section 503(b)(1)(A) to general unsecured claims under section 365(g).

Similar considerations may have motivated the debtor's motion to reject a pre-petition collective bargaining agreement in *In re Total Transportation Service, Inc.,*[255] where the debtor's operations had completely terminated. The court denied the motion to reject because (1) the labor contract was no longer executory in that "future performance pursuant to it will not take place,"[256] and (2) rejection "would serve no rehabilitative end for the employer contracting party" other than subordinating union employees' claims for $2800 in unpaid wages.[257]

Related problems involve multi-employer bargaining units. In *In re De Luca Distributing Co.*[258] the debtor, a long-standing member of a multi-employer bargaining group, filed its Chapter 11 petition the day before the group representative reached agreement with

---

[250] 734 F.2d 1020 (4th Cir. 1984).

[251] *Id.* at 1021 (*quoting* H.R. Rep. No. 595, 95th Cong., 1st Sess. 220 (1977), *reprinted in* 1978 U.S. Code Cong. & Ad. News 5787, 5844).

[252] 734 F.2d at 1022.

[253] *Id.*

[254] *See id.* at 1021 & n.2.

[255] 37 Bankr. 904 (Bankr. S.D. Ohio 1984).

[256] *Id.* at 906.

[257] *Id.* at 907–08.

[258] 38 Bankr. 588 (Bankr. N.D. Ohio 1984).

the union concerning a renewal of the current multi-employer collective bargaining agreement. The debtor had not attempted to withdraw from the multi-employer association. The bankruptcy court denied the debtor's motion to reject the labor contract because under principles of federal labor law, the debtor was bound by the multi-employer association absent timely withdrawal.[259] Consequently, the association's agreement with the union subsequent to the debtor's Chapter 11 filing was binding on the debtor.[260] As a post-petition contract, the agreement was not subject to rejection under section 365(a). The court rejected the debtor's argument that the debtor did not have authority to enter into a post-petition labor contract as a transaction "within the ordinary course of business" under section 363(c)(1). The court adopted the standard set forth in *In re James A. Phillips, Inc.*,[261] and ruled that

> where the debtor's employees have continually been covered by a collective bargaining agreement, a new collective bargaining agreement is a transaction in the ordinary course of business under 11 U.S.C. Section 363(c)(1). As such it does not require notice and a hearing; nor does it require court approval.[262]

The lesson from this case is simple but important: a debtor should withdraw from any multi-employer bargaining groups to which it belongs *prior* to filing its Chapter 11 petition.

Finally, a debtor may reject a collective bargaining agreement only pursuant to a formal order of the bankruptcy court. Moreover, an unrejected executory contract survives confirmation of the plan for reorganization and becomes binding on the reorganized corporation. In *International Union, UAW v. Miles Machinery Co.*,[263] a debtor, after failing to obtain bankruptcy court approval for rejection of a labor contract, proposed a plan of reorganization pursuant to which all of the debtor's stock would be sold to a purchaser who would continue operating the business "in basically the same form and at the same location."[264] The plan also stated that "all executory

---

[259] *See* 38 Bankr. at 590 (*citing* Charles D. Bonanno Linen Service, Inc. v. NLRB, 454 U.S. 404 (1982)).

[260] *Id.*

[261] 29 Bankr. 391 (S.D.N.Y. 1983).

[262] 38 Bankr. at 594. Likewise, outside the multi-employer bargaining context a debtor may renew or agree to a post-petition collective-bargaining agreement in its own right, in the "ordinary course of business." *See* Sealift Maritime, Inc., 265 NLRB 1219 (1982). "As with all transactions 'in the ordinary course of business' under section 363(c)(1) of the Bankruptcy Code, other creditors have no right to object to the terms of new collective bargaining agreements." McDonald, *Bankruptcy Reorganization: Labor Considerations for the Debtor-Employer,* 11 Employee Relations L.J. 7, 11 (1985).

[263] 34 Bankr. 683 (E.D. Mich. 1982).

[264] *Id.* at 685.

contracts shall be rejected."[265] Notwithstanding the bankruptcy court's confirmation of the plan, the labor contract was not thereby rejected. Instead, the district court ordered the successor to comply with the labor contract, including the grievance and arbitration provisions.[266] Again, the teaching of this case is simple but important: do not assume that a contract has been rejected unless there is a formal bankruptcy court order expressly authorizing rejection.

Ironically, the Third Circuit's decision in *Bildisco* satisfied no one. The proponents of organized labor argued for the *REA Express* standard or an even more stringent test.[267] Other commentators and some bankruptcy courts maintained that the *Bildisco/Kevin Steel* standard was too stringent and that the "business judgment" test should apply to rejection of collective bargaining agreements.[268] And nearly all commentators and courts concurred that the "new entity" theory was misconceived.[269] The Supreme Court was faced with a doctrinally and politically difficult choice among a number of competing (and conflicting) alternatives.

---

[265] *Id.*

[266] *Id.* at 688–689. For a discussion of arbitral authority in bankruptcy proceedings, see Butterfield Foods Co., 83 Lab. Arb. 1013 (Gallagher, Arb.) 1984 and chapter VIII.

[267] *See, e.g.,* Simon & Mehlsack, *Judicial Involvement in Labor Relations Under the Bankruptcy Code,* Daily Labor Report (BNA) No. 152 at E-1, E-5 (Aug. 5, 1983); Bordewieck & Countryman, *The Rejection of Collective Bargaining Agreements by Chapter 11 Debtors,* 57 Am. Bankr. L.J. 293 (1983).

[268] *See* Pulliam, *supra* note 223; *In re* Rath Packing Co., 36 Bankr. 979, 989–99 (Bankr. N.D. Iowa 1984), *aff'd,* 48 Bankr. 315 (N.D. Iowa 1985); *In Re* Concrete Pipe Machinery Co., 28 Bankr. 837, 840–42 (Bankr. N.D. Iowa 1983) and cases cited therein.

[269] *See e.g.,* Bordewieck & Countryman, *supra* note 267, at 300–11, 335–37; Pulliam, *supra* note 223, at 32–33; *In re* Brada Miller Freight System, Inc., 702 F.2d 890, 894–96 (11th Cir. 1983).

CHAPTER III

The Supreme Court's Decision in Bildisco

The Supreme Court's decision in *NLRB v. Bildisco & Bildisco,*[1] was surprisingly controversial.[2] The Court had granted certiorari[3] in the consolidated Third Circuit proceedings[4] based on a petition by the National Labor Relations Board which presented two questions:

> 1. Whether a bankruptcy court, in reorganization proceedings under Chapter 11 of the Bankruptcy Code . . ., may authorize a debtor-in-possession to reject a collective bargaining agreement without a threshold showing that the business is likely to fail unless the agreement is rejected;[5] and
>
> 2. Whether the National Labor Relations Board may properly find that a debtor-in-possession violated Section 8(a)(5) of the National Labor Relations Act . . . by unilaterally changing the terms of a collective bargaining agreement during the period between filing of a Chapter 11 petition and entry of a court order authorizing rejection of the agreement.[6]

---

[1] 465 U.S. 513 (1984), *aff'g, In re* Bildisco, 682 F.2d 72 (3d Cir. 1982).

[2] *See generally* Gregory, *Labor Contract Rejection in Bankruptcy: The Supreme Court's Attack on Labor in NLRB v. Bildisco,* 15 B.C. L. Rev. 539 (1984); Rosenberg, *Bankruptcy and the Collective Bargaining Agreement—A Brief Lesson in the Use of the Constitutional System of Checks and Balances,* 58 Am. Bankr. L. J. 293 (1984); Note, *Rejection of Collective Bargaining Agreement in Bankruptcy:* NLRB v. Bildisco & Bildisco *and the Legislative Response,* 33 Cath. U. L. Rev. 943 (1984); Note, *Rejection of Collective Bargaining Agreements Under the Bankruptcy Amendments of 1984,* 71 Va. L. Rev. 983 (1985).

[3] 103 S. Ct. 784 (1983).

[4] The cases, styled *In re* Bildisco, 682 F.2d 72 (3d Cir. 1982) below, were consolidated in the Supreme Court as *NLRB v. Bildisco & Bildisco,* No. 82-818.

[5] *See* NLRB's Petition for a Writ of Certiorari to the United States Court of Appeals for the Third Circuit, NLRB v. Bildisco & Bildisco, 465 U.S. 513 (1984) ("NLRB Petition"), at p. (I). The reference, of course, is to the standard for rejection set forth in Brotherhood of Railway, Airline and Steamship Clerks v. REA Express, Inc., 523 F.2d 164 (2d Cir.), *cert. denied,* 423 U.S. 1017 (1975).

[6] NLRB Petition at p. (I). The petition for certiorari of Teamsters Local 408 articulated the latter point somewhat differently. Local 408's petition formulated the question as whether a debtor may reject a collective bargaining agreement without first complying with "the bargaining requirement for mid-term contract modifications contained in 29 U.S.C. § 158(d) of the National Labor Relations Act." Local

The Supreme Court answered the first question in the affirmative (in Part II of its opinion) and the second question in the negative (in Part III of the opinion), thus affirming the decision of the Third Circuit. This Chapter will bifurcate the discussion of *Bildisco* consistent with the Court's analysis.

THE STANDARD FOR REJECTION

The NLRB and Local 408 argued to the Court that the Third Circuit's standard for a debtor's rejection of collective bargaining agreements under section 365 of the Code[7] impermissibly compromised the integrity of the national labor policy favoring collective bargaining.[8] According to the NLRB and Local 408, the Second Circuit's more stringent standard in *Brotherhood of Railway, Airline and Steamship Clerks v. REA Express Inc.,*[9] that union contracts can be rejected only when they are "onerous and burdensome" and if the alternative to rejection is liquidation, correctly accommodated the conflict between section 365 of the Code and the NLRA.

On this issue, decided in Part II of its opinion, the Court was unanimous. After quoting the language of section 365(a), the Court concluded that

> [t]his language by its terms includes all executory contracts except those expressly exempted, and it is not disputed by the parties that an unexpired collective bargaining agreement is an executory contract.[10]

Notwithstanding labor law decisions holding that collective bargaining agreements are different from ordinary contracts "for some purposes,"[11] the Court stated that there was no basis to conclude that Congress intended to exempt union contracts from the "general scope of § 365(a)":[12]

408's Petition for Certiorari ("Local 408 Petition"), p. (i). Local 408's petition also raised an issue concerning the judicial identity of the debtor-in-possession, the so-called "new entity" theory.

[7] The Third Circuit embraced the standard for rejection enunciated by the Second Circuit in Shopmen's Local Union No. 455 v. Kevin Steel Products, Inc., 519 F.2d 698, 707 (2d Cir. 1975): rejection of a union contract requires more than the debtor's "business judgment" that rejection will benefit the estate; a union contract may be rejected only upon the bankruptcy court's "thorough scrutiny, and a careful balancing of the equities on both sides." *In re* Bildisco, 682 F.2d at 79.

[8] NLRB Petition at pp. 15–20; Local 408 Petition at pp. 24–29; NLRB Brief at pp. 20–33; Local 408 Brief at pp. 36-48.

[9] 523 F.2d 164, 169–72 (2d. Cir.), *cert. denied,* 423 U.S. 1017 (1975).

[10] 104 S. Ct. at 1194.

[11] *Id.* (*citing* John Wiley & Sons, Inc. v. Livingston, 376 U.S. 543, 550 (1964)).

[12] 104 S. Ct. at 1194. The Court also rejected the argument of amicus United Mine Workers of America that a collective bargaining agreement is not an executory contract within the meaning of section 365(a). *Id.* n.6.

> The test of § 365(a) indicates that Congress was concerned about the scope of the debtor-in-possession's power regarding certain types of executory contracts, and purposely drafted § 365(a) to limit the debtor-in-possession's power of rejection or assumption in those circumstances. Yet none of the express limitations on the debtor-in-possession's general power under § 365(a) apply to collective-bargaining agreements. Section 1167, in turn, expressly exempts collective-bargaining agreements subject to the Railway Labor Act, but grants no similar exemption to agreements subject to the NLRA. Obviously, Congress knew how to draft an exclusion for collective bargaining agreements when it wanted to; its failure to do so in this instance indicates that Congress intended that § 365(a) apply to all collective-bargaining agreements covered by the NLRA.[13]

Having concluded that the debtor has the power to *reject* union contracts subject to the NLRA, the Court was presented with a choice of the applicable standard: the "business judgment" standard applied to ordinary executory contracts;[14] the intermediate *Kevin Steel* standard applied by the Third Circuit in *Bildisco* and the Eleventh Circuit in *In re Brada Miller Freight Systems, Inc.;*[15] or the more stringent *REA Express* standard urged by the NLRB, Local 408, amicus unions, and some commentators.[16]

The Court rejected as "wholly unconvincing" the NLRB's argument that Congress must have adopted the *Kevin Steel/REA Express* standard when it enacted § 365 in 1978[17] because, "[q]uite simply, *Kevin Steel* and *REA Express* reflect two different formulations of a standard for rejecting collective-bargaining agreements. Congress cannot be presumed to have adopted one standard over the other without some affirmative indication of which it preferred.[18]

---

[13] 104 S. Ct. at 1194–95 (footnotes omitted).

[14] *See* Pulliam, *The Rejection of Collective Bargaining Agreements Under Section 365 of the Bankruptcy Code,* 58 Am. Bankr. L. J. 1 (1984).

[15] 702 F.2d 890 (11th Cir. 1983).

[16] *See* notes 5–6 *supra;* Amicus Curiae Brief for the International Brotherhood of Teamsters, Chauffeurs, Warehousemen and Helpers at pp. 25–30; Bordewieck & Countryman, *The Rejection of Collective Bargaining Agreements by Chapter 11 Debtors,* 57 Am. Bankr. L. J. 293, 317 (1983). In its amicus curiae brief the AFL-CIO went even further, arguing that rejection should never be permitted under section 365(a) absent compliance with section 8(d) of the NLRA. *See* Amicus Brief for the AFL-CIO at pp. 2–3, 10–24. The AFL-CIO reasoned that section 8(d) creates a public duty of contract compliance, even in bankruptcy: "The status of the obligations stated in § 8(d) during a bankruptcy proceeding is therefore no different than the status of the obligation to maintain specified labor standards stated in the Fair Labor Standards Act." *Id.* at pp. 14–15. The second prong of the AFL-CIO's position was that the presence of section 1167 does not impliedly authorize rejection of non-RLA labor contracts. *Id.* at 21–26. The Court rejected both of these positions.

[17] NLRB Brief at pp. 18–19, 24–26.

[18] 104 S. Ct. at 1196

The most that could be inferred from references to *Kevin Steel* and *REA Express* in a pre-Code legislative report[19] was "that Congress approved the use of a somewhat higher standard than the business judgment rule when appraising a request to reject a collective-bargaining agreement."[20] For this reason, and "because of the special nature of a collective-bargaining contract,"[21] the Court determined, as had all of the courts of appeals to consider the issue, that a standard "somewhat stricter" than the business judgment test should apply to rejection of union contracts.[22]

The Court was left with a choice between *Kevin Steel* and *REA Express,* and Justice Rehnquist's opinion quickly disposed of *REA Express:*

> The standard adopted by the Second Circuit in *REA Express* is fundamentally at odds with the policies of flexibility and equity built into Chapter 11 of the Bankruptcy Code. The rights of workers under collective-bargaining agreements are important, but the *REA Express* standard subordinates the multiple, competing considerations underlying a Chapter 11 reorganization to one issue: whether rejection of the collective-bargaining agreement is necessary to prevent the debtor from going into liquidation. The evidentiary burden necessary to meet this stringent standard may not be insurmountable, but it will present difficulties to the debtor-in-possession that will interfere with the reorganization process.[23]

Instead, the Court adopted the intermediate *Kevin Steel* standard applied by the Third Circuit in *Bildisco* and the Eleventh Circuit in *Brada Miller:*

> [T]he Bankruptcy Court should permit rejection . . . under § 365(a) . . . if the debtor can show that the collective-bargaining agreement burdens the estate, and that after careful scrutiny, the equities balance in favor of rejecting the labor contract. The standard which we think Congress intended is a higher one than that of the 'business judgment' rule, but a lesser one than that embodied in the *REA Express* opinion of the Court of Appeals for the Second Circuit.[24]

The Court, however, elaborated on the bare legal standard and set forth specific procedural requirements to be followed by the bankruptcy court in order to accommodate the competing policies of the NLRA:

---

[19] *See* H. R. Rep. No. 94-686, 94th Cong., 1st Sess. 17–18 (1975).

[20] 104 S. Ct. at 1196.

[21] *Id.* at 1195.

[22] *Id.* The Court acknowledged, however, that "there is no indication in § 365 of the Bankruptcy Code that rejection of collective bargaining agreements should be governed by a different standard from that governing other excutory contracts." *Id.*

[23] *Id.* at 1196.

[24] *Id.*

> Before acting on a petition to modify or reject a collective-bargaining agreement, ... the Bankruptcy Court should be persuaded that reasonable efforts to negotiate a voluntary modification have been made and are not likely to produce a prompt and satisfactory solution. The NLRA requires no less.[25]

While the debtor-in-possession is obligated to bargain with the union under section 8(a)(5) of the NLRA,[26] the Court indicated that "reasonable efforts to negotiate a voluntary modification" need not amount to bargaining to "impasse."[27] The Court opined that the policies of the NLRA are "adequately served" if "reasonable efforts to reach agreement have been made."[28]

The Court also imposed the requirement that the bankruptcy court make specific findings that rejection would encourage the "successful rehabilitation" of the debtor:[29]

> The Bankruptcy Court must make a reasoned finding on the record why it has determined that rejection should be permitted. Determining what would constitute a successful rehabilitation involves balancing the interests of the affected parties—the debtor, creditor, and employees. The Bankruptcy Court must consider the likelihood and consequences of liquidation for the debtor absent rejection, the reduced value of the creditors' claims that would follow from affirmance and the hardship that would impose on them, and the impact of the rejection on the employees. In striking the balance, the Bankruptcy Court must consider not only the degree of hardship faced by each party, but also any qualitative differences between the types of hardship each may face.[30]

THE PROPRIETY OF UNILATERAL REJECTION

In Part III of its opinion, the Court addressed the question "whether the NLRB can find a debtor-in-possession guilty of an unfair labor practice for unilaterally rejecting or modifying a collective-bargaining agreement before formal rejection by the Bankruptcy Court."[31] On this issue the Court was divided 5-4; Justices Brennan, White, Marshall, and Blackmun dissented from the majority decision.

---

[25] *Id.*

[26] 29 U.S.C. § 158(a)(5).

[27] 104 S. Ct. at 1197.

[28] *Id.*

[29] *Id.*

[30] *Id.* The Court emphasized, however, that the Code "does not authorize freewheeling consideration of every conceivable equity, but rather only how the equities relate to the success of the reorganization." *Id.*

[31] *Id.*

The majority's opinion in Part III (comprised of Justices Rehnquist, Powell, Stevens, O'Connor, and Chief Justice Burger) held that a debtor does not commit an unfair labor practice under sections 8(a)(5) or 8(d) of the NLRA by unilaterally rejecting or changing the terms of a collective bargaining agreement after the bankruptcy petition has been filed but prior to the bankruptcy court's formal authorization of rejection. The majority concluded that "from the filing of a petition in bankruptcy until formal acceptance, the collective-bargaining agreement is not an enforceable contract within the meaning of NLRA § 8(d)"[32] because of the provisions of the Code which:

(1) Permit a Chapter 11 debtor to accept or reject an executory contract at any time prior to confirmation of the reorganization plan, in contrast to the requirement that a Chapter 7 trustee move to reject or accept within 60 days after the order for relief (11 U.S.C. § 365(d));

(2) Require all claims against the debtor to be presented to and administered by the bankruptcy court (11 U.S.C. §§ 501, 502, 1141) and automatically stay actions on non-bankruptcy claims against the debtor (11 U.S.C. § 362(a)); and

(3) Specify that post-petition rejection of executory contracts constitutes a breach of the contract which relates back to the date immediately preceding the filing of a bankruptcy petition (11 U.S.C. § 365(g)(1)).[33]

The majority's analysis of the provisions of the Code yielded the conclusion that all claims for post-petition violation of a union contract are governed by the Code:

> [S]uit may not be brought against the debtor-in-possession under the collective-bargaining agreement; recovery may be had only through administration of the claim in bankruptcy.[34]

The Court rejected the NLRB's argument that section 365(g)(1) "refers only to the priority of claims for damages based on rejection, not to existence of the contract in the post-petition period."[35] Rather, the Court concluded that

> the relation back of contract rejection to the filing of the petition in bankruptcy involves more than just priority of claims. Damages on the contract that result from the rejection of an executory contract . . . must be administered through bankruptcy and receive the priority provided general unsecured creditors. . . . If the debtor-in-possession

---

[32] *Id.* at 1199.
[33] *Id.* at 1198.
[34] *Id.* at 1198–99 (footnote omitted).
[35] NLRB Brief at p. 46.

> elects to continue to receive benefits from the other party to an executory contract pending a decision to reject or assume the contract, the debtor-in-possession is obligated to pay for the reasonable value of those services, which, depending on the circumstances of a particular contract, may be what is specified in the contract."[36]

Thus, permitting the NLRB, in effect, to enforce the contract by issuing unfair labor practice charges under sections 8(a)(5) or 8(d) for post-petition breaches "would run directly counter to the express provisions of the Bankruptcy Code and to the Code's overall effort to give a debtor-in-possession some flexibility and breathing space."[37]

Finally, the *Bildisco* majority rejected the arguments of Local 408 that the bankruptcy court should not authorize rejection of union contracts unless the debtor had first exhausted the mid-term modification procedures in section 8(d) of the NLRA or, in the alternative, had first bargained to impasse with the union prior to seeking rejection.[38] The majority's rationale was two-fold. First, section 8(d) does not apply because the collective-bargaining agreement is not an enforceable contract post-petition, "by operation of law."[39] Second,

> [o]ur rejection of the need for full compliance with § 8(d) procedures of necessity means that any corresponding duty to bargain to impasse under § 8(a)(5) and § 8(d) before seeking rejection must also be subordinated to the exigencies of bankruptcy.[40]

Moreover, the bankruptcy court's lack of labor law expertise would render it poorly equipped to make such determinations.[41] The majority closed with the admonition that debtors are nonetheless "employers" within the meaning of the NLRA[42] and are therefore "obligated to bargain collectively with the employees' certified representative over the terms of a new contract pending rejection of

---

[36] 104 S. Ct. at 1199 (citations omitted).

[37] *Id.*

[38] Local 408 Brief at pp. 10–36. The NLRB argued the opposite position on the subject of section 8(d). *See* NLRB Brief at 41–42.

[39] 104 S. Ct. at 1200.

[40] *Id.* One explanation for the parties' and the Court's extensive discussion of section 8(d) is that the collective bargaining agreement in *Bildisco* "expressly provided that it was binding on the parties and their successors even though bankruptcy should supervene." 104 S. Ct. at 1192. Thus, the debtor's rejection of the contract in Chapter 11, even if "by operation of law" rather than unilateral employer action (*see id.* at 1200) implicated section 8(d). In any event, the Court in *Bildisco* held that even with the foregoing contract language, "§ 8(d) procedures have no application to the employer's unilateral rejection of an already unenforceable contract." *Id.*

[41] *Id.*

[42] 29 U.S.C. § 152(1), (2).

the existing contract or following formal approval of rejection by the Bankruptcy Court."[43]

Four Justices dissented from Part III of the Court's decision. The dissent, written by Justice Brennan, would have enforced the NLRB's determination that Bildisco committed unfair labor practices by violating the terms of the union contract after it filed a bankruptcy petition but prior to formal bankruptcy court approval of rejection. In the dissenters' view, the majority erroneously reconciled the competing policies of the Code and the NLRA in a way that "seriously undermines the goals of the NLRA."[44] The dissent, however, did not embrace the argument advanced by Local 408. Justice Brennan stated in a footnote that

> I agree with the Court that the debtor-in-possession need not comply with the notice requirements and waiting periods imposed by § 8(d) before seeking rejection.... I also agree that the debtor-in-possession need not bargain to impasse before he may seek the court's permission to reject the agreement.... I believe that the test for determining whether rejection should be permitted enunciated in Part II of the Court's opinion strikes the proper balance between the NLRA and the Bankruptcy Code.[45]

Hence, the dissent disagreed with the majority only with respect to the debtor's unfair labor practice liability for post-petition alterations of terms and conditions of employment prior to rejection of a union contract. In short, the dissent reasoned that a union contract remains enforceable and in effect unless and until the bankruptcy court authorizes rejection under section 365(a).[46]

Permitting unilateral modifications by the debtor prior to bankruptcy court approval of rejection, according to Justice Brennan, would discourage interim negotiations and lead to increased industrial strife without resulting in any benefit to a financially distressed employer, who is free to reject the contract if circumstances justify.[47]

IMPACT OF BILDISCO

The Supreme Court reached an unusual degree of consensus in *Bildisco.* All nine members agreed that union contracts are subject to rejection under section 365(a); the Court was also unanimous in its adoption of the *Kevin Steel* standard for rejection, which was

---

[43] 104 S. Ct. at 1201.
[44] *Id.* at 1204 (Brennan, J., dissenting).
[45] *Id.* at 1204–05 n.9.
[46] *Id.* at 1206–08.
[47] *Id.* at 1210–11.

almost 10 years old and had already become the most widely used test among the courts of appeals. The Court also agreed that the "new entity" theory articulated by the lower federal courts as a means to accommodate the NLRA and the Code was misconceived.[48]

Significantly, the Court did *not* interpret section 365(a) literally, as some lower courts had, by applying the business judgment standard used in all other contexts.[49] All of the parties conceded that labor agreements could be rejected, and the NLRB argued against the application of section 8(d) in the rejection context. The cases applying section 365(a) following the Supreme Court's decision in *Bildisco,* prior to the effective date of section 1113, are generally less favorable to debtors than earlier cases applying the *Kevin Steel* standard.[50] What, then, made the Court's decision so controversial?

---

[48] The majority stated that if the debtor-in-possession "were a wholly 'new entity,' it would be unnecessary for the Bankruptcy Code to allow it to reject executory contracts, since it would not be bound by such contracts in the first place." 104 S. Ct. at 1197. The dissent stated that "[t]he Court today properly rejects the 'new entity' theory. . . ." *Id.* at 1206.

[49] *See* Pulliam, *supra* note 14; *In re* Rath Packing Co., 36 Bankr. 979, 989-99 (Bankr. N.D. Iowa 1984), *aff'd,* 48 Bankr. 315 (N.D. Iowa 1985); *In re* Concrete Pipe Machinery Co., 28 Bankr. 837, 839-40 (Bankr. N.D. Iowa 1983); *In re* Ateco Equipment, Inc., 18 Bankr. 915, 916–17 (Bankr. W.D. Pa. 1982).

[50] *See* Gloria Mfg. Corp. v. International Ladies' Garment Workers' Union, 734 F.2d 1020 (4th Cir. 1984) (rejection of expired collective bargaining agreement denied); *In re* Total Transportation Service, Inc., 37 Bankr. 904 (Bankr. S.D. Ohio 1984) (rejection of collective bargaining agreement denied because debtor's operations had ceased and rejection would serve no "rehabilitative end"); *In re* Schuld Mfg. Co., 43 Bankr. 535 (Bankr. W.D. Wis. 1984) (rejection of post-petition collective bargaining agreement denied); *In re* IML Freight, Inc., 37 Bankr. 556 (Bankr. D. Utah 1984) (rejection of post-petition collective bargaining agreement denied); *In re* Pesce Baking Co., 43 Bankr. 949 (Bankr. N.D. Ohio 1984) (rejection of expired collective bargaining agreement denied); *In re* Briggs Transportation Co., 39 Bankr. 343 (Bankr. D. Minn. 1984) (rejection of collective bargaining agreement granted); *In re* Allied Fabricators, Inc., No. Bk-S-282-02364-W, __ Bankr. __ (Bankr. E.D. Cal. 1984) (rejection of collective bargaining agreement denied); *In re* DeLuca Distributing Co., 38 Bankr. 588 (Bankr. N.D. Ohio 1984) (rejection of post-petition collective bargaining agreement between union and multi-employer association of which debtor was a member denied); *In re* C. & W. Mining Co., 38 Bankr. 496 (Bankr. N.D. Ohio 1984) (rejection of collective bargaining agreement denied due to debtor's lack of good faith effort to bargain with union); *In re* Bloss Glass Co., 39 Bankr. 694 (Bankr. M.D. Pa. 1984) (rejection of collective bargaining agreement granted); *In re* Fitzgeral, 44 Bankr. 628 (Bankr. W.D. Mo. 1984) (rejection of collective bargaining agreement denied due to lack of evidence that contract was burdensome or that debtor had made reasonable efforts to negotiate with the union). *See also* International Brotherhood of Teamsters v. IML Freight, Inc., 789 F.2d 1460 (10th Cir. 1986) (bankruptcy court's unreported pre-*Bildisco* decision authorizing rejection of collective bargaining agreement reversed under *Bildisco* standard due to insufficient findings of fact on balance-of-equities and reasonable efforts to negotiate a voluntary modification; debtor filed its Chapter 11 petition on July 15, 1983); *In re* Flechtner Packing Co., 63 Bankr. 585 (Bankr. N.D. Ohio 1986) (rejection of collective bargaining agreement granted under *Bildisco* standard; debtor filed its Chapter 11 petition on April 6, 1984); *In re* Crozier Bros., Inc., 52 Bankr. 402 (Bankr. S.D.N.Y. 1985) (rejection of

Perhaps organized labor did not realize until the *Bildisco* decision its vulnerability under the bankruptcy laws. This is difficult to reconcile with the existence of section 77(n) of the Act and section 1167 of the Code, which exempt RLA labor contracts from the general power to reject. Evidently some unions were aware of the consequences of rejection as early as 1933, when this exception was enacted. Moreover, employers have been rejecting labor contracts in reported cases for over 40 years. One can only speculate that most unions did not regard contract rejection as a serious threat until the Continental Airlines bankruptcy case, which undoubtedly highlighted the significance of *Bildisco.*[51]

Another possible basis for the unions' concern is that unlike the Act, the Code does not require a showing of insolvency as a condition of bankruptcy relief.[52] Accordingly, business bankruptcy filings increased sharply from 1978 to 1982, and "more companies appear[ed] to be using bankruptcy to void labor contracts prior to insolvency."[53] Moreover, on September 14, 1983 Continental Airlines filed a Chapter 11 petition and simultaneously imposed on its employees, including the approximately one-half of the workforce covered by several collective bargaining agreements, new wage rates and work

---

collective bargaining agreement denied under *Bildisco* standard due to insufficient factual showing on balance-of-equities and burdensomeness; debtor filed its Chapter 11 petition on May 23, 1984), *motion for reconsideration denied,* 60 Bankr. 683 (Bankr. S.D.N.Y. 1986); *In re* Robinson Truck Line, Inc., 47 Bankr. 631 (Bankr. N.D. Miss 1985) (rejection of union health and welfare plan granted under *Bildisco* standard; debtor filed its Chapter 11 petition on May 7, 1984); *In re S.A. Mechanical, Inc.,* 51 Bankr. 130 (Bankr. D. Ariz. 1985) (rejection of collective bargaining agreement denied under *Bildisco* standard, although court cites § 1113 authorities; debtor filed its Chapter 11 petition on March 23, 1984), *aff'd,* Case No. AZ-85-1227 (9th Cir. Bankr. App. 1985).

The NLRB has rigorously applied the Supreme Court's decision in *Bildisco* to preclude unfair labor practice liability against a debtor for failure to comply with a union contract following the filing of a Chapter 11 petition, even if the contract non-performance began pre-petition. Because under Bildisco the contract becomes unenforceable immediately upon filing for bankruptcy, the debtor's unfair labor practice liability terminates upon filing. *See* El San Juan Hotel Corp., 274 N.L.R.B. No. 3, 118 L.R.R.M. 1320 (1985); Edward Cooper Painting, Inc., 273 N.L.R.B. No. 224 (1985), *aff'd,* __ F.2d __, 123 L.R.R.M. 2905 (6th Cir. 1986). However, the NLRB will order damages against a debtor-employer for post-petition unfair labor practices independent of its rejection or noncompliance with a collective-bargaining agreement. *See* Karsh's Bakery, 273 N.L.R.B. No. 139, 118 L.R.R.M. 1297 (1984).

[51] *See* chapter IV, *infra.*

[52] *Cf.* 11 U.S.C. §§ 723, 823 (repealed 1978). *See* Kennedy, *Creative Bankruptcy? Use and Abuse of the Bankruptcy Law—Reflection on Some Recent Cases,* 71 IOWA L. REV. 199, 202 (1985) ("the Bankruptcy Code in 1978 eliminated any requirement that a voluntary petitioner be insolvent or unable to pay its debts as they mature").

[53] Rosenberg, *Bankruptcy and the Collective Bargaining Agreement—A Brief Lesson in the Use of the Constitutional System of Checks and Balances,* 58 AM. BANKR. L. J. 293, 304 (1984).

rules.[54] Although Continental filed a motion to reject its executory labor contracts on September 27, 1983, it unilaterally rejected the labor contracts prior to bankruptcy court approval; indeed, one of the stated reasons for Continental's Chapter 11 filing was to bring its labor costs into line with so-called new entrant competitors.[55] On October 4, 1983, two subcommittees of the House Education and Labor Committee held a joint hearing on the use of the Code as a "new bargaining weapon."[56] Organized labor was very concerned that other employers would follow Continental's lead.[57] Accordingly, unions were anxious to prohibit unilateral rejection and to make rejection more difficult.[58] One of the key features organized labor

---

[54] *See In re* Continental Airlines Corp., 38 Bankr. 67, 69 (Bankr. S.D. Tex 1984).

[55] 38 Bankr. at 69, 71; Rosenberg, *supra* note 53, at 306. Continental and the Air Line Pilots Association settled their dispute in November 1985, ending a 25-month strike that began on October 1, 1983. Terms included a rehiring procedure (with retention of seniority) for striking pilots wishing to return to work, severance pay for those why did not, and payment of $8.9 million for unpaid salaries and benefits owed to all pilots. "As part of the settlement, ALPA agreed to drop pending litigation against the company, including its appeal of the bankruptcy court ruling upholding Continental's abrogation of its labor contracts." *See Pilots End Two-Year Strike At Continental, Accept Terms Awarded By Bankruptcy Court,* DAILY LABOR REPORT (BNA) No. 213, at A-11 (Nov. 4, 1985).

[56] DAILY LABOR REPORT (BNA) No. 194, at E-1 (Oct. 5, 1983) (opening statement of Rep. William Clay, Chairman of Subcommittee on Labor-Management Relations).

[57]

> After *Bildisco,* union representatives complained bitterly that the decision would stimulate healthy companies with unsatisfactory labor contracts to file petitions in Chapter 11 for the sole purpose of escaping those agreements. The argument is not persuasive; no objective observer of the bankruptcy system would make such an argument.
>
> Although it is true that a company need not be insolvent in order to file under Chapter 11, there are many powerful reasons why healthy companies will not choose to exercise Chapter 11 rights. In the first place any management who files in Chapter 11 *ipso facto* loses a measurable portion of its freedom.

White, *The* Bildisco *Case and the Congressional Response,* 30 WAYNE L. REV. 1169, 1186 (1984) (footnotes omitted). Additional reasons why healthy companies will not resort to Chapter 11 are the risk that a trustee will be appointed; the negative effect such a decision would have on the companies' relationship with trade creditors, institutional lenders, and debt-holders; the alienation of shareholders, whose ownership interest would likely be diluted or destroyed; the prospect of a strike; and the possibility that the bankruptcy court would dismiss the petition under sections 305 or 1112. *See id.* at 1187–90. *Accord,* Miller, *The Rejection of Collective Bargaining Agreements Under the Bankruptcy Code—An Abuse or Proper Exercise of the Congressional Bankruptcy Power?,* 62 FORDHAM L. REV. 1120, 1131–33 (1984).

[58] *See id.; Firms Using Bankruptcy to Fight Labor,* Wall St. J., March 30, 1983, at p. 25; *Bankruptcy Filed to Erase Contract: In Unusual Maneuver, Wilson Foods Plans to Slash Wages,* L.A. Times, April 23, 1983, at I-28; *Chapter 11 Filing by Wilson Foods Roils Workers' Lives, Tests Law,* Wall St. J., May 23, 1983, at p. 29; *Continental Halts Jets, Seeks Bankruptcy Aid,* L.A. Times, Sept. 25, 1983, at I-1; *As Continental Airlines Takes Bankruptcy Step, Rivals Plan to Move In,* Wall St. J., Sept. 26, 1983, at p. 1; *More Bankruptcies for Weaker Airlines Seen,* L.A. Times, Sept. 26, 1983, at I-1; *Continental's Gamble: Using Bankruptcy Law to Break Union Pacts,* L.A. Times.

sought in legislation overturning *Bildisco* was application to cases pending upon enactment, such as the *Continental* case, even if filed prior to enactment.[59]

More than its doctrinal significance, or as a harbinger of dire consequences to organized labor, the *Bildisco* decision was symbolically important.[60] At stake was the institutional image of modern unions in the post-New Deal era. Professor James J. White offers the following symbolic interpretation:

> Unions can be characterized in quite different ways. Some regard them as the faithful alter egos of employees who, but for the union protection, would be subject to management exploitation or worse. Unions may be regarded as altruistic, as working not just for the good of their members, but for the good of society as a whole. Some of these sentiments form the basis for the Wagner Act and for the status that unions have enjoyed in the courts and legislatures for the last 45 years.
>
> Others consider unions as mature, powerful American institutions. They view unions as possessing the same qualities as other powerful (and therefore suspect) American institutions, such as corporations and governmental agencies. These persons would characterize modern unions as intensely self interested, single minded in their pursuit of power and influence, with interests often different from and conflicting with the employees' individual interests. . . .
>
> Does a 9-0 vote of the Supreme Court proceed from such an *a priori* view of modern American unions? It is that possibility that should frighten union representatives. That an occasional union might have its collective bargaining agreement rejected in bankruptcy is a small matter. That the 9-0 vote in *Bildisco* shows the Court to have adopted the negative polar view of unions is a matter of great importance. . . .
>
> If that is the basis for the *Bildisco* case, it has a meaning for every case involving union rights that comes before the Supreme Court in the foreseeable future. . . . It means that the assertion that the union speaks for and correctly represents the individual's interest will now be open to question. Worse, it may mean that lower courts, taking

---

Sept. 26, 1983, at IV-1; *Continental Air's Filing May Hinge on Bildisco Case,* Wall St. J., Sept. 27, 1983, at p. 2; White, *Management's Bankruptcy Weapon,* L.A. Times, Sept. 30, 1983, at II-7; *Labor Doubts Continental Tactic Legal,* L.A. Times, Oct. 1, 1983, at IV-1; *Besieged Unions Pressured by Newly Combative Firms,* L.A. Times, Oct. 10, 1983, at I-1.

[59] *See* Daily Labor Report (BNA) No. 70, at F-1 to F-3 (April 11, 1984) (statement of Laurence Gold, special counsel to AFL-CIO); Kennedy, *supra* note 52, at 212 ("Labor union leaders sought but did not succeed in getting legislation that would retroactively invalidate the rejection in the *Continental Airlines* case").

[60] *See* White, *supra* note 57, at 1202.

> their lead from the Supreme Court, will be more hostile to the union's interests in a whole host of ways.
>
> It is ironic therefore, that *Bildisco,* touted as a critical bankruptcy case, may have only a modest impact on the bankruptcy law, and yet, may have a far-reaching impact on labor law.[61]

In any event, the Court's decision in *Bildisco* prompted almost immediate legislative action.

---

[61] *Id.* at 1202–03 n.103. *Cf.* George, *Collective Bargaining in Chapter 11 and Beyond,* 95 YALE L. J. 300, 303 (1985) ("*Bildisco* signals a subtle yet disturbing erosion of national labor policy").

CHAPTER IV

Section 1113 and its Impact

BACKGROUND AND PASSAGE OF SECTION 1113

Apparently fearing that many employers would adopt the Continental Airlines tactic of reorganization and rejection as a means of becoming union free,[1] the AFL-CIO and other unions unleashed an intense lobbying effort. Business interests fought just as vociferously to preserve the status quo, as reflected by the *Bildisco* decision.[2] Faced also with consumer creditors' desires for greater protection, farmers clamoring for protection from insolvent grain elevator operators, and the *Marathon Pipe Line* problems of whether bankruptcy judges should have Article III or Article I standing, Congress was paralyzed by the various interest groups.[3]

After several fitful starts and eventual disagreement between the Senate and House versions of bankruptcy reform legislation, a conference committee finally agreed on the Bankruptcy Amendments and Federal Judgeship Act of 1984 ("BAFJA").[4]

Prior to *Bildisco,* the Senate had passed a bankruptcy bill curing the *Marathon Pipe Line* problem in April of 1983.[5] The House failed to act until March 21, 1984, when it passed H.R. 5174, which included a provision originally proposed by House Judiciary Com-

---

[1] *See generally Airlines in Turmoil: Labor Woes, Price Wars, and Bankruptcy Threats Rock the Industry,* Bus. Wk., Oct. 10, 1983, at p. 3.

[2] *See generally Congress Fails to Change Laws on Bankruptcy,* Wall St. J., April 2, 1984, at p. 4; *Bankruptcy Bill Divides Key Business,* Wall St. J., April 26, 1984, at p. 33.

[3] *Id., Opening for Labor in Bankruptcy Crisis,* 115 Lab. Rel. Rep. 231 (BNA News and Background Information, Mar. 19, 1984).

[4] *See* chapter I, *supra.* For a thorough analysis of the background and legislative history of the portions of BAFJA dealing with *Bildisco,* see Rosenberg, *Bankruptcy and the Collective Bargaining Agreement—A Brief Lesson in the Use of the Constitutional System of Checks and Balances,* 58 Am. Bankr. L.J. 293 (1984); Gibson, *The New Law on Rejection of Collective Bargaining Agreements in Chapter 11: An Analysis of 11 U.S.C. § 1113,* 58 Am. Bankr. L.J. 325 (1984); White, *The* Bildisco *Case and the Congressional Response,* 30 Wayne L. Rev. 1169, 1190–1204 (1984). *See also* George, *Collective Bargaining in Chapter 11 and Beyond,* 95 Yale L.J. 300 (1985).

[5] *See* S. 1013, 98th Cong., 2d Sess. S. 1013 passed the Senate on April 27, 1983. *See* 129 Cong. Rec. S5311 (daily ed. April 27, 1983).

mittee Chairman Peter W. Rodino, Jr. as H.R. 4908, designed to overturn the *Bildisco* decision. Like S. 1013, H.R. 5174 addressed the *Marathon Pipe Line* issue by vesting jurisdiction of bankruptcy matters in the Article III district courts, with the bankruptcy courts retaining their Article I status and serving as adjuncts of the district courts. H.R. 5174 also prohibited the unilateral rejection of union contracts prior to bankruptcy court approval, which would not be granted unless "absent rejection . . ., the jobs covered by such agreement will be lost and any financial reorganization of the debtor will fail," a standard virtually foreclosing rejection.[6] Despite three months of negotiation, the Senate was unable to agree on a labor provision, which required that the interim bankruptcy operating procedures necessitated by *Marathon Pipe Line* be extended four times, from April 1, 1984 to May 1, then to May 25, then to June 20, and finally until June 27, 1984.[7] Finally, on June 20, the Senate sent a bankruptcy bill to conference containing *no* labor provision.[8]

The Senate was deadlocked between a labor provision proposed by Senate Judiciary Committee Chairman Strom Thurmond, which was drafted by the National Bankruptcy Conference, and by an amendment sponsored by organized labor which was proposed by Senator Robert Packwood. The Thurmond proposal retained the *Bildisco* standard for contract rejection but required bankruptcy court approval prior to rejection, unless the court failed to act within

[6] *See House Approves Bankruptcy Bill Containing Restrictions on Rejection of Union Contracts,* Daily Labor Report (BNA) No. 56, at A-9 (March 22, 1984).

[7] *See* Pub. L. No. 98-249, 98 Stat. 116 (March 31, 1984), Pub. L. No. 98-271, 98 Stat. 163 (April 30, 1984); Pub. L. No. 98-299, 98 Stat. 214 (May 25, 1984); Pub. L. No. 98-325, 98 Stat. 268 (June 20, 1984).

[8] *See generally Revision of Labor Clause a Key Issue as Senate Nears Deadline on Bankruptcy Bill,* Daily Labor Report (BNA) No. 61, at A-6 (March 29, 1984); *Objections Raised by Management and Labor to Proposed Language in Bankruptcy Bill,* Daily Labor Report (BNA) No. 62 at A-10 (March 30, 1984); *Congress OKs Stopgap Bill to Keep Bankruptcy Court System Running,* L.A. Times, March 31, 1984, at IV-1; *Congress Extends Bankruptcy System For One Month; Senate Committees Will Consider Labor Provision,* Daily Labor Report (BNA) No. 63, at A-8 (April 2, 1984); *Agreement on Bankruptcy No Closer After Testimony Before Senate Panels,* Daily Labor report (BNA) No. 70, at A-8, F-1 (April 11, 1984); *Senate Votes to Authorize More Time for Resolution of Bankruptcy Labor Issue,* Daily Labor Report (BNA) No. 73, at A-6 (April 16, 1984); *House Joins Senate in Extending Deadline for Resolution of Bankruptcy Labor Issue,* Daily Labor Report (BNA) No. 82, at A-9 (April 27, 1984); *Senate Begins Work on Bankruptcy Bill; Labor Provision Still Focus of Debate,* Daily Labor Report (BNA) No. 99, at A-19 (May 22, 1984); *Senate Fails to Reach Agreement on Bankruptcy Labor Provisions,* Daily Labor Report (BNA) No. 100, at A-10 (May 23, 1984); *Senate Extends Bankruptcy System for Third Time, Until June 21,* Daily Labor Report (BNA) No. 102, at A-14 (May 25, 1984); *Both Sides Dig in as Bankruptcy Dispute Divides Labor, Management in Election Year,* Daily Labor Report (BNA) No. 103, at C-1 (May 29, 1984); *Senate Bypasses Vote on Bankruptcy Labor Issue; Sends Bill to Conference With One-Week Extension,* Daily Labor Report (BNA) No. 120, at A-8 (June 21, 1984).

30 days of the employer's application. Like H.R. 5174, the Thurmond proposal would have operated prospectively only, *i.e.,* to bankruptcy filings after enactment. The Packwood amendment, in contrast, required bankruptcy court approval prior to rejection, allowed a court to permit rejection only if the union had refused without justification the employer's proposed contract modifications, and operated retroactively, *i.e.,* to employers who filed bankruptcy petitions *prior* to enactment.

After lengthy negotiations, the conference committee reached a compromise early in the morning on June 28, 1984 similar in structure to the Packwood amendment. The House conferees agreed to modify the language of H.R. 5174, to permit rejection of labor contracts more easily. In return for the concession of permitting any dilution of the *Bildisco* standard, the Senate conferees extracted legislative authority to appoint 85 federal district and circuit court judges over the nest two years. Importantly, the conferees agreed that the compromise labor provision would *not* operate retroactively.[9]

The final language agreed to by the conference committee permits rejection of union contracts, but compels a debtor seeking relief to first bargain with the union in good faith over the proposed modifications to the contract. The compromise language also requires bankruptcy court approval prior to contract modifications or rejection, and authorizes rejection only if the bankruptcy court decides that the union refused to accept the debtor's proposals "without good cause," and the "balance of the equities clearly favors rejection" of the contract. The bankruptcy court must hold a hearing on a debtor's application for contract rejection within 21 days of filing, subject to extension by agreement of the parties. If the court fails to rule on the debtor's application within 30 days of the hearing, the debtor may "terminate or alter any provisions of the collective bargaining agreements pending the ruling of the court on such application."

The conferees' labor provision also permits court approval of "interim changes" in the terms of a collective bargaining agreement after notice and hearing, without the prior bargaining requirement, if the changes are "essential to the continuation of the debtor's business, or in order to avoid irreparable damage to the estate." In short, the legislation reversed the second part of the Court's decision

---

[9] *See House-Senate Conferees Resolve Disputes on Bankruptcy Bill; Approval Is Expected,* Wall St. J., June 29, 1984, at p. 2; *Bankruptcy Conferees Agree to Compromise on Labor Provision Which Overrules Bildisco,* DAILY LABOR REPORT (BNA) No. 126, at A-8 (June 29, 1984).

in *Bildisco* by increasing the bargaining obligations and requiring prior bankruptcy court approval; the statute essentially preserved the standard for rejection set forth in the first part of the *Bildisco* decision. The new legislation, unlike the prior section 365, permits interim *modification* in lieu of wholesale rejection, and upon a proper showing this may be easier to accomplish than rejection.

On June 29, 1984, Congress overwhelmingly approved the compromise reached by the Senate and House conferees.[10] On July 10, President Reagan signed the Bankruptcy Amendments and Federal Judgeship Act of 1984,[11] remarking that the bill "meets the interests of both labor and business by providing debtors with the flexibility they need to reorganize successfully and preserve jobs for workers" while "prohibiting unilateral rejection of labor agreements without court review of whether rejection is necessary."[12]

THE TEXT AND MEANING OF SECTION 1113

Under the new statute,[13] codified as 11 U.S.C. section 1113, most Chapter 11 filings[14] after the date of its enactment (July 10, 1984) are subject to a new standard and procedure for rejection of collec-

---

[10] *See Congress Approves Bankruptcy Bill With Compromise Labor Law Provision,* DAILY LABOR REPORT (BNA) No. 127, at A-9 (July 2, 1984).

[11] Pub. L. No. 98-353, 98 Stat. 33 (1984).

[12] *See President Reagan Signs Bankruptcy Bill Including* Bildisco *Labor Clause,* DAILY LABOR REPORT (BNA) No. 134, at A-9 through A-10 (July 12, 1984).

[13] Subtitle J of the BAFJA states in its entirety as follows:

> Subtitle J—*Collective Bargaining Agreements*
>
> Sec. 541. (a) Title 11 of the United States Code is amended by adding after section 1112 the following new section:
>
> § 1113. Rejection of collective bargaining agreements
>
> (a) The debtor in possession, or the trustee if one has been appointed under the provisions of this chapter, other than a trustee in a case covered by subchapter IV of this chapter and by title I of the Railway Labor Act, may assume or reject a collective bargaining agreement only in accordance with the provisions of this section.
>
> (b)(1) Subsequent to filing a petition and prior to filing an application seeking rejection of a collective bargaining agreement, the debtor in possession or trustee (hereinafter in this section "trustee" shall include a debtor in possession), shall—
>
>> (A) make a proposal to the authorized representative of the employees covered by such agreement, based on the most complete and reliable information available at the time of such proposal, which provides for those necessary modifications in the employees benefits and protections that are necessary to permit the reorganization of the debtor and assures that all creditors, the debtor and all of the affected parties are treated fairly and equitably; and
>>
>> (B) provide, subject to subsection (d)(3), the representative of the employees with such relevant information as is necessary to evaluate

tive bargaining agreements. Section 1113 states that a debtor-in-possession or trustee (if one has been appointed) "may assume or reject a collective bargaining agreement only in accordance with

---

the proposal.

(2) During the period beginning on the date of the making of a proposal provided for in paragraph (1) and ending on the date of the hearing provided for in subsection (d)(1), the trustee shall meet, at reasonable times, with the authorized representative to confer in good faith in attempting to reach mutually satisfactory modifications of such agreement.

(c) The court shall approve an application for rejection of a collective bargaining agreement only if the court finds that—

(1) the trustee has, prior to the hearing, made a proposal that fulfills the requirements of subsection (b)(1);

(2) the authorized representative of the employees has refused to accept such proposal without good cause; and

(3) the balance of the equities clearly favors rejection of such agreement.

(d)(1) Upon the filing of an application for rejection the court shall schedule a hearing to be held not later than fourteen days after the date of the filing of such application. All interested parties may appear and be heard at such hearing. Adequate notice shall be provided to such parties at least ten days before the date of such hearing. The court may extend the time for the commencement of such hearing for a period not exceeding seven days where the circumstances of the case, and the interests of justice require such extension, or for additional periods of time to which the trustee and representative agree.

(2) The court shall rule on such application for rejection within thirty days after the date of the commencement of the hearing. In the interests of justice, the court may extend such time for ruling for such additional period as the trustee and the employees' representative may agree to. If the court does not rule on such application within thirty days after the date of the commencement of the hearing, or within such additional time as the trustee and the employees' representative may agree to, the trustee may terminate or alter any provisions of the collective bargaining agreement pending the ruling of the court on such application.

(3) The court may enter such protective orders, consistent with the need of the authorized representative of the employee to evaluate the trustee's proposal and the application for rejection, as may be necessary to prevent disclosure of information provided to such representative where such disclosure could compromise the position of the debtor with respect to its competitors in the industry in which it is engaged.

(e) If during a period when the collective bargaining agreement continues in effect, and if essential to the continuation of the debtor's business, or in order to avoid irreparable damage to the estate, the court, after notice and a hearing, may authorize the trustee to implement interim changes in the terms, conditions, wages, benefits, or work rules provided by a collective bargaining agreement. Any hearing under this paragraph shall be scheduled in accordance with the needs of the trustee. The implementation of such interim changes shall not render the application for rejection moot.

(f) No provision of this title shall be construed to permit a trustee to unilaterally terminate or alter any provisions of a collective bargaining agreement prior to compliance with the provisions of this section.

(g) The table of sections for chapter 11 of title 11, United States Code, is amended by inserting after the item relating to section 1112 the following item:

the provisions of this section."[15] With one narrow exception, section 1113 prohibits any form of unilateral modification or rejection of a labor contract by a debtor.[16]

A debtor seeking rejection of a labor contract ordinarily must make a proposal to the union subsequent to filing its Chapter 11 petition but prior to filing an application with the bankruptcy court authorizing rejection.[17] The debtor's proposal must "provide[] for those necessary modifications in the employees['] benefits and protections that are necessary to permit the reorganization of the debtor."[18] Moreover, the debtor's proposal must be "based on the most complete and reliable information available at the time,"[19]

1113. Rejection of collective bargaining agreements.

(c) The amendments made by this section shall become effective upon the date of enactment of this Act; provided that this section shall not apply to cases filed under title 11 of the United States Code which were commenced prior to the date of enactment of this section.

[14] Section 1113 does not apply to Chapter 7 liquidation proceedings, to Chapter 9 municipal bankruptcies, or to Chapter 13 proceedings involving the adjustment of individuals' debts. *See* 11 U.S.C. § 103(f). Section 1113 also does not apply to railroad reorganizations governed by subchapter IV of Chapter 11. *See* 11 U.S.C. § 1113(a). Rejection of collective bargaining agreements subject to the Railway Labor Act, 45 U.S.C. § 151 *et seq.*, is prohibited by 11 U.S.C. § 1167, except in accordance with section 6 of the RLA, 45 U.S.C. § 156.

[15] 11 U.S.C. § 1113(a). The "assume or reject" language in section 1113(a) is derived from section 365(a). The cases under both sections of the Code deal overwhelmingly with rejection rather than assumption. Collier notes in the context of section 365 that "[a]ssumption or adoption of the contract can only be effected through an express order by the court." 2 COLLIER ON BANKRUPTCY ¶ 365.03 at 365-25 (15th ed. 1985). The lack of authorities dealing with assumption is explained by the fact that "[a]s long as rejection is not ordered the contract continues in existence. . . . [I]f the contract is not affected by the plan, it rides through the proceeding having neither been assumed nor rejected and will thereafter be binding on the debtor." *Id.* at 365-25 to -26. The same principle presumably governs under section 1113.

Under section 365(d)(2), in a Chapter 11 reorganization a party to an executory contract or lease may move the court for an order requiring the debtor to reject or assume within a specified period prior to confirmation. Under section 365(d)(1), in a Chapter 7 liquidation all executory contracts are deemed rejected unless assumed within 60 days after the order for relief. Under section 1113(d)(1), creditors committees are presumably "interested parties" which are entitled to appear at the hearing on the debtor's motion to reject. However, there is no statutory mechanism with which creditors can force a debtor to reject a contract, other than possibly by converting the Chapter 11 reorganization to a Chapter 7 liquidation, at which point section 1113 would no longer apply.

[16] 11 U.S.C. § 1113(f). The debtor may act without prior bankruptcy court approval only if the court fails to act on the debtor's application for rejection within 30 days of the hearing. 11 U.S.C. § 1113(d)(2).

[17] 11 U.S.C. § 1113(b)(1). The only exception to the requirements set forth in § 1113(b)–(d) is the "interim change" procedure contained in § 1113(e), which must be predicated on a showing that modification or rejection of the labor contract is "essential to the continuation f the debtor's business, or in order to avoid irreparable damage to the estate." Even "interim changes," however, require prior bankruptcy court approval "after notice and hearing." 11 U.S.C. § 1113(e).

[18] 11 U.S.C. § 1113(b)(1)(A).

[19] *Id.*

and must "assure[] that all creditors, the debtor, and all of the affected parties are treated fairly and equitably."[20]

After making such a proposal to the union, the debtor may file an application for rejection with the bankruptcy court; the bankruptcy court must schedule a hearing on the debtor's application within fourteen days,[21] unless "the circumstances or the case" and "the interests of justice" require an extension not to exceed seven days[22] or the debtor and union agree to continue the hearing.[23] After the debtor's proposal to the union and prior to the hearing on the debtor's application, the debtor must provide the union "with such relevant information as is necessary to evaluate the proposal"[24] (subject to the bankruptcy court's entry of a protective order to prevent the union's disclosure of the debtor's sensitive trade secret or proprietary information)[25] and must meet with the union "at reasonable times ... to confer in good faith in attempting to reach mutually satisfactory modifications" of the union contract.[26]

If these conditions have been met, at the hearing on the debtor's application[27] the court "shall approve" the application "only if the court finds that the [union] has refused to accept [the debtor's] proposal without good cause"[28] and "the balance of the equities clearly favors rejection of such agreement."[29] The debtor must wait for the court's approval prior to implementing any modification or rejection of the union contract unless the court fails to rule on the application within 30 days "after the date of the commencement of the hearing."[30] If the court has not acted within the 30-day period, or within such additional period as the debtor and union agree to,[31] the debtor "may terminate or alter any provisions of the collective bargaining agreement pending the ruling of the court on such application."[32]

---

[20] *Id.*

[21] 11 U.S.C. § 1113(d)(1).

[22] *Id.*

[23] *Id.*

[24] 11 U.S.C. § 1113(b)(1)(B).

[25] 11 U.S.C. § 1113(d)(3).

[26] 11 U.S.C. § 1113(b)(2).

[27] Section 1113(d)(1) provides that "[a]ll interested parties may appear and be heard at such hearing. Adequate notice shall be provided to such parties at least ten days before the date of such hearing." The statute does not define the term "interested parties" and does not specify who is obligated to provide notice.

[28] 11 U.S.C. § 1113(c)(2).

[29] 11 U.S.C. § 1113(c)(3).

[30] 11 U.S.C. § 1113(d)(2).

[31] *Id.*

[32] *Id.* By failing to act, the bankruptcy court apparently could authorize the debtor to reject only part of the union contract, such as the provisions dealing with wages, benefits, work rules, and arbitration, while preserving the no-strike clause and provisions establishing a binding grievance procedure. *Cf.* 130 CONG. REC. S8898

Section 1113 sets forth an alternative procedure permitting the debtor to implement "interim changes in the terms, conditions, wages, benefits, or work rules" provided by a union contract.[33] The interim change procedure, whether exercised independently or in conjunction with the conventional rejection procedure,[34] requires prior court approval, a hearing, and notice.[35] The interim change procedure may be invoked if immediate modification or rejection of a union contract is "essential to the continuation of the debtor's business, or in order to avoid irreparable damage to the estate."[36] Consistent with this showing, the statute states that "[a]ny hearing under this paragraph shall be scheduled in accordance with the needs of the [debtor]."[37] The granting and implementation of interim changes does not affect the debtor's obligation to obtain bankruptcy court approval for rejection of a union contract.[38]

Section 1113 unmistakably overrules the second part of the Supreme Court's decision in *Bildisco* by prohibiting unilateral action by the debtor and encouraging negotiated solutions whenever possible. There is no indication in the text or legislative history of section 1113, however, that Congress intended to alter the procedure for calculating or recovering claims against the debtor arising from rejection.[39] Thus, while under section 1113 a bankruptcy court may authorize rejection of a union contract prospectively only,[40] pursuant to section 502(g) "[a] claim arising from the rejection ... of any executory contract ... shall be determined, and shall be allowed

---

(daily ed. June 29, 1984)(statement of Sen. Packwood); *id.* at S8899 (statement of Sen. Kennedy) (union can strike if debtor acts unilaterally under section 1113(e)).

[33] 11 U.S.C. § 1113(e).

[34] The statute specifies only that the bankruptcy court may authorize interim changes "during a period when the collective bargaining agreement continues in effect." 11 U.S.C. § 1113(e). *See* 130 CONG. REC. S8892 (daily ed. June 29, 1984) (statement of Sen. Hatch).

[35] The statute does not specify how much notice is required or who is responsible for giving notice.

[36] *Id.* 11 U.S.C. § 1113(e).

[37] *Id.*

[38] The statute states that "[t]he implementation of such interim changes shall not render the application for rejection moot." *Id.* If interim changes were authorized but rejection was ultimately denied, the union would presumably be able to recover damages from the debtor for breach of the collective bargaining agreement, which claim would have first priority as administrative expenses. *See* 11 U.S.C. §§ 503(b)(1)(A), 507(A)(1). The same would presumably be true if the debtor modified or rejected the union contract due to the court's failure to rule within 30 days, if the court eventually denied the debtor's application. *See* 130 CONG. REC. S8898 (daily ed. June 29, 1984)(statement of Sen. Packwood.).

[39] *See* 11 U.S.C. §§ 502(g) & 365(g)(1); chapter II at notes 52–55, 68, and 243–257 and accompanying text, and chapter X *infra*.

[40] Courts have so held. *See In re* Mile Hi Metal Systems, Inc., 51 Bankr. 509 (Bankr. D. Colo. 1985), *rev'd on other grounds*, __ Bankr. __ (D. Colo. 1986).

. . . the same as if such claim had arisen before the date of the filing of the petition."[41]

Many of the provisions of section 1113 lack specific statutory definition, and the courts will have to provide content to some of these vague terms.[42] Many of the concepts embraced in section 1113, however, had pre-existing meaning in bankruptcy or labor law, and the legislative history of the statute, though not perfectly clear, sheds light on some of the new concepts. Moreover, section 1113 does not completely overrule *Bildisco,* and the Supreme Court's decision illuminates many aspects of section 1113.[43]

According to Senator Edward Kennedy, the intent of section 1113 was "to overturn the *Bildisco* decision which had given the trustee all but unlimited discretionary power to repudiate labor contracts and to substitute a rule of law that encourages the parties to solve their mutual problems through the collective bargaining process."[44]

The bargaining requirement contains several components. The provisions dealing with meeting at reasonable times, conferring in good faith, and providing relevant information, although superficially similar to the concept of good faith bargaining under section 8(a)(5) of the NLRA,[45] were not intended to import labor law principles into bankruptcy court proceedings.[46] Senator Orrin Hatch

---

[41] 11 U.S.C. § 502(g).

[42] The Senate conferees noted that "[l]egitimate concerns have been raised regarding the broadness and vagueness of this language. I would hope that courts will interpret both provisions in the most practical and workable manner possible." 130 CONG. REC. S8888 (daily ed. June 29, 1984) (statement of Sen. Thurmond). *See also* White, *supra* note 7, at 1197 (language of § 1113 is "purposefully ambiguous"; "Surely it makes the law measurably less certain; it will make the trial judge's decision more discretionary and speculative; it will introduce greater guesswork into the lives of those who must advise management and unions about their rights.").

[43] *See* Kennedy, *Creative Bankruptcy? Use and Abuse of the Bankruptcy Law—Reflection on Some Recent Cases,* 71 IOWA L. REV. 199, 213 (1985) ("the unions received considerably less than they had hoped. The Senate resisted the effort to overrule *Bildisco,* and the *Bildisco* balance-of-the-equities test survived."); Wines, *An Overview of the 1984 Bankruptcy Amendments: Some Modest Protections for Labor Agreements,* 36 LABOR L.J. 911, 917 (1985) (section 1113 codified the "common law standard [for rejection] embraced by the *Bildisco* court"); Bendixsen, *Enforcing the Duty to Arbitrate Claims Arising Under a Collective Bargaining Agreement Rejected in Bankruptcy: Preserving the Parties' Bargain and National Labor Policy,* 8 INDUS. REL. L.J. 401, 404 (1986) ("Section 1113 largely codified the standard for rejection imposed by *Bildisco*"); Note, *Collective Bargaining Agreements in Bankruptcy Proceedings: Congressional Response to Bildisco,* 1985 U. ILL. L. REV. 997, 998 ("Congress adopted the *Bildisco* 'balance of the equities' standard of rejection"). *See also* notes 69–70 *infra* & accompanying text.

[44] 130 CONG. REC. S8898 (daily ed. June 29, 1984). See *also id.* (statement of Sen. Packwood) ("The bill should stimulate collective bargaining and limit the number of cases when a judge will have to authorize the rejection of a labor contract").

[45] 29 U.S.C. § 158(a)(5).

[46] *See* Gibson, *supra* note 7, at 329 ("Congress did not appear to intend this provision

stated, for example, that "[t]he conference's compromise adheres to the spirit of [the] unanimous Supreme Court opinion [in *Bildisco*]."[47] The Supreme Court had emphatically distinguished between the procedural requirements it imposed and the bargaining requirements of federal labor law.[48] Senator Hatch stated that the conference "preserved the spirit of that ... holding by requiring good faith efforts to confer in an effort to reach an agreement between the business and its union employees which will both preserve the labor contract with modifications and save the business."[49]

This view is supported by Senator Thurmond's statement in a related context that the bargaining requirement "is obviously not intended to import traditional labor law concepts into a bankruptcy forum or turn the bankruptcy courts into a version of the National Labor Relations Board."[50] Thus, the bankruptcy court should interpret the bargaining requirements in section 1113 "in a nontechnical fashion, and limit its determination to a ruling on whether or not the debtor appeared to have a serious desire to reach an agreement with the union."[51]

The substantive requirements of the debtor's proposal, that it provide for "necessary modifications ... that are necessary to permit the reorganization" and assure that all affected parties are treated "fairly and equitably," pose greater challenges for interpretation.

Senator Packwood provided some guidance with his statement that

> only modifications which are necessary to a successful reorganization may be proposed. Therefore, the debtor will not be able to exploit the bankruptcy procedure to rid itself of unwanted features of the labor agreement that have *no relation to its financial condition and its reorganization* and which earlier were agreed to by the debtor. The word 'necessary' inserted twice into this provision clearly emphasizes

---

to be interpreted in light of labor precedent"); George, *supra* note 7, at 318–19 ("Congress apparently shared the concern of the *Bildisco* Court that the bankruptcy judges not be burdened by traditional Board determinations"); Note, *The Rejection of Collective Bargaining Agreements in Chapter 11 Reorganizations: The Need for Informed Judicial Decisions,* 134 U. PA. L. REV. 1235, 1247 (1986) ("Congress ... provid[ed] that the bankruptcy judges were not to follow established labor law precedent in enforcing Section 1113.").

[47] 130 CONG. REC. S8892 (daily ed. June 29, 1984).

[48] See chapter III, notes 25–28 and 38–43 and accompanying text.

[49] 130 CONG. REC. S8892 (daily ed. June 29, 1984).

[50] *Id.* at S8888.

[51] Gibson, *supra* note 4, at 330. This commentator opines that "the debtor can make an application for rejection immediately after it makes its proposal to the union. As this application must normally be heard within ten to fourteen days, ... the process of negotiation under section 1113 will be extremely short." *Id.*

> this required aspect of the proposal which the debtor must offer and guarantees the sincerity of the debtor's good faith in seeking contract changes.[52]

Hence, the debtor's proposal must address economic or operational barriers to reorganization contained in the current labor contract; "[i]n cases in which no reorganization is possible, save selling the firm's assets for their scrap value, then no modifications can be justified as necessary to permit rehabilitation of the debtor."[53] In any event, the conference committee intended that this provision

---

[52] 130 Cong. Rec. S8898 (daily ed. June 29, 1984) (emphasis added). *See also id.* S8892 (statement of Sen. Hatch) ("The intent of this provision is to allow the business to make whatever changes in the collective bargaining agreement [that] are reasonably necessary to ensure the likelihood of a successful reorganization."). Gibson, *supra* note 4, at 336–38, suggests that the effect of this language is to overturn decisions such as *In re* Alan Wood Steel Co., 449 F. Supp. 165, 4 B.C.D. 850 (Bankr. E.D. Pa. 1978) and *In re* Allied Technology, Inc., 7 B.C.D. 233 (Bankr. S.D. Ohio 1980) and to uphold the approach of *In re* Total Transportation Service, Inc., 37 Bankr. 904 (Bankr. S.D. Ohio 1984), which involved debtors whose operations had ceased. In *Alan Wood* and *Allied Technology*, the court authorized rejection of labor contracts primarily to reduce the priority of the union's claim for damages and thereby generate greater assets for the general unsecured creditors. In *Total Transportation*, the court denied rejection because, among other reasons, it would "serve no rehabilitative end."

[53] Gibson, *supra* note 4, at 338. In contrast, one student commentator has concluded that "[t]he logic and legislative history of section 1113 lead inexorably to the necessity standard of REA Express for review of a debtor's decision to reject a collective bargaining agreement." Note, *Rejection of Collective Bargaining Agreements Under the Bankruptcy Amendments of 1984*, 71 Va. L. Rev. 983, 1008 (1985). Thus, even though this commentator recognizes that section 1113(b)(1)(A) can be plausibly interpreted to "allow the debtor to propose any modifications substantially related to the reorganization effort," *id.* at 1006, he argues that

> [o]nly if the debtor limits his offer to modifications necessary to prevent liquidation should rejection follow a union refusal to accept, and then only if the equities balance in favor of rejection. Conversely, if the debtor cannot show that modifications in the collective bargaining agreement are necessary to prevent liquidation, the bankruptcy court should not permit rejection at all. . . . If, at an early stage of the reorganization, it is unclear whether modifications of the agreement will be necessary, the court should still deny rejection.

Id. at 1008 & n. 173 (footnote omitted). This argument actually goes beyond *REA Express* by requiring the debtor to demonstrate both that liquidation is the only alternative to rejection *and* that the balance of equities favors rejection. As a practical matter, it is hard to imagine a situation in which the equities would favor liquidation over rejection. The better-reasoned view, which more accurately comports with the legislative history of section 1113, is that the proposed revisions must be reasonably calculated to contribute to a successful reorganization. *See* George, *supra* note 4, at 319 n.108 (construing § 1113(b)(1)(A) to "require only that the [proposed] revisions contribute to a successful reorganization," in the light of a "legislative history suggest[ing] that the statute be interpreted liberally with concern for the debtor's financial well-being"); note 52 *supra* & accompanying text. Most of the cases applying section 1113 have so concluded. *See also* note 43 *supra* and note 66 *infra*.

not become "an attempt to devise an entire reorganization plan at a premature stage."[54]

According to Senator Packwood, "fair and equitable treatment of all affected parties" means that

> the focus for cost cutting must not be directed exclusively at unionized workers. Rather the burden of sacrifices in the reorganization process will be spread among all affected parties.[55]

Senator Packwood specifically referred to the approach taken in *In re Blue Ribbon Transportation Co.*[56] as indicative of "this kind of analysis."[57] In *Blue Ribbon* the bankruptcy court denied the debtor's motion to reject a collective bargaining agreement unless it shared the economic sacrifice by reducing management salaries, eliminating company cars, cancelling gasoline credit cards, and reducing management's health insurance and pension contributions proportionately to those sought for by the unioned employees.[58]

In order to authorize rejection of a labor contract, the bankruptcy court must find that (1) the debtor has made a proposal to the union complying with the requirements of the statute,[59] (2) that the union has refused to accept the proposal "without good cause,"[60] and (3) the balance of the equities "clearly favors rejection."[61] The first element of the court's finding is merely a determination that the debtor's proposal was substantively sufficient, a requirement which has already been discussed.

The second element is seemingly the converse of a proper proposal; if the union refuses to accept the "necessary modifications" proposed by the debtor, it has done so "without good cause."[62] Senator Thurmond made it clear that the union's refusal is not to

---

[54] 130 CONG. REC. S8892 (daily ed. June 29, 1984) (statement of Sen. Hatch).

[55] *Id.* at S8898.

[56] 113 L.R.R.M. 3505 (Bankr. D. R.I. 1983).

[57] 130 CONG. REC. S8890 (daily ed. June 29, 1984).

[58] *Id.;* 113 L.R.R.M. at 3508–09. *Accord, In re* Parrot Packing Co., 115 L.R.R.M. 2607 (N.D. Ind. 1983).

[59] 11 U.S.C. §§ 1113(b)(1), (c)(1).

[60] 11 U.S.C. § 113(c)(2).

[61] 11 U.S.C. § 1113(c)(3).

[62] *See* 130 CONG. REC. S8890 (daily ed. June 29, 1984) (statement of Sen. Dole); *id.* S8892 (statement of Sen. Hatch):

> [T]he unions must not reject the business offer without good cause. This opportunity to accept or reject the proposal should be assessed in light of the essentiality of the swift and fair resolution of the initial phases of the reorganization. Accordingly, rejection of a proposal should only happen if the cause for the rejection is good enough to risk the damage to the business as well as its creditors and employees that delay or protacted negotiations could produce.

be evaluated in terms of "impasse" or other labor law standards[63]; "the intent is for these provisions to be interpreted in a workable manner."[64] Senator Packwood confirmed that the "without good cause" language

> imposes no barrier to rejection if the debtor's proposal has contained only the specified 'necessary' modifications. Thus, the language serves to prohibit any bad faith conduct by an employer, while at the same time protecting the employer from a Union's rejection of the proposal without good cause.[65]

The final element, that the equities clearly favor rejection, is simply a clarification of the Supreme Court's holding in *Bildisco.*[66] Senator Hatch explained that "[t]he word 'clearly' is merely intended to assure that rejection is not warranted where the equities balance exactly equally on each side."[67]

The remaining problem areas in section 1113 are the impact of the bankruptcy court's failure timely to act and the standard for authorizing "interim changes."

Senator Thurmond described the conference committee compromise on H.R. 5174 as

> essentially the same as those of the Packwood amendment. Certain provisions were added . . . to insure the flexibility and finality of the labor language. A provision was added, for example, to clarify that, should a judge fail to rule on an application for rejection within 30

---

[63] 130 Cong. Rec. S8888 (daily ed. June 29, 1984).

[64] *Id.* (statement of Sen. Thurmond).

[65] *Id.* at S8898. *See also* Gibson, *supra* note 4, at 341 & n.69; Ehrenwerth & Lally-Green, *The New Bankruptcy Procedures For Rejection of Collective-Bargaining Agreements: Is the Pendulum Swinging Back?,* 23 Duq. L. Rev. 939, 964 (1985) ("it appears that the phrase ['without good cause'] can be interpreted to require the union to both confer in 'good faith' and, at a minimum, to compromise on proposals which meet the section 1113(b)(1) test").

[66] 130 Cong. Rec. S8890 (daily ed. June 29, 1984) (statement of Sen. Dole) ("the court will apply the balancing of equities test enunciated in *Bildisco,* with a clarification of that standard to ensure that rejection is accomplished only where the equities balance clearly in favor of rejection"); Gibson, *supra* note 4, at 343. Note, *supra* note 53, at 1007–08 ("Congress plainly imported [the 'balance of the equities'] language from *Bildisco,* and effectively codified the equities listed in the Supreme Court's opinion.") Most commentators have concluded that the standard for rejection set forth in section 1113 is similar to the *Bildisco* standard. *See* note 43 *supra;* Note, *supra* note 43, at 1011–13; *id.* at 1016 ("the legislative history does not indicate clearly that Congress intended to require that a debtor in possession meet a higher standard under section 1113 than under *Bildisco.*"); Roukis & Charnov, *Section 1113 of the Bankruptcy Amendments and Federal Judgeship Act of 1984: A Management-Labor Compromise That Will Not Work,* 37 Labor L.J. 273, 279 (1986) (rejection standard under § 1113 similar to *Bildisco/Kevin Steel*).

[67] 130 Cong. Rec. S8892 (daily ed. June 29, 1984). Senator Hatch also observed that "the equities will almost always balance in favor [of] one resolution or another. In such cases, the court will surely rule in accordance with the tilt of the balance." *Id.*

> days of the commencement of the hearing on such application, the debtor may unilaterally terminate or alter the collective bargaining agreement pending the court's final ruling on the application. At that point in time, the debtor would essentially be in the same position he is now in under the *Bildisco* decision—that is he may unilaterally abrogate the contract pending the court's decision.[68]

Senator Packwood stated that

> if the court ultimately refused to approve rejection of the contract, then the trustee will have to pay back any wages or benefits withheld unilaterally and unpaid wages and benefits will be treated as costs of administration.[69]

The interim change provision in section 1113(e) is largely self-explanatory. Senator Thurmond described the provision as "a very important addition to the labor provisions and allows the necessary flexibility to prevent a debtor from being forced into liquidation."[70] Although some of the conferees stated that the standard for authorizing interim changes is the *REA Express* text,[71] there is no clear consensus in the legislative history to support this position. Senator Packwood stated that section 1113(e) "essentially requires the court to apply the [*REA Express*] test."[72] Representatives Hughes and Morrison made a similar statement,[73] but this interpretation did not go unchallenged.[74] In any event, the judicial authorities applying the *REA Express* standard doubtless will be persuasive precedents in cases under section 1113(e).[75]

CASES DECIDED UNDER SECTION 1113

Section 1113 governs Chapter 11 filings made on or after July 10, 1984. Although the bargaining requirements of section 1113, if successful, may prevent many debtors' resort to bankruptcy court

---

[68] *Id.* S8888. *See also id.* S8893 (statement of Sen. Hatch); S8898 (statement of Sen. Packwood).

[69] *Id.* S8898. Representatives Hughes and Morrison further stated that

> The courts are expected as a matter of course to meet the time limits set by Congress. In the unlikely event that a particular court should not do so, expeditious mandamus relief would be available in the appellate courts.

130 Cong. Rec. H7496 (daily ed. June 29, 1984).

[70] 130 Cong. Rec. S8888 (daily ed. June 29, 1984). *See also id.* S8892 (statement of Sen. Hatch).

[71] Brotherhood of Railway, Airline and Steamships Clerks v. REA Express, Inc., 523 F.2d 164, 172 (2d Cir.) (rejection should not be authorized unless the debtor will otherwise collapse and the employees will no longer have their jobs). *cert. denied,* 423 U.S. 1017 (1975).

[72] 130 Cong. Rec. S8898 (daily ed. June 29, 1984).

[73] 130 Cong. Rec. H7496 (daily ed. June 29, 1984)(the standard for qualifying for interim relief is, in essence, the *REA Express* standard).

[74] *Id.* (statement of Rep. Lundgren).

[75] *See* Gibson, *supra* note 4, at 333–34.

for authorization to reject collective bargaining agreements,[76] there is a growing number of judicial decisions applying section 1113.

The reported decisions suggest that a debtor must make more than superficial and "perfunctory" attempts to negotiate concessions from the union prior to seeking rejection, particularly when the current union contract is shortly due to expire.[77] Moreover, courts will deny interim relief under section 1113(e) unless the debtor presents specific and credible evidence that the relief sought is essential to the continuation of operations.[78] As was the case prior to *Bildisco,* the bankruptcy court decisions tend to favor the debtor, and the court of appeal decisions are in conflict. In general, however, the reported cases confirm the wisdom of Professor White's prediction that notwithstanding section 1113, "the courts will continue routinely to reject collective bargaining agreements."[79]

In one of the earliest cases, *In re Wright Air Lines, Inc.,*[80] the court denied a debtor's application for section 1113(e) interim relief from its executory contract with the Air Line Pilots Association (ALPA). Focusing on the requirement in section 1113(e) that interim relief be granted only if "essential to the continuation of the debtor's business," or "in order to avoid irreparable damage to the estate," the court found that the debtor had failed to meet its burden

---

[76] *Cf. Eastern Airlines Outside Report Urges Severe Wage Cuts or Chapter 11 Filing,* Wall St. J., Jan. 8, 1986, at p. 2; *Eastern Air's Borman Badly Underestimated Obduracy of Old Foe,* Wall St. J., Feb. 25, 1986, at p. 1. In NLRB v. Manley Truck Line, Inc. 779 F.2d 1327 (7th Cir. 1985), the court upheld the NLRB's refusal to recognize an "economic necessity" defense under section 8(d) to unilateral wage reductions by a non-bankrupt employer, because "[t]he language of section 8(d) neither expressly conditions its enforcement upon the continuing economic survival of the employer's business, nor invites such a condition." *Id.* at 1331. The court elaborated in a footnote that Congress' enactment of section 1113 in response to the Supreme Court's decision in Bildisco

> suggests the inference that [Congress] disfavors unilateral mid-term modifications by an employer absent the economic hardship which warrants a filing for bankruptcy, and then, only under the meticulous procedural safeguards provided by § 1113.
>
> We also note that through § 1113 Congress has provided an economically distressed employer an avenue for relief from excessive burdens under a collective-bargaining agreement. Substantially similar relief was available to [the employer] under 11 U.S.C. § 365(a), the predecessor to § 1113.

Id., n.7.

[77] *See In re* American Provision Co., 44 Bankr. 907 (Bankr. D. Minn. 1984).

[78] *See In re* Wright Air Lines, Inc. 44 Bankr. 744 (Bank. N.D. Ohio 1984) (interim relief denied); *In re* K & B Mounting Inc., 122 L.R.R.M. 2541 (Bankr. N.D. Ind. 1986) (same). *But see In re* Salt Creek Freightways, 46 Bankr. 347 (Bank. D. Wyo. 1985) (interim relief granted under REA Express standard, notwithstanding debtor's failure to make a proposal to union or to file application for rejection).

[79] White, *supra* note 4, at 1198.

[80] 44 Bankr. 744 (Bankr. N.D. Ohio 1984).

of proof.[81] The deficiency was three-fold. First, some of the proffered "evidence" was inconclusive:

> The financial information presented by the Debtor-In-Possession was largely incomplete, and no reliable projections were presented as to the probable income and expenses for the months of November and December. All of the figures presented were based on assumptions which the chief witness for the Debtor-In-Possession admitted were not valid assumptions for purposes of financial projections. None of the witnesses for the Debtor-In-Possession was able to testify as to what dollar amount of savings would be required to enable the company to survive.[82]

Second, the evidence did not prove enough. The debtor sought to discontinue pilot training, which would save $71,000. The court pointed out, however, that

> [t]he financial information which was presented indicates that Wright Air Lines is presently losing upwards of Eight Hundred Thousand ($800,000.00) each month. Thus the cost of the training amounts to less than ten percent of Wright's monthly losses.
>
> There is no question that the pilot training . . . is burdensome and uneconomical. However, the evidence presented by Wright does not show that the relief sought is essential to permit the company to continue its operations.[83]

Finally, the court chided the debtor for failing to explain in its application how the operating changes sought could, as a practical matter, be implemented on an interim basis. Because the interim relief would extend only until the court ruled on the pending motion to reject the ALPA contract in its entirety, the court reasoned that "the issue of what will occur in the event that rejection were not granted would appear to impact strongly upon the instant application."[84] The debtor was apparently attempting to implement an interim system for recall of laid-off pilots that would be based on seniority within particular aircraft rather than seniority generally. If rejection was denied, the court stated, the pilots recalled on this basis would "have to be furloughed immediately."[85] The lesson of *Wright Air Lines* is that a debtor must present detailed and convincing evidence in order to obtain interim relief under section 1113(e).

Another early decision, *In re American Provision Co.,*[86] denied a debtor's motion to reject an executory Teamsters contract because

---

[81] *Id.* at 745.
[82] *Id.*
[83] *Id.*
[84] *Id.*
[85] *Id.* at 746.
[86] 44 Bankr. 907 (Bankr. D. Minn. 1984).

the debtor only met with the union once to discuss the proposal, the projected monthly savings of $1,185 would amount to only two percent of the debtor's total monthly operating expenses of $58,000, and the contracts were due to expire in eight months. In so ruling, the court distilled from section 1113 nine elements, for which the debtor bears the burden of persuasion by a preponderance of evidence:

> 1. The debtor in possession must make a proposal to the Union to modify the collective bargaining agreement.
>
> 2. The proposal must be based on the most complete and reliable information available at the time of the proposal.
>
> 3. The proposed modifications must be necessary to permit the reorganization of the debtor.
>
> 4. The proposed modifications must assure that all creditors, the debtor and all of the affected parties are treated fairly and equitably.
>
> 5. The debtor must provide to the Union such relevant information as is necessary to evaluate the proposal.
>
> 6. Between the time of the making of the proposal and the time of the hearing on approval of the rejection of the existing collective bargaining agreement, the debtor must meet at reasonable times with the Union.
>
> 7. At the meetings the debtor must confer in good faith in attempting to reach mutually satisfactory modifications of the collective bargaining agreement.
>
> 8. The Union must have refused to accept the proposal without good cause.
>
> 9. The balance of the equities must clearly favor rejection of the collective bargaining agreement.[87]

These nine elements for court approval of the rejection of collective bargaining agreements have been followed in subsequent decisions.

In *In re Salt Creek Freightways*,[88] the court declined to apply the *American Provision* test in the context of *interim* relief under section 1113(e) because "the standard for the rejection of collective bargaining agreements is separate and distinct from the standard for the authorization of interim changes under subsection (e)."[89] Instead, the court concluded that Congress enacted as the standard for interim changes under section 1113(e) the strict requirements of *Brotherhood of Railway Employees v. REA Express, Inc.*,[90] "Thus, a debtor seeking interim relief must show a more immediate level

[87] *Id.* at 909.

[88] 46 Bankr. 347 (Bankr. D. Wyo. 1985).

[89] *Id.* at 350. *See In re* K & B Mounting, Inc., 122 L.R.R.M. 2541, 2542 (Bankr. N.D. Ind.) ("In order to obtain [interim] relief, the debtor's evidence must establish that the provisions of 11 U.S.C. § 1113(e) are satisfied.").

[90] 523 F.2d 164 (2d Cir.), *cert. denied*, 423 U.S. 1017 (1975). *See* 46 Bankr. at 350.

of economic emergency than it would need to show as support for an application for rejection."[91]

Employing the *REA Express* standard, the court in *Salt Creek Freightways* granted the debtor interim relief because the uncontradicted evidence showed that, without the interim change, the debtor would be unable to remain in business more than another week.[92] The debtor had not yet sought rejection of the union contract, which was due to expire in less than two months.[93] The court disagreed with the union's argument that interim relief is only available after an unsuccessful attempt at rejection.[94] Looking to the legislative intent of section 1113 as a whole, the court interpreted the phrase in subsection (e), "during a period when the collective bargaining agreement continues in effect," to mean "any one of the various times in which a collective bargaining agreement remains in effect," whether before or after an application for rejection has been filed.[95] Limiting interim relief to the period after an unsuccessful attempt at rejection would "thwart" Congress' intent that bankruptcy courts "have the flexibility to effectuate the overriding objective of Chapter 11, the preservation of a failing business for the benefit of all, including the employees who would otherwise lose their jobs."[96]

The debtor in *In re Salt Creek Freightways* had made a proposal to the union containing requests for direct economic as well as non-economic relief. The debtor and the union had met twice to discuss the proposal.[97] The court limited its authorization of interim relief to the debtor's six specific proposals for reductions of wages and benefits.[98] Although the court warned that its ruling on interim relief "does not render moot the issues ultimately to be decided on an application for rejection" of the union contract,[99] the court noted the debtor's long-standing record of losses, large current and projected continuing losses, and reductions in the salaries and benefits of non-union employees, including management personnel.[100]

After this ruling, but prior to expiration of the union contract, the debtor in *In re Salt Creek Freightways* filed a motion to reject

[91] 46 Bankr. at 350.
[92] *Id.*
[93] *Id.* at 348.
[94] *Id.*
[95] *Id.* at 351.
[96] *Id.*
[97] *Id.* at 348.
[98] *Id.* at 351.
[99] *Id.*
[100] *Id.* at 348–49.

its collective bargaining agreement with the union.[101] Citing *American Provision Co.* as "[t]he only reported decision construing § 1113" since its enactment,[102] the court in *Salt Creek II* found that the debtor met each of the nine requirements. In so ruling the court clarified the meaning of the nine elements. The court held that all of the debtor's proposed modifications, including modification of grievance procedure, were necessary to permit the reorganization of the debtor because they "impacted upon operations."[103] Thus, absent specific proof that proposed changes would have no impact, any proposal having economic consequences favorable to the debtor, even if indirect, will qualify as "necessary to permit reorganization."

The court also construed the duty to provide information in the fifth requirement as applying only to information necessary to evaluate the debtor's proposal. Thus, the debtor's failure to furnish the union with copies of the written cost estimates it had prepared to evaluate the union's counter-proposals did not violate section 1113(b)(1)(B).[104] In addition, the court construed the duty to "confer in good faith" in the seventh requirement to permit a debtor to take a "hard and fast stand" on certain issues in negotiations, so long as it meets with the union and considers the union's counter-proposals, even if it is unwilling to accept the union's position or negotiate further.[105]

Significantly, the court interpreted, for the first time, the "refusal without good reason" standard in the eighth requirement. After considering the various statements in the legislative history of section 1113(c)(2), the court concluded that

> it is not necessary to find that a Union has rejected the debtor's proposal in 'bad faith' or for some contrary motive. In fact, the Union may often have a principled reason for deciding to reject the debtor's proposal and which may, when viewed subjectively and from the standpoint of its self-interest, be a perfectly good reason. However, the court must review the Union's rejection utilizing an objective standard which narrowly construes the phrase "without good cause"

---

[101] *See In re* Salt Creek Freightways ("Salt Creek II"), 47 Bankr. 835 (Bankr. D. Wyo. 1985).

[102] *Id.* at 837.

[103] *Id.* at 839. *Cf. In re* Valley Kitchens, Inc., 52 Bankr. 493, 495–97 (Bankr. S.D. Ohio 1985) (debtor's inclusion of items in proposal to union that did not involve direct economic savings, such as overtime, shutdowns, job classifications, promotions and transfers, absenteeism, and tardiness, made the proposal defective under § 1113(b)(1)(A)).

[104] 47 Bankr. at 839.

[105] *Id.* at 839–40.

> in light of the main purpose of Chapter 11, namely reorganization of financially distressed businesses.[106]

This "objective standard," however, is not a reasonableness standard. The court specifically found that the union's basis for rejecting the debtor's proposal, though "not an unreasoned basis . . .[,] does not constitute 'good cause' within the meaning of § 1113(c)(2)."[107] What then, does "good cause" mean? The court suggested that any refusal of a proper proposal would be "without good cause":

> [I]n view of the fact that the company has negotiated in good faith and the debtor's proposal contains only the specified "necessary" modifications, the court concludes that the Union's refusal to accept the debtor's proposal in this case was "without good cause."[108]

Finally, the court held that the balance of equities "clearly favored" rejection and adopted the Supreme Court's approach in *Bildisco,* which considers only how the equities relate to the success of reorganization.[109] Notwithstanding that the union contract was due to expire less than three days after the court's ruling, and that a major consequence of rejection would be to reduce the priority of union employees' claims for unpaid pension contributions,[110] the certain alternative of liquidation convinced the court that "the balance of the equities clearly favor rejection of the collective bargaining agreement."[111]

The debtor in *In re Russell Transfer, Inc.,*[112] sought simultaneously to reject and to modify its union contracts on an interim basis. At the hearing an officer of the debtor testified without contradiction that it could not continue to operate unless it reduced union employees' salaries and holiday benefit payments by approximately 20 percent.[113] The debtor did not intent to reduce administrative employees' salaries because their wages had been frozen for the prior three years, whereas the union employees had received regular increases under their contract. The union argued that no interim relief should be ordered without corresponding reductions of administrative salaries. The court took a middle course:

> [I]t is incumbent upon courts to equitably apportion the reduction of overhead even where the debtor does not so recommend. In this case, where the administrative employees have not received increases as

[106] *Id.* at 840.
[107] *Id.* at 841.
[108] *Id.*
[109] *Id.* (*citing* Bildisco, *supra,* 465 U.S. 513, 527 (1984)).
[110] *Id.* at 841–42 & n.2.
[111] *Id.* at 842.
[112] 48 Bankr. 241 (Bankr. W.D. Va. 1985).
[113] *Id.* at 242–43.

> Union employees have in the last three (3) years, a smaller reduction is in order. It is, therefore, the conclusion of the Court that the twenty per cent (20%) reduction outlined by the Debtor in Union employees' salaries and benefits will be granted, and a ten per cent (10%) reduction in salaries of administrative employees will likewise be ordered.[114]

In *In re K & B Mounting, Inc.,*[115] a debtor's motion to reject an executory collective bargaining agreement was denied under sections 1113(c)(1) and (c)(2) because, *inter alia,* the debtor did not accompany its proposal to the union with sufficient information with which the union could evaluate the proposal. Citing the nine requirements for rejection set forth in *American Provision Co.* and independently reviewing the text and legislative history of section 1113, the court concluded that the debtor's proof was "woefully inadequate" and that its initial proposal was flawed.[116]

The parties had never met in person to discuss the debtor's proposal, and the debtor's initial written proposal lacked any analysis or explanation of the financial consequences of the proposed modifications.[117] Accordingly, the court held that

> neither the union nor the court could assess the necessity of [the debtor's proposed] modifications, since the debtor did not substantiate its proposal with "relevant" information selected from "the most complete and reliable information available" when the debtor made its proposal. As stated above, the debtor's bankruptcy filings are hardly sufficient. The union should be supplied with detailed projections and recommendations, perhaps made by a management consultant, preferably one who is independent of the interested parties. The debtor should present full and detailed disclosure of its difficulties and its proposed short-run and long-run solutions.[118]

The court's analysis seems to confuse the second and fifth requirements of *American Provision Co.;* there was no contention that the debtor's proposal was not based on "the most complete and reliable information available at the time,"[119] and the union never requested any supporting documentation "to evaluate the proposal."[120] Instead, the court fashioned from section 1113(b)(1)(B) an affirmative

---

[114] *Id.* at 244.
[115] 50 Bankr. 460 (Bankr. N.D. Ind. 1985).
[116] *Id.* at 467–68.
[117] *Id.* at 463, 467–68.
[118] *Id.* at 467.
[119] 11 U.S.C. § 1113(b)(1)(A).
[120] 11 U.S.C. § 1113(b)(1)(B). *See* 50 Bankr. at 468 & n.10.

duty to furnish "full information to the union," whether requested or not.[121]

The court may also have been influenced by other defects in the debtor's proposal: "The proposal clearly does not assure that all creditors and affected parties are treated fairly and equitably [as required by section 1113(b)(1)(A)]."[122] Although management salaries were reduced, all equipment had been purchased with cash rather than debt.

> The result of this management decision ... was that, upon filing in bankruptcy the company had no secured debtors, and the only major debt owed was that obligation of employee benefits under the labor contract. Therefore the proposal of [the debtor] affects only one party in interest, the employees.[123]

Moreover, the court held that "[s]ince no meetings took place between the debtor and the union, the debtor has not met the requirement of meeting at reasonable times to confer in good faith over the modifications."[124] Although the union's refusal to recognize or meet with the debtor's attorney "reflected its lack of good faith in these proceedings,"[125] the union had good cause to refuse to accept the proposal because the proposal itself was flawed.[126]

In *In re Allied Delivery System Co.*,[127] in contrast, the court authorized a debtor's rejection of a collective bargaining agreement even though the parties had met only twice to discuss the debtor's proposal prior to the hearing on the motion to reject, the debtor proposed a greater percentage reduction of wages and benefits for union employees than for non-union employees, and the contract itself was due to expire in less than six weeks. The debtor's distressed financial condition was apparently not disputed: direct labor costs attributable to the debtor's union employees constituted 87 percent of the debtor's gross revenues, and indirect costs such as pension health and welfare benefits brought that percentage even higher;[128]

---

[121] 50 Bankr. at 568. Similarly, in *In re* Fiber Glass Industries, Inc., 49 Bankr. 202, 207 (Bankr. N.D.N.Y. 1985), the court ruled that debtor had not provided "such relevant information as is necessary to evaluate the proposal," as required by 11 U.S.C. § 1113(b)(1)(B), by failing to disclose to the union an anticipated layoff of one-third of the union workforce. A better interpretation of section 1113(b)(1)(B) would limit its application to *financial* information bearing on the debtor's proposal which is *requested* by the union.

[122] 50 Bankr. at 468.

[123] *Id.*

[124] *Id.*

[125] *Id.*

[126] *Id.*

[127] 49 Bankr. 700 (Bankr. N.D. Ohio 1985).

[128] *Id.* at 702.

the debtor lost $287,000 in 1984 and faced a decline in projected revenues for 1985 of approximately $1 million.[129]

On these facts, the court held, first, that the requirement of section 1113(b)(1)(A) that the debtor's proposal contain only "necessary modifications" is less stringent than the "essential to the continuation of the debtor's business" standard for interim relief under section 1113(e).[130] Thus, a proposal contains "necessary modifications" if it will promote the successful reorganization of the debtor; a debtor is not required to prove that reorganization will fail otherwise.[131] The court concluded that the debtor's proposal met this standard:

> Clearly the modifications proposed by the debtor would have substantially reduced the debtor's labor costs, and such cost reduction is absolutely required if this debtor is to reorganize.[132]

Second, the court ruled that a debtor's proposal of disproportionate reduction of the wages and benefits of union employees was not necessarily unfair or inequitable under section 1113(b)(1)(A).[133] The court stated that the requirement of fair and equitable treatment does not mean that all employees' wages must be reduced by the same percentage:[134]

> The evidence clearly demonstrated that the wages of all non-union employees were reduced on a graduated scale based on earnings, and that the earnings and benefits of most of the non-union employees did not equal in value those of the union employees. In particular, the non-union employees have no pension plan. Fair and equitable treatment does not of necessity mean identical or equal treatment.[135]

Third, the court rejected the union's argument that the debtor failed to comply with section 1113(b)(1)(B) by withholding "such relevant information as is necessary to evaluate the proposal." With its January 16, 1983 proposal the debtor had included "the most current financial statement available at that time, which was complete through November 30, 1984."[136] The union requested, but did not receive, previous financial statements covering a period of 2

---

[129] *Id.* at 703.

[130] *Id.* at 702. *Cf.* Wheeling-Pittsburgh Steel Corporation v. United Steelworkers of America, 791 F.2d 1074, 1088–89 (3d Cir. 1986) (terms "necessary" and "essential" are synonymous), discussed at notes 230–43 and accompanying text.

[131] 49 Bankr. at 702.

[132] *Id.*

[133] *Id.* at 702–03.

[134] *Id.* at 702.

[135] *Id.* at 702–03.

[136] *Id.* at 701.

and 3 years prior to the debtor's Chapter 11 filing on December 24, 1984.[137] The court held that

> once the debtor has produced evidence that it provided information to the union, the burden is on the union to demonstrate that that information was not sufficient, for whatever reason. The union herein has not met this burden. . . . This Court finds that in the absence of the union's showing of a need for specific information beyond the current financial information provided by the debtor, the debtor has complied with [section 1113(b)(1)(B)].[138]

Fourth, the court held that the debtor had reasonably met and conferred with the union in good faith to discuss its proposal, as required by section 1113(b)(2), even though only two meetings were held prior to the hearing, one of which occurred prior to filing the motion to reject:

> [T]he reason more sessions were not held . . . was mutual scheduling difficulties. Neither the debtor nor the union will be penalized for that. It is also clear that the debtor did, during the course of these negotiations, make reductions in its demands to the union. The Court finds that the requirement of good faith negotiations has in fact been complied with.[139]

Fifth, the court concluded that the union's refusal of the debtor's final proposal was "without good cause" under section 1113(c)(2). The union argued that the debtor's final proposal called for reductions in excess of its 1984 losses. The court concluded, however, that the final proposal did not exceed projected 1985 losses and was therefore proper under section 1113(b)(1)(A).[140]

> The Court finds further that the union's refusal to accept the proposal, while understandable, is not for good cause. If the proposal is necessary and is fair and equitable, which this Court finds that it is, then the union's refusal to accept it on the basis that the proposal is unjust, as the union representative has testified, is not for good cause.[141]

Finally, the court ruled that the balance of equities clearly favored rejection even though the underlying contract was due to expire just 10 days after the court's decision. The court reasoned that

> the financial drain on this debtor is enormous. The cutting of labor costs is essential. There has been no showing of any other area in which substantial savings could be realized by the debtor. Furthermore, the testimony established that the cost of living increase which

[137] *Id.* at 703.
[138] *Id.*
[139] *Id.*
[140] *Id.* at 703–04.
[141] *Id.* at 704.

> will become effective pursuant to the collective bargaining agreement on April 1, 1985, applies to this debtor, even though the collective bargaining agreement itself expires on March 31, 1985. . . . The debtor herein is in no position to continue to pay salaries and benefits at the current level, much less to be subject to a cost-of-living increase.[142]

In *In re Carey Transportation,*[143] the court eschewed reliance on the legislative statements accompanying passage of section 1113 and instead was "guided by the plain meaning of the statutory language . . . and by what little case law exists."[144] The debtor in *Carey Transportation* sought to reject two Teamsters contracts after extensive remedial actions, both before and after filing a voluntary petition for reorganization, failed to solve its financial difficulties. The debtor had operated at a loss for over 3 years and had lost approximately $2.5 million in the fiscal year just ended. The union had rejected the debtor's package of proposals, which would have resulted in projected economies of $1.8 million for each of the next 3 fiscal years.[145] A group of union members, described as "believing themselves disaffected,"[146] alternately boycotted the bargaining sessions and submitted its own counter-proposals.[147] The employees participated in the hearing on the debtor's motion to reject.

The union and the ad hoc committee of union employees separately challenged the debtor's proposal on the ground that the debtor had failed to provide sufficient financial information. The court rejected the committee's argument because the financial information it requested did not relate to the debtor's proposal. The court adopted the reasoning of *Salt Creek II* that the debtor's duty to provide information under section 1113(b)(1)(B) is limited to data necessary to evaluate the debtor's proposal, not the union's own counter-proposals.[148] While *Salt Creek II* also involved interim relief under section 1113(e), the court held that there is "no policy difference behind the financial information requirement in the context of § 1113(b) and that required under § 1113(e)."[149] The court in *Carey Transportation* likewise overruled the union's objection on the information issue:

---

[142] *Id. Cf. In re* Valley Kitchens, Inc., 52 Bankr. 493, 497 (Bankr. S. D. Ohio 1985) (rejection denied, in part because contract was due to expire only six weeks after hearing on debtor's motion).

[143] 50 Bankr. 203 (Bankr. S.D.N.Y. 1985).

[144] *Id.* at 207 (citations omitted).

[145] *Id.* at 208.

[146] *Id.* at 205.

[147] *Id.*

[148] *Id.* at 208 (*citing In re* Salt Creek Freightways, 47 Bankr. 835, 839 (Bankr. D. Wyo. 1985)).

[149] *Id.*

> While claiming an initial lack of supplied relevant financial information, the Union chose not to avail itself of [the debtor's] offer to permit the Union's auditors to examine the Debtor's books and records on location. . . . That the Union is not satisfied with the Debtor's proposals and that the Debtor did not adopt one of the [committee's] counter-proposals are insufficient bases to support a finding that [the debtor] failed to provide relevant financial information.[150]

At the hearing, officers of the debtor "testified generally but credibly"[151] that its proposals were necessary to successful reorganization. The union "argued to the contrary without developing any factual contradiction."[152] The court held that the debtor's proposals were "necessary" within the meaning of section 1113(b)(1)(A), steering a middle course between the holdings of *Allied Delivery* and *American Provision.*[153] The court did not attempt to "quantify" its approach or to adopt any "set formula" as to the degree of distress necessary to justify certain levels of proposed savings.[154] "Any analysis must be undertaken on a case by case basis with due consideration given to the nature of the business and industry patterns."[155] The court ultimately followed the reasoning of *Salt Creek II* and held that the debtor's proposed modifications were necessary because they would have impacted upon the debtor's operations.[156]

The union in *Carey Transportation* also challenged the debtor's proposal on the ground that it did "not include concomitant wage cuts and other economies for management, supervisory and other non-union personnel."[157] In fact, while the number of management personnel had been reduced pre-petition, the debtor maintained five company cars, gave two managers pay raises and made profit-sharing contributions to eight others.[158] The debtor had, however, implemented various reductions of personnel among the non-union ranks pre-petition.[159] On these facts the court held that the debtor's proposal was fair and equitable under section 1113(b)(1)(A):

> Equity requires management to tighten its belt along with labor, and the record herein supports a finding that [the debtor] has com-

---

150 *Id.* at 208–09.
151 *Id.* at 209.
152 *Id.*
153 *Id.*
154 *Id.*
155 *Id.*
156 *Id.* (*citing In re* Salt Creek II, 47 Bankr. at 838).
157 *Id.* at 210.
158 *Id.* at 209.
159 *Id.* at 210.

> plied with this requirement. *These pruning efforts may occur prior to or concurrent with the Chapter 11 filing.*[160]

Thus, the proposal itself does not have to contain reductions in the wages and benefits of non-union employees if the debtor's actions result in company-wide economies:

> Although [the debtor] has not reduced the wages and salaries of its remaining managerial and supervisory employees, it has gradually reduced the number of these personnel by approximately sixty-five percent, which has certainly resulted in economies of scale.[161]

Accordingly, the court held that the debtor's proposal "treats all affected parties fairly and equitably, without placing a disproportionate burden on the members of the Union."[162]

The court concluded that nine meetings held after the debtor's proposal and prior to the conclusion of the hearing met the good faith meet and confer requirements of section 1113(b)(2); that the debtor failed to accept the union's counter-proposal was not dispositive, particularly since uncontradicted testimony showed that the union's counter-proposal was inadequate to permit a reorganization.[163] Moreover, the court adopted the approach of *Allied Delivery* and *Salt Creek II* on the "good cause" requirement in section 1113(c)(2):

> Having found that [the debtor's] proposal contained necessary modifications and was fair and equitable when all the economies made by [the debtor] pre-petition are combined with those proposed post-petition, it must be found that the Union's refusal to accept [the debtor's] proposal was without good cause within the meaning of the statute.[164]

In other words, if a proposal meets the requirements of section 1113(b)(1), there is no good cause for the union to refuse to accept it.

---

[160] *Id.* (emphasis added).

[161] *Id.* As in *Allied Delivery,* the court rejected the notion that the requirement of fair and equitable treatment means identical or equal treatment. *Id.* Further, the court criticized the holding of *In re* Russell Transfer, Inc., *supra,* in which the court ordered the debtor to implement reductions in administrative salaries. The *Carey Transportation* court described this as "an unsanctioned exercise in discretion" and observed that

> where management has failed to make concomitant belt-tightening cuts in its compensation, this fact may clearly tip the equities in favor of denying a motion to reject a collective bargaining agreement under § 1113(b) and (c) or for interim relief under (e). However, nothing in § 1113 affirmatively empowers the court to order management to reduce salaries involuntarily. 50 Bankr. at 210 n.4.

[162] *Id.* at 211.

[163] *Id.*

[164] *Id.* at 212.

Finally, the court found that the balance of equities clearly favored rejection of the union contract.[165] Embracing the standard set forth by the Supreme Court in *Bildisco,* the court considered the interests of the affected parties, the likelihood and consequences of liquidation absent rejection, and the effect of affirmance on creditors and of rejection on the employees.[166] The court refused to consider "whether or not the Union asserts a claim that the [Chapter 11 petition] was filed solely to jettison [the debtor's] union contract."[167] The court concluded that the union's assertion that this was the case was unsupported by the record.[168]

The court in *In re Cook United, Inc.,*[169] denied a debtor's motion for interim relief under section 1113(e) on the basis of the debtor's failure to comply with two of the nine requirements set forth in *American Provision.* Specifically, the court held that the proposed modifications of the debtor, a department store chain, were not "necessary" because "[w]ithout the anticipated labor savings, [the debtor's] operating plan would still show a positive cash flow of $1.9 million."[170] The court could have reached the same result under the applicable standard for interim relief in section 1113(e), which requires that the requested modification be either "essential to the continuation of the debtor's business" or "in order to avoid irreparable injury to the estate." (It is unclear from the court's opinion whether the debtor simultaneously sought rejection of the union contracts; if not, the court's reliance on the "necessary" standard of section 1113(b)(1)(A) was simply mistaken.) The court alternatively found that the balance of the equities did not clearly weigh in favor of rejection because the debtor "has simply failed to demonstrate that the adverse effects of a denial of its motion to reject or modify the collective bargaining agreement outweigh the adverse effects rejection will have on [the debtor's] employees."[171]

In *In re Kentucky Truck Sales, Inc.,*[172] the bankruptcy court applied the *American Provision Co.* analysis and granted a debtor's motion to reject its contract with General Drivers, Warehousemen, and Helpers Union, Local No. 89. The court described the debtor's financial condition as "precarious, but not beyond salvage."[173] Al-

---

[165] *Id.*

[166] *Id.* (*citing* Bildisco, *supra,* 465 U.S. 513, 527 (1984)).

[167] *Id.*

[168] *Id.* at 213.

[169] 50 Bankr. 561 (Bankr. N.D. Ohio 1985).

[170] *Id.* at 563.

[171] *Id.* at 565.

[172] 52 Bankr. 797 (Bankr. W.D. Ky. 1985).

[173] *Id.* at 799.

though its assets considerably exceeded its liabilities, the debtor was competing in a declining industry and had experienced three consecutive years of operating losses.[174] Prior to filing under Chapter 11 on March 18, 1985, the debtor had implemented a number of remedial measures affecting its non-union and managerial personnel.[175] A certified public accountant hired as a consultant conducted an "intensive analysis" of the debtor's operations and concluded that it would have to reduce its operating expenses in the parts and service department by $100,000 in order to continue as a viable business.[176] The consultant concluded that the only area where these savings could be realized was in labor cost.[177]

Accordingly, the consultant recommended, and the debtor proposed to the union, a package of modifications consisting of (1) a 12 percent cut in salary; (2) substitution of a private health plan for existing coverage under Central States, Southeast and Southwest Areas Health and Welfare Fund; (3) reduction of paid vacation time to two weeks; (4) elimination of one paid holiday; and (5) no increase in the debtor's contribution to the union's pension fund.[178] The consultant estimated that these modifications would save the debtor approximately $100,000 a year.[179] The union refused the debtor's proposed modifications without explanation, and the debtor promptly moved to reject the contract. The parties met a total of four times: twice between the filing of the Chapter 11 petition and the motion to reject, once after the motion was filed and prior to the hearing, and once during a recess in the hearing. Only at the last meeting did the union make a counter-offer, which the debtor rejected as inadequate.[180] At the hearing the union did not contest the accuracy of the debtor's financial information, but challenged the good faith of the proposals and the necessity of the proposed modifications.[181]

After reviewing the legislative history of section 1113(b)(2) and the Supreme Court's decision in *Bildisco,* the court concluded that

> the 'good faith' requirements of section 1113 can be satisfied by the debtor showing that it has seriously attempted to negotiate reasonable modifications in the existing collective bargaining agreement with the union prior to the rejection hearing.[182]

[174] *Id.*
[175] *Id.* & n.3.
[176] *Id.*
[177] *Id.*
[178] *Id.* at 799–800.
[179] *Id.* at 800.
[180] *Id.*
[181] *Id.* at 801.
[182] *Id.*

Based on this standard, rather than the labor law definition of "impasse," the court held that the debtor negotiated in good faith with the union.[183] In light of the union's failure "to affirmatively demonstrate that any of the debtor's proposed modifications were unnecessary" or that "a major reduction in labor costs [was not necessary] to successfully reorganize," the court found in the debtor's favor on the fifth requirement of *American Provision Co.*[184]

The court held that the debtor's proposal treated all affected parties fairly and equally, even though the president and principal shareholder of the debtor, a closely held corporation, leased to the debtor at a profit a building he owned, and had purchased one of the debtor's profitable branches and now ran it as a separate company.[185] The court examined each of the alleged instances of self-dealing and found no evidence that the owner treated the debtor unfairly.[186]

On the other issues raised by the union, the court concluded that the proposed concessions for union employees were proportionate to those made by non-union employees; the debtor "constantly" offered to make its financial records available to the union (which offer the union "for the most part" declined); the union's refusal to accept any alternative to union-administered health insurance, although reasonable, did not constitute "good cause" within the meaning of section 1113(c)(2);[187] and that the balance of equities clearly favored rejection because "[t]he debtor has shown that without the rejection of its present collective bargaining agreement it will soon be forced to cease operations and liquidate."[188]

The difference between the result in *Kentucky Truck Sales,* authorizing rejection, and in *Fiber Glass Industries,* denying rejection, is as stark as it is inexplicable. The debtor in *Kentucky Truck Sales* showed a positive net worth and had no serious cash flow problems, aside from relatively small operating losses. The debtor in *Fiber Glass Industries,* in contrast, had debts substantially in excess of assets and was being foreclosed upon by its creditors. The debtor's financial evidence in *Kentucky Truck Sales,* particularly the testimony of the CPA-consultant, was accorded a great deal more weight than the internal projections offered by the debtor in *Fiber Glass Industries.* Whenever possible, then, debtors should utilize inde-

---

[183] *Id.* at 801–02.
[184] *Id.* at 802.
[185] *Id.* at 803.
[186] *Id.* at 803–04.
[187] The court adopted the reasoning of *Salt Creek II* that the union's rejection of a procedurally proper proposal is *a fortiori* "without good cause." *Id.* at 804–05.
[188] *Id.* at 806.

pendent financial experts to prove that the proposed modifications are necessary to facilitate reorganization. The apparent lesson for unions is that courts are unsympathetic to an uncompromising position during negotiations and unsupported allegations at the hearing. Unless prepared to offer competent and detailed rebuttal evidence, unions would be unable to oppose the debtor's showing under section 1113. In *Kentucky Truck Sales,* the debtor's evidence was weak but uncontradicted.

BILDISCO *REDUX:* WHEELING-PITTSBURGH *AND THE CONFLICT AMONG THE COURTS OF APPEALS*

In terms of the number of employees involved, the most significant ruling under section 1113 came in *In re Wheeling-Pittsburgh Steel Corp.*[189] Wheeling-Pittsburgh Steel Corp., the nation's seventh largest steel maker, filed for protection under Chapter 11 in April 1985 after posting large losses beginning in early 1982.[190] The debtor, which incurred a record $50.1 million loss for the second quarter of 1985,[191] sought a five-year, thirty percent reduction in the total hourly labor costs, from $21.40 to $15.20, under its contract with the United Steelworkers of America.[192] The union contract covered approximately 8,500 of the debtor's employees.[193] This proposal was made on May 9, 1985.[194] The motion to reject was filed on May 31, 1985.[195]

The court granted the debtor's motion to reject, and in the course of its lengthy opinion recited the company's longstanding financial woes and the history of concession bargaining with the union, dating to as early as 1980–81. Synthesizing the previous decisions applying section 1113, the court reformulated the nine *American Provision* requirements into nine elements of its own:

Prior to the § 1113 Hearing

1. The debtor-in-possession must make a proposal to the Union to modify the collective bargaining agreement. [1113(b)(1)(A)].
2. The debtor-in-possession then must meet at reasonable times with the Union until the date set forth the § 1113 hearing. [1113(b)(2)].

---

[189] 50 Bankr. 969 (Bankr. W.D. Pa.), *aff'd,* 52 Bankr. 997 (W.D. Pa. 1985), *rev'd,* 791 F.2d 1074 (3d Cir. 1986).

[190] *See Wheeling-Pittsburgh Posts Record Loss of $50.1 Million as Labor Ruling Nears,* Wall St. J., July 16, 1985, at p. 14.

[191] *Id.*

[192] *Id.*

[193] 50 Bankr. at 973.

[194] *Id.* at 974.

[195] *Id.*

3. At these meetings, the debtor-in-possession must confer in good faith in attempting to reach mutually satisfactory modifications of such agreement. [1113(b)(2)].

At the § 1113 Hearing

The court shall approve the application for rejection only if the court finds that:

4. The proposal was based on the most complete and reliable information available at the time of its creation. [1113(b)(1)(A)].
5. The proposed modifications are necessary to permit the reorganization of the debtor-in-possession. [1113(b)(1)(A)].
6. The proposed modifications assure that all creditors, the debtor-in-possession, and all of the affected parties are treated fairly and equitably. [1113(b)(1)(A)].
7. The debtor-in-possession provided the Union with such relevant information as was necessary to evaluate the proposal. [1113(b)(1)(B)].
8. The Union has refused to accept the proposal without good cause. [1113(c)(2)] and
9. The balance of the equities clearly favors rejection of the collective bargaining agreements. [1113(c)(3)].[196]

It was undisputed, and the court found, that the debtor complied with the first, second, and fourth elements. On the third element, the union challenged the debtor's good faith because it filed its motion to reject only three weeks after submitting its proposal and allegedly failed to cooperate with the union's financial experts. Mindful of admonitions in the legislative history that section 1113 was not to be construed in accordance with labor law precedents, the court ruled that

> the "good faith" element in § 1113(b)(2) can be satisfied by showing that the debtor made reasonable efforts to negotiate a voluntary modification, and those efforts were not likely to produce a prompt and satisfactory solution.[197]

Applying this standard, the court concluded that a three-week hiatus between making a proposal and filing a motion to reject is "not inherently unreasonable."[198] Because the debtor provided adequate information for the union to evaluate its proposal, in sufficient time to conduct meaningful negotiations, and because the debtor in fact

[196] *Id.* at 974–75.
[197] *Id.* at 976.
[198] *Id.*

made reasonable efforts to negotiate, the timing of the motion did not evidence bad faith.[199]

On the issue of the debtor's failure to cooperate with the union's financial experts, specifically by refusing to allow a plant tour and to explain its standard wage cost system, the court found that the request for a plant tour had not been refused, but was merely postponed, and that the standard cost system had already been reviewed by the same accounting organization that represented the union.[200]

On the fifth element, the court found that the debtor's proposals contained "necessary" modifications, despite the union's proof that the debtor could afford to pay the contractual labor rate for the remaining 13 months of the contract.[201] The court assumed this to be true, but determined that the appropriate inquiry is whether the *proposed* labor cost rate is necessary to permit the debtor's reorganization.[202] In light of the debtor's financial condition and the state of the industry, the court ruled that both the proposed $15.20 labor rate and the proposed five-year contract term were necessary "if a reorganization is to be achieved and a liquidation avoided."[203]

Following the analysis of *Allied Delivery* on the sixth element, the court rejected the union's claim that the proposal was unfair and inequitable.[204] The terms "fair and equitable" in section 1113(b)(1)(A) do not mean that management salaries must be reduced to an identical or equal degree.[205] The union argued that fixing union employees' compensation for five years without any opportunity for upward adjustment if the debtor's financial condition improved imposed a disproportionate burden on the union employees. The court rejected this argument because the proposed labor rate was both a ceiling and a floor; the employees were not being asked to share in possible future shortfalls.[206] Moreover, cred-

---

[199] *Id.* In *In re* Century Brass Products, Inc., 55 Bankr. 712, 716 (D. Conn. 1985), *rev'd on other grounds,* 795 F.2d 265 (2d Cir. 1986), the court held that a debtor's filing of a rejection petition only four days after it had presented its proposed contract modifications to the union was not "inherently unreasonable" absent any showing of bad faith by the debtor or prejudice to the union.

[200] 50 Bankr. at 976–77.

[201] *Id.*at 977–78. However, another court has cautioned that "[m]erely demonstrating a resultant savings to the debtor to justify a modification does not appear to meet the statutory standard [of "necessary" modifications] without the additional showing that but for the particular savings reorganization cannot be achieved." *In re* Fiber Glass Industries, Inc., 49 Bankr. 202, 206 (Bankr. N.D.N.Y. 1985).

[202] 50 Bankr. at 978.

[203] *Id.* at 979.

[204] *Id.* at 979–80.

[205] *Id.* at 980.

[206] *Id.*

itors were being asked to make substantial sacrifices, amounting to over $250 million.[207] Finally, the court found that the debtor's salaried employees were being paid below competitive rates, had their salaries frozen since 1981, and had suffered a salary reduction in 1982. Hence, the burden on the union employees was not disproportionate.[208]

The court revisited the issue of financial information in its discussion of the seventh element. The union contended that not enough information was given and that the motion to reject was filed too soon to permit adequate evaluation of the information provided. The court rejected both contentions. First, even prior to filing under Chapter 11 the debtor had provided detailed financial information to the union. This information could be considered in the context of section 1113(b)(1)(B).[209] Moreover, in January 1985 the debtor had submitted to an intensive five-week financial analysis by the same accounting organization that represented the union, which resulted in an "exhaustive" twenty-seven-page report.[210] Similarly, at the union's request Lazard-Freres conducted a three-week analysis of the debtor's pre-petition financial condition.[211] After the petition was filed, the debtor produced "reams" of additional financial information.[212] In short, the union had sufficient information with which to evaluate the debtor's proposal.

The court also rejected the union's argument that three weeks was an inadequate period to evaluate the information:

> Nothing in Section 1113 says that the Union must be given a certain period of time to evaluate the information given by the Company . . . [T]here simply is not the time during a Chapter 11 proceeding in general and a § 1113 scenario in particular, to do a completely exhaustive financial analysis.[213]

Under the circumstances, then, three weeks was adequate. The court followed the trend of the courts on the good cause component of the eighth element and concluded that because the debtor's pro-

---

[207] *Id.*

[208] *Id.* In light of section 1113(b)(1)(A), the existence of concessions by non-union employees logically should aid a debtor in obtaining court approval of rejection or modification of a union contract. In *In re* Fiber Glass Industries, Inc., 49 Bankr. 202, 207 (Bankr. N.D.N.Y. 1985), however, the court inexplicably disregarded such evidence with the statement that "these employees did not have the protection afforded by a collective bargaining agreement and the debtors were largely free to dictate new employment terms."

[209] 50 Bankr. at 981.

[210] *Id.*

[211] *Id.* at 981–82.

[212] *Id.* at 982.

[213] *Id.*

posal met the requirements of section 1113(b)(1), "the Union rejected the Company's proposal without good cause."[214]

Addressing the last element, the balancing of the equities, the court applied the *Bildisco* criteria and concluded that the alternative to rejection would be a liquidation disastrous to all parties.[215] Keeping the contractual labor rates in place until expiration of the contract, as urged by the union, would amount to "the liquidation of a debtor's assets for the benefit of one group of interested parties at the expense of the others."[216] Consequently, the equities clearly favored rejection.

Notwithstanding that "[t]he controlling facts . . . lead necessarily to the conclusion that the labor agreement must be rejected and renegotiated," the court encouraged the parties to "work out a solution at the bargaining table taking into consideration the hard realities that face them economically."[217] After the court granted Wheeling-Pittsburgh's motion to reject the contract and to implement its proposal, the company reduced hourly labor rates 18 percent, from \$21.40 to \$17.50.[218] Although this was less than the bankruptcy court authorized, on July 21, 1985 the union called a strike, resulting in 8,200 employees walking off their jobs.[219]

On August 28, 1985, the United States District Court for the Western District of Pennsylvania affirmed the decision of the bank-

---

[214] *Id.* at 983.

[215] *Id.* at 983–84.

[216] *Id.* at 984.

[217] *Id.*

[218] *See Wheeling-Pittsburgh Strike Is Possible As Steelmaker Moves To Cut Costs 18%,* Wall St. J., July 19, 1985, at p. 32.

[219] *See Wheeling-Pittsburgh Steelworkers Strike Over Proposed Wage Cuts,* Wall St. J., July 22, 1985, at p. 3. The strike continued until Dennis Carney, Wheeling-Pittsburgh's chairman, resigned in September 1985. *See Nisshin Steel Co.'s Chairman Resigns As a Director of Wheeling-Pittsburgh,* Wall St. J., Aug. 30, 1985, at p. 2; *Wheeling Steel Chairman, Five Directors Resign,* San Diego Union, Sept. 21, 1985, at E-2. Negotiations then progressed, with the company and the United Steelworkers of America reaching tentative agreement on October 15, 1985 on an hourly wage rate of \$18 and termination of the existing pension plan. *See Tentative Accord With Steelworkers Could End Three-Month Strike At Wheeling-Pittsburgh,* Daily Labor Report (BNA) No. 200, at A-15 (Oct. 16, 1985); *Wheeling Steel, Union Tentatively Agree On Accord Cutting Labor Costs by 16%,* Wall St. J., Oct. 16, 1985, at p. 3; *Wheeling Steel, in Final Proposal, Offers Employees a Labor Rate of \$18 an Hour,* Wall St. J., Oct. 16, 1985, at p. 17; *Resumption of Wheeling-Pittsburgh Operations Depends on Ratification Vote, Court Approval,* Daily Labor Report (BNA) No. 201, at A-11 (Oct. 17, 1985). Following ratification by union members on October 26, and approval by the bankruptcy court on October 25, the striking employees returned to work on October 28, ending the three-month walkout. *See Wheeling Steel's Creditor Banks Balk At \$18-an-Hour Tentative Labor Pact,* Wall St. J., Oct. 25, 1985, at p. 4; *Wheeling-Pittsburgh Employees Are Set To Return To Work Under New Contract,* Wall St. J., Oct. 28, 1985, at p. 2.

ruptcy court[220] pursuant to the "clearly erroneous" standard.[221] The thrust of the union's appeal was that the debtor's proposal was not "necessary" because the debtor could comply with the contractual labor rates and still have cash on hand at the contract's expiration.[222] Following the reasoning of the bankruptcy court, however, the district court ruled that

> [t]he question is *not* simply whether Wheeling-Pittsburgh can continue to pay the $21.40 rate required by the current *collective bargaining agreement* and still emerge with enough cash in hand at the contract term to meet current operational expenses. The relevant question is whether it is necessary for Wheeling-Pittsburgh to pay the $15.20 rate found in its *proposal* in order to successfully reorganize. The questions are not the same.[223]

The district court emphasized that "[t]he paramount goal of Chapter 11 is reorganization of the Company, not preservation of the collective bargaining agreement."[224] The district court agreed with the bankruptcy court's "conclusion that the 'necessary' standard of § 1113 does not mean 'absolutely essential' as the [union] contends here."[225]

The court also overruled the union's arguments that the proposal placed a disproportionate burden on the union employees[226] and that the debtor had not bargained in good faith, adopting the bankruptcy court's findings and reasoning on these issues. On the subject of good faith, the court held that "the debtor in possession [must] make reasonable efforts to negotiate a voluntary modification but a failure to achieve mutually satisfactory modifications indicates no more than the difficulty of the task."[227]

Finally, the court rejected the union's argument that section 1113 was intended to completely overrule *Bildisco* and in effect adopt the *REA Express* standard for rejection.[228] The court stated that

---

[220] *See In re* Wheeling-Pittsburgh Steel Corp., 52 Bankr. 997 (W.D. Pa. 1985).

[221] Bankruptcy Rule 8013 provides as follows:

> On an appeal the district court or bankruptcy appellate panel may affirm, modify, or reverse a bankruptcy court's judgment, order, or decree or remand with instructions for further proceedings. Findings of fact shall not be set aside unless clearly erroneous, and due regard shall be given to the opportunity of the bankruptcy court to judge the credibility of the witnesses.

[222] 52 Bankr. at 1000–01.

[223] *Id.* at 1001–02 (emphasis in original).

[224] *Id.* at 1002.

[225] *Id.* at 1003. *Accord, In re* Century Brass Products, Inc., 55 Bankr. 712 (D. Conn. 1985), *rev'd on other grounds,* 795 F.2d 265 (2d Cir. 1986).

[226] 52 Bankr. at 1004–05.

[227] *Id.* at 1005.

[228] *Id.* at 1004, 1006–07.

> we cannot accept interpretations of § 1113 which attribute to Congress an intent to temporarily shield employees from the consequence of the employer's financial plight with the attendant risk that such temporary protection will exacerbate the crisis and fuel the possibility of total fiscal disaster which would jeopardize future job availability for those employees.[229]

Despite the wage reduction agreed to by the union in October 1985 in settlement of the three-month strike, the United Steelworkers of America appealed the district court's decision to the U.S. Court of Appeals for the Third Circuit, "because of the precedent-setting effect" of the company's rejection of the prior contract.[230] The Third Circuit held that the case was not moot, notwithstanding the negotiation of a new contract, because in the settlement the union reserved the right to assert claims for lost pay of plant guards who worked during the strike.[231] If the union succeeded in establishing that the prior contract was rejected erroneously, the difference between the pay rate set forth in the rejected contract and the rate unilaterally set by the company for plant guards who worked during the strike was approximately $146,000.[232]

The Third Circuit, in a decision by Judge Dolores Sloviter, concluded on the merits that the company was procedurally entitled to seek rejection of its former contract with the union, even though it had sufficient cash on hand to perform the duration of the contract. In other words, the court rejected the union's argument that a debtor must make a *threshold* showing of necessity prior to seeking judicial authorization to implement its proposal under section 1113(c).[233]

However, the court was more receptive to the union's argument that the company's proposal did not meet the requirements of section 1113(b)(1)(A) in that it did not contain only "necessary" modifications that treated all affected parties "fairly and equitably." After reviewing the legislative history of section 1113, the court concluded that in section 1113 "the *REA Express* standard, or something close to it, had been reinstated."[234] Accordingly, the court held that

[229] *Id.* at 1007.

[230] *Wheeling Steel Loses Court Ruling on Labor Contract,* Wall St. J., May 30, 1986, at p. 43.

[231] Wheeling-Pittsburgh Steel Corp. v. United Steelworkers of America, 791 F.2d 1074, 1078 (3d Cir. 1986).

[232] *Id.* at 1079.

[233] *Id.* at 1085.

[234] *Id.* at 1088. The court held that the "essential to the continuation of the debtor's business" standard for interim relief under section 1113(e) is "synonymous" with

> [t]he "necessary" standard cannot be satisfied by a mere showing that it would be desirable for the trustee to reject a prevailing labor contract so that the debtor can lower its labor costs. . . . "[N]ecessity" [must] be construed strictly to signify only modifications that the trustee is constrained to accept because they are directly related to the Company's financial condition and its reorganization.[235]

The court further held that the appropriate focus is not on "the long-term economic health of the debtor," but on "the somewhat shorter term goal of preventing the debtor's liquidation."[236]

The Third Circuit concluded, in contrast, that the district court had erroneously applied a rejection standard closer to that set forth in *Bildisco,* which in addition incorrectly focused on the long-term economic health of the debtor.[237] Because of the district court's apparent failure to apply the correct statutory standard, and because it improperly reviewed the bankruptcy court's mixed findings of fact and law under a "clearly erroneous" standard, the court vacated the district court's ruling and remanded the case for reconsideration of whether the company's proposal met the "necessary" standard, in light of the absence of a "snap back" feature which would restore some of the wage reductions over the proposed five-year term of the contract if experience was more favorable than the anticipated "worst case" scenario.[238]

The Third Circuit also vacated for reconsideration the "snap back" issue under the "fair and equitable treatment" standard because the district court did not adequately justify the proposal's failure to include the possibility of an upward adjustment:

> Equity demands that concessions and benefits to the various interested parties be examined from a realistic standpoint and on the basis of record evidence. . . . In the circumstances of this case, the bankruptcy court's failure to recognize the need for some parity in this regard flaws the court's conclusion that the proposal was "fair and equitable." Therefore, we cannot affirm the district court's order approving the debtor's rejection of the collective bargaining agreement.[239]

---

the "necessary to permit the reorganization of the debtor" standard under section 1113(b)(1)(A). *Id.*

[235] *Id.*

[236] *Id.* at 1089. The court also noted that under section 1113(b)(1), a proposal must meet *both* of the "necessary" and "fair and equitable treatment" requirements. *Id.*

[237] *Id.* at 1090–91. The Third Circuit stated that "[t]he district court appeared to regard the congressional response to *Bildisco* as limited to prevention of the trustee's unilateral rejection of the contract before formal rejection by the bankruptcy court. . . . *Apparently, the court failed to appreciate Congress' substantial modification of the standard for rejection.*" *Id.* (emphasis added).

[238] *Id.*

[239] *Id.* at 1093.

Finally, the court ordered the district court to reconsider its conclusion that three weeks of negotiations were sufficient due to the company's need for haste.[240]

The most significant—and controversial—aspect of the Third Circuit's decision in *Wheeling-Pittsburgh* was its ruling that section 1113(b)(1)(A) codified the *REA Express* standard for rejection of collective bargaining agreements, and that the appropriate focus is on the likelihood of short-term liquidation, rather than the likelihood of the debtor's successful reorganization in the long run. This holding, which is diametrically at odds with the conclusion reached by most bankruptcy courts and commentators, means that Congress overruled *both* aspects of the *Bildisco* decision, and not just the unilateral rejection holding.

In fact, the Third Circuit's ruling goes farther than *REA Express,* because it requires that the debtor demonstrate that its proposed concessions are the only alternative to imminent liquidation *and* that the proposed concessions do not disproportionately burden union employees. The court's reasoning on this point seems to support a conclusion that a proposal, although necessary to prevent the debtor's liquidation in the short term, would not satisfy the requirements of section 1113(b)(1)(A) if it favored non-union employees or creditors.[241]

The court stated that the "requirement that the proposal provide only for 'necessary' modifications in the labor contract is conjunctive with the requirement that the proposal treat 'all of the affected parties . . . fairly and equitably.' "[242] The court reasoned that

> [t]he language as well as the legislative history makes plain that a bankruptcy court may not authorize rejection of a labor contract merely because it deems such a course to be equitable to the other affected parties, particularly creditors.[243]

The opposite would presumably be true also, that rejection may not be authorized if only the "necessary" requirement had been satisfied.

Ironically, the U.S. Court of Appeals for the Second Circuit has indicated that it believes the Third Circuit went too far in *Wheeling-*

---

[240] *Id.* The court also held that the district court's ruling that the company provided the union with the information necessary to evaluate its proposal was not clearly erroneous. *Id.* at 1094.

[241] *Id.* at 1089. *See, e.g., In re* William P. Brogna & Co., Inc., 64 Bankr. 390, 392–93 (Bankr. E.D. Pa. 1986).

[242] 791 F.2d at 1089.

[243] *Id.* Neither District Judge Mencer nor Bankruptcy Judge Bentz even had an opportunity to consider the case can remand because the parties stipulated to a resolution of the plant guard claim.

Pittsburgh.[244] In *Bildisco,* it may be recalled, the Third Circuit refused to follow the Second Circuit's decision in *REA Express,* leading to the Supreme Court's resolution of the conflict. In *Century Brass Products* the Second Circuit refused to follow the Third Circuit's decision in *Wheeling-Pittsburgh.* If the conflict is not resolved, the Supreme Court may once again be forced to intervene.

In *In re Century Brass Products, Inc.,*[245] the United States District Court for the District of Connecticut had affirmed an unreported decision of the bankruptcy court authorizing the debtor's rejection of a collective bargaining agreement. The union argued that the debtor's proposal was improper because it called for a reduction in the benefits paid to current retirees. Thus, the union argued that it was entitled to reject the debtor's proposed modifications because (1) under sections 1113(b)(1)(A) and 1113(c)(2), the union is not the "authorized representative" of retired employees, and (2) under section 1113(b)(1)(A), the proposal did not provide for "necessary modifications in the employees' benefits and protections."[246] The union relied primarily on *Allied Chemical & Alkali Workers v. Pittsburgh Plate Glass Co.,*[247] which held that current retirees' benefits were not a mandatory subject of bargaining because they did not "vitally affect" the terms and conditions of active employees. The court rejected this argument, reasoning that

> in this case, unlike *Pittsburgh Plate Glass,* the level of benefits provided to retirees "vitally affects" the level of wages and benefits available to current employees and, indeed, the ability of Century Brass to remain in business. . . . [*Pittsburgh Plate Glass*] merely states that neither an employer nor a union is required to bargain about such matters unless they "vitally affect" the interests of active employees. The Congress that enacted Section 1113 most likely assumed, consistently with *Pittsburgh Plate Glass,* that the rights of retired workers "vitally affect" the rights of current workers whenever their common employer files for protection under Chapter 11.
>
> Accordingly, the court finds that the [union] lacked "good cause" under Section 1113(c)(2) for its failure to negotiate with Century Brass concerning modification of their collective bargaining agreement."[248]

The Second Circuit reversed, not because the union per se lacked authority to represent retired workers, but because it found that a

[244] *In re* Century Brass Products, Inc., 795 F.2d 265 (2d Cir. 1986), *rev'g* 55 Bankr. 712 (D. Conn. 1985).
[245] 55 Bankr. 712 (D. Conn. 1985), *rev'd,* 795 F.2d 265 (2d Cir. 1986), *cert. denied,* 107 S. Ct. __, 55 U.S.L.W. 3335 (1986).
[246] *Id.* at 714.
[247] 404 U.S. 157, 179 (1971).
[248] 55 Bankr. at 714–15 (footnote omitted).

conflict of interest existed between the active and retired employees, and the retired employees were not separately represented in the negotiations.[249] Accordingly, the court concluded that the debtor failed to negotiate with an authorized representative of the retired employees and therefore "failed to comply with the procedural requirements of § 1113."[250]

More significantly, the court interpreted the language and legislative history of section 1113 to mean that Congress overruled only the unilateral rejection holding of *Bildisco;* section 1113 preserved the "balance-of-equities" standard for rejection set forth in *Bildisco.* Thus, the Second Circuit decision written by Judge Cardamone is directly at odds with *Wheeling-Pittsburgh.* The extent of the courts' disagreement is reflected in the reasoning of *Century Brass Products.*

The court's analysis of the legislative history focused on unions' dissatisfaction with the controversial unilateral rejection holding of *Bildisco,* which divided the Supreme Court by a 5-4 vote:

> This second part of *Bildisco,* which held that a debtor could rescind the labor contract immediately upon filing under Chapter 11, fueled the already noted lobbying effort by organized labor to have Congress amend the law. . . .
>
> *Section 1113 reversed the second part of Bildisco.* It created an expedited form of collective bargaining with several safeguards designed to insure that employers did not use Chapter 11 as a medicine to rid themselves of corporate indigestion. . . . Only if the expedited bargaining fails does § 1113 permit a debtor to apply for rejection of the labor agreement. *At that point, a modified version of the unanimously decided first part of Bildisco applies.*[251]

Unlike the Third Circuit, the court in *Century Brass Products* did not place a great deal of importance on the word "necessary" in section 1113(b)(1)(A):

> The use of the word "necessary" twice in § 1113(b)(1)(A) emphasizes the requirement of *the debtor's good faith in seeking to modify its existing labor contract.* 130 Cong. Rec. S 8898 (statement of Senator Packwood). The court must also assure itself that "all creditors, the debtor and all affected parties are treated fairly and equitably." The

---

[249] *In re* Century Brass Products, Inc., 795 F.2d 265, 275–76 (2d Cir. 1986), *cert. denied,* 107 S. Ct. __, 55 U.S.L.W. 33335 (1986). The Second Circuit stated that retired employees are "generally capable of being represented by the union as their 'authorized representative,'" but that it "may not always be appropriate for a union to represent both active and retired workers in modification negotiations." *Id.* at 275. Because the interests of the debtor's active and retired workers were divergent, the court concluded as a matter of law that a conflict existed. *Id.* at 275–76.

[250] *Id.* at 276.

[251] *Id.* at 272 (emphasis added).

> purpose is to spread the burdens of saving the company to every constituency while ensuring that all sacrifice to a similar degree.[252]

The Second Circuit emphatically embraced an interpretation of section 1113 that rejected the *REA Express* standard for rejection: "the 'balance of equities' [in section 1113(c)] codifies the unanimous holding set forth in the first part of *Bildisco.*"[253] The court indicated that "[o]ur construction of the statute follows from its plain language and the comments of its sponsors in Congress. *Moreover, a number of courts have generally adopted the same approach in interpreting the statute in cases arising under it.*"[254] As if to highlight its divergent analysis of section 1113, the court in *Century Brass Products* stated that:

> [o]ur sister circuit in *Wheeling-Pittsburgh Steel Corp. v. United Steel Workers of America,* 791 F.2d 1074 (3d Cir. 1986) apparently thought that Congress swung the pendulum back in favor of labor as a reaction to *Bildisco.* The predicate of this opinion is rather that the Senate and House Conferees made the point clear that the road to resolution of the conflict between labor and bankruptcy lies in honest compromise.[255]

The Second Circuit's analysis of section 1113, particularly its interpretation of the "necessary" standard in section 1113(b)(1)(A), is more faithful to the text and legislative history of the statute. Doubtless other courts of appeals will add to, rather than diminish, the conflict.[256] The supreme irony would be a split of authority in

---

[252] *Id.* at 273.

[253] *Id.*

[254] *Id.* at 273–74 (emphasis added) (*citing In re* Kentucky Truck Sales, Inc., 52 Bankr. 797 (Bankr. W.D. Ky. 1985); *In re* K & B Mounting, Inc., 50 Bankr. 460 (Bankr. N.D. Ind. 1985); *In re* Salt Creek Freightways, 47 Bankr. 835 (Bankr. D. Wyo. 1985)).

[255] *Id.* at 276. A bankruptcy court within the jurisdiction of the Second Circuit, writing after *Wheeling-Pittsburgh* but prior to *Century Brass Products,* showed little respect for the Third Circuit's analysis. Granting a debtor's motion to reject, the court in *In re* Royal Composing Room, Inc., 62 Bankr. 403, 417 (Bankr. S.D.N.Y. 1986) sharply disagreed that the terms "essential" and "necessary" are synonymous:

> [T]he final modifications, dealing as they must with the uncertainties created by a longer period of time and the larger picture of a debtor's reorganization and economic future . . ., neither can nor should be so finely tuned to bare survival. . . . A debtor can live on water alone for a short time but over the long haul it needs food to sustain itself an retain its vigor. *Id.* at 418.

[256] The Tenth Circuit has stated in dictum that while under section 1113 "new procedural requirements have been imposed, the approach to the required balancing of the equities should not be different from the instruction provided in *Bildisco.*" International Brotherhood of Teamsters v. IML Freight, Inc., 789 F.2d 1460, 1461 (10th Cir. 1986). The Seventh Circuit has also intimated its belief that section 1113 overruled only the unilateral rejection holding of Bildisco. *See* NLRB v. Manley Truck Line, Inc., 779 F.2d 1327, 1331 n.7 (7th Cir. 1985). The United States Bankruptcy Appellate Panel of the Ninth Circuit has stated that "[t]he enactment of §

the circuits requiring resolution by the Supreme Court: *Bildisco* and the subsequent legislation would have come full circle.

THE RELATIONSHIP BETWEEN SECTION 1113 AND THE NLRA BARGAINING DUTY

Determining section 1113's meaning will keep courts busy for a considerable time. But regardless of what the section means, there is still the troublesome issue of how it relates to the parallel bargaining provisions of the NLRA.

To begin with, one must consider the new prohibition against unilateral termination or alteration of the collective bargaining agreement. The bankruptcy law power of a debtor-in-possession to suspend performance under an executory contract pending court approval of its rejection was the predicate of the Supreme Court's conclusion in *Bildisco* that a collective bargaining agreement was no longer an "enforceable contract," and therefore NLRA section 8(d) was inapplicable. But does section 1113's prohibition of unilateral suspension make the collective bargaining agreement an "enforceable contract" once again, thus activating NLRA section 8(a)(5) and 8(d) prohibitions?

Although there may be some logic to the argument that it does,[257] that interpretation should be rejected. The new provision does not expressly overrule the judicial gloss that *Bildisco* put on section 8(d) of the NLRA. Congress disagreed with the Court over an interpretation of the Bankruptcy Code not the NLRA, and amended the code rather than the NLRA. The Court thought that the exigencies of a Chapter 11 reorganization required that the debtor-in-possession have power to unilaterally terminate or alter the collective bargaining agreement pending court approval of rejection. Congress thought otherwise, but provided procedures to expedite rejection. Both the Court and Congress thought, however, that bankruptcy law and not labor law controls the debtor-employer's power to terminate or alter the terms of a collective bargaining agreement. The bankruptcy court has adequate power to deal with a debtor-in-possession who fails to adhere to provisions of section 1113; simultaneously to subject that debtor to NLRA unfair labor practice procedures would be both pointless and counterproductive. In this

---

1113 . . . substantially adopted the rejection standard set forth by the Supreme Court in *Bildisco.*" *See In re* S.A. Mechanical, Inc., Case No. AZ-85-1227 (9th Cir. Bankr. App., May 15, 1986).

[257] *See* Note, NLRB v. Bildisco & Bildisco: *Rejection of Collective Bargaining Agreements by Chapter 11 Debtors Receives High Court Approval,* 1984 N. Ill. U.L. Rev. 295, 326–27.

regard, section 1113 should be deemed totally preemptive of the NLRA.

Under *Bildisco,* as a condition of obtaining bankruptcy court approval of rejection, the employer was required at least to attempt to negotiate a change in the collective bargaining agreement. The Court also held that the NLRA duty to bargain applied to these negotiations. The new section 1113 now expressly imposes a bargaining duty on a debtor-in-possession who seeks to reject its collective bargaining agreement. Although the statute is loaded with various NLRA-sounding terms—like "good faith," a phase that does not appear in the *Bildisco* decision—legislative history, such as it is, suggests that the intent was merely to codify the limited *Bildisco* requirement,[258] not to require bankruptcy courts to enforce NLRA collective bargaining duties.[259] But if section 1113 duties are somehow less demanding (and even if they are not), the question remains whether the debtor-in-possession is also subject to provisions of the NLRA, as construed and enforced by the NLRB, during the pre-rejection negotiation period. Although the Supreme Court may have been reluctant to read a duty to bargain into the Bankruptcy Code and then to say that this implied duty nevertheless preempted the analogous but specific provisions of the NLRA, for Congress itself to impose a limited bargaining duty as part of the Bankruptcy Code with the intention of thereby superseding more general bargaining provisions of the NLRA is an entirely different matter. Indeed, it would be senseless and futile for a bankruptcy court to determine that a debtor-in-possession's bargaining was adequate for contract rejection purposes only to have the NLRB hold later that the bargaining was not in "good faith" under NLRA precedent.[260]

---

[258] Senator Hatch noted that

> [t]he first step of this process [leading to rejection of the contract] will of course involve good faith negotiations between the parties. This was a requirement articulated by the Supreme Court in the Bildisco case. The conference, once again, preserved the spirit of that Court holding by requiring good faith efforts to confer. . . .

130 CONG. REC. S8892 (daily ed. June 29, 1984) (statement of Sen. Hatch).

[259] In reference to the bargaining standard to be applied in evaluating the union's rejection of proposed modifications, Senator Thurmond stated that the statute "is obviously not intended to import traditional labor law concepts into a bankruptcy forum or turn the bankruptcy courts into a version of the National Labor Relations Board." 130 CONG. REC. S8888 (daily ed. June 29, 1984) (statement of Sen. Thurmond).

[260] "Application of the requirements of both section 1113 of the Bankruptcy Code and section 8 of the NLRA would be ludicrous. The result of the concurrent jurisdiction of the bankruptcy court and the NLRB could only be chaotic, and would

Just as the section 8(d) (unilateral changes) and section 8(a)(5) (state-of-mind) aspects of NLRA bargaining law should be deemed preempted by narrower provisions of the Bankruptcy Code, so too should the NLRA duty to supply information. Originating simply as a duty to substantiate claims regarding an employer's alleged inability to pay a demanded increase,[261] the NLRA duty to supply the union with relevant bargaining information has burgeoned into a significant and complex area of labor law.[262] Whether the Bankruptcy Code section 1113(b)(1)(B) duty to supply the union "with such relevant information as is necessary to evaluate the [debtor-in-possession's] proposal"[263] regarding contract modification is broader, narrower, or essentially the same as the NLRA duty is not clear. In any event, whatever the Bankruptcy Code requires should be regarded as exclusive. By the time the NLRB could process and obtain judicial enforcement of a duty-to-supply information order, a bankruptcy court would have long since acted on the petition to modify or reject the contract. In addition, the debtor-in-possession, in the interest of preserving assets of the estate, should be protected from having to litigate the NLRA issue.

In sum, pending bankruptcy court action on a petition to reject a collective bargaining agreement, irrespective of bargaining duties an employer would otherwise have under sections 8(a)(5) and 8(d) of the NLRA, the employers' NLRA bargaining duties should be suspended in favor of the more specific provisions of the Bankruptcy Code.

POSTREJECTION BARGAINING ISSUES

Bildisco held that even after an existing contract has been rejected, a debtor-in-possession is still subject to the NLRA section 8(a)(5) duty to bargain over the terms of a new collective bargaining agreement.[264] Section 1113 does not deal specifically with this matter, and one may assume that Congress also intended continued applicability of the NLRA duty to bargain. This assumption, however, causes some complications.

---

certainly imperil, if not prevent, effective reorganization." Comment, Bildisco: *Are Some Creditors More Equal Than Others?,* 35 S.C.L. Rev. 573, 611 (1984).

[261] NLRB v. Truitt Mfg. Co., 351 U.S. 149 (1956).

[262] *See generally* J. O'Reilly, Unions' Rights To Company Information Rev. Ed. (Labor Relations and Public Policy Series No. 21 1987).

[263] 11 U.S.C. § 1113(b)(1)(B) (Supp. II 1984).

[264] NLRB v. Bildisco & Bildisco, 465 U.S. 513, 534 (1984). This was consistent with prior court and board authority. *See* Brotherhood of Ry. Clerks v. REA Express, Inc., 523 F.2d 164, 169 (2d Cir.), *cert. denied,* 423 U.S. 1017 (1975); Oxford Structures, Ltd., 245 N.L.R.B. 1180, 1183 (1979).

If the bankruptcy court has approved only a modification or partial rejection, then the unrejected portion of the contract remains in effect. Thus, in the period following bankruptcy court action, the debtor-in-possession's unilateral abrogation of the terms of the remaining contract would be an unfair labor practice under NLRA section 8(d).[265] Complications may arise, however, with respect to provisions that have been removed from the contract by a court-approved modification.

Subject to the limitations discussed in the next chapter, the NLRA bargaining duties generally apply during the postrejection period. Section 8(d), however, provides that these duties "shall not be construed as requiring either party to discuss or agree to any modification of the terms and conditions contained in a contract for a fixed period."[266] The "contained in" requirement is generally met if a topic has been "'fully discussed' or 'consciously explored,'" and it can be fairly concluded that the matter was put to rest for the term of the contract; the omission of that topic from the contract is considered part of the contemporaneous bargain.[267] There is no reason why bargaining that precedes court approval or rejection of a particular contract term, pursuant to provisions of section 1113, should be treated any differently. The result is that there will be no contract limitations or provisions with respect to that topic.

This result means that the debtor-in-possession would have no duty to bargain further. But it also means that any attempt to force the debtor to bargain over this topic by means of a strike would itself be an unfair labor practice under NLRA section 8(d), and strike participants would lose their status as employees because such conduct would be a breach of the section 8(d) duty to continue "in full force and effect, without resorting to strike or lock-out, all the terms and conditions of the existing contract"[268]—including the implied term about omission.[269] In this instance, provisions of section

---

[265] For a discussion of the conflict that would exist if an alleged contract "breach" also involved a court approved change in the debtor's business operations, see chapter V, *infra.*

[266] 29 U.S.C. § 158(d) (1982).

[267] *See, e.g.,* Jacobs Mfg. Co., 94 N.L.R.B. 1214, 1228 (1951), *enforced,* 196 F.2d 680 (2d Cir. 1952); Proctor Mfg. Corp., 131 N.L.R.B. 1166, 1169 (1961). *See generally* F. Bartosic & R. Hartley, Labor Relations Law In The Private Sector 176–77 (1977); 1 A.B.A. Section of Labor and Employment Law, The Developing Labor Law 672–74 (C. Morris 2d ed. 1983) [hereinafter The Developing Labor Law].

[268] 29 U.S.C. § 158(d)(4); *see* Local No. 3, United Packing House Workers v. NLRB, 210 F.2d 325 (8th Cir.), *cert. denied,* 348 U.S. 822 (1954) (loss of employee status); Carpenters' Dist. Council. 172 N.L.R.B. 793 (1968) (strike as an unfair labor practice).

[269] If the unrejected portion of the contract contains a broad no-strike clause (*e.g.,* one that is not limited by the scope of the arbitration clause), then a strike in this

8(d) actually complement and reinforce the binding effect that a section 1113 modification is intended to have.

If the old contract is rejected in its entirety, the debtor-in-possession will presumably have an NLRA section 8(a)(5) duty to bargain with the union over the terms of a new agreement. Although as a practical matter the debtor-in-possession would simply continue the bargaining that occurred prior to rejection, this bargaining would now be governed by NLRA standards. If negotiations are successful, the debtor-in-possession will then have the duty under NLRA section 8(d) to execute "a written contract incorporating any agreement reached during the bargaining process." At this point, however, there is a potential conflict with the requirements of the Bankruptcy Code.

In *Local Joint Executive Board v. Hotel Circle, Inc.,*[270] which was decided under the Bankruptcy Act of 1898, the Ninth Circuit held that a trustee lacked authority either to affirm a collective bargaining agreement without court approval, now an express requirement,[271] or to enter into a new agreement without court approval. Although the court conceded that a trustee has authority to enter into contracts "incidental and usual" to operations of the business, it thought that this authority referred only to contracts for supplies and services needed by the trustee in daily business operations.[272] Major long-term contracts extending beyond the receivership, such as collective bargaining agreements, required bankruptcy court approval.[273] However, a contrary result was reached in *In re DeLuca Distributing Co.,*[274] which was decided under the current Bankruptcy Code. The court noted that while the former act, under which *Hotel Circle* was decided, required a high degree of judicial supervision over the debtor's estate, one of the code's purposes was to relieve bankruptcy judges from the business details involved in case administration.[275] Thus, section 363(c)(1) authorized the trustee to "enter into transactions ... in the ordinary course of business, without notice or a hearing. ..."[276] The court further defined "ordinariness" in terms of "the interested parties' reasonable expectations of what transactions the debtor in possession is likely to

---

situation would also be a breach of contract and actionable on that basis as well. *Accord* Pacemaker Yacht Co. v. NLRB, 663 F.2d 455 (3d Cir. 1981).

[270] 613 F.2d 210 (9th Cir. 1980).

[271] 29 U.S.C. § 158(d) (1982).

[272] *Hotel Circle,* 613 F.2d at 217–18.

[273] *Accord* Chicago Deposit Vault Co. v. McNulta, 153 U.S. 554, 561 (1894).

[274] 38 Bankr. 588 (Bankr. N.D. Ohio 1984).

[275] *Id.* at 592–93.

[276] 11 U.S.C. § 363(c)(1) (1982). *See also* International Assoc. of Machinists v. Dalford Corp., 117 L.R.R.M. 2257, 2263 (N.D. Tex. 1984).

enter in the course of its business."[277] The debtor-employer in this case was a member of a multi-employer bargaining unit. After the bankruptcy petition was filed the employer bargaining association renegotiated the group's contract with the union. The debtor-employer was clearly bound by the new contract as a matter of federal labor law, but maintained that since the bankruptcy court had not approved the new agreement, it could not be enforced against him. The court, however, concluded that the creditors had a reasonable expectation that this debtor would continue to be subject to collective bargaining agreements and found, therefore, "that where the debtor's employees have continually been covered by a collective bargaining agreement, a new collective bargaining agreement is a transaction in the ordinary course of business. . . ."[278]

Although it seems a bit anomalous to hold that assuming an existing collective bargaining agreement requires court approval but negotiating a new one does not, the *DeLuca* result may be proper under the facts of that case: the collective bargaining agreements were apparently not a point of controversy in the bankruptcy; the employer had acquiesced in the new contract without objection; it had enjoyed the benefits of labor peace under the agreements during its peak business period; and the court obviously thought that the employer's after-the-fact attempt to escape the agreement bordered on fraud.

The *DeLuca* case, however, should not be read as holding that the negotiation of a new collective bargaining agreement by a debtor-in-possession is *always* a transaction "in the ordinary course of business," which *never* requires prior court approval. To the contrary, when the debtor under section 1113 rejects a contract that had burdened the estate, and then negotiates a new contract, the new agreement can hardly be considered "in the ordinary course of business." If the debtor-in-possession actually signs the new agreement and none of the creditors later object,[279] then he should probably be bound. On the other hand, the debtor or any objecting

[277] *DeLuca,* 38 Bankr. at 593 (quoting *In re* James A. Phillips, Inc., 29 Bankr. 391, 394 (S.D.N.Y. 1983)).

[278] *DeLuca,* 38 Bankr. at 594; *accord* Sealift Maritime, Inc., 265 N.L.R.B. 1219 (1982). In *Sealift,* the debtor-in-possession first assumed the collective bargaining agreement with bankruptcy court approval, but later agreed to a modification. The NLRB found that this modification was "in the ordinary course of business" under the Bankruptcy Code, that court approval was not required, and that the modified contract was thus valid for the purposes of the "contract bar doctrine." *Id.* at 1220; *see also In re* IML Freight, Inc., 37 Bankr. 556, 559 (Bankr. D. Utah 1984) ("[t]he delicate mechanism of negotiations leading to post-petition contracts should not be influenced by the expectation of court approval or disapproval").

[279] In *Dalford, supra* note 276, at 2263, the contracting union unsuccessfully at-

creditor should have the right to request court review of the new contract, and if approval is not given, then the debtor's NLRA section 8(d) duty to sign the agreement and abide by its terms should be abrogated in favor of the exigencies of bankruptcy.

---

tempted to void the contract on the grounds that the employer entered into it without bankruptcy court approval.

PART THREE

CHAPTER V

Mandatory Bargaining Over Changes in the Operation of the Debtor-Employer's Business[1]

Bankruptcy and labor law bargaining duty conflicts can occur even if the Chapter 11 debtor-in-possession does not formally attempt to modify or reject its collective bargaining agreement. For example, as a part of its reorganization plan, a Chapter 11 employer may find it necessary to close, relocate, or substantially alter the nature of its business operation. Decisions of this kind may implicate three different kinds of NLRA bargaining duties.[2]

THE SECTION 8(d) DUTY TO HONOR THE TERMS OF AN EXISTING AGREEMENT

In *Milwaukee Spring I,*[3] the NLRB held that relocation of unit work from a union to a nonunion facility during the term of a collective bargaining agreement constituted a midterm repudiation of the agreement in violation of section 8(d). Later in *Milwaukee Spring II,*[4] the board reversed itself, holding that the section 8(d) prohibition against midterm modification or repudiation applied only to terms "contained in" the agreement. Since the board could find no express or implied agreement to preserve work at the Milwaukee plant for the duration of the contract, the relocation did

[1] Portions of this chapter originally appeared in Haggard, *The Continuing Conflict Between Bankruptcy and Labor Law—The Issues that* Bildisco *and the 1984 Bankruptcy Amendments Did Not Resolve,* 1986 BRIGHAM YOUNG L. REV. 1.

[2] *See generally* P. MISCIMARRA, THE NLRB AND MANAGERIAL DISCRETION: PLANT CLOSINGS, RELOCATIONS, SUBCONTRACTING AND AUTOMATION (1983).

[3] 265 N.L.R.B. 206 (1982), *rev'd,* 268 N.L.R.B. 601 (1984); *see also* Los Angeles Marine Hardware Co., 235 N.L.R.B. 720 (1978), *enforced,* 602 F.2d 1302 (9th Cir. 1979); The Boeing Co., 230 N.L.R.B. 696 (1977), *enforcement denied,* 581 F.2d 793 (9th Cir. 1978); University of Chicago, 210 N.L.R.B. 190 (1974), *enforcement denied,* 514 F.2d 942 (7th Cir. 1975).

[4] 268 N.L.R.B. 601 (1984), *enforced sub nom.* Local 547, UAW v. NLRB, 765 F.2d 175 (D.C. Cir. 1985).

not breach the contract and thus did not violate section 8(d). *Milwaukee Spring II* was affirmed on appeal, albeit on a slightly different theory—namely, the decision to relocate was either an inherent "reserved right" or was authorized by the management rights clause. Either construction obviated any possible section 8(d) violation.

Although the law in this area is still somewhat obscure, it would appear that in certain narrow circumstances a decision to relocate or close a facility might still be covered by section 8(d); the employer would then be required to obtain union approval before implementing the decision. The conflict arises when relocation or closing has also been made part of a Chapter 11 reorganization plan approved by the bankruptcy court.

This conflict, however, is fairly easy to resolve. If a decision to relocate or close a facility is of a kind that would violate section 8(d), then *a fortiori* it is also a partial modification if not total repudiation of the collective bargaining agreement. If the closure or relocation is so construed, it necessarily follows that section 1113 of the Bankruptcy Code applies. But since an employer's *right* to modify or repudiate a contract under section 1113 supersedes its *duty* to adhere to terms of that contract under section 8(d) of the NLRA, the employer must only satisfy the section 1113 requirements. Thus, although an employer should be required to engage in some degree of "bargaining" with the union about a decision to relocate or close, it is not required to obtain the union's approval as would be the case under the NLRA.

In sum, bankruptcy law should take labor law interests into account in the following fashion. If, but only if, the decision to close or relocate a facility would otherwise qualify as a section 8(d) violation, the court should treat it as a partial modification or repudiation of the contract requiring exhaustion of all section 1113 procedures. But, as with literal contract modification or rejection, duties imposed by the Bankruptcy Code completely supersede those imposed by section 8(d).[5]

[5] Bankruptcy court approval of the change should also be dispositive of any alleged antiunion discrimination under section 8(a)(3). 29 U.S.C. § 158(a)(3) (1982). Regardless of the debtor's subjective motivation, if the change is found to be justified by the exigencies of bankruptcy, then that should be controlling. From the bankruptcy perspective, it is irrelevant whether the NLRB interference flows from section 8(a)(3), rather than sections 8(a)(5) and 8(d). Other aspects of section 8(a)(3), such as the prohibition against discrimination toward specific individuals, would of course remain in effect.

THE SECTION 8(a)(5) DUTY TO BARGAIN TO IMPASSE BEFORE MAKING UNILATERAL CHANGES

The second NLRA bargaining duty that may be implicated by a Chapter 11 reorganization is an employer's section 8(a)(5) duty to bargain to impasse before making any changes with respect to a matter statutorily defined as a mandatory subject of bargaining.[6] This duty goes beyond the section 8(d) duty to honor terms of an existing agreement, and thus applies even when the contract is silent. As was seen earlier, except in the contract rejection context, Congress apparently intended that normal section 8(a)(5) bargaining duties would continue to apply to a debtor-in-possession. The duty to bargain before making changes in wages, hours, and working conditions is an integral part of section 8(a)(5). It would thus seem that unilateral change by a debtor-in-possession or trustee should be considered an unfair labor practice.[7] In most instances, imposition of such a duty would implicate no bankruptcy law interests. But if the change also requires bankruptcy court approval, then the question becomes whether the debtor's duty to obtain approval supersedes its duty under the NLRA to also bargain first with the union.

The problem is probably not significant since the issue would arise only when the change in question is one that would otherwise be subject *both* to bankruptcy court approval *and* NLRA bargaining requirements. Bankruptcy court approval, however, would normally be required only for major operational changes—plant closures, relocations, sales, large-scale subcontracting, and other matters necessarily included in a reorganization plan. The NLRA duty to bargain over matters of this genre is somewhat limited. The Supreme

---

[6] NLRB v. Katz, 369 U.S. 736 (1962). *See generally* 1 A.B.A. SECTION OF LABOR AND EMPLOYMENT LAW, THE DEVELOPING LABOR LAW, 563–66 (C. Morris 2d ed. 1983) [hereinafter THE DEVELOPING LABOR LAW]; Turner, *Impasse in the "Real World" of Labor Relations: Where Does the Board Stand?*, 10 EMPLOYEE REL. L.J. 468 (1985).

[7] *Bildisco*'s implications for this issue are unclear. The Supreme Court suggested in a footnote that changes in working conditions and other mandatory subjects of bargaining that would necessarily accompany contract rejection could not be considered § 8(a)(5) violations of the "unilateral change" variety. It is not an 8(a)(5) violation because that interpretation would simply be another way of achieving what the Court said § 8(d) itself did not achieve, namely interim enforcement of the contract pending court approval of its rejection. NLRB v. Bildisco & Bildisco, 465 U.S. 513, 533 n.14 (1984); *see also* Durand v. NLRB, 296 F. Supp. 1049, 1056 (W.D.Ark. 1969). But the opinion leaves open the question of whether a unilateral change that did not also involve a potential section 8(d) violation could still be considered an unfair labor practice under section 8(a)(5).

Court in *First National Maintenance Corp. v. NLRB*[8] held that a decision to close part of a business for economic reasons unrelated to wages did not involve a mandatory subject of bargaining. Although the Court limited the decision to the facts before it and expressly declined to rule on "other types of management decisions, such as plant relocations, sales, other kinds of subcontracting, automation, etc. . . .",[9] subsequent decisions have used the underlying philosophy of *First National Maintenance* as justification for limiting the duty to bargain over those kinds of business decisions as well.[10]

Nevertheless, cases will doubtless still arise in which the debtor-in-possession's court-approved reorganization plan includes some kind of operational change that is arguably also a mandatory subject of bargaining. The question is whether the two laws can both apply in this context. At first blush, it would seem that the debtor-in-possession should be able to discharge its NLRA duty without much difficulty or interference with the bankruptcy process. The NLRA requires only notice and good faith bargaining, possibly to impasse; it does not require that the employer necessarily obtain union agreement to the change.[11]

On the other hand, while *discharge* of the NLRA bargaining duty over operational changes would not seem to impose any significant impediments to the bankruptcy process, *administrative enforcement* of that duty would. Whether the change involved a mandatory subject of bargaining, whether the debtor-in-possession evidenced the required amount of "good faith,"[12] and whether impasse was reached before the change was made,[13] are all complicated issues. Participation in unfair labor practice proceedings would be burdensome to the debtor-in-possession, to the estate, and to all other creditors.[14] If the charge is found to have been without merit, then

---

[8] 452 U.S. 666 (1981).

[9] *Id.* at 686 n.22.

[10] *See e.g.,* Gar Wood-Detroit Truck Equipment, Inc., 274 N.L.R.B. No. 23 (1985) (subcontracting); Bostrom Div., UOP, Inc. 272 N.L.R.B. 999 (1984) (closure, consolidation of operations, and subcontracting); Fraser Shipyards, Inc., 272 N.L.R.B. 496 (1984) (closure and subcontracting); Otis Elevator Co. (II), 269 N.L.R.B. 891 (1984) (relocations and sales).

[11] Bi-Rite Foods, Inc., 147 N.L.R.B. 59, 64–65 (1964).

[12] *See generally* 1 The Developing Labor Law, *supra* note 6, at 570–606.

[13] *Id.* at 634–36.

[14] Judicial notice may be taken of the fact that proceedings before the Board and review or enforcement proceedings in the courts are protracted and expensive, and to the extent that expenses of litigation are paid out of the bankruptcy estate, the burden will fall ultimately on the former employees of the bankrupt or on the secured claimants. Durand v. NLRB, 296 F. Supp. 1049, 1054 (W.D.Ark. 1969). *See generally* E. Miller, An Administrative Appraisal of the NLRB (rev. ed. 1980).

the estate will have been unnecessarily burdened. Even if the charge is ultimately upheld, by then there will be no remedy that the NLRB can impose that will not be blatantly inconsistent with bankruptcy court approval of change.

For example, in the nonbankruptcy context, the board has sometimes ordered an employer to first restore the *status quo ante* and then bargain about the desired change.[15] The NLRB, however, should not be allowed to unravel a Chapter 11 court-approved reorganization plan in that fashion. Alternatively, the board has sometimes held that the employer is liable for backpay to terminated employees because of the change, with liability running from the date of termination until the earliest of four conditions: (1) the parties reach an "agreement" about the change that the employer has already made; (2) they bargain about it to impasse; (3) the union fails to promptly request or commence bargaining; or (4) the union bargains in bad faith.[16] But backpay liability here is simply the "wages equivalent" or "counterpart" of actually reopening the facility. After the bankruptcy court has authorized a closure, the debtor-in-possession should have *no* further liability for its operation—either literally, by being required to reopen the facility, or figuratively, by being required to pay employees the wages they would have received "but for" closure. Either remedy is equally inconsistent with bankruptcy court authorization of facility closure. The threat of either remedy being imposed could significantly retard the development of a workable reorganization plan.

The presence of such a threat suggests that the NLRA duty to bargain over major operational changes, to the extent that it exists at all, should be abrogated when the employer is in Chapter 11 reorganization. Legitimate interests of the employees and union could be better served through bankruptcy law itself. The union may already be involved in making decisions about the change, either as a member of the creditors' committee[17] or, more properly, as a "party in interest" with a right to be heard on the reorganization plan.[18] If not, then the bankruptcy court should make a *Bildisco*-like accommodation of labor and bankruptcy law interests by requiring, as a condition of plan approval, that the debtor-in-

[15] Weather Tamer, Inc. 253 N.L.R.B. 293 (1980), *enforced in part, enforcement denied in part,* 676 F.2d 483 (11th Cir. 1982); Smyth Mfg. Co. 247 N.L.R.B. 1139 (1980). *See generally* D. McDowell & K. Huhn, NLRB Remedies For Unfair Labor Practices 210–11 (1976).

[16] National Family Opinion, Inc., 246 N.L.R.B. 521, 521 (1979).

[17] *In re* Altair Airlines, Inc., 727 F.2d 88 (3d Cir. 1984).

[18] *See* Haggard, *The Appointment of Union Representatives to Creditors' Committees under Chapter 11 of the Bankruptcy Code,* 35 S.C.L. Rev. 517 (1984).

possession first notify and "bargain" with the union over the matter. This requirement would serve the same objectives as section 8(a)(5), but without involving the NLRA's technical labor law nuances or the NLRB's time-consuming and ultimately futile processes.[19]

THE SECTION 8(a)(5) DUTY TO ENGAGE IN "EFFECTS BARGAINING"

The third area in which an NLRA bargaining duty may conflict with the exigencies of bankruptcy involves so-called "effects bargaining." Even if a particular management decision is not itself a mandatory subject of bargaining, the employer still has the duty to bargain with the union over the decision's effect on employees.[20] The NLRB has held that filing a petition in bankruptcy does not relieve an employer of this duty.[21] "Effects bargaining" usually encompasses such matters as severance pay, letters of reference, preferential hiring at other facilities owned by the employer, and payments into a pension fund. What, then, of "effects bargaining" when the decision to close or relocate a plant is made by a debtor-in-possession or a bankruptcy trustee?

The Seventh Circuit was confronted with this issue in *Yorke v. NLRB.*[22] There, the Seeburg Corporation filed under Chapter 11, and Nathan Yorke was eventually appointed as trustee. Yorke decided it was necessary to terminate operations completely, and obtained bankruptcy court authorization to do so. Yorke did not know that the seven employees who remained on the payroll were represented by a union, but discovered this fact when he received a letter from the union demanding a meeting to "discuss the decision and effects that your action has on our bargaining unit employees."[23] Yorke's reply was apparently not satisfactory, and the union filed unfair labor practice charges. A complaint was filed which claimed that Yorke's "failure to give notice that he was terminating operations and his subsequent failure to bargain over the effects of that decision [violated] . . . §§ 8(a)(5) and 8(a)(1) of the [NLRA]."[24]

---

[19] Section 8(a)(3) discrimination charges growing out of the change should be dealt with in the manner suggested in *supra* note 5.

[20] First National Maintenance Corp. v. NLRB, 452 U.S. 666, 681–82 (1981).

[21] Briggs Trans. Co., 276 N.L.R.B. No. 149, 120 L.R.R.M. 1267 (1985).

[22] 709 F.2d 1138 (7th Cir. 1983). *cert. denied,* 465 U.S. 1023 (1984).

[23] *Id.* at 1141.

[24] *Id.* at 1142.

The board ultimately found that Yorke had violated the NLRA,[25] issued a bargaining order, and "requir[ed] the Trustee to pay the seven employees their normal daily wage from five days after the board's decision until agreement or impasse over effects bargaining," provided the total was "not less than an amount equivalent to two weeks pay and not greater than an amount the employees would have received had they worked until the time they found alternative employment."[26]

In reviewing the board's decision, the court of appeals began with the proposition that "a Trustee in Bankruptcy, like any other employer, must abide by the labor laws, as long as they prescribe conduct consistent with the duties imposed by the Bankruptcy Code."[27] The court then concluded that bargaining over the effects of a decision to terminate operations was consonant with a trustee's functions under the code. A trustee has responsibility for "preserving the estate," and the court reasoned that a Trustee thus had the power to terminate an operation if necessary. Costs or losses stemming from such actions are "administrative expenses," and the court concluded that "effects bargaining" fell into that category. The court admitted that "[w]hile the Trustee's discretion might be constrained by his need for authorization from the bankruptcy court, that limitation can be taken into account in any bargaining."[28]

The trustee also challenged the backpay order, alleging that it was punitive and unjustified in a bankruptcy context. The court, however, justified the order on two grounds. First, if the trustee had bargained when it was supposed to, the union would have had greater leverage in obtaining concessions than it was going to have when it bargained some three years after plant shutdown; second, such an award would in general create an incentive for good faith bargaining. The court did hold, however, that the two-week minimum should be computed from the date if its decision rather than from the date of the board's decision. The money was to come from

---

[25] *Id; see also* Burgmeyer Bros. Inc., 254 N.L.R.B. 1027, 1028 (1981) ("[A]n employer is not relieved of its obligation to bargain over the effects of its decision to close merely because it has become a debtor-in-possession under the Bankruptcy Act and believes that, as a result thereof, it would be financially unable to meet any of the Union's bargaining demands.").

[26] *Yorke,* 709 F.2d at 1144. The award was based on the so-called "Transmarine formula," the remedy the Board normally orders when there has been a failure to engage in effects bargaining. Transmarine Navigation Corp., 170 N.L.R.B. 389 (1968).

[27] *Yorke,* 709 F.2d at 1142.

[28] *Id.* at 1143.

the $55,000 the bankruptcy court had set aside for this purpose when it approved the reorganization plan.[29]

The *Yorke* decision drew a sharp dissent from Judge Coffey. He said that the "majority's rote and mechanistic application of principles that may be appropriate in the normal employer-employee relationship ignores that fact that this case arises in the context of a Federal Bankruptcy Chapter XI proceeding."[30] He considered the context important because the trustee or debtor-in-possession does not in fact have the same legal powers as the employer, but is subject to the restrictions of the Bankruptcy Code. Further,

> It is clear that the Trustee was not authorized to bargain with the Union without first receiving the approval of the Court. In light of the fact that "it is well settled bankruptcy law that on important decisions, whatever their character, the Trustee must get the court's approval," bargaining with a Union over the effects of the plant closing (e.g. severance pay, payments into the pension fund, etc.) obviously would entail making "important decisions" affecting the bankrupt corporation. Thus, the Trustee would be engaging in an exercise in futility were he to meet with the Union in an attempt to bargain, as he was without authority to bind the bankrupt corporation absent specific prior approval of the bankruptcy judge. If, on the other hand, the Trustee did purport to bind the bankrupt corporation, he would breach his duty as an officer of the court by acting on "important matters" without prior court approval.[31]

It is clear, however, that Judge Coffey merely objected to the union's precipitous filing of unfair labor practice charges. Rather than construing the trustee's letter as an unequivocal refusal to bargain, he viewed it as an invitation to further negotiations that the union should have accepted. The trustee, or even the union itself, could then appear before the bankruptcy court and seek authorization to bargain. "If the Bankruptcy Court refused to allow the Trustee to bargain, or if the Trustee subsequently failed to bargain in good faith, *then, and only then,* should the Union be permitted to bring an unfair labor practice charge before the NLRB.[32]

Judge Coffey correctly thought that the majority position failed to accommodate adequately the exigencies of bankruptcy. But he did not carry the logic of that premise to its ultimate conclusion, which would entirely abrogate the section 8(a)(5) duty to bargain over the effects of a court-approved change in business operations.

[29] *Id.* at 1145–46.
[30] *Id.* at 1147 (Coffey, J., dissenting).
[31] *Id.* at 1149 (citation omitted).
[32] *Id.* at 1150.

Again, Judge Coffey's position is correct not because such bargaining is necessarily burdensome or inconsistent with bankruptcy processes; rather, it is because administrative enforcement of the duty is both futile and harmful from the bankruptcy perspective. *Yorke* is a good example of why the bankruptcy court should have exclusive jurisdiction over virtually all aspects of liquidation of the assets of a business.

In *Yorke,* it was almost three and one-half years after termination of the business before the trustee was actually forced to bargain with the union over the effects of termination. Although it is possible that the trustee might have agreed to write letters of recommendation or ask the company that purchased the assets to hire some of the displaced employees, it is unlikely that the trustee could have agreed to any kind of financial arrangements with the terminated employees. Assets of the estate had long since been distributed, and money set aside by the court was for satisfaction of the board's backpay order only; it was not available for distribution as part of effects bargaining. As a practical matter, the only result of the mandated effects bargaining was that the trustee and the union agreed to a settlement whereby the seven "discharged" employees were paid $27,500 out of the amount the bankruptcy court had set aside.[33]

The other creditors, however, were obviously disadvantaged by this use of estate assets. Employees received money not because they had earned it, but only because the trustee unwittingly breached an NLRA duty to bargain over the effects of plant closing.[34] That duty, or its equivalent, could have been more effectively imposed as a matter of bankruptcy law through a union's participation on the creditors' committee,[35] or by making such bargaining a condition of court approval of the closing or of the reorganization plan itself. The whole issue and expense of the NLRB proceedings could

---

[33] Letter from Narcisse A. Brown, of Schwartz, Cooper, Kolb & Gaynor, attorneys for the trustee, to the author (July 19, 1985).

[34] In a somewhat analogous context, the court in Durand v. NLRB, 296 F. Supp. 1049, 1058 (W.D. Ark. 1969), noted that "[t]aking money out of a bankruptcy estate to pay back wages to persons who did not work is certainly of no benefit to the estate or to security interests therein." The court also noted that secured creditors were responsible for neither the rejection of the contract nor the subsequent unfair labor practice, and said that the NLRB backpay award would thus be subordinated to secured claims, *Id.*

[35] *See* Division of Advice Memorandum, Cooper-Jarrett, Inc., Case Nos. 6-CA-15414 and 6-CA-15424-2 (Nov. 29, 1982), 10 A.M.D. 20009 (1982). In recommending dismissal of a charge of an alleged breach of duty to bargain over effects of a closing, the memorandum noted that "the Union is the major creditor on the creditors committee in the bankruptcy proceeding and will therefore have a substantial role in the implementation of liquidation. . . ."

have been avoided if the NLRA duty to engage in effects bargaining were thus abrogated in favor of a bankruptcy law duty of like effect.

In sum, to the extent that operational changes or effects of operational changes by a debtor-in-possession or trustee require some degree of bargaining with a union, the duty to so bargain should be a matter of bankruptcy law and enforced by imposing the duty as a condition of plan approval. This approach serves the legitimate interests of not only the affected employees, but also of the debtor and its other creditors. Involvement by the NLRB, in contrast, would be a time-consuming and expensive exercise in futility. In the words of Judge Coffey, "[i]t is the height of absurdity for the NLRB to exert a fatal chokehold on Congress's specific intent to allow mortally wounded businesses a chance to make a financial comeback at a time when our basic industries are struggling to survive.[36]

---

[36] *Yorke,* 709 F.2d 1151 (Coffey, J., dissenting).

CHAPTER VI

Labor Law Successorship Doctrines as Applied to the Purchaser of the Assets of a Bankruptcy Estate[1]

Under the NLRA, one business entity can be considered the "successor" of another for at least four different purposes: (1) being fully bound by the terms of the predecessor's collective bargaining agreement,[2] (2) being bound by the contractual duty to arbitrate,[3] (3) having a duty to continue to recognize and bargain with the union as the employees' representative,[4] and (4) being responsible for remedying the predecessor's unfair labor practices.[5]

The NLRA successorship doctrine could conflict with bankruptcy law in several ways. For example, a debtor-in-possession, a trustee, or a receiver under the old law would appear to be a successor for almost all NLRA purposes, and has been so regarded by the board.[6] In contrast, some courts regarded the debtor-in-possession as a "new entity," and thus not responsible for anything that the debtor himself had done.[7] The Supreme Court's rejection of the "new entity" theory in *Bildisco* has apparently put that conflict to rest.[8]

---

[1] Portions of this chapter originally appeared in Haggard, *The Continuing Conflict Between Bankruptcy and Labor Law—The Issues that* Bildisco *and the 1984 Bankruptcy Amendments Did Not Resolve,* 1986 Brigham Young L. Rev. 1.

[2] Crawford Door Sales Co., 226 N.L.R.B. 1144 (1976) (an employer who is a successor in this sense is referred to as an "alter ego").

[3] John Wiley & Sons v. Livingston, 376 U.S. 543 (1964).

[4] NLRB v. Burns Int'l Sec. Servs., Inc., 406 U.S. 272 (1972).

[5] Golden State Bottling Co. v. NLRB, 414 U.S. 168 (1973).

[6] *See* Ohio Container Service, Inc., 277 N.L.R.B. No.25, 120 L.R.R.M. 1279 (1985). Oxford Structures, Ltd., 245 N.L.R.B. 1180 (1979); Jersey Juniors, Inc., 230 N.L.R.B. 329 (1977); *see also In re* Bel Air Chateau Hosp., Inc., 611 F.2d 1248, 1251 (9th Cir. 1979) (holding that "[w]hether a new employer [a federal bankruptcy receiver] is an 'alter ego' or a 'successor' to an earlier employer is a question of substantive federal labor law, the resolution of which is committed to the Board and the courts that review its determinations.").

[7] *See, e.g.,* Brotherhood of Ry. Clerks v. REA Express, Inc., 523 F.2d 164 (2d Cir.), *cert. denied,* 423 U.S. 1017 (1975).

[8] NLRB v. Bildisco & Bildisco, 465 U.S. 513, 528 (1984) ("For our purposes, it is sensible to view the debtor-in-possession as the same 'entity' which existed before the filing of the bankruptcy petition. . . .").

The remaining conflict is between NLRA successorship doctrine and the bankruptcy law theory that, subject to some limitations, the purchaser of assets at a liquidation sale takes title to property free of all claims.[9] Here, no single resolution is possible. Rather, whether the predecessor's labor law obligations bind a purchaser should turn on the nature of the obligation.

THE SUCCESSOR'S DUTY TO REMEDY UNFAIR LABOR PRACTICES

Under NLRB law, "one who acquires and operates a business of an employer found guilty of unfair labor practices in basically unchanged form under circumstances which charge him with notice of unfair labor practice charges against his predecessor should be held responsible for remedying his predecessor's unlawful conduct."[10] The board has consistently held that a trustee in bankruptcy is the alter ego of the debtor-employer and thus responsible for remedying its unfair labor practices.[11] In *International Technical Products Corp.* (ITP),[12] the board also applied that doctrine to the purchaser of the physical assets of a bankrupt company. The trustee had obtained bankruptcy court approval to sell the assets "free and clear of all liens and encumbrances"[13] and to transfer all liens to proceeds of the sale. ITP then purchased the assets and continued operations with the same employees and in essentially the same manner as had the bankrupt. The NLRB had previously found the predecessor liable for unfair labor practices, and after the sale the General Counsel initiated backpay proceedings against ITP. The board held that ITP's liability was not extinguished by the bankruptcy court order authorizing the sale free of all liens, claims, and encumbrances. It reasoned that enforcement of a remedial order "rests exclusively with the Board and the appropriate reviewing Federal courts, and not the bankruptcy courts."[14] The board held that allowing the bankruptcy court to effectively nullify a board order by exonerating a successor from liability for backpay would

---

[9] 11 U.S.C. § 363(f) (1982); *see* 2 COLLIER ON BANKRUPTCY ¶ 363.07, at 363-29 to 30 (L. King 15th ed. 1984).

[10] Perma Vinyl Corp., 164 N.L.R.B. 968, 969 (1967), *enforced sub nom.* United States Pipe & Foundry Co. v. NLRB, 398 F.2d 544 (5th Cir. 1968). The *Perma Vinyl* test was approved and applied by the Supreme Court in Golden State Bottling Co. v. NLRB, 414 U.S. 168, 171 n.2 (1973).

[11] *See* Ohio Container Service, Inc., 277 N.L.R.B. No.25 n.5 (1985) (holding that these decisions were not overruled by the *Bildisco* decision).

[12] 249 N.L.R.B. 1301 (1980).

[13] *Id.* at 1302.

[14] *Id.* at 1303.

be tantamount to a relinquishment of its statutory obligation. Moreover, although the order in the case apparently involved only financial reimbursement, an order would ordinarily also require an employer to take other kinds of action of a nonmonetary nature; a board order, it argued, thus "cannot be classified or treated simply as a 'lien, claim or encumbrance' within the common usage of those terms."[15] and the judicial sale did not have the effect of extinguishing ITP's liability.

Member Penello dissented, arguing that the majority "improperly fail[ed] to interpret [the NLRA] in comity with other important Federal objectives,"[16] namely those served by operation of the Bankruptcy Code. He then noted that the purpose of a "free and clear" sale is to enhance the value of assets being sold and thus ensure that proceeds will equal or exceed the amount of liens on the property, so that *all* general unsecured creditors will receive at least something. He also noted that the sale of assets would be more difficult, if the purchaser remained liable for the debtor's backpay obligations. Moreover, Penello noted that in *Nathanson v. NLRB,*[17] the Supreme Court held that the purposes of the NLRA were adequately served by treating the board, in enforcing a backpay award against a bankrupt entity, like any other unsecured creditor. The board's preference over other creditors was then determined by bankruptcy law whose theme is equality of distribution. Penello concluded that by seeking to recover the full amount of the backpay award from ITP rather than filing a claim against the estate and taking its equal share vis-à-vis other creditors, the board simply attempted an "end run" around the Bankruptcy Act.[18]

It is not surprising that in analogous contexts bankruptcy courts have sided with Penello. *In re New England Fish Co.*[19] involved a backpay claim that arose, not under the NLRA, but under Title VII of the Civil Rights Act of 1964. Title VII, however, has a successorship doctrine virtually identical to the one applied by the NLRB. The trustee and the would-be purchaser asked for and received a declaratory judgment that the sale of assets would be clear of any monetary liability growing out of alleged civil rights violations by the debtor. Like Penello, the court thought that the *Nathanson* requirement that statutory backpay claims be afforded no special priority was controlling, and that allowing certain claimants but

---

[15] *Id.* at 1304.
[16] *Id.* (Penello, dissenting).
[17] 344 U.S. 25 (1952).
[18] *Technical Products,* 249 N.L.R.B. at 1307 (Penello, dissenting).
[19] 19 Bankr. 323 (Bankr. W.D. Wash. 1982).

not others to recover directly from the purchaser of assets would subvert that requirement. Also like Penello, the court was sensitive to practical consequences. It noted that the purchaser "would not and will not take the business burdened with civil rights litigation. No purchaser would. Such a prospect would chill or render impossible any sale. Those who would suffer from the uncertainty and delay would be creditors, including the [instant] claimants themselves."[20]

Penello and the bankruptcy court were clearly correct. Their approach does not leave employee-victims of unfair labor practices without relief; beneficiaries of NLRB backpay awards have the same rights vis-à-vis assets of the estate or proceeds of the sale thereof as any other general unsecured creditor. The award, thus, does not become a complete nullity due to inapplicability of the successorship doctrine.

That, at least, is true with respect to the backpay aspects of an award. But what of the prospective aspects of an award, such as an order requiring reinstatement of a wrongfully discharged employee? If the original violator is now completely out of business and the purchaser is not regarded as a successor, then as a practical matter the victim is left without any prospective remedies. The district court in *Forde v. Kee-Lox Manufacturing Co.* recognized this problem, but concluded the "[t]his state of affairs is one of the unfortunate yet unavoidable consequences of our bankruptcy system."[21] There is, however, some justification for that result. In order to promote free alienability of the bankrupt's assets, the purchaser must have maximum freedom to select and structure its own work force. This freedom could be significantly curtailed if the purchaser were bound to honor a reinstatement order that covered a substantial number of former employees. Moreover, even under NLRA law, the purchaser of assets is not required to hire all of the predecessor's employees.[22] The purchaser, however, may not discriminatorily re-

---

[20] *Id.* at 328–29. In Durand v. NLRB, 296 F. Supp. 1049 (W.D. Ark. 1969), the court noted that the successor's fear of being held liable for the predecessor's unfair labor practices made it unwilling to put the plant into operation except on a limited basis, and that the employees allegedly injured by the unfair labor practice were thus injured even further by the threat of successor liability. *See also* Forde v. Kee-Lox Mfg. Co., 437 F.Supp. 631, 633–34 (W.D.N.Y. 1977) ("If the trustee in a liquidation sale is not able to transfer title to the bankrupt's assets free of all claims, including civil rights claims, prospective purchasers may be unwilling to pay a fair price for the property, leaving less to the creditors").

[21] 437 F. Supp. 631, 634 (W.D.N.Y. 1977).

[22] Howard Johnson Co. v. Detroit Joint Executive Bd., Hotel & Restaurant Employees, 417 U.S. 249, 261 (1974); NLRB v. Burns Int'l Sec. Servs., Inc, 406 U.S. 272, 280 n.5. (1972).

fuse to hire these employees either because of union activities or membership or because of a desire to avoid a duty to recognize and bargain with the incumbent union.[23] Thus, in order to avoid giving beneficiaries of an NLRB reinstatement order a "windfall" not enjoyed by other employees, the purchaser should not be bound to honor the reinstatement order *as such.* But beneficiaries of the reinstatement order are entitled to be treated as if they too were active employees on the date of the sale, which means that in making its initial hiring decisions the purchaser has a duty not to discriminate against them on an impermissible basis. In this way, the interests of bankruptcy law in facilitating the sale of assets and the interests of "wronged" employees are both adequately and fairly served.

THE SUCCESSOR'S DUTY TO REMEDY CONTRACT BREACHES

The purchaser of the assets of a bankrupt company is generally not obligated to remedy the predecessor company's breaches of the collective bargaining agreement. In *Cliquot Club Bottling Co.,*[24] the union demanded that the successor pay vacation benefits that had accrued under an expired agreement with the predecessor company. The arbitrator denied the claim.

> The very essence of a purchase at bankruptcy sale is legally to buy without incurring *any* obligations which the bankrupt may have had. The slate is wiped clean. Creditors, and that is actually what these unfortunate employees were, have either been paid in full or part from the sale at bankruptcy, or (as more often happens) have lost what was due them.[25]

THE SUCCESSOR'S DUTY TO HONOR THE COLLECTIVE BARGAINING AGREEMENT

Under the successorship doctrine, a purchaser is normally not bound by the terms of the seller's collective bargaining agreement unless the subsequent employer is but a disguised continuation or alter ego of the predecessor employer or "the two enterprises have 'substantially identical' management, business purpose, operation,

---

[23] Howard Johnson Co. v. Detroit Joint Executive Bd., Hotel & Restaurant Employees, 417 U.S. 249, 262 n.8 (1974); NLRB v. Burns Int'l Sec. Servs., Inc, 406 U.S. 272, 280 n.5. (1972).

[24] 14 Lab Arb. 260 (Cornsweet, Arb., 1950).

[25] *Id.* at 261–62.

equipment, customers, and supervision, as well as ownership."[26] The board has not been quick to find alter ego status in the bankruptcy context or elsewhere.[27] But it is possible that a Chapter 11 reorganization plan may produce a new corporate entity, which would be free of the predecessor's liabilities and contractual obligations as a matter of bankruptcy law, but would nevertheless be an alter ego for purposes of labor law.[28] Such an after-the-fact imposition of contract liability should be avoided,[29] and can be only if bankruptcy law is allowed to control.

This is not to say that the bankruptcy court should be oblivious to labor law interests. Rather, when it appears that the Chapter 11 reorganization plan will produce a corporate entity qualifying as an alter ego under labor statutes, the court should either expressly require that the new corporation honor the existing collective bargaining agreement or that the debtor-in-possession use section 1113 procedures for contract rejection before proceeding further with reorganization. Conversely, if the bankruptcy court finds that the new corporate owner is not an alter ego under the labor statutes, that finding should be determinative and not subject to relitigation before the board.

---

[26] Crawford Door Sales Co., 226 N.L.R.B. 1144 (1972).

[27] *See* Blazer Indus., Inc., 236 N.L.R.B. 103, 110 (1978) (held that it was an arm's length sale, with no evidence of fraud or intent to circumvent the labor statute); Jersey Juniors, Inc., 230 N.L.R.B. 329, 334 (1977) (held that respondent was a "successor" for the purpose of being required to recognize and bargain with the union, but that it was not an "alter ego" for the purpose of being bound by the terms of the predecessor's collective bargaining agreement).

[28] In William B. Allen, 267 N.L.R.B. 700 (1983), *enforced,* 758 F.2d 1145 (6th Cir. 1985), *cert. denied,* 106 S. Ct. 882 (1986), the board held that the named respondent was the alter ego of the original employer, and thus bound to remedy the predecessor's unfair labor practices, recognize and bargain with the union, and honor the collective bargaining agreement. *Id.* at 705. In *Allen,* however, it appears that the employer simply changed names and went through what the ALJ referred to as "a series of chameleonlike corporate metamorphoses," *id.* at 706, and it is not clear how involved the bankruptcy court was, or whether there was any court involvement at all. In Century Printing Co., 242 N.L.R.B. 659 (1979) *enforced per curiam,* 108 L.R.R.M. (BNA) 2279 (3d Cir. 1981), the board applied the alter ego label to the purchaser of assets in a sale approved by the bankruptcy court. Contract survival, however, was not at issue there since the court had previously approved the contract's rejection. *See also* Marquis Printing Corp., 213 N.L.R.B. 394 (1974) (purchaser from assignee for benefit of creditors held to be an alter ego; debtor was not in bankruptcy, however).

[29] Comment, *The Unenforceable Successorship Clause: A Departure From National Labor Policy,* 30 UCLA L. Rev. 1249, 1276–77 (1983) ("It would serve no purpose for the courts to rigidly enforce the collective bargaining agreement against the successor employer when to do so would either prevent the transfer of the business altogether (and push the predecessor into bankruptcy) or drive the successor employer into economic collapse.").

THE SUCCESSOR'S DUTY TO HONOR THE ARBITRATION CLAUSE OF THE OLD CONTRACT

In *John Wiley & Sons, Inc. v. Livingston,*[30] the Supreme Court held that under certain limited circumstances, while the contract as a whole did not necessarily survive as a matter of statutory law, a successor employer could be bound by the predecessor's contractual duty to arbitrate; the arbitrator would then decide as a matter of contract law whether the successor was bound by any other contract provisions. It is not clear how much of *Wiley,* if any, survives the Supreme Court's later and more restrictive interpretations of the successorship doctrine.[31] But if, *as a matter of bankruptcy law,* none of the collective bargaining agreement survives a "free and clear" sale and the purchaser is not otherwise liable for the predecessor's contract breaches, there is simply nothing left to arbitrate. A section 301 action against the purchaser to compel arbitration should, therefore, be dismissed.[32]

THE SUCCESSOR'S DUTY TO RECOGNIZE AND BARGAIN WITH THE INCUMBENT UNION

The final way in which the successorship doctrine is traditionally used in labor law involves a successor's duty to continue to recognize and bargain with the union that represented the predecessor's employees. The board has held that if the purchaser of assets in a bankruptcy sale otherwise qualifies as a successor in this sense, the duty to recognize and bargain remains intact.[33] That position would seem correct. The right being asserted is in no way analogous to a "claim" against the predecessor for which the purchaser is now being held liable. Such a claim grows out of something the predecessor has done, like agreeing to a contract or discharging an employee in violation of law. The duty to recognize and bargain, in contrast, grows out of the situation at the time the purchaser begins

---

[30] 376 U.S. 543 (1964).

[31] *See* Severson & Willcoxon, *Successorship Under* Howard Johnson: *Short Order Justice for Employees,* 64 Calif. L. Rev. 795 (1976); Note, *The Impact of* Howard Johnson *on Labor Obligations of the Successor Employer,* 74 Mich. L. Rev. 555 (1976).

[32] *See generally* Owens-Illinois, Inc. v. District 65, Retail Store Union, 276 F. Supp. 740 (S.D.N.Y. 1967) (employer's action against union for declaratory judgment).

[33] Jersey Juniors, Inc., 230 N.L.R.B. 329, 332–33 (1977); *see* William B. Allen, 267 N.L.R.B. 700 (1983).

operation.[34] It is not a duty that the purchaser "inherits" from the seller. Rather it is a new and independent duty. Moreover, the only effect that application of the successorship doctrine has here is to raise a presumption that the union continues to enjoy majority status.[35] The presumption would be irrebuttable during the year following original certification.[36] but after that could be rebutted by a showing of good faith doubt based on "objective considerations."[37] Even if the presumption cannot be rebutted by the successor, its duty is merely to bargain with the union before making changes in wages, hours, and working conditions; the purchaser/successor is not required to obtain the union's actual assent to these changes.[38]

Thus, while a "free and clear" purchaser would undoubtedly prefer that the burden be on the union to reestablish its majority status through an NLRB election, the advantage that gives the purchaser (over having the burden to rebut the presumption of continued majority support) is probably not significant enough to affect a decision about whether to purchase assets. Therefore, application of the successorship doctrine here would not seriously implicate any bankruptcy law interests.

---

[34] The determination of "bargaining duty successorship" focuses upon whether there is a substantial continuity in work force, continuity in the employing industry, continuity in the appropriateness of the bargaining unit, and the impact of a hiatus in operations. *See generally* 1 A.B.A. Section of Labor and Employment Law, The Developing Labor Law, (C. Morris 2d ed. 1983), at 712–35.

[35] Ranch-Way, Inc., 203 N.L.R.B. 911, 912 (1973).

[36] Dynamic Mach. Co., 221 N.L.R.B. 1140, 1142 (1975), *enforced,* 552 F.2d 1195 (7th Cir. 1977).

[37] Virginia Sportswear, Inc., 226 N.L.R.B. 1296, 1301 (1976).

[38] Ranch-Way, Inc., 203 N.L.R.B. 911, 912–13 (1972).

CHAPTER VII

Bankruptcy Versus NLRB Jurisdiction Over Labor Matters Affecting the Debtor's Estate[1]

Bankruptcy has been described as "a distinct system of jurisprudence the nature of which is to sort out *all* of the debtor's legal relationships with others, and to apply the principles and rules of the bankruptcy laws to those relationships. . . ."[2] Once the bankruptcy system acquires jurisdiction over a failing business, it is usually not willing to surrender it "except under exceptional circumstances,"[3] and even mere interference with the court's exercise of jurisdiction over the debtor and its assets is subject to constraint.[4]

On the other hand, the triangular relationship among employers, employees, and unions is governed extensively by the National Labor Relations Act (NLRA). Violations of this act often result in an order requiring an employer to give back wages to employees it has wronged.[6] Adjudication and enforcement of such claims is normally the exclusive prerogative of the National Labor Relations Board (NLRB).[7]

Who, then, has jurisdiction to resolve a claim that arises under the NLRA, but is being asserted against an employer who has filed in bankruptcy? Although it is not unheard of for the NLRB to attempt to prevent a bankruptcy court from exercising its jurisdiction,[8] the matter usually comes up the other way around: the bankruptcy court is asked to forestall NLRB action and bring the case

---

[1] Portions of this chapter originally appeared in Haggard, *The Continuing Conflict Between Bankruptcy and Labor Law—The Issues that Bildisco and the 1984 Bankruptcy Amendments Did Not Resolve,* 1986 BRIGHAM YOUNG L. REV. 1.

[2] 1 BANKR. SERV. § 1:1, at 4–5 (L. Ed. 1985) (emphasis added).

[3] *In re* Muskegon Motor Specialities Co., 313 F.2d 841, 842 (6th Cir.), *cert. denied,* 375 U.S. 832 (1963) (citing Mangus v. Miller, 317 U.S. 178, 186 (1942)).

[4] *See Ex parte* Baldwin, 291 U.S. 610, 615 (1934).

[6] 29 U.S.C. § 160(c) (authorizing the board to order reinstatement of employees "with or without backpay").

[7] Amalgamated Util. Workers v. Consolidated Edison Co., 309 U.S. 261, 264–65 (1940).

[8] *See, e.g., In re* Unit Parts Co., 9 Bankr. 386 (Bankr. W.D. Okla. 1981).

into its own bailiwick. Various mechanical and procedural devices available to the bankruptcy court in its assertion of exclusive or preemptive jurisdiction over NLRB matters and the propriety of their use in any given situation are discussed below.

REMOVAL

Removal of actions to bankruptcy courts was authorized for the first time in the Bankruptcy Reform Act of 1978. In relevant part, the removal section currently provides that "[a] party may remove any claim or cause of action in a civil action other than . . . a civil action by a governmental unit to enforce such governmental unit's police or regulatory power. . . ."[9]

In *In re Adams Delivery Service, Inc.,*[10] a bankruptcy judge used the removal section to remove from the NLRB determination of a backpay award for an employee whom the board had previously found was unlawfully discharged. A bankruptcy appellate panel of the Ninth Circuit held that removal was improper for two reasons.

First, the panel noted that the removal section is limited to "civil actions," that "the concept of a civil action is inseparable from a court proceeding," that "with respect to backpay liquidation proceedings the NLRB is not acting as a court,"[11] and that removal

---

[9] 28 U.S.C.A. § 1452(a) (West Supp. 1985). The statute further provides that removal shall be "to the district court for the district where such civil action is pending." This position is consistent with the jurisdictional section itself, which vests jurisdiction over bankruptcy matters in the federal district court; the bankruptcy court is nowhere mentioned in the jurisdictional sections. Section 157(a), however, allows the district court to refer bankruptcy matters "to the bankruptcy judges for the district." *Id.* § 157(a). In practice, apparently, the district court automatically refers all matters affecting the bankrupt or its estate to the bankruptcy judge within the district. *See generally* B. WEINTRAUB & A. RESNICK, BANKRUPTCY LAW MANUAL ¶ 6.03, § 6–8; ¶ 6.03A, § 6–13 & 14 (Cumulative Supp. No. 2 1984); Developments, *Jurisdiction: A New System for the Bankruptcy Courts,* 2 BANKR. DEV. J. 1, 9, 13 (1985). It has been suggested that matters coming before the district court by removal would probably be handled in the same fashion. 1 COLLIER ON BANKRUPTCY ¶ 3.01, at 3–54 (L. King 15th ed. 1985); D. COWANS, BANKRUPTCY LAW AND PRACTICE § 1.4 (1985). However, once the unfair labor practice claim was before the bankruptcy judge, it would still be subject to section 157(d), which requires the district judge, on timely motion by any party, to withdraw from the bankruptcy court "a proceeding if the court determines that resolution of the proceeding requires consideration of both title 11 and other laws of the United States regulating organizations or activities affecting interstate commerce." 28 U.S.C.A. § 157(d) (West Supp. 1985). The NLRA is certainly such a law. *But see In re* Continental Airlines Corp., 60 Bankr. 459, 461 (Bankr. S.D. Tex. 1986) (applies only when resolution would "require direct interpretation or application of the statutory language of [a] . . . federal statute regulating interstate commerce").

[10] 24 Bankr. 589 (Bankr. 9th Cir. 1982).

[11] *Id.* at 592.

was therefore improper. Second, the court held that removal was improper because it fell within the exception for actions by a governmental unit to enforce its regulatory power. The court construed the relevant language of the removal section *in pari materia* with the similarly worded exception to the automatic stay provision, which it noted had been found to apply to NLRB proceedings.[12]

Construing the "police or regulatory power" exception of the removal statute by reference to similarly worded exceptions to the automatic stay provision would, at first blush, appear to be a reasonable approach for the bankruptcy court to have taken. While the automatic stay provision cases that the court relied on seem to support its position, the problem with the court's approach is that this area of bankruptcy law is confused and unclear.[13] The certainty and consistency that the court was striving for in taking the approach was, therefore, more illusory than real.

The court's construction of the term "civil action" is also open to question. As a general rule, removal jurisdiction should be equated with original jurisdiction, removal jurisdiction being narrower only if the statute specifically provides.[14] Given that rule, the court should have construed the bankruptcy removal statute by reference to the bankruptcy jurisdictional statute.[15] Since a good argument can be made that an unfair labor practice proceeding, particularly one that merely liquidates a backpay award as in *Adams,* is a "civil proceeding" for section 1334(b) jurisdictional purposes,[16] it should similarly qualify as a "civil action" for section 1452 removal purposes.

Finally, it should be noted that the two grounds on which the court relied in disallowing removal are mutually inconsistent. Enforcement of a "governmental unit's police or regulatory power," which the court held applicable to an NLRB proceeding to liquidate a backpay award, is specifically characterized as a "civil action" by the removal section itself. The language of the removal section is thus contrary to the court's holding that the term does not encompass such administrative proceedings.

---

[12] *Id.* at 593; *see also In re* Unit Parts Co., 9 Bankr. 386, 391 (W.D. Okla. 1981).

[13] *See infra* text accompanying notes 22–35.

[14] C. Wright, The Law of Federal Courts 210, 214 (4th ed. 1983). The bankruptcy removal statute lists two such exceptions: "a proceeding before the United States Tax Court" and "a civil action by a governmental unit to enforce such governmental unit's police or regulatory power." 28 U.S.C.A. § 1452(a) (West Supp. 1985).

[15] 28 U.S.C.A. § 1334(b) (West Supp. 1985).

[16] *See infra* text accompanying notes 76–85.

THE AUTOMATIC STAY PROVISION

Section 362(a) of the code provides that the filing of a petition in bankruptcy

> operates as a stay, applicable to all entities, of . . . the commencement or continuation, including the issuance or employment of process, of a judicial, *administrative*, or other action or proceeding against the debtor that was or could have been commenced before the commencement of the case under this title, or to recover a claim against the debtor that arose before the commencement of the case under this title. . . .[17]

Section 362(a)(2) similarly stays "the enforcement, against the debtor or against property of the estate, of a judgment obtained before the commencement of the case under this title."[18] This language would certainly seem to cover unfair labor practice proceedings, which are administrative in nature, and any attempt by the board to enforce backpay orders or other monetary remedies.

The automatic stay provision, however, is subject to several exceptions. The stay in subsection (a)(1) does not apply to "the commencement or continuation of an action or proceeding by a governmental unit to enforce such governmental unit's *police or regulatory power.*"[19] Furthermore, the subsection (a)(2) stay does not apply to "the enforcement of a judgment, other than a money judgment, obtained in an action or proceeding by a governmental unit to enforce such governmental unit's *police or regulatory power.*"[20] Regardless of which exception applies, the critical question is whether the NLRB (including the general counsel and its staff) is acting within its "police or regulatory power' when it processes unfair labor practices, makes backpay determinations, and conducts representation proceedings and elections.

This is not an easy question to answer.[21] To be sure, all the NLRB functions listed represent actions to "enforce [its] regulatory powers." But, in the broad sense, the same is true of any administrative agency action. Read literally, therefore, the exception is as broad as the rule; what subsection (a) "gives," by mandating a stay, subsections (b)(4) and (b)(5) "take away." But that is a silly and erroneous way to interpret statutes. Rather, one must assume that something qualifies as an administrative proceeding under subsec-

[17] 11 U.S.C. § 362(a) (1982) (emphasis added).
[18] *Id.* § 362(a)(2).
[19] *Id.* § 362(b)(4) (emphasis added).
[20] *Id.* § 362(b)(5) (emphasis added).
[21] The NLRB, however, is of the definite opinion that its proceedings are not automatically stayed. Goldstein Co., 274 N.L.R.B. No. 95, 118 L.R.R.M. 1435 (1985).

tion (a) but is not an action to enforce the agency's police or regulatory power under subsection (b) exceptions.

The courts have not had an easy time identifying this middle ground even in non-NLRA contexts.[22] The analysis inevitably proceeds from legislative history. For example, legislative history of the operative provisions of section 362 suggests that this section was intended to have very broad scope. It states that "*[a]ll proceedings* are stayed, including arbitration, *license revocation, administrative,* and judicial proceedings."[23] However, description of the exception's scope is equally broad:

> Paragraph (4) excepts commencement or continuation of actions and proceedings by governmental units to enforce police or regulatory powers. Thus, where a governmental unit is suing a debtor to prevent or stop violation of fraud, environmental protection, consumer protection, safety, or similar police or regulatory laws, or attempting to fix damages for violation of such a law, the action or proceeding is not stayed under the automatic stay. *Paragraph (5) makes clear that the exception extends to permit an injunction ... and to permit the entry of a money judgment, but does not extend to permit enforcement of a money judgment.* Since the assets of the debtor are in the possession and control of the bankruptcy court, and since they constitute a fund out of which all creditors are entitled to share, enforcement by a governmental unit of a money judgment would give it preferential treatment to the detriment of all other creditors.[24]

The other bit of legislative history relevant to this issue involves observations of Congressman Don Edwards:

> This section [364(b)(4)] is intended to be given a narrow construction in order to permit governmental units to pursue actions to protect the public health and safety and not to apply to actions by a governmental unit to protect a pecuniary interest in property of the debtor or property of the estate.[25]

Several sets of distinctions may be drawn from the legislative history. For example, the proper distinction may be between regulation of conduct, on the one hand, and recovery of monetary

---

[22] For a thorough discussion of the controlling precedent, see NLRB v. Edward Cooper Painting, Inc. __ F.2d __ (6th Cir. 1986); *In re* Rath Packing Co., 35 Bankr. 615 (Bankr. N.D. Iowa 1983); Donovan v. TMC Indus., 20 Bankr. 997 (Bankr. N.D. Ga. 1982); Hennigan, *Accommodating Regulatory Enforcement and Bankruptcy Protection,* 59 Am. Bankr. L.J. 1, 9–38 (1985).

[23] H.R. Rep. No. 595, 95th Cong., 1st Sess. 340 (1977) (emphasis added).

[24] *Id.* at 343 (emphasis added).

[25] 124 Cong. Rec. H11089 (1978) (statement of Rep. Edwards), *reprinted in* 1978 U. S. Code & Ad. News 6436, 6444–45.

amounts, on the other.[26] Under this view, if the unfair labor practice proceeding merely may result in a cease-and-desist or "affirmative action" order against the offending employer, it would be within the exception to the automatic stay; but if backpay is possible, the stay remains operative.

Alternatively, the distinction may be between agency actions that primarily affect the health, safety, and welfare of the public, in contrast to administrative proceedings where the object is merely to achieve some pecuniary benefit on behalf of private claimants. The bankruptcy court in *In re Theobold Industries*[27] was apparently operating on this theory. The exact nature of the alleged unfair labor practice in that case was unclear, but it somehow related to the employer's claim that it was no longer bound by the collective bargaining agreement. In any event, the general counsel of the NLRB was seeking an order compelling the payment of $25,910.74 for vacation pay, severance pay, clothing allowance, and interest. The court rejected the contention that the NLRB proceeding was "somehow relate[d] to the protection of the public health and safety, and thus [fell] within the contemplation of a restrictively construed § 362(b)(4) exception. . . ."[28] Rather, the court determined that "the claims asserted by the N.L.R.B. in behalf of the union are essentially monetary in nature, impacting directly and ineluctably on the assets of the estate."[29]

---

[26] Dicta in the recent Supreme Court case of Ohio v. Kovacs, 105 S. Ct. 705, 709 (1985), suggests that this may be a reasonable distinction. The Sixth Circuit in an earlier but related case had held that the automatic stay applied to the state's attempt to recover monetary damages for a violation of a state environmental law. Ohio v. Kovacs, 681 F.2d 454 (6th Cir. 1982), *vacated and remanded,* 459 U.S. 1167 (1983) (to consider the question of mootness). With respect to this decision, the Supreme Court said that "[i]n that court's view, while § 362(b) allowed governmental units to continue to enforce police powers through mandatory injunctions, it denied them the power to collect money in their enforcement efforts." 105 S. Ct. at 707 n.2. In slightly less clear terms, the Court itself then stated that "[t]he automatic stay provision does not apply to suits to enforce the regulatory statutes of the State, but the enforcement of such a judgment by seeking money from the bankrupt . . . is another matter." *Id.* at 711 n.11.

[27] 16 Bankr. 537 (Bankr. D.N.J. 1981).

[28] *Id.* at 539.

[29] *Id.* at 538. *But see* NLRB v. Edward Cooper Painting, Inc., *supra,* note 22 (held that the NLRB "does not proceed on behalf of private persons"); EEOC v. Rath Packing Co., 787 F.2d 318 (8th Cir. 1986) (court held that even though the ultimate objective of the EEOC proceedings was to achieve some pecuniary benefit for private claimants, the Commission's enforcement of Title VII of the Civil Rights Act of 1964 was primarily a vindication of public rather than private interests, and that the exception thus applied); EEOC v. Sambo's Restaurants, Inc., 34 Fair Empl. Prac. Cas. (BNA) 1451 (S.D. Tex. 1982). A private employment discrimination suit is however, subject to the stay. *In re* Page Wilson Corp., 37 Bankr. 962 (Bankr. D. Conn. 1984).

A third possible distinction, and one that the legislative history reflects most clearly, is between administrative proceedings that *fix* the amount of recovery and administrative attempts to *enforce* collection of such amounts outside the bankruptcy process.[30] This was the approach taken by the bankruptcy court in *In re D.M. Barber, Inc.*[31] The court believed that the board would not and legally could not independently enforce its money judgments against the employer,[32] and thus saw "no reason to grant a discretionary stay to prohibit the Board from liquidating its claim against the debtor for purposes of filing a claim in the bankruptcy estate."[33] The court also reserved the right "to determine the extent to which any such proof of claim should be allowed and the priority treatment accorded it under the distribution hierarchy set forth in the Bankruptcy Code."[34]

The court, in short, allowed the NLRB to fix the amount of the award, but would have applied provisions of the automatic stay to any attempt by the board to independently enforce its award.[35] But since the board has apparently been content to file its claims in bankruptcy court rather than seek enforcement through normal channels,[36] this distinction—if indeed it is the controlling one—is more or less moot.

---

[30] This is suggested by the italicized language of the legislative history. *See supra* note 24 and accompanying text.

[31] 13 Bankr. 962 (Bankr. N.D. Tex. 1981).

[32] *Id.* at 965 n.1.

[33] *Id.* at 965; NLRB v. Edward Cooper Painting, Inc., *supra* note 22 at __; *see also* NLRB v. Evans Plumbing Co., 639 F.2d 291, 293 (5th Cir. 1981); *In re* Nicholas, Inc., 55 Bankr. 212 (Bankr. D.N.J. 1985).

[34] *Valverde,* 13 Bankr. at 965. The court in *In re* Tucson Yellow Cab Co., 27 Bankr. 621 (Bankr. 9th Cir. 1983), similarly held that the NLRB had exclusive jurisdiction to determine the amount of money the debtor owed employees as a result of its unfair labor practice, but reserved to the bankruptcy court the right to examine allowability and priority of these claims. *Id.* at 623; *see also* EEOC v. Rath Packing Co., 787 F.2d 318 (8th Cir. 1986); General Highway Express, Inc. v. Teamsters Local 20, 118 L.R.R.M. (BNA) 3402 (Bankr. N.D. Ohio 1985); Armour Oil Co. v. NLRB, 120 L.R.R.M. 3006 (Bankr. C.D. Calif. 1985); *In re* Daryl Indus., 74 Lab. Cas. (CCH) ¶ 10,126 (Bankr. S.D. Fla. 1973); Airport Bus Service, Inc. 273 N.L.R.B. No. 84, 118 L.R.R.M. 1343 (1984).

[35] *Accord In re* Shippers Interstate Serv., 618 F.2d 9 (7th Cir. 1980); *In re* Bel Air Chateau Hosp., 611 F.2d 1248 (9th Cir. 1979). These cases suggest that the stay might apply if administrative proceedings "threaten the assets" of the estate. *In re* Shippers Interstate Serv., 618 F.2d 9, 13 (7th Cir. 1980); *In re* Bel Air Chateau Hosp., 611 F.2d 1248, 1251 (9th Cir. 1979). This is also one test used by courts in evaluating the propriety of a discretionary injunction. *See infra* text accompanying notes 54–55. In that regard it has been suggested that this "threat" would arise only if the board attempted to enforce a backpay award outside the bankruptcy process. *See infra* text accompanying note 58. Indirectly, therefore, these cases may be cited in support of the distinction between fixing and enforcing monetary awards, as the basis for deciding when the exception applies and when the stay itself applies.

[36] *But see* NLRB v. Deena Artware, Inc., 251 F.2d 183 (6th Cir. 1958). The board

The debate over the applicability of the automatic stay provision may not be as important as it seems. Even if the stay provision applies, the Bankruptcy Code gives the bankruptcy court broad discretion to lift, modify, or condition a stay "for cause."[37] Conversely, notwithstanding the inapplicability of stay provisions, a bankruptcy court still has the power under section 105 to issue injunctions.[38] While this approach shifts the burden from the administrative agency seeking relief from the stay to the party seeking an injunction against that agency, the test would probably be about the same.[39]

SECTION 105 INJUNCTIONS AGAINST THE NLRB

Since its inception, the bankruptcy court has been regarded as a court of equity with inherent power to protect its processes and property by injunctive decree.[40] Section 105(a) codifies this power, providing that "the bankruptcy court may issue any order, process, or judgment that is necessary or appropriate to carry out the provisions of this title."[41] Finally, the power of the bankruptcy court to issue an injunction is unaffected if the conduct to be enjoined otherwise falls within an exception to the automatic stay. The legislative history states that "[t]he effect of an exception is not to make the action immune from injunction.... By excepting an act or action from the automatic stay, the [Code] simply requires that the trustee move the court into action...."[42] Under what circumstances, then, would it be appropriate for the bankruptcy court to enjoin an NLRB proceeding?

---

here filed a motion with the court of appeals for discovery proceedings for the ultimate purpose of enforcing monetary awards in favor of employees who had been discriminated against by the debtor. The court held that supervision of discovery was part and parcel of collection of the award, and thus something that should be handled by a court of original jurisdiction, presumably the bankruptcy court. *Id.* at 186. The court also suggested, however, that enforcement of an award by a court of appeals through exercise of contempt power might present a different situation. *Id.* at 185. Although the court of appeals would have jurisdiction to issue a contempt citation for nonpayment, an action by the NLRB to enforce an award in that way would appear to "threaten the assets" of the estate, and would thus be subject to a bankruptcy court injunction.

[37] 11 U.S.C. § 362(d)(1) (1982).

[38] 11 U.S.C. § 105(a) (Supp. II 1984).

[39] Compare cases cited *supra* note 35 (using a "threaten the assets of the estate" test for determining when the automatic stay applies) with the case cited *infra* note 45 (using the same test to determine when an injunction should be issued); *see also In re* Atlantic Int'l Corp., 101 L.R.R.M. (BNA) 2128, 2129 (D. Md. 1979).

[40] *Ex parte* Baldwin, 291 U.S. 610, 615 (1934); *Ex parte* Christy, 44 U.S. (3 How.) 292, 312 (1845).

[41] 11 U.S.C. § 105(a) (Supp. II 1984).

[42] H.R. Rep. No. 595, 95th Cong., 1st Sess. 342 (1977).

THE LIMITATIONS IMPOSED BY THE NORRIS-LAGUARDIA ACT

The 1932 Norris-LaGuardia Act provides that "[n]o court of the United States shall have jurisdiction to issue any ... injunction in any case involving or growing out of a labor dispute," except in those cases provided for in the statute.[43] The act further defines "labor dispute" very broadly, as including "any controversy concerning terms or conditions of employment, or concerning the association or representation of persons in negotiating ... terms or conditions of employment. . . ."[44]

In *In re Rath Packing Co.,*[45] the company sought an injunction to bar the union and the NLRB from continuing an unfair labor practice proceeding on a charge alleging that the company had illegally circumvented the union in negotiating a wage deferral agreement. The bankruptcy court denied the injunction, in part because of the Norris-LaGuardia Act. First it determined, probably correctly, that a bankruptcy court was a "court of the United States" for purposes of the Norris-LaGuardia Act. Second, it determined that the unfair labor practice charge involved a controversy concerning "representation of persons" in negotiations changing "terms and conditions of employment" (the wage deferral), and that the case thus involved a "labor dispute" for purposes of the Norris-LaGuardia Act. Having thus brought the controversy within the purview of that act, the court then concluded that the statutory standing requirements were not satisfied, specifically the requirement that the person seeking injunctive relief show "irreparable injury." The court regarded as inadequate the company's reference to "the expense and inconvenience of litigating before the Board" and the effect that a potential award of monetary damages might have on potential purchasers of Rath assets.[46]

The court's analysis was simplistic at best. To begin with, its treatment of the "irreparable injury" issue seemed to ignore that the plaintiff was not simply another party trying to avoid the expense and inconvenience of litigation, but a debtor-in-possession attempting to salvage assets of the estate, not only for the debtor's benefit but also for the benefit of creditors.[47] But that is a mere quibble.

---

[43] 29 U.S.C. § 104 (1982).
[44] 29 U.S.C. § 113(c) (1982).
[45] 38 Bankr. 552 (Bankr. N.D. Iowa 1984).
[46] *Id.* at 558–63 & n.6.
[47] *See* Durand v. NLRB, 296 F. Supp. 1049, 1054, (W.D. Ark. 1969).

More troublesome is the court's literal and thus overly broad interpretation of the term "labor dispute." Although couched in jurisdictional terms, the Norris-LaGuardia Act had a substantive purpose:[48] to remove from the proscriptions of federal antitrust law all attempts by labor unionists to achieve legitimate ends by peaceful purposes. Congress had tried to do this through a substantive enactment, the Clayton Act,[49] but had been frustrated by the Supreme Court.[50] Therefore Congress took a jurisdictional approach; it gave a broad definition to the term "labor dispute," and generally denied federal courts power to issue injunctions or assess damages in matters arising out of such disputes.

The substantive purpose of the Norris-LaGuardia Act, to provide federal immunity to strikes and other forms of "peaceful" concerted activity, must be taken into account when construing the term "labor dispute" since existence of such a dispute is what triggers the applicability of the act. Adjudication of unfair labor practice claims by the NLRB is far removed from anything Congress intended to cover when it enacted the Norris-LaGuardia Act, and it would be nonsensical to apply the act to those proceedings simply because they can be construed as falling within the literal definition of a "labor dispute." The problem lies in accommodating the provisions of the Bankruptcy Code with those of the NLRA; that is difficult enough. There is no need to complicate matters further by forcing into the equation a statue designed to deal with different problems at another time in the history of industrial relations.

Finally, even if an injunction against the NLRB were within the literal prohibitions of the Norris-LaGuardia Act, specific reference to "administrative" proceedings in the automatic stay provisions without any exception for the NLRB, and the even broader grant of injunctive power in section 105(a) of the Bankruptcy Code should be construed as a *pro tanto* repeal.[51] The *Rath* court expressly declined to pass on that issue,[52] holding that the automatic stay did not apply and an injunction would be inappropriate anyway.

Rath is the only decision to consider the applicability of the Norris-LaGuardia Act in bankruptcy proceedings. Apparently, all

---

[48] *See generally* Haggard, *The Power of the Bankruptcy Court to Enjoin Strikes: Resolving the Apparent Conflict Between the Bankruptcy Code and the Anti-Injunction Provisions of the Norris-LaGuardia Act,* 53 Geo. Wash. L. Rev. 703 (1985) at 705–06.

[49] 29 U.S.C. §§ 52, 53 (1982).

[50] Duplex Printing Press Co. v. Deering, 254 U.S. 443 (1921).

[51] *See generally* Haggard, *Norris-LaGuardia, supra* note 48.

[52] *Rath,* 38 Bankr. at 560.

other courts have simply assumed[53]—correctly so—that in an appropriate case that act imposes no obstacles to a bankruptcy court injunction against an NLRB proceeding.

THE PROPER TEST FOR GRANTING INJUNCTIVE RELIEF

In evaluating the propriety of a bankruptcy court injunction, one must necessarily begin with the Supreme Court's decision in *Nathanson v. NLRB.*[54] The narrow issue in that case was whether the bankruptcy court or the NLRB was the proper forum for liquidation of backpay awards pursuant to a board finding that the employer had committed unfair labor practices. But in resolving that issue, the Court articulated what has become the controlling principle in the relationship between bankruptcy courts and the NLRB. The Court noted that

> [t]he bankruptcy court normally supervises the liquidation of claims.... But the rule is not inexorable. A sound discretion may indicate that a particular controversy should be remitted to another tribunal for litigation.... And where the matter in controversy has been entrusted by Congress to an administrative agency, the bankruptcy court normally should stay its hand pending an administrative decision.[55]

From this case has emerged a general presumption against bankruptcy court interference with NLRB proceedings, although that principle is subject to several possible exceptions.

The first and most commonly recognized exception allows the bankruptcy court to issue a stay if administrative or regulatory proceedings "threaten the assets of the estate."[56] No case really

---

[53] The court in *In re* Brada Miller Freight Systems, 16 Bankr. 1002 (N.D. Ala. 1981), was asked to enjoin any interference with the debtor's business (including strikes) and the continuance of unfair labor practice proceedings. The court, after extensive analysis, held that the Norris-LaGuardia Act precluded the requested strike injunction. The injunction against the NLRB proceedings was also denied, but solely on the grounds that those proceedings posed no threat to assets of the estate; the Norris-LaGuardia Act was not even given passing mention as to this issue, which seems to suggest that the court thought that the act did not need to be considered.

[54] 344 U.S. 25 (1952).

[55] *Id.* at 30 (citations omitted).

[56] *See, e.g., In re* Shippers Interstate Serv., 618 F.2d 9, 13 (7th Cir. 1980); *In re* Bel Air Chateau Hosp., 611 F.2d 1248, 1251 (9th Cir. 1979); *In re* Brada Miller Freight Systems, 16 Bankr. 1002, 1013 (N.D. Ala. 1981); Gen. Highway Express, Inc. v. Teamsters Local 20, 118 L.R.R.M. (BNA) 3402, 3406 (Bankr. N.D. Ohio 1985).

explains what this means,[57] and apparently no injunction has ever been issued on a finding that assets were threatened. One leading labor law text suggests that an NLRB action might threaten assets of the estate only if the board attempted to enforce a monetary award outside normal channels of bankruptcy.[58] But apparently the board has never done that. Conceivably, a board order requiring a debtor-employer to reopen a plant or facility could also threaten assets of the estate, but a case involving those facts has not yet arisen.

Second, some courts have suggested that an exception allowing an injunction against the NLRB may be more appropriate in a total liquidation than in a mere reorganization.[59] The theory is that disappearance of the employing entity renders moot any remedial order requiring the now defunct employer to cease-and-desist from coercion or domination, bargain with the union, reinstate employees, or post notices of compliance.[60] Since it would be an exercise in futility and a drain on assets to force the estate to participate in such proceedings, an injunction would appear proper. Again, however, no injunction has ever been issued on that basis.

The third exception, though not clearly recognized as such, focuses not so much on threats to assets of the estate as it does on threats to the bankruptcy process itself. This exception is perhaps what the

---

[57] The court in *In re* Tucson Yellow Cab, 27 Bankr. 621, 623–24 (Bankr. 9th Cir. 1983) adopted the "threatened assets" test, but admitted that there is little or no authority available to instruct us when an action of NLRB represents an enjoinable threat." The court did hold, however, that the mere possibility that backpay claims might have priority was not sufficient to constitute an enjoinable "threat" against the estate. Similarly, in *In re* GHR Energy Corp., 33 Bankr. 449 (Bankr. D. Mass. 1983), the court held that the "cloud" on the bankrupt's assets created by continuance of unfair labor proceedings and the threat of liability flowing therefrom, which the debtor said would deter potential purchasers of assets, still did not constitute a "threat" to assets of the the estate in the sense of justifying an injunction. Finally, the court in *In re* Nicholas Inc., 55 Bankr. at 212, 218 (Bankr. D. N.J. 1985), held that litigation expenses did not constitute a "threat" to assets of the estate, especially since the amount was neither substantiated nor related to total assets of the estate.

[58] 2 A.B.A. Section of Labor and Employment Law, The Developing Labor Law (C. Morris 2d ed. 1983), at 1598.

[59] *See In re* Shippers Interstate Service, Inc., 618 F.2d 9 (7th Cir. 1980). *GHR Energy Corp.* construed that as meaning a literal "liquidation" (the extinguishment of the business as a going concern) rather than just a "liquidation" (sale) in the Chapter 7 sense. In the latter situation the court felt that the purchaser of assets might still be liable to remedy the predecessor's unfair labor practices. *In re* GHR Energy Corp., 33 Bankr. 449, 450 n.4 (Bankr. D. Mass. 1983); *see also In re* Seeburg Corp., 11 Bankr. 121, 123 (N.D. Ill. 1980) (the possibility of successorship liability caused the court to evaluate the injunction issue from the perspective of a reorganization rather than a liquidation, even though it was a Chapter 7 proceeding). *But see* chapter VI, *supra.*

[60] *In re* Shippers Interstate Service, Inc., 618 F.2d 9, 12 & n.3 (7th Cir. 1980); D.M. Barber, Inc. v. Valverde, 13 Bankr. 962, 965 (Bankr. N.D. Tex. 1981).

district court in *In re Airport Iron & Metal, Inc.* had in mind when it held that an injunction against the NLRB was not appropriate "as long as the administration of the debtor's estate is not being embarrassed or delayed, to the point of threatened or impending irreparable injury."[61] The court in *In re Accurate Die Casting, Inc.*,[62] specifically defined the test in terms of harm to the debtor's "successful reorganization."[63] This "threatened process" test was more clearly articulated in a recent article by attorney Peter A. Jackson.[64]

Drawing from the language of section 105(a) itself, which empowers the bankruptcy court to issue all orders "necessary or appropriate to carry out the provisions of this title,"[65] he argues that the provisions in question "constitute a process aimed at protecting the reorganization potential of an ailing business. Thus, an injunction may be justified when an NLRB action threatens the orderly processing of a promising reorganization effort."[66] He then suggests that the three most common threats to a reorganization effort potentially posed by an NLRB proceeding are delay, expense, and duplication of effort.[67] Jackson makes a compelling case for the "threatened process" test, and argues that it is a reasonable alternative to, if not a complete substitute for, the more common "threatened assets" and "liquidation versus reorganization" tests.

APPLICATION OF THE TEST

One can assume that all NLRB unfair labor practice proceedings, if participated in by the trustee or debtor-in-possession, are going to impose substantial administrative expenses on the estate. In addition, the NLRB processes will probably take much longer than a normal Chapter 11 reorganization or Chapter 7 liquidation, thus either delaying bankruptcy proceedings or tying up funds that could otherwise be distributed to creditors or used in revitalizing the

---

[61] 90 L.R.R.M. (BNA) 3108, 3111 (S.D.N.Y. 1974).

[62] 59 Bankr. 853 (Bankr. N.D. Ohio 1986).

[63] *Id.* at 855.

[64] Jackson, *Bankruptcy Courts and the NLRB: A Clash of Jurisdiction Over Unfair Labor Practices*, 1 Bankr. Dev. J. 27 (1984).

[65] 11 U.S.C. § 105(a) (Supp. II 1984).

[66] Jackson, *supra* note 64, at 37.

[67] A duplication of effort would occur only if the board were allowed to continue to adjudicate an issue even after the bankruptcy court had asserted jurisdiction over it. *See In re* Unit Parts Co., 9 Bankr. 386 (W.D. Okla. 1981) (court assumed jurisdiction over the unfair labor practice, but refused to enjoin the NLRB).

debtor.[68] It would thus seem that absent compelling considerations to the contrary, an injunction would almost always be appropriate.

The most obvious instance in which these "compelling considerations" are *not* present is an NLRB charge against the debtor-in-possession based on conduct which, *because of the preemptive effect of the bankruptcy laws,* cannot as a matter of law be considered an unfair labor practice at all. Here, substantive law is dispositive of jurisdiction, providing what is undoubtedly the cleanest and thus the best resolution of the conflict.

NLRB v. Superior Forwarding, Inc. is a recent example of this resolution.[69] In that case, the debtor-in-possession sought to enjoin the NLRB from prosecuting unfair labor practice charges that the debtor claimed arose out of its unilateral modification and ultimate rejection of a collective bargaining agreement, conduct that it argued was declared by the Supreme Court in *Bildisco* not to be an unfair labor practice. The NLRB responded that the unfair labor practice charges pertained to the debtor's failure to bargain in good faith over a new contract, a duty which survived *Bildisco.*[70] The Eight Circuit, however, held that this question was for the bankruptcy court to decide, and that an injunction would be appropriate if the board was acting outside its authority and the proceedings would threaten assets of the estate.

The same approach should be followed with respect to the effect of section 1113 provisions. For example, when a debtor-in-possession follows section 1113 procedures for contract rejection, it clearly has immunity from any section 8(d) liability, and an attempt by the NLRB to process a section 8(d) and 8(a)(5) unfair labor practice charge should be enjoined. While the preemptive quality of section 1113 may not be so clear in other situations, that determination can be more quickly and authoritatively made through bankruptcy processes than through NLRB processes.[71]

The NLRB proceeding next most likely to be enjoined by a bankruptcy court is a backpay liquidation proceeding. After the NLRB

---

[68] *See* Durand v. NLRB, 296 F. Supp. 1049, 1054 (W.D. Ark. 1969). The debtor in *In re* Nicholas, Inc., 55 Bankr. 212, 217 (Bankr. D.N.J. 1985), claimed that it would cost between $25,000 and $50,000 to litigate the unfair labor practice charge, including an appeal, but this figure was unsubstantiated.

[69] 762 F.2d 695 (8th Cir. 1985); *see also In re* San Juan Hotel Corp., 111 L.R.R.M. (BNA) 2877 (D.P.R. 1982).

[70] *Cf.* El San Juan Hotel, NLRB Dec. (CCH) ¶ 17,063 (1985) (board dismissed complaint alleging section 8(a)(5) and 8(d) violations that fell squarely within the *Bildisco* holding). The court in *In re* Nicholas, Inc., 55 Bankr. at 216–17, construed *Superior Forwarding* as applying only to *Bildisco*-type issues, and not to unfair labor practices that are independent of the collective bargaining agreement.

[71] *See Superior Forwarding,* 762 F.2d at 700.

decides an unfair labor practice case and all appeals, if any, have been exhausted, the agency conducts a separate hearing to determine the amount of backpay to which each employee is entitled.[72] As the Supreme Court recognized in *Nathanson v. NLRB,* "[t]he bankruptcy court normally supervises the liquidation of claims."[73] Section 502(c) of the code expressly grants the court that power; indeed, it *requires* the court to estimate "any contingent or unliquidated claim, the fixing or liquidation of which ... would unduly delay the closing of the case.[74] Notwithstanding the desirability of having backpay determinations made by someone with labor law expertise and a familiarity with the controlling substantive law,[75] it would seem that the section 502 mandate should apply to NLRA claims.

This position is consistent with *Nathanson,* which merely required that the bankruptcy court give the NLRB a "reasonable time"[76] to liquidate the claim. Presumably, a reasonable time would be determined by the exigencies of the bankruptcy process, which vary from case to case. Moreover, as the court noted in *In re Wilson Foods Corp.,* "[c]ounsel for the Board has stated that it expedites proceedings upon request. We assume the Board will be mindful of the harm that can befall an estate in reorganization proceedings due to unreasonable delay, and will seek to accommodate itself to the bankruptcy process. . . ."[77] The alternative is for the bankruptcy court to either set aside an amount that it thinks will be sufficient to cover the claims or to enjoin further NLRB proceedings and liquidate the claims itself.[78]

---

[72] *See generally* K. McGuiness, How To Take a Case Before the National Labor Relations Board § 18-6, at 319 (4th ed. 1976).

[73] 344 U.S. 25, 30 (1952).

[74] 11 U.S.C. § 502(c) (Supp. II 1984).

[75] The computation of the amount due may not be a simple matter. It may require, in addition to the projection of earnings which the employee would have enjoyed had he not been discharged and the computation of actual interim earnings, the determination whether the employee willfully incurred losses, whether the back pay period should be terminated because of offers of reinstatement or the withdrawal of the employee from the labor market, whether the employee received equivalent employment, and the like. Congress made the relation of remedy to policy an administrative matter, subject to limited judicial review, and chose the Board as its agent for the purpose. Nathanson v. NLRB, 344 U.S. 25, 29–30 (1952) (citations omitted).

[76] *Id.* at 30.

[77] 31 Bankr. 269, 271 (Bankr. W.D. Okla. 1983).

[78] This approach is supported by the existence of an exception to the automatic stay for "the enforcement of a judgment, *other than a money judgment,* obtained in an action or proceeding by a governmental unit to enforce such governmental unit's police or regulatory power. . . ." 11 U.S.C. § 362(b)(5) (1982) (emphasis added).

A hearing on the unfair labor practice complaint may be a third type of NLRB proceeding subject to an injunction. The principal bankruptcy law interest at stake here is expeditious resolution of the controversy. If monetary relief is going to be awarded (pursuant to the bifurcated procedure discussed above), it should be awarded quickly. It is one thing for the NLRB to expedite liquidation of damages proceedings so that it can file its claims in the bankruptcy court. It would be quite another for the board to expedite its entire unfair labor practice proceedings—from the trial by an administrative law judge through review by the board itself. Indeed, since board orders are not "self-enforcing," in a technical sense the "process" on the merits is not complete until the board's order has been approved by a federal court of appeals. At that point there is still the liquidation proceeding. For an alleged unfair labor practice occurring just prior to or during bankruptcy proceedings, this process would be far too long.

On the other hand, an injunction against these proceedings seems almost unthinkable. If an injunction is issued, one of three things can happen to employee claims: they are either permanently lost, they will have to be heard by the NLRB after the bankruptcy proceedings are over, or they will have to be heard by the bankruptcy court itself. None of these alternatives is fully tenable. The first would simply mean that a bankrupt employer or a trustee is no longer answerable for its labor law violations, a result so extreme as to be rejected as obviously inconsistent with congressional intent.[79] The second alternative, however, would have a similar effect since confirmation of a plan would discharge monetary claims thus leaving nothing for the NLRB to adjudicate.[80] Finally, the third alternative poses enormous legal and practical problems.

On the legal side, it is debatable whether the bankruptcy court would even have jurisdiction to hear an unfair labor practice claim. Section 1334(b) provides that "[n]otwithstanding any Act of Congress that confers exclusive jurisdiction on a *court* or *courts* other than the district courts, the district courts shall have original but not exclusive jurisdiction of all *civil proceedings* arising under title 11, or arising in or related to cases under title 11.[81] Construing this section's similarly worded predecessor,[82] the court in *NLRB v. Brada*

[79] The National Labor Relations Act expressly includes within its definition of "person" "trustees in [bankruptcy], or receivers." 29 U.S.C. § 152(1) (1982).

[80] *See* Jackson, *supra* note 64, at 40. Of course, the court could always set aside an amount sufficient to cover the potential liability, but tying up assets of the estate in this fashion is generally undesirable.

[81] 28 U.S.C.A. § 1334(b) (West Supp. 1985) (emphasis added).

[82] 28 U.S.C. § 1471 (1982).

Miller Freight Systems[83] apparently felt that the word "court" in the introductory clause modified the term "civil proceeding" in the following clause. It thus concluded that "[o]n its face, the provision is not applicable to NLRB proceedings, for the NLRB is not a 'court,' within the plain meaning of the statute."[84]

While there is some merit to that argument, the conclusion that the bankruptcy court lacks jurisdiction over unfair labor practice claims may be countered on several grounds. The legislative history, for example, states that the term "proceeding here is used in its broadest sense, and would encompass what are now called contested matters, adversary proceedings, and plenary actions. . . ."[85] The history thus suggests that the focus should be on the nature of the controversy, not the specific forum in which Congress originally contemplated its adjudication. In short, if the controversy between the debtor and a claimant is adversarial in nature, and thus suitable for judicial resolution, then its adjudication should be regarded as involving a "civil proceeding." It should not make any difference that in the nonbankruptcy context the controversy would be resolved by an agency *acting in its quasi-judicial capacity* rather than by a court. Moreover, the intended breadth of the term "proceedings" is simply a manifestation of the more generalized intent "to bring all litigation within the umbrella of the bankruptcy court, irrespective of Congressional statements to the contrary in the context of certain specialized litigation."[86] In other words, as the court in *In re Unit Parts Co.* stated, "[b]y conscious design, Congress endowed the Bankruptcy Court with *wide* latitude to deal with all money problems touching the financially threatened."[87]

The legislative history of section 157(d), though not conclusive, also suggests the possibility of bankruptcy court jurisdiction over unfair labor practices. Section 157(d) requires the district court, on motion, to withdraw from the bankruptcy court any proceeding that involves a consideration of both bankruptcy law and any other law "regulating organizations or activities affecting interstate commerce."[88] The legislative history states that this includes "cases

---

[83] 16 Bankr. 1002 (Bankr. N.D. Ala. 1981), *vacated and remanded on other grounds,* 702 F.2d 890 (11th Cir. 1983).

[84] *Id.* at 1009; *see also In re* Adams Delivery Serv., 24 Bankr. 589 (Bankr. 9th Cir. 1982). *Contra In re* Theobald Indus., Inc., 16 Bankr. 537, 538 (Bankr. D.N.J. 1981) (treats the adjudication of claims arising under the NLRA as "civil proceedings" for purposes of bankruptcy court jurisdiction).

[85] S. Rep. No. 989, 95th Cong., 2d Sess. 153 (1978).

[86] *In re* Unit Parts Co., 9 Bankr. 386, 389 (W.D. Okla. 1981).

[87] *Id.*

[88] 28 U.S.C.A. § 157(d) (West Supp. 1985).

involving the National Labor Relations Act."[89] Although direct judicial enforcement of the NLRA is provided for in a few narrow instances,[90] the act is most often thought of in terms of its unfair labor practice provisions, which are enforced through the quasi-judicial administrative processes of the NLRB. Withdrawal of an NLRA case from the bankruptcy court to the district court under section 157(d), however, necessarily presupposes proper jurisdiction of that case under section 1334.

Finally, even if an unfair labor practice proceeding does not fall within the literal language of section 1334, bankruptcy court jurisdiction can nevertheless be implied from the other sections of the Bankruptcy Code. The Court in *Nathanson,* for example, assumed that the bankruptcy court had the power to liquidate a claim arising under the NLRA, although it went on to hold that the court should normally defer to the NLRB.[91] The court in *Unit Parts* relied on section 502(c) to support its assertion of jurisdiction;[92] it noted that section 502(c) *requires* the bankruptcy court to estimate the amount of a contingent or unliquidated claim, when actual liquidation (by the NLRB in its unfair labor practice and backpay determination proceedings) "would unduly delay the closing of the case."[93] This requirement, if applicable to NLRA-based claims (and there is no reason to suggest that it is not), again presupposes that the threshold problem of jurisdiction under section 1334 has been crossed. Peter Jackson similarly argues that "the bankruptcy court's labor claim adjudication power can best be seen as an extension of its claim jurisdiction and injunctive power that is necessary to avoid discharge of labor claims."[94]

In sum, while the jurisdictional issue is a difficult one, it can be resolved. However, even assuming solution of the jurisdictional issue, there would still be enormous practical problems involved in litigating an unfair labor practice action in bankruptcy court. The NLRA forms and procedures—to say nothing of the complex relationship between the administrative law judge who hears the case, the board that finally decides it, and the court of appeals that

---

[89] 130 CONG. REC. H1850 (daily ed. Mar. 21, 1984) (statement of Rep. Kastenmeier).

[90] 29 U.S.C. §§ 160(j), 160(l), 161(2), 178, 185, 186(e), 187(b) (1982).

[91] The Court said that "the bankruptcy court *normally* should stay its hand pending an administrative decision," Nathanson v. NLRB, 344 U.S. 25, 30 (1952) (emphasis added), a grant of discretion which presupposes the bankruptcy court's jurisdiction to try the claim itself.

[92] *Unit Parts,* 9 Bankr. at 390.

[93] 11 U.S.C. § 502(c)(1) (1982).

[94] Jackson, *supra* note 64, at 43.

reviews it on a limited basis[95]—would all have to be jettisoned if the unfair labor practice charge were heard by the bankruptcy judge and treated like any other civil dispute. Such a radical change in procedures would undoubtedly affect the substantive result.

However, the greater practical difficulty lies in the substantive law itself. The NLRA is a complex statute with its own arcane terminology and a vast body of interpretative precedent. The enforcement scheme of this statute places primary enforcement responsibility on the administrative agency whose administrative law judges and board members supposedly have the expertise necessary for proper and consistent application of the law.[96] Judicial involvement normally comes only at the end of the process by way of limited federal appellate court review. It would be unrealistic to ask a bankruptcy court judge, who will usually have absolutely no prior experience with the complexities of labor law, to suddenly assume a role as the primary adjudicator of an unfair labor practice charge.

Moreover, while the purpose of giving section 1334 a broad reading is to insure that all the money claims against a debtor are consolidated and resolved in a single forum,[97] that purpose would not be served by the exercise of bankruptcy court jurisdiction over unfair labor practice claims. Such claims obviously fall under the mandatory withdrawal provisions of section 157(d).[98] And if someone other than the bankruptcy court is going to hear the claim anyway, it is undoubtedly better for the NLRB to hear it than the district court.

Therefore, the bankruptcy court should exercise jurisdiction (assuming that it even has jurisdiction) over an unfair labor practice charge only in the most extreme and compelling of situations.[99] If

---

[95] *See* Universal Camera Corp. v. NLRB, 340 U.S. 474 (1951). This restriction on elections presumably applies to other substantial corporate changes besides a fluctuating work force.

[96] Referring to bankruptcy and labor law, Durand v. NLRB, 296 F. Supp. 1049, 1055 (W.D. Ark. 1969), recognized that "[e]ach of those fields of law is a specialized one, and persons having day to day familiarity with one field may have little familiarity with or expertise in the other."

[97] *See supra* note 86 and accompanying text.

[98] *See supra* note 9.

[99] *Unit Parts,* while holding that a bankruptcy court had jurisdiction over NLRA claims, nevertheless conceded that "[m]any instances may arise wherein the Bankruptcy Courts will do well to abstain from pre-empting claim determinations by administrative bodies possessing special expertise where such neither delays, complicates nor clouds rehabilitation prospects. . . ." 9 Bankr. at 391. The court in *In re* Nicholas, Inc., 55 Bankr. 212, 216 (Bankr. D.N.J. 1985), stated that "[g]iven the inescapable weight of the authorities in support of the Board's exclusive jurisdiction, it is incumbent upon the debtor to demonstrate a cognizable reason for this court

the interests of bankruptcy law can be substantially satisfied in any other way, then that alternative ought to be pursued. Occasionally, the board may be able to deal with the problem by simply expediting its processes. Or, if the amount at stake is not extremely large, the bankruptcy court may simply set that amount aside to cover any potential liability by the debtor-in-possession and then proceed with confirmation of the plan. The board can then proceed at its own pace with the unfair labor practice charge. But the more probable, and possibly the most desirable, resolution of this conflict will often be through the avoidance of any formal adjudication. The debtor-in-possession, the union, and the general counsel of the NLRB all have a strong incentive to settle the dispute.[100] Although the interests of the other creditors may be compromised to some extent, the bankruptcy court should approve any settlement that appears reasonable.

A representation election proceeding is the last type of NLRB proceeding that may be subject to a bankruptcy court injunction. Under section 9 of the NLRA, upon petition and a showing of support for the union by at least thirty percent of the employees in an appropriate bargaining unit, the NLRB is empowered to conduct an election among these employees to determine if they desire union representation.[101] NLRB elections are often hotly contested and may involve considerable time and expense on the employer's part. Although there is no direct conflict between section 9's authorization of elections and any specific provision of the Bankruptcy Code, the reorganization period "is undoubtedly an inauspicious time to introduce into the affairs of the debtor any . . . industrial or economic instability.[102] Moreover, the election and its consequences may precipitate secondary or indirect conflicts. For example, during the pendency of an NLRB election, an employer is normally precluded from making changes which either improve or worsen wages, hours, or working conditions, if the purpose is to affect the election's outcome.[103] As a practical matter, any changes in the dynamic status quo will be deemed objectionable unless the employer can establish some justification unrelated to pendency of the election.[104] However, during a reorganization the debtor-in-possession will often need to

---

to override the presumptive jurisdiction of the N.L.R.B." The debtor was unable to do so in that case.

[100] This approach was urged upon the parties in *Durand,* 296 F. Supp. at 1054, but apparently without success.

[101] 29 U.S.C. § 159(e)(1982).

[102] *In re* American Buslines, Inc., 151 F. Supp. 877, 887 (D. Neb. 1957).

[103] NLRB v. Exchange Parts Co., 375 U.S. 405, 408–09 (1964).

[104] *See* American Sunroof Corp., 248 N.L.R.B. 748 (1980).

make changes in wages, hours, and working conditions. Saddling a debtor-in-possession with a duty not to make these changes unless it can satisfy a burden of justifying them before the NLRB will significantly inhibit any reorganization effort. Furthermore, if the union wins the election, a duty will arise on the part of the employer (through the debtor-in-possession or trustee) to recognize and bargain with this union over all matters involving wages, hours, and working conditions. This duty will then bring to a head the issues discussed earlier and all the complications that flow from them. Finally, a successful union election coupled with a subsequent sale of the facility will require the resolution of some of the difficult "successor" issues also discussed earlier.

While various bankruptcy law interests would be jeopardized by an NLRB election, the labor law interests in holding one are not especially strong. The board itself has recognized the impropriety of holding an election if the work force is fluctuating.[105] A Chapter 11 reorganization would certainly seem to qualify in that regard.[106]

Under the "threatened process" test, an NLRB election proceeding would seem to be the very kind of administrative action that a bankruptcy court should have discretion to enjoin. After the dust has cleared from the Chapter 11 reorganization, employees can make a more intelligent choice about whether they want to have a union represent them in the future. The courts, however, have been reluctant to issue such injunctions.

In *In re American Buslines, Inc.*,[107] the district court held that representation questions were within the exclusive jurisdiction of the NLRA and nothing in the Bankruptcy Act empowered it to enjoin election proceedings. More importantly, however, the court indicated that even if it had the power, it would not exercise it in this case. The trustee sought an injunction against a proceeding which involved a claim by the Brotherhood of Railroad Trainmen that it represented certain of the debtor's employees. Many of the debtor's employees, however, were already represented by two locals of the Amalgamated Association of Street, Electric Railway and

---

[105] *See* K-P Hydraulics Co., 219 N.L.R.B. 138 (1975).

[106] *But see* Coastal Plywood & Timber Co., 102 N.L.R.B. 300 (1953), in which the Board noted:

> There is no certainty that the Employer's operations will cease or change. Nor does the record disclose that any definite plans have yet been completed for closing or selling the Employer's plant. Accordingly, in the absence of evidence that the Employer will necessarily terminate its operations in the immediate future, we shall process the present [election] petition.

Id. at 300 n.1 (citations omitted).

[107] 151 F. Supp. 877 (D. Neb. 1957).

Motor Coach Employees of America with which the debtor had a collective bargaining agreement. Yet another union claimed to represent other of the debtor's employees. In spite of these facts, the court was unconvinced that the NLRB proceedings posed any threat of injury to the estate. It regarded the controversy essentially as being between several competing unions concerning who was entitled to represent which employees, and it noted "in theory at least, that problem is not the concern of the employer."[108] The court recognized that the trustee would be required to bargain with whomever the employees selected, but observed that "[i]t may not be assumed at the present time that these negotiations will either result in injury to the trust or even be rendered more onerous by the yet undeterminable identity of the employees' negotiators."[109]

The more recent case of *In re Continental Airlines Corp.*[110] reached essentially the same result. The Teamsters Union had originally been certified by the National Mediation Board (NMB) as the collective bargaining representative of all office, clerical, fleet service, and passenger service employees of Texas International Airlines (TIA). When TIA merged with Continental Airlines, the new company refused to recognize the union or to honor the collective bargaining agreement. After the Fifth Circuit upheld the company's refusal to bargain, the union filed an application with the NMB to divide the Continental workforce into three separate units, a division which Continental opposed. The board, however, approved an election in the units requested. Later, Continental filed under Chapter 11 of the Bankruptcy Code, and the bankruptcy court specifically stayed the election pursuant to the automatic stay provision.

On appeal to the district court, the union argued that the election was not a "proceeding against the debtor" under section 362(a)(1) of the automatic stay provisions, and that specific enforcement of the section against the NMB was thus inappropriate. The court found five different reasons for agreeing with the union on that point: (1) Continental's alleged lack of any legitimate interest in the representation proceeding; (2) Congress's intent that the debtor-in-possession continue to be subject to the Railway Labor Act; (3) prior cases giving a narrow construction to actions "against the debtor's property;" (4) the fact that neither purpose of the automatic stay (giving the debtor a breathing spell *from his creditors* and providing equality of distribution among all the creditors) would

[108] *Id.* at 887.
[109] *Id.*
[110] 50 Bankr. 342 (S.D. Tex. 1985).

be served by its application in this instance; and (5) the analogous *American Buslines* case.[111]

The district court then addressed the propriety of the stay from the perspective of section 105 of the Bankruptcy Code, which it admitted went beyond what is literally prohibited by the automatic stay provisions. The court focused on some legislative history which indicated that, when enjoining administrative agencies under section 105, bankruptcy courts should be most careful in "protecting the legitimate interests of the State."[112] It concluded that these state interests would be unduly jeopardized by even a *delay* in the NMB election.

That analysis, however, is fatally flawed. Although Congress presumably believed that election mechanisms of the RLA and the NLRA would in the long run promote industrial peace and thus serve the public interest,[113] Congress never suggested that this interest extends to any particular election. Indeed, administrative agencies were given a rather wide range of discretion to decide when, if at all, an election should be held. The public interest is remote; therefore, the court should have balanced this interest with the public's far more immediate and compelling interest in the successful reorganization of a major air carrier. The issue in the *Continental* case thus should have been whether the election would have significantly affected, interfered with, or threatened the Chapter 11 reorganization effort. Although the court stated in this context that "these NMB proceedings inflict little or no harm upon Continental,"[114] its conclusion in that regard seems to have been dictated more by devotion to the primacy of labor laws than by any realistic evaluation of the effect an immediate election would have on a Chapter 11 employer.

---

[111] *Id.* at 350–57.

[112] *Id.* at 358 (quoting H.R. Rep. No. 595, 95th Cong., 1st Sess. 6135 (1977)).

[113] Professor Richard Epstein's appraisal is a more realistic one. He observes that "[t]he present system of labor law is an elaborate form of special interest legislation that benefits some workers at the expense of other workers and society at large." N.Y. Times, July 21, 1985. § 3, at 2, col.6.

[114] *Continental,* 50 Bankr. at 358.

CHAPTER VIII

Bankruptcy Versus Arbitral Jurisdiction Over Disputes Arising Under a Debtor-Employer's Collective Bargaining Agreement[1]

The employer/employee relationship, though heavily regulated by statute, is still basically contractual in nature. In the unionized sector of the economy the collective bargaining agreement defines wages, hours, and other terms and conditions of employment for each employee represented by the union. Because of the complex and specialized nature of this contract, the parties customarily agree that all disputes arising under it will be resolved by private arbitration rather than the normal judicial processes.[2] Nourished by a favorable legal climate, labor arbitration has evolved into an extensive and sophisticated system of industrial jurisprudence, drawing its sustenance from the practices and traditions of the workplace, from the expertise of labor arbitrators, and from the fact that it deals with an ongoing relationship between an employer and the union that represents its employees.

When a business is or threatens to become insolvent, however, its contract and other legal disputes are normally removed to another specialized forum, that of bankruptcy. Which forum, then, has jurisdiction over a dispute arising under a labor contract of an employer who is also in bankruptcy? This chapter will explore the competing jurisdictional claims of bankruptcy and arbitration and suggest a possible accommodation.[3]

---

[1] Portions of this chapter originally appeared in Haggard, *Labor Arbitration and Bankruptcy: A Trek into the Serbonian Bog,* 17 LOYOLA UNIVERSITY L. J. 171 (1986).

[2] *See* A. ZACH & R. BLOCH, LABOR AGREEMENT IN NEGOTIATION AND ARBITRATION 83 (1983).

[3] *See generally* Berger, *The Collective Bargaining Agreement in Bankruptcy: Does the Duty to Arbitrate Survive?,* 35 LAB L.J. 685 (1984); Comment, *Partial Repudiation and the Survivability of Labor Arbitration Agreements in the Context of Bankruptcy,* 1 BANKR. DEV. J. 177 (1984). A similar conflict has arisen between the bankruptcy laws and the Federal Arbitration Act, 9 U.S.C. §§ 1–208 (1982), which manifests a

THE NATURE AND SCOPE OF THE COMPETING JURISDICTIONAL CLAIMS

Labor Arbitration

The jurisdictional claims of arbitration are firmly embedded in federal law. Section 203(d) of the National Labor Relations Act (NLRA) states that the preferred method for resolving industrial disputes is that chosen by the parties themselves.[4] In the vast majority of cases the parties negotiate a collective bargaining agreement which contains an arbitration clause.[5] Section 301 of the NLRA also gives the federal district courts jurisdiction over suits alleging violations of such agreements.[6] Moreover, in *Textile Workers Union v. Lincoln Mills,*[7] the Supreme Court held that section 301 authorized the federal courts to create a federal "common law" of labor contracts, one tenet of which was that arbitration provisions could be specifically enforced.[8]

Subsequently, in the famous *Steelworkers Trilogy*[9] of cases, the Court further enhanced the status of arbitration as the nearly exclusive forum for the resolution of labor contract disputes. In *United Steelworkers v. American Manufacturing Co.,*[10] the first case of the trilogy, the Court held that courts "have no business weighing the merits of the grievance, considering whether there is equity in a particular claim, or determining whether there is particular language in the written instrument which will support the claim."[11]

---

federal policy in favor of and facilitates the use of arbitration in commercial disputes. *See* Deitrick, *The Conflicting Policies Between Arbitration and Bankruptcy,* 40 Bus. Law. 33 (1984); Kreindler, *The Convergence of Arbitration and Bankruptcy,* 26 Arb. J. 34 (1971); Note, *Balancing Section 3 of the United States Arbitration Act and Section 1471 of the Bankruptcy Reform Act of 1978; A Bankruptcy Judge's Exercise of "Sound Discretion",* 53 Cin. L. Rev. 231 (1984); Note, *Bankruptcy Law—Arbitration Agreements in Bankruptcy Proceedings: The Clash Between Policies and the Proper Forum for Resolution,* 57 Temple L.Q. 855 (1984); Annot., 72 A.L.R. Fed. 890 (1985).

[4] 29 U.S.C. § 173(d) (1982).

[5] *See* 2 Collective Bargaining Negotiations and Contracts § 1:1 (BNA 1983) (grievance and arbitration provisions found in all 400 labor contracts examined in the BNA survey).

[6] 29 U.S.C. § 185 (1982).

[7] 353 U.S. 448 (1957).

[8] *Id.* at 456–58. At common law, executory agreements to arbitrate were revocable at any time by either party, and thus could not be specifically enforced. D. Nolan, Labor Arbitration Law and Practice 36 (1979).

[9] United Steelworkers v. American Mfg. Co., 363 U.S. 564 (1960); United Steelworkers v. Warrior & Gulf Navigation Co., 363 U.S. 574 (1960); United Steelworkers v. Enterprise Wheel & Car Corp., 363 U.S. 593 (1960).

[10] 363 U.S. 564 (1960).

[11] *Id.* at 568.

Rather, "[w]hether the moving party is right or wrong is a question of contract interpretation for the arbitrator."[12]

In *United Steelworkers v. Warrior & Gulf Navigation Co.,*[13] the second case in the trilogy, the Court indicated that the existence of a contractual duty to submit to arbitration is a threshold issue that the court must necessarily decide before it can order arbitration. Nonetheless, the Court, in order to avoid the possibility of inadvertently resolving the issue on the merits, held that "[a]n order to arbitrate the particular grievance should not be denied unless it may be said with positive assurance that the arbitration clause is not susceptible of any interpretation that covers the asserted dispute."[14] And in the final case of the trilogy, *United Steelworkers v. Enterprise Wheel & Car Corp.,*[15] the Court held that an arbitrator's decision is final on the merits; a reviewing court can set an arbitration award aside only if the arbitrator has clearly gone beyond the terms of the contract and the scope of his authority.[16] In sum, federal law posits that the arbitration forum should have virtually exclusive jurisdiction over labor contract disputes, leaving the federal district courts with only a narrow channeling and supervisory function.

Bankruptcy

The jurisdictional claims of bankruptcy, on the other hand, are more uncertain and complicated than those of the arbitration forum. Under the Bankruptcy Act of 1898 (the "1898 Act"),[17] the bankruptcy court had "summary jurisdiction" over two kinds of matters: proceedings in bankruptcy and controversies arising in proceedings in bankruptcy.[18] The former pertained to administrative and other matters internal to the bankruptcy system itself, and the latter were limited to matters in which the court had actual or constructive possession of the *res* involved in the dispute.[19] If a dispute did not fall within the summary jurisdiction of the Bankruptcy Court, then it was necessary for a party to bring a plenary action in a state court or the federal district court.[20]

[12] *Id.*

[13] 363 U.S. 574 (1960).

[14] *Id.* at 582–83.

[15] 363 U.S. 593 (1960).

[16] *Id.* at 596–97.

[17] Bankruptcy Act of 1898, ch. 541, 30 Stat. 544 (1898), amended by Chandler Act, ch. 575, 52 Stat. 883 (1938) (codified at 11 U.S.C. §§ 1–1200 (1976) (repealed 1979).

[18] *See generally* 2 Collier on Bankruptcy §§ 23.02–.06 (14th ed. 1976).

[19] *Id.*

[20] *Id.*

This divided jurisdiction proved unsatisfactory because of the delay that it caused and the expense it imposed on the bankruptcy estate.[21] Accordingly, Congress enacted the Bankruptcy Reform Act of 1978 (the "1978 Act"),[22] which significantly extended the jurisdiction of the bankruptcy courts by giving them original and exclusive jurisdiction over all "bankruptcy cases."[23] The 1978 Act also provided for original but not exclusive jurisdiction in the bankruptcy courts over all "civil proceedings arising out of, arising under, or relating to a bankruptcy proceeding."[24] The 1978 Act's broad jurisdictional grant give the bankruptcy court both in personam and in rem jurisdiction to handle everything that arises in a bankruptcy case.[25] As a result, actions that formerly had to be tried in state court or in federal district court, at great cost and delay to the estate, could now be tried in the bankruptcy courts.[26]

However, in *Northern Pipeline Construction Co. v. Marathon Pipe Line Co.,*[27] the Supreme Court held that this broad grant of jurisdiction was unconstitutional. The Court reasoned that the 1978 Act granted article III powers to the bankruptcy court which, because its judges were not appointed for life, was not itself an article III court.[28] Congress, after much travail and delay, finally responded to the *Marathon* decision in the Bankruptcy Amendments and Federal Judgeship Act of 1984 (BAFJA).[29] The jurisdictional provisions of BAFJA, which are patterned after the emergency rule promulgated by the Court following its *Marathon* decision, are extremely obscure and confusing. As one leading commentator recently put it, "[U]nderstanding the matter is not easy. At least until some gifted judicial mind definitively resolves certain matters, it defies simple summarization."[30] But in relevant part, this is what the law provides:

Section 1334(a) of the BAFJA states that "[e]xcept as provided in subsection (b) of this section, the district courts shall have orig-

---

[21] S. Rep. No. 989, 95th Cong., 2d Sess. 17 (1978) (referring to the need "to eliminate the serious delays, expense and duplications associated with the current dichotomy between summary and plenary jurisdiction").

[22] 11 U.S.C. §§ 1–1330 (1982 & Supp. I 1983); 28 U.S.C. §§ 1471–82 (1982).

[23] 28 U.S.C. §§ 1471(a),(c) (1982).

[24] 28 U.S.C. § 1471(b) (1982).

[25] H.R. Rep. No. 595, 95th Cong., 1st Sess. 445 (1977).

[26] *Id.*

[27] 458 U.S. 50 (1982).

[28] *Id.* at 87.

[29] Pub. L. No. 98-353, 98 Stat. 333 (1984).

[30] Cowans, *The Bankruptcy Court and its Jurisdiction,* 42 Bankr. 17, 25 (1984) (printed in supplement to advance sheet only; materials taken from ch. 1, §§ 1.1–1.4 of the forthcoming Cowans Bankruptcy Law and Practice, to be published by West Publishing Co.).

inal and *exclusive* jurisdiction of all cases under title 11 [the Bankruptcy Code]."[31] The exclusive jurisdiction covers the filing of the bankruptcy petition itself and the issuance of the final order for relief; how much more it covers is a matter of some dispute.[32] Section 1334(b) provides that the "the district courts shall have original but *not exclusive* jurisdiction of all civil proceedings arising under title 11, or arising in or related to cases under title 11."[33] The use of the phrases "arising under," "arising in," and "related to" was apparently intended to make federal bankruptcy jurisdiction as broad and all-encompassing as possible—although the precise meaning and constitutionally permitted scope of these terms has yet to be determined by the courts.[34]

Section 1334 of the BAFJA is very similar to section 1471 of the 1978 Act.[35] The difference, however, lies in the fact that section 1334 grants jurisdiction to the federal district court rather than to the bankruptcy court as such. Indeed, the 1984 Amendments contain no express grant of jurisdiction to any bankruptcy court—a change obviously intended to obviate the constitutional difficulty found by the Court in *Marathon Oil.* While section 1334 does not expressly grant jurisdiction to a bankruptcy court, section 151 of title 28 provides that "[in] each judicial district, the bankruptcy judges in regular active service shall constitute a unit of the district court to

---

[31] 28 U.S.C.A. § 1334(a) (West Supp. 1977–1984) (emphasis added).
[32] Cowans, *supra* note 30 at 27.
[33] 28 U.S.C.A. § 1334(b) (West Supp. 1977–1984) (emphasis added).
[34] *See* Cowans, *supra* note 30 at 28.
[35] Section 1471 of the 1978 Act provides:

> a) Except as provided in subsection (b) of this section, the district courts shall have original and exclusive jurisdiction of all cases under title 11. . . .
> b) Notwithstanding any Act of Congress that confers exclusive jurisdiction on a court or courts other than the district courts, the district courts shall have original but not exclusive jurisdiction of all civil proceedings arising under title 11. . . . or arising in or related to cases under title 11. . . .
> c) The bankruptcy court for the district in which a case under title 11 . . . is commenced shall exercise all of the jurisdiction conferred by this section on the district courts.
> d) Subsection (b) or (c) of this section does not prevent a district court or a bankruptcy court, in the interest of justice, from abstaining from hearing a particular proceeding arising under title 11 . . . or arising in or related to a case under title 11 . . . Such abstention, or a decision not to abstain, is not reviewable by appeal or otherwise.
> e) The bankruptcy court in which a case under title 11 . . . is commenced shall have exclusive jurisdiction of all of the property, wherever located, of the debtor, as of the commencement of such case.

28 U.S.C. § 1471 (1982).

Section 1334 of the 1984 Amendments provides: "The district courts shall have original jurisdiction exclusive of the courts of the States, of all matters and proceedings in bankruptcy." 28 U.S.C.A. § 1334 (West Supp. 1977–1984).

be known as the bankruptcy court for that district."[36] And section 157(a) of the same title states that "[e]ach district court *may* provide that any or all cases under title 11 and any or all proceedings arising under title 11 or arising in or related to a case under title 11 shall be referred to the bankruptcy judges for the district."[37] Notwithstanding the merely permissive nature of this grant of authority which suggests some degree of discretion on the part of the district courts, practice under the emergency rules and the probable intent of Congress suggest that the district court refer all section 1334 matters to the bankruptcy judges for initial consideration.[38] However, section 157(d) provides that for cause shown the district court may withdraw all or part of the cases it refers to the bankruptcy judge and that "the district court *shall,* on timely motion of a party, ... withdraw a proceeding [referred under this section] if the court determines that resolution of the proceeding requires consideration of both title 11 and other laws of the United States regulating organizations or activities affecting interstate commerce."[39]

Some of the matters that can be referred under section 157 are designated by the statute as "core proceedings."[40] As the name suggests, these are integral to the bankruptcy process itself, and Congress apparently intended that these particular matters should be dealt with by the bankruptcy court.[41] More specifically, "core proceedings" are matters over which the bankruptcy judge may issue final orders or judgments; unless the parties assent, only the district court may issue a final order or judgment over non-core proceedings.[42] Core proceedings include "matters concerning the administration of the estate,"[43] the "allowance or disallowance of claims against the estate,"[44] "counterclaims by the estate against persons filing claims against the estate,"[45] "motions to terminate, annul, or modify the automatic stay,"[46] "determinations as to the

---

[36] 28 U.S.C.A. § 151 (West Supp. 1968–1984).

[37] 28 U.S.C.A. § 157(a) (West Supp. 1968–1984 (emphasis added).

[38] *See generally* B. WIENTRAUB & A. RESNICK, BANKRUPTCY LAW MANUAL §§ 6.03, 6.03A (Cum. Supp. No. 2 1984); Developments, *Jurisdiction: A New System for the Bankruptcy Courts,* 2 BANKR. DEV. J. 1, 9, 13 (1985).

[39] 28 U.S.C.A. § 157(d) (West Supp.1968–1984) (emphasis added).

[40] 28 U.S.C.A. § 157(b)(2) (West Supp. 1968–1984).

[41] *See* King, *Jurisdiction and Procedure Under the Bankruptcy Amendments of 1984,* 38 VAND. L. REV. 675, 679–80 (1985).

[42] 28 U.S.C.A. § 157(c)(1) (West Supp. 1968–1984).

[43] 28 U.S.C.A. § 157(b)(2)(A) (West Supp. 1968–1984).

[44] 28 U.S.C.A. § 157(b)(2)(B) (West Supp. 1968–1984).

[45] 28 U.S.C.A. § 157(b)(2)(C) (West Supp. 1968–1984).

[46] 28 U.S.C.A. § 157(b)(2)(G) (West Supp. 1968–1984). The automatic stay referred to in the list of core proceedings applies to, among other things, "the commencement or continuation, including the issuance or employment of process, of a judicial,

dischargeability or particular debts,"[47] and "other proceedings affecting the liquidation of the assets of the estate or the adjustment of the debtor-creditor . . . relationship."[48] Each of these "other proceedings" is potentially relevant to the enforcement, through arbitration, of a collective bargaining agreement.[49]

To be sure, this collage of statutory provisions presents a confusing and obscure jurisdictional picture, and it is difficult to know where even some of the more traditional bankruptcy law issues fit into the statutory scheme. However, it does seem relatively clear that the statute gives bankruptcy judges the power to hear and finally resolve most breach of contract claims against the debtor or the estate[50]—subject, of course, to the district courts' exercise of the referral power, the assent of the parties in some instances, and the right to appeal.

FRAMING THE ISSUE

The question, then, is this: How can the jurisdiction of the bankruptcy forum over the debtor's general contract liabilities be reconciled with the jurisdiction of the arbitration forum over the debtor's breaches of a special kind of contract, the collective bargaining agreement? Or more precisely, as between the federal district court, the bankruptcy judge, and a labor arbitrator, *who* shall decide *which* issues?

There is no easy answer to the question. In resolving it one can, however, look to the literal words of BAFJA, to the broader purposes and policies of both bankruptcy and labor law, and to the cases that were decided under the 1978 and 1898 statutes, to the extent that they remain relevant. In addition, one would hope that a fair amount of common sense and due regard for the practicalities of the situation would influence the resolution of the issue.

---

administrative, *or other action or proceeding* against the debtor that was or could have been commenced before the commencement of the case under this title, or to recover a claim against the debtor that arose before the commencement of the case under this title. . . ." 11 U.S.C. § 362(a)(1) (Supp. II 1984) (emphasis added).

[47] 28 U.S.C.A. § 157(b)(2)(I) (West Supp. 1968–1984).

[48] 28 U.S.C.A. § 157(b)(2)(O) (West Supp. 1968–1984).

[49] 11 U.S.C. § 362(a)(1) (Supp. II 1984).

[50] "Contract claims, while not explicitly mentioned by § 157(a)(2)(B), are drawn squarely within the powers of the bankruptcy judge to determine the allowance or disallowance of claims." W. Norton & R. Lieb, Norton on Bankruptcy 105–06 (Monograph No. 1, 1985). The authors question the constitutionality of allowing a non-article III court to decide a breach of contract claim. *Id.* at 106–10.

ALLOCATING JURISDICTION: SOME GENERAL PRINCIPLES

The two sets of "jurisdictional" struggles which occur in this area are first, between the federal district court and the bankruptcy component of that court, and second, between the bankruptcy court and arbitration. Some general principles or "presumptions" about how jurisdiction ought to be allocated will be outlined first.

The District Court versus the Bankruptcy Court

The allocation of jurisdiction under the BAFJA, though obscure, recognizes that:

> [t]here are certain types of problems which seem to many people to be so inherently a part of what happens in a bankruptcy that it is agreed that the bankruptcy court should decide them ["core proceedings"]. At the other extreme are disputed rights and causes of action that involve no points of bankruptcy law and have no other connection with bankruptcy than that they are asserted by or against a debtor or trustee.[51]

Presumably, the bankruptcy court should hear cases falling in the first category, and the district court should hear the others. But those are the clear cases; the problem is with cases that fall between the two extremes.

One can, however, begin with the proposition that the 1978 Act was intended to vest the bankruptcy courts with as broad a jurisdiction as was possible.[52] The 1984 Amendments, which were necessitated by the *Marathon Oil* decision, should be read as narrowing that jurisdiction only to the extent necessary to obviate the constitutional problems. Thus, if there are labor contract issues involving a bankrupt employer which clearly require a judicial resolution, then the presumption should be that it is the bankruptcy court rather than the district court that should hear them, at least initially. In such a case the burden is on the party asserting district court jurisdiction to show that such a forum is either constitutionally or statutorily required.

---

[51] Cowans, *supra* note 30, at 25.

[52] The *House Report* states that "the combination of the three bases for jurisdiction, 'arising under title 11,' 'arising under a case under title 11,' and 'related to a case under title 11,' will leave no doubt as to the scope of the bankruptcy court's jurisdiction over disputes." H. R. Rep. No. 595, 95th Cong., 1st Sess. 445–46 (1977). Cowans states that in the above quoted sentence "the authors seem to be saying that . . . the bankruptcy court has jurisdiction in every way they could." Cowans, *supra* note 30, at 28.

The Bankruptcy Court versus an Arbitration Tribunal

The current Bankruptcy Code contains no express reference to arbitration or its relationship with the bankruptcy process.[53] Indirectly, however, section 1334(c)(1) permits absention "in the interest of justice."[54] Although this section is worded in terms of the "district court," it probably also applies to the bankruptcy court and could perhaps be used in favor of the arbitration forum in an appropriate case. Moreover, section 362(d)(1) allows for relief from the operation of the automatic stay,[55] again suggesting that in some instances a forum other than that of bankruptcy, such as arbitration, may be the proper one in which to resolve a particular issue. The question is *when* the arbitration forum should be used.

Courts should begin with the presumption that claims predicated on an alleged breach of a collective bargaining agreement should be established in the manner agreed to by the parties. As contemplated by federal law, this should be done through the arbitration process by a person with expertise in construing this type of contract.[56] But it is clear that a claim involving an interpretation of the federal Bankruptcy Code must be decided by the bankruptcy court itself. Among the issues that bankruptcy courts have reserved to themselves in the past, and which they should continue to reserve, are whether the duty to arbitrate survives a filing in bankruptcy,[57]

---

[53] Section 26 of the Bankruptcy Act of 1898 authorized the trustee in bankruptcy or the receiver to submit matters to arbitration and outlined the procedures that were to be followed. 11 U.S.C. § 49 (repealed 1978). This provision was omitted in the Bankruptcy Code, although an abbreviated version of it has been carried forward in Bankruptcy Rule 9019(c) which provides: "On stipulation of the parties to any controversy affecting the estate the court may authorize the matter to be submitted to final and binding arbitration." 11 U.S.C. Rule 9019(c) (Supp. II 1984). Some courts had held that these statutory arbitration procedures were intended to apply only where the parties had not otherwise agreed to arbitration. *See e.g.,* Truck Drivers Local 807 v. Bohack Corp., 541 F.2d 312, 319 (2d Cir. 1976), *on remand,* 431 F. Supp. 646 (E.D.N.Y.), *aff'd per curiam,* 567 F.2d 237 (2d Cir. 1977), *cert. denied,* 439 U.S. 825 (1978). *But see* Johnson v. England, 356 F.2d 44 (9th Cir.), *cert. denied,* 384 U.S. 961 (1966).

[54] 28 U.S.C.A. § 1334(c)(1) (West Supp. 1977–1984).

[55] 11 U.S.C. § 362(d)(1) (Supp. II 1984).

[56] *See In re* Smith Jones, Inc., 17 Bankr. 126, 128 (Bankr. D. Minn. 1981) (suggesting that while "certain exigent circumstances" might justify denial of the arbitration forum, this would be an "extraordinary action" which this court would not take when the grievance involves merely a wrongful discharge); *In re* Continental Airlines Corp., 60 Bankr. 472, 479 (Bankr. S.D. Tex. 1986) (court refused to defer to arbitration because there was nothing "technical and esoteric" about the issue and because the court felt that it knew more about the background facts than an arbitrator would).

[57] *See* Truck Drivers Local 807 v. Bohack Corp., 431 F. Supp. 646, 655 (E.D.N.Y.), *aff'd per curiam,* 567 F.2d 237 (2d Cir. 1977), *cert. denied,* 439 U.S. 925 (1978).

the effect of a court-approved rejection of the contract,[58] the extent to which an order confirming a reorganization plan operates as a discharge of workers' claims under the contract,[59] and the status and priority of contract claims.[60]

The difficulty arises when the underlying issue is basically one of contract interpretation rather than bankruptcy law as such, but an arbitration decision on that issue might nevertheless impact negatively on legitimate bankruptcy interests. In this situation the general rule should be that the policy in favor of arbitration must bend to the policy in favor of the primacy of bankruptcy court jurisdiction. The interests of creditors in the assets of the estate and of society as a whole in the successful revitalization of the business should take precedence over the narrow interests of the employer and its employees in obtaining the bargained-for forum for resolution of their contract disputes.[61]

---

[58] Truck Drivers Local 807 v. Bohack Corp., 541 F.2d 312, 320–21 (2d Cir. 1976), *on remand,* 431 F. Supp. 646 (E.D.N.Y.), *aff'd per curiam,* 567 F.2d 237 (2d Cir. 1977), *cert. denied,* 439 U.S. 825 (1978).

[59] L.O. Koven & Bros. v. Local 5767, United Steelworkers, 381 F.2d 196, 201 (3d Cir. 1967).

[60] Truck Drivers Local 807 v. Bohack Corp., 541 F.2d 312, 321 n.15 (2d Cir. 1976), *on remand,* 431 F.Supp. 646 (E.D.N.Y.), *aff'd per curiam,* 567 F.2d 237 (2d Cir. 1977), *cert. denied,* 439 U.S. 825 1978); *see also* L.O. Koven & Bros. v. Local 5767, United Steelworkers, 381 F.2d 196, 205–06 (3d Cir. 1967) (whether vacation benefits constituted wages for priority purposes); Johnson v. England, 356 F.2d 44, 51 (9th Cir.), *cert. denied,* 384 U.S. 961 (1966) (whether the claimed monies were "trust funds" and whether employees were entitled to a preference in payment); *In re* Penn Fruit Co., 1 Bankr. 714 (Bankr. E.D. Pa. 1979) (whether a claim was entitled to priority as an administrative expense); *accord In re* Braniff Airways, Inc., 33 Bankr. 33 (Bankr. N.D. Tex. 1983).

[61] L.O. Koven & Bros. v. Local 5767, United Steelworkers, 381 F.2d 196, 205 (3d Cir. 1967).

> [W]e hold that questions involving an interpretation of the Bankruptcy Act should be decided by the court, while questions involving an interpretation of the collective bargaining agreement should *if feasible* be decided by the arbitrator, *unless they involve special bankruptcy interests.* If such interests are present, then the proper forum should be dictated by the needs of the particular case, and this is a matter best left to the discretion of the trial court.

Id. (emphasis added). The court expressly recognized that some issues may affect bankruptcy interests even though their resolution does not necessarily involve an interpretation of bankruptcy law as such. *Id.* at 202. The *Koven* court further held that the effect of a release on claims later asserted by the union was a matter for the arbitrator to decide, since the interests of the receiver were not involved and since the decision on that issue would have no effect on claims actually processed in the Chapter 11 proceeding. *Id.* at 204.

FACTORS MILITATING AGAINST DEFERRAL TO ARBITRATION

If the accepted principle is that arbitrators should decide contract disputes unless those disputes implicate important bankruptcy interests, then the next determination is what those interests are and how they might be jeopardized by the use of arbitration. One area of concern involves the remedies or relief that an arbitrator might order. For example, in *Local 807, International Brotherhood of Teamsters v. Bohack Corp.*,[62] the bankruptcy court had authorized the arbitrator to decide whether the contract rejected by the employer should be specifically enforced by the reinstatement of each employee who had been laid off by the alleged breach. The district court felt that such a remedy would encroach upon the prerogatives of bankruptcy. The district court noted that "in allowing rejection of the contract, the bankruptcy judge found that Bohack could not attain financial viability and at the same time employ Local 807 drivers. If the arbitrator is now allowed to reinstate terminated employees, the rejection of the contract becomes meaningless."[63]

Similarly, in *Local 692, United Food Workers v. Pantry Pride*,[64] the union first petitioned the bankruptcy court for relief from an automatic stay so that it could sue to compel arbitration. The petition was granted, but on the condition that no court or arbitrator would have jurisdiction "to interfere with the going-out-of-business sales presently being conducted by the debtors, the sale of leases, or the closing of the Baltimore area stores."[65] The union then sued to compel arbitration and for an injunction compelling the employer to continue to provide health care coverage pending the outcome of that arbitration. The district court granted the motion to compel arbitration, but denied the injunction. The court reasoned that the union's sole remedy against Pantry Pride for closing its stores was monetary damages. Neither the district court nor an arbitration forum had the jurisdiction or authority to stop the closing of the area stores or to preserve the jobs of the affected employees. Even after arbitration Pantry Pride would not be required to continue paying health and welfare premiums.[66]

---

[62] 431 F. Supp. 646 (E.D.N.Y.), *aff'd per curiam,* 567 F.2d 237 (2d Cir. 1977), *cert. denied,* 439 U.S. 825 (1978).

[63] *Id.* at 654 (footnote omitted).

[64] 522 F. Supp. 1009 (D. Md. 1981).

[65] *Id.* at 1014.

[66] *Id.*; *see infra* text accompanying notes 129–39.

Even if an arbitrator is allowed to determine the amount of damages arising from a breach of contract, the bankruptcy court should still have ultimate jurisdiction over enforcement of the award.[67] This will allow the court to determine the status and priority of the claim[68] and whether it is subject to equitable subordination.[69]

In the past, some courts have declined to defer to arbitration if the grievance involved a monetary claim that would have to be paid out of funds in which other creditors also had an interest. For example, in *Johnson v. England,*[70] the union demanded arbitration over the debtor-employer's past failure to fund adequately a pension plan as required by the collective bargaining agreement. The Ninth Circuit held that this was not an appropriate issue for arbitral determination. The court, emphasizing that this case involved a complete liquidation of the business rather than merely a reorganization, noted that:

> [t]his does not present the type of grievance which is ordinarily the subject of arbitration under a collective bargaining agreement pursuant to § 301(a) [of the NLRA]. Such controversies usually involve disputes between the union and the current operating employer and are generally of such character that they lend themselves most readily to solution through arbitration. In that type of case the arbitrators "sit to settle disputes at the plant level—disputes that require for their solution knowledge of the customs and practices of a particular factory or of a particular industry as reflected in particular agreements."[71]

The court also noted that although the employer had breached the contract, "the result was merely that the employees became creditors to the extent of that default,"[72] with just another claim on the assets of the debtor-employer. Thus, the court concluded that "the controversy which now arises is between two groups of cred-

---

[67] *See e.g., In re* Allen & Hein, Inc., 59 Bankr. 733 (Bankr. S.D. Cal. 1986); *In re* Sterling Mining Co., 21 Bankr. 66 (Bankr. W.D. Va. 1982); *In re* Smith Jones, Inc., 17 Bankr. 126, 128 (Bankr. D. Minn. 1981); *see also* Gottfried Baking Co., 46 Lab. Arb. (BNA) 386 (Benewitz, Arb., 1966); Marathon City Brewing Co., 45 Lab. Arb. (BNA) 453 (McCormick, Arb., 1965).

[68] *See supra* note 60.

[69] P. Murphy, Creditors' Rights in Bankruptcy § 9-6 (1982). *See generally* DeNatale & Abram, *The Doctrine of Equitable Subordination As Applied to Nonmanagement Creditors,* 40 Bus. Law. 417 (1985).

[70] 356 F.2d 44 (9th Cir.), *cert. denied,* 384 U.S. 961 (1966); *see also In re* F & T Contractors, Inc., 649 F.2d 1229, 1232 (6th Cir. 1981) (commercial arbitration); *In re* Continental Airlines Corp., 60 Bankr. 472, 478–79 (Bankr. S.D. Tex. 1986). *In re* Brookhaven Textiles, 21 Bankr. 204, 207 (Bankr. S.D.N.Y. 1982) (commercial arbitration).

[71] 356 F.2d at 51 (quoting United Steelworkers v. Enterprise Wheel & Car Corp., 363 U.S. 593, 596 (1960)).

[72] 356 F.2d at 51.

itors. . . . On the one hand we have the employees and on the other we have the other general creditors such as creditors for merchandise sold."[73] The court reasoned that "a decision of an arbitrator here would involve interests of parties who never consented to arbitration, namely, the trustee in bankruptcy and the general creditors. They ought not to be bound by the decision of an arbitrator selected by the employer and the union."[74]

The court's reasoning, however, is not persuasive on either point. The assertion that the dispute was not of the kind ordinarily handled by arbitration was apparently predicated on the belief that arbitrators function more as informal mediators of disputes about working conditions and employment practices[75] than as adjudicators of claims for monetary amounts, and that bankruptcy should thus defer to arbitration only when the former function is being performed, rather than the latter. This is a two-fold misconception. The subject matter or arbitration involves both kinds of disputes, and in either event the arbitrator's exclusive function is to construe the contract, not to act as some roving, ad hoc "problem solver." Moreover, the expertise of a labor arbitrator is in construing the specialized contract, whether the dispute involves an alleged failure to follow agreed-upon work practices, an alleged breach of the duty to pay the agreed-upon wages, or an alleged breach of the duty to pay into the pension fund, as in *Johnson v. England.*[76] In sum, federal policy in favor of arbitration does not recognize the distinction the *Johnson* court was apparently drawing between various types of arbitral disputes.

Also, the fact that, in *Johnson,* the union's pension fund claims would have to be paid out of the liquidation assets of the employer does not necessarily mean that only the bankruptcy court could decide the claim. Indeed, the *Johnson* court suggested that another form of arbitration could be resorted to in order to determine the

---

[73] *Id.*

[74] *Id; see* L.O. Koven & Bros. v. Local 5767, United Steelworkers, 381 F.2d 196, 203 (3d Cir. 1967); *accord In re* Ludwig Honold Mfg. Co., 22 Bankr. 436 (Bankr. E.D. Pa. 1982), *aff'd sub nom.* Zimmerman v. Continental Airlines, Inc., 712 F.2d 55 (3d Cir. 1983), *cert. denied,* 464 U.S. 1038 (1984).

[75] *See In re* F & T Contractors, Inc., 649 F.2d 1229 (6th Cir. 1981).

> Now, if this were a situation where the internal affairs of the Defendant [the bankrupt employer], based upon maybe its rules of procedures such as a union might have, were at issue, working conditions, et cetera, then I would think that this would be particularly within the realm of arbitration, but every one of these issues . . . are tried out every day before a Court as a part of a law suit.

Id. at 1232–33.

[76] *See Johnson,* 356 F.2d at 51–52; *supra* note 53 and accompanying text.

amount of the claim, namely, the arbitration forum provided for by the 1898 Act itself.[77] But if another forum can decide the amount, then it would seem that the forum used should be the one that the parties themselves have selected. If the theory is that an arbitrator is required in order to construe properly the terms of a collective bargaining agreement, then the *amount* of money to which the claimants have a right (an issue which the court said someone else could decide) is inexorably connected to the *forum* that the parties have selected for the resolution of the controversy. The fact that the other creditors have not consented to that forum is no more relevant than the fact that they have also not consented to a contract giving the employees a pension fund in *any* amount.

The Supreme Court has stated that "an arbitration agreement must be enforced notwithstanding the presence of other persons who are parties to the underlying dispute but not to the arbitration agreement."[78] Moreover, if the amount to which the employees are contractually entitled is fairly determined by a labor arbitrator,[79] the status and priority of that claim are still subject to determination by the bankruptcy court. There the interests of the other creditors can be adequately protected.

The fact that the *Johnson* case involved a straight bankruptcy rather than a reorganization may be relevant in another respect, however. In a reorganization, the contracting employer generally will also be appointed the debtor in possession, and it is this combined entity that will defend against the union's claim before the arbitrator. The cost of this defense is no greater than it would be in a non-Chapter 11 situation. But in a straight bankruptcy, the contracting employer fades out of the picture, and the responsibility for contesting claims against the estate falls on the appointed trustee.[80] This trustee will normally be an attorney who, though

---

[77] *Id.*

[78] Moses H. Cone Memorial Hosp. v. Mercury Constr. Corp., 460 U.S. 1, 20 (1983).

[79] The *Johnson* court implied that it would not be fair for the other creditors to be bound by the decision of an arbitrator picked only by the now defunct employer and the contracting union. 356 F.2d at 51. Similarly, if only the employer had standing to contest the union's claim in the arbitration forum, resort to that forum would be obviously unfair since, in a straight bankruptcy, the employer may lack both the interest and the resources to contest adequately the claim against the estate. Neither concern, however, is valid. The trustee in a straight bankruptcy would assume the employer's responsibilities both in selecting the arbitrator and defending against the claim.

[80] In Coar v. Brown, 29 Bankr. 806, 807 (N.D. Ill. 1983), the court emphasized that the trustee, as a representative of the other creditors, had never agreed to arbitration. That is true, but irrelevant; the trustee inherited both the rights and the duties of

familiar with business and commercial matters, may be totally unfamiliar with the practice and procedure of labor arbitration. The retention of special labor counsel may be required, thus putting an additional financial burden on the estate. Of course, even if the litigation occurs in court rather than before an arbitrator, the trustee may still find it necessary to retain labor counsel to deal with the substantive issues. In any event, this is a matter that the courts should take into account in deciding whether or not to defer to arbitration.

Two other factors that the courts sometimes consider, albeit sometimes in the context of deferral under a commercial rather than a labor arbitration agreement, are the delaying effect deferral may have on the bankruptcy proceeding itself and the underlying unfairness of forcing the bankrupt (or its representative) into a forum which may lack adequate discovery procedures.[81] These considerations usually arise when the bankrupt himself files a breach of contract claim against another party, that party demures on the ground that the contract calls for the arbitration of disputes arising under it, and the bankrupt raises delay and lack-of-discovery issues. The interests of bankruptcy clearly dictate that the bankrupt's claims against third parties be resolved as quickly as possible and that the success of this litigation not be hampered by the inadequacy of discovery and other processes, since this will affect the size of the estate.

These concerns are equally pressing when labor arbitration is at issue. Although labor arbitration was originally thought of as a speedy and inexpensive alternative to litigation, in recent years it has become increasingly slow and costly.[82] Moreover, discovery and other forms of compulsory process are somewhat limited in the

---

the debtor under the contract being sued upon, even though the trustee consented to neither.

[81] *See, e.g., In re* Flechtner Packing Co., 63 Bankr. 585, 587 (Bankr. N.D. Ohio 1986); *In re* Cross Elec. Co., 9 Bankr. 408, 412 (Bankr. W.D. Va. 1981).

[82] One commentator has estimated that a normal arbitration case with a one-day hearing costs each party $2,200 or more and that the average time from the filing of the grievance to the issuance of the award is eight months. LABOR RELATIONS YEARBOOK 1977, at 206 (BNA 1978). In *In re* Allen & Hein, Inc., 59 Bankr. 733 (Bankr. S.D. Cal. 1986), the court, noting the slow pace of the reorganization, found that the debtor had failed to demonstrate that arbitration would be any less expeditious than a bankruptcy resolution of the issue. The court also found that since a substantial amount of money had already been expended on the arbitration at the time the petition was filed, it would be more expensive to relitigate the issue in bankruptcy than it would be to simply allow the arbitration to proceed by lifting the stay. *But see In re* Flechtner Packing Co., *supra,* note 81 (citing delay and cost as grounds for non-deferral).

arbitration context.[83] Courts must be sensitive to these concerns. If the interests of the estate or other creditors would be adversely affected by delay or other procedural inadequacies, then the court should either refuse to defer to arbitration or defer only on the condition that the arbitration be conducted in a manner that may go beyond the scope of the collective bargaining agreement.[84]

These are the factors that militate against deferral to arbitration. However, in some instances, deferral to arbitration may actually enhance, rather than harm, the interests of other creditors—and thus serve, rather than retard, the purposes of bankruptcy. For example, some courts have noted that deferral to arbitration is particularly appropriate when it promotes "labor peace."[85] Such courts are apparently referring to the legal theory that treats arbitration as the substitute for industrial strife (strikes).[86] If an employer can be compelled to arbitrate an issue, then the union cannot go out on strike over it.[87] But if the same issue is not going to be resolved by arbitration and is, rather, going to be resolved by the bankruptcy court, this presumably frees the union from its contractual "no-strike" obligations.[88] It is widely recognized that a strike against an employer who has gone into a Chapter 11 reorganization may be devastating.[89] Indeed, it may defeat the entire reorganization effort and drive the business into a total liquidation to the considerable detriment of the creditors. Thus, where there is the likelihood of a strike, bankruptcy law interests may weigh in favor of arbitration rather than against it.

This "labor peace" theory, however, is valid only if the strike is not subject to the automatic stay provisions of the Bankruptcy Code or could not otherwise be enjoined under the bankruptcy court's section 105 equity powers—an issue over which there is considerable

---

[83] *See* O. Fairweather, Practice and Procedure in Labor Arbitration 133–59 (2d ed. 1983).

[84] *Accord* Alexander v. Gardner-Denver Co., 415 U.S. 36, 60 n.21 (1974).

[85] *See, e.g.,* Truck Drivers Local 807 v. Bohack Corp., 431 F. Supp. 646, 653 (E.D.N.Y.), *aff'd per curiam,* 567 F.2d 237 (2d Cir. 1977), *cert. denied,* 439 U.S. 825 (1978); *In re* Muskegon Motor Specialties Co., 313 F.2d 841, 843 (6th Cir.), *cert. denied sub nom.* International Union, UAW v. Davis, 375 U.S. 832 (1963).

[86] *See* United Steelworkers v. American Mfg. Co., 363 U.S. 564, 567 (1959).

[87] Boys Markets, Inc., v. Retail Clerks Local 770, 398 U.S. 235, 254 (1970).

[88] *See In re* Smith Jones, Inc., 17 Bankr. 126, 127–28 (Bankr. D. Minn. 1981).

[89] In Truck Drivers Local 807 v. Bohack Corp., 541 F.2d 312 (2d Cir. 1976), *on remand.* 431 F. Supp. 646 (E.D.N.Y.), *aff'd per curiam,* 567 F.2d 237 (2d Cir. 1977), *cert. denied,* 439 U.S. 825 (1978), the court of appeals noted that "[t]he argument is made that to allow picketing in the case of this financially troubled debtor is to put it out of business. That is, unfortunately, sometimes the sad outcome when a union and an employer cannot come to terms." *Id.* at 318; *see also* Crowe & Assoc., Inc. v. Bricklayers Local 2, 713 F.2d 211, 216 (6th Cir. 1983); Briggs Transp. Co. v. Teamsters, 116 L.R.R.M. (BNA) 2241, 2244 (D. Minn. 1984).

dispute.[90] Moreover, "labor peace" is a relevant consideration only in the context of a Chapter 11 reorganization. If the case involves a straight bankruptcy and the employer has already gone out of business, then there is nothing for the union to strike against and the "labor peace" issue does not even come into consideration.

The interests of bankruptcy may be infringed or enhanced by arbitration in other ways as well. The point, however, is that the effect of arbitration on bankruptcy interests is the critical factor in deciding whether a labor contract issue should be resolved by an arbitrator or by the bankruptcy court.[91]

TRACKING A PATH THROUGH THE JURISDICTIONAL MAZE: A LOOK AT SPECIFIC SITUATIONS IN WHICH THE ISSUE MAY ARISE

The jurisdictional frameworks of arbitration and bankruptcy have been described, some general principles have been proposed, and the interests that must be taken into account in applying those principles have been identified in part. We can now address the more specific situations in which the triangular conflict among district court, bankruptcy court, and arbitration is most likely to occur.

When the Grievance Occurs During Bankruptcy Proceedings

Under section 1113 of the Bankruptcy Code, a collective bargaining agreement remains in full force and effect until its rejection is approved by the bankruptcy judge or other interim relief is allowed.[92] Thus, the debtor in possession or trustee has the contractual duty to adhere to the substantive provisions of the agreement *and* the duty to arbitrate any alleged breaches of those provisions.

With respect to such an alleged breach, one of three things might happen. First, the parties (employer and union) may agree that the grievance over the alleged breach is arbitrable and may be perfectly willing to proceed with the arbitration process. Second, the employer may contend that the grievance is not arbitrable, that the bankruptcy court should decide the issue itself, or both. And third, while

---

[90] *See generally* Haggard, *The Power of the Bankruptcy Court to Enjoin Strikes: Resolving the Apparent Conflict Between the Bankruptcy Code and the Anti-Injunction Provisions of the Norris-LaGuardia Act,* 53 Geo. Wash. L. Rev. 703 (1985); Comment, *The Automatic Stay of the 1978 Bankruptcy Code Versus the Norris-LaGuardia Act: A Bankruptcy Court's Dilemma,* 61 Tex. L. Rev. 321 (1982).

[91] *See In re* Muskegon Motor Specialties Co., 313 F.2d 841, 843 (6th Cir.), *cert. denied sub nom.* International Union, UAW v. Davis, 375 U.S. 832 (1963).

[92] 11 U.S.C. § 1113(f) (Supp. II 1984).

the union may be content to have the grievance heard and resolved by the bankruptcy judge, the employer may insist that the arbitration forum be used, as provided for in the contract. Problems can arise under each scenario.

First, although the parties themselves may be willing to submit to arbitration, once a bankruptcy petition is filed the parties cannot simply proceed in blithe disregard of the jurisdiction of the bankruptcy tribunal.[93] As one court has noted, "there must be judicial control over the exercise of the right to arbitrate just as there is over other rights and duties of the bankrupt. For now [in bankruptcy], an additional consideration has been added, the rights of the creditors."[94] This is particularly true with respect to breaches that occur between the time of filing and the court's approval of the rejection of the contract, and with respect to the liabilities the debtor in possession incurs as a result of these breaches. These are technically classified as "administrative expenses," which section 157 includes within the list of "core proceedings"[95] (that is, matters within the presumed unique expertise of the bankruptcy court).

In *L. O. Koven & Brothers v. Local 5767, United Steelworkers,*[96] the union asserted a claim for vacation benefits arising during three periods: prior to the bankruptcy filing, during the bankruptcy proceeding itself, and after the order of confirmation.[97] The Third Circuit held that during the bankruptcy proceedings "the bankruptcy court [has] the exclusive right and duty under its basic custodial power to decide what were proper administration expenses and to shield the estate from unnecessary and improvident expenditures." The court further noted that "until any expense was allowed by the bankruptcy court as an administrative expense, Koven had no obligation to pay it."[98] Thus, although the court allowed arbitration over the portions of the vacation pay claims that were attributable to the prefiling period and to the period following the order of confirmation, the bankruptcy court itself was held to be the proper forum to consider the eligibility and amount of vacation pay claims that accrued during the reorganization period.

Although the court in *Koven* was undoubtedly correct in concluding that the allowance of "administrative expenses" was within

---

[93] Truck Drivers Local 807 v. Bohack Corp., 541 F.2d 312, 320 (2d Cir. 1976), *on remand,* 431 F. Supp. 646 (E.D.N.Y.), *aff'd per curiam,* 567 F.2d 237 (2d Cir. 1977), *cert. denied,* 439 U.S. 825 (1978).

[94] *Id.*

[95] 28 U.S.C.A. § 157(b)(2)(A) (West Supp. 1968–1984).

[96] 381 F.2d 196 (3d Cir. 1967).

[97] *Id.* at 199.

[98] *Id.* at 208 (footnote omitted).

the exclusive purview of the bankruptcy court, there is no reason why the amount of those expenses could not have been determined by the arbitrator when it determined the amount of vacation benefits that arose during the other two periods. This was the approach taken in *In re Penn Fruit Co.,*[99] in which the court held that:

> [a]lthough the determination of whether a claim is entitled to priority as an administrative expense is within the province of the bankruptcy court, the determination of the amount due employees who have filed grievances under the collective bargaining agreement is a contractual matter which . . . should be decided according to the procedure to which both the debtor in possession and the employees (through the union) agreed and by which both are bound.[100]

The procedure for accomplishing this result is provided in section 1334(c)(1) of the 1984 Amendments,[101] which allows the court, "in the interest of justice," to abstain from hearing a particular proceeding arising under Chapter 11 or arising in or related to a case under Chapter 11.[102] If deference to arbitration is otherwise appropriate, it would seem that the fact that the grievance arose during the bankruptcy proceeding itself should not be controlling, and that in such a situation abstention under section 1334(c)(1) is appropriate.

Under the second scenario, where the employer refuses to submit the grievance to arbitration, the union will have additional problems. If the employer were not in bankruptcy, the union would simply file a NLRA section 301 action, and the federal district court would use the *Warrior Gulf* criteria to determine whether or not the grievance was arbitrable under the contract.[103] But when the employer is in bankruptcy, presumably any action against it that is filed in the federal district court will be automatically referred to the bankruptcy court. This referral, however, is subject to section 157(d) of the Bankruptcy Code, which requires the district court, on timely motion of any party, to withdraw from the bankruptcy judge any proceeding which involves a construction of both the Bankruptcy Code and a federal law regulating interstate commerce.[104] An action to enforce the arbitration provisions of a collective bargaining agreement arises under section 301 of the NLRA and involves an interpretation of section 301 "common-law" standard of arbitrability articulated in *Warrior Gulf.* Moreover, the legislative history of section 157(d) of the Bankruptcy Code, though

[99] 1 Bankr. 714 (Bankr. E.D. Pa. 1979).
[100] *Id.* at 716–17.
[101] 28 U.S.C.A. § 1334(c)(1) (West Supp. 1977–1984).
[102] *Id.*
[103] *See supra* text accompanying note 13.
[104] *See supra* text accompanying note 39.

scant, does cite the National Labor Relations Act (and that presumably includes the Taft-Hartley Act amendments) as the kind of nonbankruptcy federal statute to which the mandatory withdrawal provision was intended to apply.[105] It would thus seem that the district court is required, pursuant to appropriate motion, to withdraw from the bankruptcy court an action to compel arbitration.

This allocation of jurisdiction between the district court and the bankruptcy court certainly is reasonable when the employer's only defense is that the grievance is not in fact arbitrable under the contract. Federal district courts have traditionally handled this issue, while the bankruptcy courts have not. Therefore, if there is no danger that an arbitration award will somehow impinge upon the prerogatives of the bankruptcy system, or if any such danger will be obviated by the bankruptcy court's ultimate control over the enforcement of the award, then the district court appears to be the proper forum for resolution of the arbitrability issue.

This jurisdictional dilemma is complicated further if, in addition to the employer's traditional section 301 defenses, a claim is also made (by the employer or some other interested party) that deferral to arbitration is not appropriate for reasons related to the proper administration of the bankruptcy laws. Section 157(d) of the Bankruptcy Code still seems to require that the district court resolve the NLRA section 301 arbitrability issue. And while bankruptcy court input on the bankruptcy law implications might seem desirable, the Bankruptcy Code apparently does not contemplate a bifurcated proceeding of that nature. Thus the district court will of necessity determine both the labor law and the bankruptcy law issues.[106]

On the other hand, if the employer's objections to arbitration pertain solely to arbitration's alleged impact on bankruptcy interests and processes, then it appears that the bankruptcy court is the forum in which those determinations should be made. The mandatory withdrawal provisions of section 157(d) might be avoided by arguing that such a case does not in fact require "consideration of" a nonbankruptcy law. The legislative history suggests that actual consideration is required.[107] Indeed, one court has held that this

---

[105] 130 CONG. REC. H1849–50 (daily ed. March 21, 1984) (remarks of Rep. Kastenmeier).

[106] *See, e.g.,* International Union, UAW v. Miles Machinery Co., 113 L.R.R.M. (BNA) 3616 (E.D. Mich. 1982) (district court decided a combination of section 301 labor law and bankruptcy law issues).

[107] "The district court should withdraw such proceedings only if the court determines ... that other laws regulating organizations affecting interstate commerce *are in fact likely to be considered.*" 130 CONG. REC. S6081 (daily ed. June 19, 1984) (remarks of Sen. DeConcini) (emphasis added).

consideration must be of a "substantial and material" nature,[108] and another has held that unless the section is "narrowly construed" it "could create substantial potential difficulties in the administration of this bankruptcy case and to the bankruptcy system in general."[109] Thus, although an action to enforce an arbitration agreement will necessarily involve section 301 in the sense that it provides the basis for federal jurisdiction, that alone should not be deemed sufficient to trigger the mandatory withdrawal provision.[110]

In any event, if the case is not withdrawn from the bankruptcy court and that court determines that arbitration would impinge upon legitimate bankruptcy interests, the bankruptcy judge should proceed to resolve the contract issue himself. But if, as is more likely to be the case, the bankruptcy judge determines that arbitration would not have that impact (and assuming that there are no genuine section 301 issues at stake), then he should have the power to order the employer to submit to arbitration. Since this determination does not appear to be within the definition of a "core proceeding," the bankruptcy judge's findings of fact and conclusions of law will still have to be submitted to the district court for the entry of a final order.[111] But despite the apparent cumbersomeness of this process (in contrast to allowing the district court to decide the issue in the first instance), the expertise of the bankruptcy judge appears necessary here.

Finally, there is the problem of inducing a union to use arbitration when it, but not the debtor-employer, would prefer to litigate the contract dispute in the bankruptcy forum. As a general rule, a union with a grievance against an employer is not affirmatively required to use the arbitration process, but it must use that process before it can pursue other relief. That is, in the nonbankruptcy context, if the union files a section 301 breach of contract action in federal district court, the employer will simply move to have the action dismissed for failure to exhaust contract remedies.[112] But when the employer is in bankruptcy, the situation again becomes more complicated. Here, the breach of contract claim is automatically referred

---

[108] *In re* White Motor Corp., 42 Bankr. 693, 704 (Bankr. N.D. Ohio 1984). *See also In re* Continental Airlines Corp., 60 Bankr. 459, 461 (Bankr. S.D. Tex. 1986) (applies only when resolution would "require direct interpretation or application of the statutory language of [a] . . . federal statute regulating interstate commerce").

[109] *Id.* at 462.

[110] *See* W. Norton & R. Lieb, *supra* note 50, at 145.

[111] 28 U.S.C.A. § 157(c)(1) (West Supp. 1968–1984) (unless under § (c)(2) all parties consent to district court's referral of proceeding to bankruptcy judge for entire proceeding, including issuance of final order).

[112] *See* Carpenters Local 1846 v. Pratt-Farnsworth, Inc., 106 L.R.R.M. (BNA) 2968, 2972 (E.D. La. 1981).

to the bankruptcy judge. The union will contend that the claim constitutes an "administrative expense" or "claim against the estate" and that it is thus a "core proceeding" under section 157.[113] If the employer files a motion to have the claim dismissed for failure to exhaust contract remedies, the union will presumably defend on the grounds that the grievance is not arbitrable, or that bankruptcy interests require the adjudication of the dispute in the bankruptcy forum, or both.[114]

Such action on the part of the union raises issues requiring "consideration" of section 301 of the NLRA, and thus allows the employer to request that the district court withdraw the matter from the bankruptcy judge and decide the issue itself.[115] If the union's position is predicated solely or even primarily on a section 301 interpretation of the contract, this bifurcated allocation of decisional authority is reasonable. But if the defense is predicated exclusively on bankruptcy considerations, then the matter should be resolved by the bankruptcy judge. And in this situation the union again can argue that the "resolution of the proceeding" (whether to dismiss the claim for failure to exhaust contract remedies) does not require "consideration" of section 301 at all, in which case withdrawal under section 157(d) will not be required.

If the district court determines that the grievance is arbitrable and that no bankruptcy interests will be jeopardized by arbitration, then it should grant the employer's motion to dismiss the breach of contract action—thereby inducing the union to resort to arbitration. On the other hand, if the court determines that the grievance is not arbitrable, the question remains of who, as between the district court and the bankruptcy court, should decide the contract breach issue. The union will continue to contend that this is a "core proceeding" which the bankruptcy court must resolve. The employer, however, may contend that *any* suit on a collective bargaining agreement is necessarily predicated on section 301, thus activating the mandatory withdrawal provisions of section 157(d).[116]

The employer's contention, however, represents an extremely broad reading of a section of the statute intended to have only a narrow application.[117] In *In re Continental Airlines*[118] the bankruptcy court thus held that as used in section 157(d) the phrase "laws of the United States" means "statutes"; since a breach-of-

---

[113] *See supra* notes 41–50 and accompanying text.
[114] 28 U.S.C.A. § 157(d) (West Supp. 1977–1984).
[115] 29 U.S.C. § 185 (1982).
[116] *See supra* note 39 and accompanying text.
[117] *See* W. Norton & R. Lieb, *supra* note 50, at 145.
[118] 57 Bankr. 845, 850 (Bankr. S.D. Tex. 1985).

contract action would be resolved by an "application of evolving federal common law grounded in national labor policy" rather than by the literal words of the Railway Labor Act (or its NLRA counterpart, section 103), section 157(d) did not apply in this context. Moreover, with a view to who is best qualified to construe the contract (since it is not going to be construed by an arbitrator), it should be noted that direct judicial enforcement of the substantive provisions of collective bargaining agreements is relatively infrequent. Thus, it is unlikely that the district court judge will have any greater expertise in construing such a contract than does the bankruptcy judge. Consistent with the general principle favoring bankruptcy court resolution of all issues affecting the bankrupt, the better approach is to treat the union's breach of contract claim no differently than any other contract claim against the estate, and to have it resolved by the bankruptcy court.

Arbitration of Issues Flowing from the Rejection of the Contract

In *Local 807, International Brotherhood of Teamsters v. Bohack Corp.,*[119] the court noted that when the contract is rejected, the law treats the rejection as a breach as of the moment prior to the filing in bankruptcy—thus making the nonbreaching party a general unsecured creditor. But "like any other unilateral breach of contract, it does not destroy the contract so as to absolve the parties . . . from a contractual duty to arbitrate their disputes."[120] Breaches occurring prior to filing thus remain arbitrable, while conduct occurring after an effective rejection does not constitute a "breach." That much is clear. However, two problems remain.

The first involves the status of alleged breaches that occur between the filing date and the court's approval of the contract rejection. On remand from the Second Circuit, the district court in *Bohack* held that the contract rejection constituted not only a breach of the contract retroactive to the date of filing, but also a unilateral "termination" of the contract as of that date. The question of any subsequent breach was thus mooted.[121] The issue in *Bohack* was mooted, however, only because the nature of the original claim involved an objection to the subcontracting that Bohack arranged during the reorganization period. Since the employees

[119] 541 F.2d 312 (2d Cir. 1976), *on remand,* 431 F. Supp. 646 (E.D.N.Y.), *aff'd per curiam,* 567 F.2d 237 (2d Cir. 1977), *cert. denied,* 439 U.S. 825 (1978).

[120] *Id.* at 321 n.15.

[121] Bohack Corporation v. Truck Drivers Local Union No. 807, 431 F. Supp. 646, 656 (E.D.N.Y.), *aff'd per curiam,* 567 F.2d 237 (2d Cir. 1977), *cert. denied,* 439 U.S. 825 (1978).

would have lost their jobs anyway, because of the court-approved termination of this portion of the employer's business under the reorganization plan, it was irrelevant whether the job loss was also a breach of the collective bargaining agreement. The employees suffered no injury beyond that flowing from the terms of the bankruptcy reorganization—thus the contract violation issue was mooted in fact as well as law.[122]

But this might not always be the case. Suppose the contract is rejected, but the affected portion of the business stays in operation. What is the status of the employee who is "wrongfully discharged" between the time the employer files in bankruptcy and the time the contract rejection is approved? If *Bohack* is to be taken literally, the collective bargaining agreement covering the employee (which we will assume contains a discharge clause) is retroactively terminated on the date of filing. This means that the discharge, however "wrongful" it was at the time it occurred, is nevertheless not a contract violation and that there is nothing to arbitrate.

This result also seems to be dictated by the logic of *NLRB v. Bildisco,*[123] which held that the collective bargaining agreement ceases to be an "enforceable contract" once the petition is filed.[124] The court in *In re Midwest Emery Freight System, Inc.,*[125] citing *Bildisco,* held that grievances arising between the filing of the petition in bankruptcy and the approval of rejection of the contract cannot be submitted to arbitration.[126]

The *Emery* decision, however, seems inconsistent with section 1113 of BAFJA.[127] Although a rejected contract is still treated as being breached and terminated as of the date prior to the filing of

---

[122] *Id.*

[123] 104 S. Ct. 1188 (1984).

[124] *Id.* at 1199. Since there was no "enforceable contract," the Court concluded that section 8(d) of the National Labor Relations Act, 29 U.S.C. § 158(d) (1982), which normally imposes a duty on an employer to adhere to the terms of an agreed-upon contract simply does not apply to a trustee or debtor in possession. 104 S. Ct. at 1199.

[125] 48 Bankr. 566 (Bankr. N.D. Ill. 1985).

[126] *Id.* at 569. *See also In re* Fletchner Packing Co., 63 Bankr. 585, (Bankr. N.D. Ohio 1986).

[127] 11 U.S.C. § 1113 (Supp. II 1984). This section, which was part of the Bankruptcy Amendments and Federal Judgeship Act of 1984, Pub. L. No. 98-353, 98 Stat. 390 (1984), overrules *Bildisco* in part and requires a Chapter 11 employer to honor the terms of the agreement until such time as the bankruptcy court approves its rejection. Thus between the time of filing and the rejection, a collective bargaining agreement continues to be a viable legal instrument, with breaches subject to whatever grievance and arbitration provisions the contract contains. *But see* 11 U.S.C. § 1113(d)(2) (Supp. II 1984) (granting a trustee power to terminate or alter provisions of the collective bargaining agreement if the court does not rule on the rejection application within 30 days after commencement of hearing or agreed-upon additional time).

the bankruptcy petition, the whole thrust of section 1113 is to ensure that the contract remains in effect and is honored by the parties until its rejection is approved by the bankruptcy court. Conduct that violated the contract at the time it occurred remains a "contract violation" for purposes of arbitration, even though for other purposes the relation-back theory regards the contract as being nonexistent at the time of the alleged breach. While this result may be somewhat lacking in terms of conceptual tidiness, it makes up for this in terms of fundamental fairness to the employees.

The second problem involves the liquidation of damages that flow from the contract rejection. As previously indicated, a rejected contract is deemed totally breached as of the time of filing, and the nonbreaching party is a general unsecured creditor with respect to the damages that flow from such a breach. But should those damages be determined by an arbitrator or by the bankruptcy court?[128] In the *Bohack* case, both the bankruptcy court and the district court concluded that "the amount of damages suffered by the employees as a result of the rejection ... [is] appropriate for arbitration."[129]

In most cases, the breach flows from the rejection of the contract and the damages caused by the breach can thus be characterized as a dispute "arising under the contract." Such damages appear to be covered by most arbitration clauses. While the liquidation of damages flowing from a total repudiation of the contract is not the kind of issue that labor arbitrators customarily handle,[130] they do have expertise in dealing with the component parts of such a breach.[131] That is, the damages that flow from the rejection of the contract will usually pertain to entitlements which have vested as of the date of breach, such as vacation benefits, unused sick leave, severance pay, health and life insurance premiums and pension

[128] On the question of whether the breach of contract damages issue is subject to withdrawal under section 157(d), see text at notes 117–118, *supra.* Moreover, if liquidation "would involve the unnecessary expenditure of enormous amounts of time, effort and money," then it will be performed by neither the bankruptcy court nor an arbitrator; the court, rather, will simply estimate the claims under section 502(c), as was done in *In re* Continental Airlines Corp., 57 Bankr. 842, 844 (Bankr. S.D. Tex. 1985).

[129] 431 F. Supp. at 654. The parties, however, settled the grievance short of arbitration. Letter from J. Warren Mangan, counsel for Truck Drivers Local 807 (Sept. 24, 1984).

[130] *But see* Dynamics Corp. of Am., 57 Lab Arb. (BNA) 674 (Smith, Arb., 1971); Sidele Fashions, Inc., 36 Lab. Arb. (BNA) 1364 (Dash, Arb., 1961).

[131] *See generally* Krotseng, *Judicial and Arbitral Resolution of Contractual Plant Closing Issues,* 35 Lab. L.J. 393, 398–404 (1984). One commentator has also suggested that arbitration of the liquidation issues might make the contract rejection itself somewhat more palatable to the union. *See* Gregory, *Labor Contract Rejection in Bankruptcy: The Supreme Court's Attack on Labor in* NLRB v. Bildisco, 25 B.C.L. Rev. 539, 603–04 (1984).

fund contributions.[132] Arbitrators often deal with these matters and, indeed, their expertise may well be necessary to a decision of who is entitled to what under the contract in question. Damages flowing from an employer's repudiation of an obligation to make payments for a fixed or indefinite term in the future, as in the case of retirement benefits or pensions, are also within the scope of an arbitrator's expertise.

Arbitral expertise is also required in resolution of some other damages issues that arise from the rejection of the collective bargaining agreement. In *Bohack,* for example, the court stated:

> [V]aluing seniority rights under the unfulfilled portion of the collective bargaining agreement, as well as ascertaining the mitigating value of the new seniority rights of terminated employees who subsequently obtained employment, does not appear to be simply a matter of dollars and cents, rather it involves knowledge of the likelihood of attrition and advancement of employees within the industry and an interpretation of contract provisions respecting seniority rights.[133]

A word of caution is in order here. An arbitral determination of the current and future entitlements that had vested at the time of breach would seem to implicate few bankruptcy interests. Once the arbitrator determines the amount of a claim, the bankruptcy court can then determine its status and priority and deal with it in conjunction with other claims against the estate.

The matter is more complicated, however, when the claimed damages are predicated on postrejection "might have beens"—that is, when damages are sought to put the employees in the position they would have been in *but for* the breach. As a matter of combined bankruptcy/labor law, it may be that once a collective bargaining agreement has been effectively rejected, prospective damages should never be allowed. For example, where the bankruptcy court has approved a plant closure, claims for entitlements predicated on work the employees would have performed if the plant had stayed open are legitimate only on the assumption that the employees had a right of continued employment, which is to say that the closure itself violated the contract.[134] This is not often the case.[135] But if

---

[132] *See In re* Continental Airlines Corp., 57 Bankr. 845, 848 (Bankr. S.D. Tex. 1985) (list of claims flowing from the rejection of the contract).

[133] 431 F. Supp. at 654.

[134] *See generally* Krotseng, *supra* note 131, at 397–98.

[135] Truck Drivers Local 807 v. Bohack Corp., 541 F.2d 312, 321 n.16 (2d Cir. 1976), *on remand,* 431 F. Supp. 646 (E.D.N.Y.), *aff'd per curiam,* 567 F.2d 237 (2d Cir. 1977), *cert. denied,* 439 U.S. 825 (1978); Local 692, United Food Workers v. Pantry Pride, Inc., 522 F. Supp. 1009, 1014 (D. Md. 1981). *See generally* Krotseng, *supra* note 131, at 397–98.

the contract is construed as prohibiting a closure, allowing the full measure of damages is inconsistent with the bankruptcy court's decision to allow the employer to reject the contract and close the plant. And even if the plant is not closed and the employees continue to work, albeit for lower postrejection wages, the awarding of employee damages measured as the difference between the wages to which employees were entitled under the contract and the wages they later received defeats the purpose of allowing the employer to reject the contract in the first place.[136]

The court in *Bohack* was apparently unconcerned about prospective damages, since it allowed the arbitrator to determine the value of the seniority rights that the employees lost by virtue of the plant closure and contract rejection. But in *In re Muskegon Motor Specialties Co.,*[137] the court may have had this difficulty in mind when it refused to defer to arbitration. In *Muskegon,* the employees sought the recover vacation pay for a period which extended beyond the date of the termination of the debtor-employer's business. The court refused to defer to arbitration, reasoning ambiguously that the claim involved merely a "question of law" rather than "working conditions or practices in a shop."[138] Whether the contract required payment for this period certainly is a "question of law," in the sense that it is a matter of contract interpretation.[139] But presumably an arbitrator should decide that issue. On the other hand, whether the allowance of vacation pay under those circumstances is inconsistent with bankruptcy interests is also a "question of law." If this is what the court had in mind, then it properly reserved the issue to itself.

In sum, before the district court or the bankruptcy court allows arbitration of damages flowing from the rejection of the collective bargaining agreement, the union's claims should be carefully scrutinized and the feasibility of any prospective damages determined in advance. It is senseless for an arbitrator to make these compli-

---

[136] *See supra* notes 62–66 and accompanying text; *cf. In re* Butterfield Foods Co., 83 Lab Arb. (BNA) 1013 (Gallagher, Arb., 1984). *Accord, In re* Continental Airlines Corp., 64 Bankr. 865, 872 (Bankr. S.D. Tex. 1985) (disallowed claims for lost future wages and fringe benefits). *But see* Teamsters v. IML Freight, 789 F.2d 1460, 1463 (10th Cir. 1986) (suggesting that following contract rejection, "claims may be filed for all losses attributable to the non-performance of the contracts, including payments due to all fringe benefit plans, loss of seniority rights, and all other provisions of the agreement).

[137] 313 F.2d 841 (6th Cir.), *cert. denied sub nom.* International Union, UAW v. Davis, 375 U.S. 832 (1963).

[138] *Id.* at 843.

[139] *See* L.O. Koven & Bros. Inc. v. Local Union 5767, United Steelworkers, 381 F.2d 196, 203 n.27 (3d Cir. 1967).

cated computations, only to have the claims subsequently disallowed as inconsistent with bankruptcy interests.

Arbitration of Grievances Arising Prior to the Bankruptcy Filing

Under a 1974 Second Circuit decision, an unenforced pre-petition arbitration award is apparently rendered totally unenforceable by a bankruptcy filing. The court in *Robb v. New York Joint Board, Amalgamated Clothing Workers,*[140] thus dismissed as moot a suit to vacate the award. Since the award was legally unenforceable, it made no difference whether it was legally correct or not. The court also suggested that while the award would not have res judicata effect on the union's bankruptcy claim for damages (based on the same alleged breach of the contract), the award was "entitled to some consideration" and the bankruptcy court should thus give it "such weight as may be appropriate."[141]

The decision is questionable. Rather than declaring the award totally "unenforceable," the better approach would have been to treat it like any other unenforced claim or judgment against the estate and have the bankruptcy court review it under the criteria that will be discussed subsequently.[142]

When an alleged contract breach has occurred at some time prior to the employer's filing in bankruptcy and has not yet been arbitrated, the union faces essentially the same procedural choices previously discussed. There is, however, another Bankruptcy Code provision implicated here. The automatic stay provision prohibits the initiation or continuance of any legal proceedings against the debtor on claims which arose before the commencement of the bankruptcy case.[143] The legislative history of this section indicates that it was intended to apply to arbitration, as well as to more traditional legal proceedings.[144]

In order to proceed with arbitration, the party desiring that course of action will have to file a motion for relief from the provisions of the automatic stay.[145] Such a motion is regarded as a "core pro-

---

[140] 506 F.2d 1246 (2d Cir. 1974).

[141] *Id.* at 1247 n.1.

[142] See text at nn. 152–160, *infra.*

[143] 11 U.S.C. § 362(a)(1) (1982).

[144] H.R. Rep. No. 595, 95th Cong., 1st Sess. 340 (1977); S. Rep. No. 989, 95th Cong., 2d Sess. 50 (1978); *see also In re* Penn Fruit Co., 1 Bankr. 714, 716 (Bankr. E.D. Pa. 1979) ("under the stay provisions . . . , the parties may not proceed to arbitration without the permission of the bankruptcy court").

[145] *See In re* Allen & Hein, Inc., 59 Bankr. 733 (Bankr. S.D. Cal. 1986) (arbitration in progress at the time the petition was filed); *In re* Sterling Mining Co., 21 Bankr. 66 (Bankr. W.D. Va. 1982).

ceeding" by section 157(b)(2)(G) of the Bankruptcy Code,[146] and is thus within the jurisdiction of the bankruptcy court. The court's decision whether to grant relief from the stay should be governed by the principles that have already been discussed.[147]

Arguably, a motion for abstention might have the same effect as a motion for relief from the stay.[148] The difference is that the latter can be appealed, while the former cannot.[149] In either event, a decision by the bankruptcy court to lift the stay or abstain will merely permit the parties to proceed with arbitration; it does not compel them to do so. If the employer resists arbitration of the dispute, the union will have to file an additional action to compel arbitration. As discussed above, this action will probably be subject to section 157(d) withdrawal for resolution by the district court rather than the bankruptcy court.

Enforcement of Arbitration Awards

Like any other judgment against a debtor, an arbitration award must be filed with the bankruptcy court; the automatic stay provisions prohibit any independent attempts to enforce or collect the judgment. If the award involves the payment of money, this is a "claim against the estate"[150] and thus a core proceeding within the jurisdiction of the bankruptcy court. The same is true if the enforcement of the award results in an order approving the use[151] or sale[152] of the debtor's property, or affects the liquidation of the assets of the estate.[153] But an arbitration award that requires the employer to take some other kind of affirmative action, such as adjustment of seniority ranking or reinstatement of an employee, appears not to be a core proceeding but, rather, a proceeding within the "relating to" coverage of section 1334(b) of the Bankruptcy Code.[154]

---

[146] 28 U.S.C.A. § 157(b)(2)(G) (West Supp. 1968–1984).

[147] *See supra* notes 40–49 and accompanying text.

[148] The court in *In re* Sterling Mining Co., 21 Bankr. 66 (Bankr. W.D. Va. 1982), apparently regarded the two motions as being interchangeable; it formally granted the union's motion for relief from the stay under § 364(b), but characterized its action in terms of a § 1471(d) (now § 1334(c)(1)) abstention. *Id.* at 62; *see also In re* Smith Jones, Inc., 17 Bankr. 126, 127 (Bankr. D. Minn. 1981).

[149] 28 U.S.C.A. § 1334(c)(2) (West Supp. 1977–1984).

[150] 28 U.S.C.A. § 157(b)(2)(B) (West Supp. 1968–1984).

[151] 28 U.S.C.A. § 157(b)(2)(M) (West Supp. 1968–1984).

[152] 28 U.S.C.A. § 157(b)(2)(N) (West Supp. 1968–1984).

[153] 28 U.S.C.A. § 157(b)(2)(O) (West Supp. 1968–1984).

[154] 28 U.S.C.A. § 1334(b) (West Supp. 1977–1984).

Generally, an action to enforce an arbitration award is brought in federal district court pursuant to section 301 of the NLRA.[155] If the award is presented to the bankruptcy court, it appears to be subject to the withdrawal provisions of section 157(d) of the Bankruptcy Code.[156] However, if the validity of the award is not at issue, status questions, priority, and equitable subordination should be decided by the bankruptcy court. Again, a good argument can be made that this is not a proceeding which requires "consideration" of the labor statutes and that section 157(d) is therefore inapplicable.

However, if questions are raised about the underlying validity of the arbitration award, complications will arise. Normally, the bankruptcy court can "inquire into the validity of any claim asserted against the estate and . . . disallow it if it is ascertained to be without lawful existence,. . . [and] the mere fact that a claim has been reduced to judgment does not prevent such an inquiry."[157] Putting aside the meaning of this as a matter of pure bankruptcy law,[158] it is clear that as a matter of labor law judicial review of arbitration decisions is extremely limited.[159] In this instance, the labor law standard of review should prevail, particularly if the award is the result of an arbitration previously permitted by the court to proceed. Presumably in making that determination the court has already considered the bankruptcy law interests and found that they will not be adversely implicated. Moreover, the whole purpose of initially deferring to arbitration would be defeated if the parties were later permitted to substantially relitigate the merits in the bankruptcy court. If the award results from an arbitration that occurred prior to bankruptcy, review on the merits should still be limited; the bankruptcy court should, however, have the power to refuse to honor the award if conditions are such that the initial deferral to arbitration was inappropriate.

If the employer has legitimate objections to the validity of the award, section 301 issues are clearly raised and the matter should be subject to withdrawal under section 157(d). If, after reviewing the award under the truncated *Enterprise Wheel & Car* standards,[160]

---

[155] 29 U.S.C. § 160 (1982).

[156] 28 U.S.C.A. § 157(d) (West Supp. 1977–1984).

[157] Pepper v. Litton, 308 U.S. 295, 305 (1939).

[158] The arbitration of a commercial dispute under § 26 of the Bankruptcy Act was generally considered reviewable on the merits. *See* Kreindler, *supra* note 3, at 35. *But see In re* Mastercraft Record Plating, Inc., 39 Bankr. 654, 658–59 (S.D.N.Y. 1984).

[159] *See supra* text accompanying note 16.

[160] *See* United Steelworkers v. Enterprise Wheel & Car Corp., 363 U.S. 593 (1960); *supra* notes 15–16 and accompanying text.

the district court determines that the award should be enforced, this judgment should be filed with the bankruptcy court before compliance. This allows the bankruptcy court to consider and decide all relevant bankruptcy law issues, such as priority, status, and subordination.

Union Breaches of the Collective Bargaining Agreement

Collective bargaining agreements are notoriously one-sided, since duties are imposed principally on the employer while corresponding rights are conferred upon the employees and their union. The primary exception arises when the union agrees to a no-strike clause.[161] If the agreement has an arbitration provision which covers union as well as employer breaches and the union violates the no-strike clause, the employer will be entitled to both equitable relief and damages. The employer, however, must pursue its claims against the union through arbitration.[162]

When the union breaches the collective bargaining agreement the fact that the employer is in bankruptcy does not unduly complicate the matter. Basically, the issues are the same as discussed previously; only the parties have changed. There are, however, two additional considerations. First, unless the union has filed its own claim against the employer, the employer's claim for damages flowing from the breach of the no-strike clause is not a core proceeding.[163] Similarly, an order requiring the union to end the strike is not a core proceeding regardless of the union's status as claimant. This suggests that bankruptcy interests are more attenuated when the union, rather than the employer, is in breach. Second, the interest of bankruptcy in this situation is mainly in ensuring that the employer's rights are vigorously and speedily vindicated. A substantial award of damages will certainly inure to the benefit of both the estate and its creditors, and ending the strike may be essential to the success of the reorganization.[164] Yet it seems that these interests can be adequately served by arbitration. A Chapter 11 debtor-in-possession has the incentive necessary to press the matter in the

---

[161] *See* R. Gorman, Labor Law 605-20 (1976); C. Morris, The Developing Labor Law 410 (1971).

[162] *See* Buffalo Forge Co. v. United Steelworkers, 428 U.S. 397, 405 (1976) ("Whether the . . . strike . . . violated the no-strike clause, and the appropriate remedies if it did, are subject to the agreed-upon dispute settlement procedures of the contract and are ultimately issues for the arbitrator.").

[163] 28 U.S.C.A. § 157(b)(2)(C) only applies to "*counterclaims* by the estate *against persons filing claims against the estate.*" 28 U.S.C.A. § 157(b)(2)(C) (West Supp. 1977–1984) (emphasis added).

[164] *See supra* note 89 and accompanying text.

arbitration. forum. Similarly, in a straight bankruptcy the appointed trustee's standing to compel arbitration is unquestioned. Delay and inadequacy of process — problems inherent in the arbitration forum—might be prejudicial in some instances. However, if an order enjoining the strike is the primary objective and the necessary injunctive relief is not otherwise available,[165] arbitration may be not only the *best* forum, but the *only* forum. For unless such an order is processed through the legitimizing portals of arbitration, it can be held invalid under the anti-injunction provisions of the Norris-LaGuardia Act.[166]

---

[165] Under Boys Markets, Inc. v. Retail Clerks Local 770, 398 U.S. 235, 254 (1970), an employer can obtain an injunction only if the strike is over a dispute that is itself arbitrable. *But see supra* text accompanying note 90.

[166] 29 U.S.C. §§ 101–15 (1982). This does not, however, prevent a court from specifically enforcing an arbitrator's order to end a strike that is in breach of the no-strike clause. *See e.g.,* New Orleans Steamship Ass'n v. General Longshore Workers I.I.L. Local Union 1418, 389 F.2d 369 (5th Cir.), *cert. denied,* 393 U.S. 828 (1968).

CHAPTER IX

The Power of the Bankruptcy Court to Enjoin Strikes[1]

The American bankruptcy courts have always exercised an inherent, nonstatutory power to protect by injunction the property and assets of the debtor or his estate.[2] Although the law governing the exercise of this power has, at times, been somewhat complex, if not confusing,[3] section 362 of the Bankruptcy Reform Act of 1978[4] addresses the bankruptcy courts' power in a straightforward and unambiguous manner.[5] Section 362 broadly provides for an automatic stay of all litigation, lien enforcements, and other actions that interfere with the property or assets of the debtor. Two particularly relevant provisions automatically stay "any act to obtain possession of property of . . . or . . . from the estate"[6] and "any act to collect, assess, or recover a claim against the debtor that arose before the commencement of the case."[7] These automatic-stay provisions provide crucial protection for both the debtor's estate and the creditors' claims.[8]

---

[1] Portions of this chapter originally appeared in Haggard, *The Power of the Bankruptcy Court to Enjoin Strikes: Resolving the Apparent Conflict Between the Bankruptcy Code and the Anti-Injunction Provisions of the Norris-LaGuardia Act,* 53 GEO. WASH. L. REV. 703 (1985).

[2] *See, e.g., Ex parte* Baldwin, 291 U.S. 610, 615 (1934); *Ex parte* Christy, 44 U.S. (3 How.) 292, 312 (1845).

[3] *See* 2 COLLIER ON BANKRUPTCY ¶ 362.01, at 362–6 (15th ed. 1985) (section 362 replaced by a single section—an agglomeration of language under the prior Bankruptcy Act and the former Bankruptcy Rules).

[4] 11 U.S.C.A. § 362 (West Supp. 1985).

[5] *See generally* Johnson & O'Leary, *Automatic Stay Provisions of the Bankruptcy Act of 1978,* 13 N.M.L. REV. 599 (1983) (setting out the powers of the bankruptcy courts under section 362 and delineating between actions stayed and actions not stayed by the automatic stay provisions of the Bankruptcy Code).

[6] 11 U.S.C. § 362(a)(3) (1982).

[7] *Id.* § 362(a)(6).

[8] In the words of the House Committee Report:

> The automatic stay is one of the fundamental debtor protections provided by the bankruptcy laws. It gives the debtor a breathing spell from his creditors. It stops all collection efforts, *all harassment,* and all foreclosure actions. It permits the debtor to attempt a repayment or reorganization plan, or simply

The stay provisions of section 362 become effective automatically upon the filing of the petition in bankruptcy, and courts will void actions that violate these provisions.[9] In addition, section 105(a) gives the bankruptcy court the general powers of a court of equity[10]—powers that are broad enough to further enforce the automatic stay provisions by injunctive decree and to do whatever is necessary to aid and protect the court's jurisdiction over bankruptcy proceedings.[11] Congress clearly intended section 105 and the automatic-stay provisions to give bankruptcy courts the broad power to stop any actions detrimental to the debtor's financial recovery or the fair distribution of his assets among all creditors.

On the other hand, in 1932 Congress enacted the Norris-LaGuardia Act[12] to severely limit the involvement of federal courts in labor disputes.[13] Influenced heavily by a book entitled *The Labor*

> to be relieved of the financial pressures that drove him into bankruptcy.
>
> The automatic stay also provides creditor protection. Without it, certain creditors would be able to pursue their own remedies against the debtor's property. Those who acted first would obtain payment of the claims in preference to and to the detriment of other creditors.

H.R. Rep. No. 595, 95th Cong., 1st Sess. 340 (1977) (emphasis added); *see also* Kennedy, *Automatic Stays Under the New Bankruptcy Law,* 12 U. Mich. J.L. Ref. 3, 61–65 (1978) (finding automatic stays necessary to protect both debtor and creditor). Most of the claims that unions will assert in a bankruptcy proceeding involve unpaid wages or pension-fund contributions. It is by no means clear that the union is technically the creditor with respect to these claims. *See* Haggard, *The Appointment of Union Representatives to Creditors' Committees Under Chapter 11 of the Bankruptcy Code,* 35 S.C.L. Rev. 517 (1984) at 524–30. The union, however, is the agent of those who are the proper claimants, the employees, and thus would be subject to the automatic stay provisions affecting the rights of claimants in a Chapter 11 proceeding. Thus, a striking union would be subject to the court's equity powers, regardless of whether it qualifies as a creditor, so long as the Norris-LaGuardia Act's anti-injunction provisions are not applicable. *See* Crowe & Assocs. v. Local 2, Bricklayers & Masons Union, 713 F.2d 211, 214 (6th Cir. 1983) (per curiam).

[9] *In re* Wheeler, 5 Bankr. 600, 604 (Bankr. N.D. Ga. 1980). The newly enacted section 362(h), which was a part of the Bankruptcy Amendments and Federal Judgeship Act of 1984, Pub. L. No. 98-353 § 304, 98 Stat. 333, 352, specifically authorizes actual damages, costs, attorneys' fees, and even punitive damages for willful violations of the automatic stay. 11 U.S.C.A. § 362(h) (West Supp. 1985).

[10] 11 U.S.C. § 105(a) (1982).

[11] *See* 2 Collier on Bankruptcy ¶105.02 (15th ed. 1983). Creditors are subject to contempt and possible monetary liability if they violate an injunction. *See* Meek Lumber Yard, Inc. v. Houts, 23 Bankr. 705, 707 (Bankr. W.D. Mo. 1982); *In re* Eisenberg, 7 Bankr. 683, 687 (Bankr. E.D.N.Y. 1980). *See generally* Stoops, *Monetary Awards to the Debtor for Violations of the Automatic Stay,* 11 Fla. St. U.L. Rev. 423 (1983) (describing equitable relief available to a bankrupt debtor against actions by a creditor and recommending statutory authority to enable recovery of damages).

[12] Norris-LaGuardia Act, ch. 90, 47 Stat. 70 (1932) (current version at 29 U.S.C.A. §§ 101–115 (West Supp. 1985)).

[13] *See generally* Kerian, *Injunctions in Labor Disputes: The History of the Norris-LaGuardia Act,* 37 N.D.L. Rev. 88 (1961) (analyzing the Norris-LaGuardia Act's provisions designed to curb the abuse by the federal courts in issuing injunctions

Injunction,[14] coauthored by then Harvard law professor and later Supreme Court Justice Felix Frankfurter and Nathan Greene, Congress concluded that the federal judiciary was biased in favor of management and that courts were abusing their equity powers by issuing, often on a purely ex parte basis, overly broad injunctions against strikes and other forms of collective activity by labor unionists. Moreover, the antitrust and tort doctrines upon which the courts relied either reflected some of the influence of the old criminal-conspiracy doctrine or were otherwise regarded as open-ended vehicles through which the courts expressed their predilections about labor relations and social policy. Nevertheless, at that time, Congress was allegedly in a laissez faire mood—not yet willing to legislate affirmatively in favor of labor unions, but also unwilling to let the courts "legislate" in favor of management. The Norris-LaGuardia Act was thus designed to prod the judiciary into a hands-off or neutral policy toward labor unions' activity.[15]

The Norris-LaGuardia Act sets forth Congress's clear message to the judiciary: federal courts should not enjoin labor disputes, except in the narrowest of circumstances. The Act provides: "No court of the United States ... shall have jurisdiction to issue any ... injunction in a case involving or growing out of a labor dispute, *except* in strict conformity with the provisions of this chapter. . . .[16] The Act then lists conduct that cannot be enjoined under any circumstances, including peaceful strikes and picketing.[17] Additionally, even if the Act does not affirmatively protect a form of union activity, federal courts still cannot enjoin that activity unless certain procedural and substantive requirements are satisfied, including proof that "unlawful acts have been threatened and will be com-

---

during labor disputes); Wimberly, *The Labor Injunction—Past, Present and Future,* 22 S.C.L. REV. 689 (1970) (explaining the Norris-LaGuardia Act's regulation of federal courts' equity jurisdiction); Winter, *Labor Injunctions and Judge-Made Labor Law: The Contemporary Role of Norris-LaGuardia,* 70 YALE L. J. 70 (1960) (discussing the Norris-LaGuardia Act's attack on judge-made labor law and its administration).

[14] F. FRANKFURTER & N. GREENE, THE LABOR INJUNCTION (1930). Scholars recently have raised serious questions about the selectivity of the data reported in this study, the validity of the inferences and sweeping conclusions drawn from these data, and even the objectivity of the authors themselves. *See* Petro, *Injunctions and Labor Disputes: 1880–1932. Part I: What the Courts Actually Did—and Why,* 14 WAKE FOREST L. REV. 341 *passim* (1978).

[15] *See* 75 CONG. REC. 4915 (1932) (statement of Sen. Wagner) ("The policy and purpose which gives meaning to the present legislation is its implicit declaration that the Government shall occupy a neutral position, lending its extraordinary power neither to those who would have labor unorganized nor to those who would organize it. . . ."); A. COX, LAW AND THE NATIONAL LABOR POLICY 8 (1960).

[16] 29 U.S.C. § 101 (1982) (emphasis added).

[17] *Id.* § 104.

mitted . . . or have been committed and will be continued unless restrained. . . ."[18]

The conflict between the automatic stay provisions and section 105 of the Bankruptcy Code, on the one hand, and the anti-injunction provisions of the Norris-LaGuardia Act, on the other, is readily apparent. If, in the words of the Norris-LaGuardia Act, a group of employees is "refusing to perform any work"[19] and is publicizing this dispute "by advertising, speaking, patrolling or by any other method not involving fraud or violence,"[20] then the Act precludes the federal courts from enjoining these activities. On the other hand, if the employer's business has been brought under the protective jurisdiction of the bankruptcy court and the object of the strike is to "obtain possession of property"[21] of the employer (by forcing him to agree to new contract terms or make current wage payments)[22] or to "collect, assess, or recover a claim against"[23] the employer (such as forcing him to make delinquent payments into a pension fund), then the strike is an "act" that the Bankruptcy Code automatically stays and that federal courts can enjoin. Beyond that, section 105 seemingly vests the bankruptcy court with equity powers broad enough to enjoin any other strike that threatens to interfere with bankruptcy processes.

Although this chapter focuses primarily on the apparent conflict between the Bankruptcy Code and the Norris-LaGuardia Act, a bankruptcy court's injunction against a strike raises other possible conflicts. For example, although workers certainly have no absolute

---

[18] *Id.* § 107(a); *see infra* text accompanying notes 57–81.

[19] 29 U.S.C. § 104(a) (1982).

[20] *Id.* § 104(e) (1982).

[21] 11 U.S.C.A. § 362(a)(3) (West Supp. 1985).

[22] There is no direct bankruptcy law authority for this interpretation of the statutory language. However, the federal anti-extortion statute, the Hobbs Act, 18 U.S.C. § 1951 (1982), which similarly prohibits "the obtaining of property from another" by the use of force, *id.* § 1951(b)(2), has been applied to unions' attempts to compel employers to agree to collective bargaining and other wage demands. United States v. Green, 350 U.S. 415, 418–20 (1956); *cf.* United States v. Enmons, 410 U.S. 396, 408–11 (1973) (dismissing indictment because the attempt to obtain the property in question—wages and other employment benefits—was not wrongful). *See generally* A. Thieblot & T. Haggard, Union Violence: The Record and the Response by Courts, Legislatures, and the NLRB 245–300 (1983) (contending the use of threats or violence by unions to coerce employers to acquiesce to their demands constitutes extortion under the Hobbs Act notwithstanding the legitimacy of the bargaining objectives); Haggard, *Labor Violence: The Inadequate Response of the Federal Anti-Extortion Statutes,* 59 Neb. L. Rev. 859 (1980) (positing that legislative history reveals Congress intended the Hobbs Act to prohibit labor from using force or violence to compel employers to agree to concessions).

[23] 11 U.S.C. § 362(a)(6) (1982).

constitutional right to strike or picket,[24] these activities do at least represent a constitutionally based interest that a bankruptcy court should consider.[25] Moreover, strikes and picketing are an integral part of the industrial-relations scheme created by the National Labor Relation Act (NLRA),[26] and a bankruptcy court's injunction might, in some instances, frustrate the interests of that statute.[27] When relevant, this chapter considers these other federal sources of the "right" to strike.

Courts employ one of two broad approaches to this apparent conflict between the Bankruptcy Code and the Norris-LaGuardia Act: they either avoid the conflict through statutory construction or analysis of underlying policy;[28] or resolve the conflict in favor of one statute.[29]

ATTEMPTS TO AVOID THE CONFLICT

When confronted with a set of apparently contradictory statutory commands, courts follow a natural inclination to avoid the conflict altogether by denying its existence. Courts do this either by construing the statutory language narrowly, or by construing the underlying policies broadly. In the context of bankruptcy and labor law, courts have considered, and at times adopted, both of these approaches.

The Alleged Absence of a "Labor Dispute"

The Norris-LaGuardia Act applies only when there is a "labor dispute"; absent such a dispute, the Act poses no obstacle to the issuance of appropriate injunctive relief.[30] The judicial response defining away a conflict with the Norris-LaGuardia Act on this basis has been mixed; however, most recent decisions have found this option unavailing because the facts simply could not be construed to involve anything but a labor dispute, at least in the purely conventional sense of the term. The Norris-LaGuardia Act defines "labor dispute" rather broadly, to include "any controversy concerning terms or conditions of employment, or concerning the as-

---

[24] *See, e.g.,* Dorchy v. Kansas, 272 U.S. 306, 311 (1926); United Fed'n of Postal Clerks v. Blount, 325 F. Supp. 879, 882–84 (D.D.C.), *aff'd,* 404 U.S. 802 (1971).

[25] *See* Cox, *Strikes, Picketing and the Constitution,* 4 Vand. L. Rev. 574, 575 (1951).

[26] 29 U.S.C. §§ 141–188 (1982).

[27] *See* 2 C. Morris, The Developing Labor Law 1002–06 (2d ed. 1983).

[28] *See infra* notes 96–133 and accompanying text.

[29] *See infra* notes 133–155 and accompanying text.

[30] *See* Ashley, Drew & N. Ry. v. United Transp. Union, 625 F.2d 1357, 1362 (8th Cir. 1980).

sociation or representation of persons in negotiating . . . [such] terms and conditions of employment, regardless of whether or not the disputants stand in the proximate relation of employer and employee."[31] As the Sixth Circuit, allegedly quoting the Supreme Court, recently stated: "The term labor dispute should be most broadly and liberally construed. [It] comprehends disputes growing out of labor relations. . . . All such disputes seem to be clearly included."[32]

For the most part, courts have adhered to this broad reading of the Norris-LaGuardia Act when analyzing the conflict between bankruptcy and labor law. In *Petrusch v. Teamsters Local 317,*[33] for example, the Second Circuit ruled that a labor dispute existed when a union picketed to protest a debtor-employer's failure to make payments into the union's health, hospital, pension, and retirement funds, as required by the collective bargaining agreement.[34] The Second Circuit reasoned that these fringe benefits were clearly part of the "terms and conditions of employment," that a "controversy" existed over them, and that there was thus a "labor dispute" under the Norris-LaGuardia Act.[35]

Courts generally consider disputes over wages and benefits to be labor disputes under the Norris-LaGuardia Act. For example, *Briggs Transportation Co. v. Local 710, International Brotherhood of Teamsters*[36] arose when a union struck to contest a reduced-wage schedule instituted by the employer after the bankruptcy court approved the employer's rejection of the collective bargaining agreement.[37] The district court aptly reasoned that wages and fringe benefits are central to the employee-employer relationship and, thus, the strike involved a labor dispute.[38] Additionally, strikes to obtain a reduction in hours without a diminution of take-home pay,[39]

---

[31] 29 U.S.C. § 113(c) (1982).

[32] Crowe & Assocs. v. Local 2, Bricklayers & Masons Union, 713 F.2d 211, 213–14 (6th Cir. 1983) (per curiam). Although the quotation is consistent with what the Supreme Court said in Jacksonville Bulk Terminals, Inc. v. International Longshoremen's Ass'n, 457 U.S. 702, 712 (1982), the Court did not use those exact words.

[33] 667 F.2d 297 (2d Cir.) (per curiam), *cert. denied,* 456 U.S. 974 (1981).

[34] 667 F.2d at 299.

[35] *Id. see also* Crowe & Assocs. v. Local 2, Bricklayers & Masons Union, 713 F.2d 211, 213 (6th Cir. 1983) (per curiam) (ruling that a "labor dispute" existed under similar facts).

[36] 40 Bankr. 972 (D. Minn.), *aff'd,* 739 F.2d 341 (8th Cir.), *cert. denied,* 105 S. Ct. 295 (1984).

[37] 40 Bankr. at 973.

[38] *Id.*

[39] Third Ave. Transit Corp. v. Quill, 192 F.2d 971, 973 (2d Cir. 1951). Although the Second Circuit cited *Third Avenue* as authority supporting the proposition that section 362 of the Bankruptcy Code did not override the prohibitions of the Norris-

strikes in protest of allegedly unfair labor practices,[40] and strikes to compel compliance with an arbitration award[41] have also been ruled labor disputes within the meaning of the Norris-LaGuardia Act, thus bringing the Act into conflict with the bankruptcy court's power to enjoin the strikes.

On the other hand, in *Converse v. Highway Construction Co.,*[42] a 1939 decision, the Sixth Circuit held that a union's attempt to force a debtor-employer to join a contractors' association was not a labor dispute because there was no underlying controversy between the employer and his employees concerning the terms and conditions of employment.[43] The court, instead, characterized the dispute as an attempt to destroy competition in the highway-construction business.[44] But that was an unduly narrow reading of the situation. The union clearly purported to represent all the superintendents, foremen, and timekeepers of the employers who were members of this association, and the union's objective in forcing an additional contractor to join the association was undoubtedly to attain a similar status with respect to his employees.[45] This was, in other words, simply an attempt to unionize a nonunion contractor—a recognized form of labor union activity.

Although the *Converse* holding may seem inconsistent with the meaning of "labor dispute" as the term has since evolved, it is supported by a Fifth Circuit decision. In *Scott v. Moore,*[46] the court held *en banc* that violence and picketing directed against a nonunion construction firm did not involve a labor dispute under the Norris-LaGuardia Act because there was no strike by the employees, no underlying collective bargaining agreement, and no connection at all with any legitimate, ongoing union activity.[47] Eight of the twenty-four judges vigorously dissented on this point, arguing that a union's

---

LaGuardia Act, Petrusch v. Teamsters Local 317, 667 F.2d 297, 299 (2d Cir.) (per curiam), *cert. denied,* 456 U.S. 974 (1981), the Second Circuit decided *Third Avenue* before the passage of the 1978 Code; thus the Second Circuit's reliance on this decision is questionable, as is the continued precedential value of *Third Avenue* itself.

[40] Teamsters Local 886 v. Quick Charge, Inc., 168 F.2d 513,515 (10th Cir. 1948).

[41] Truck Drivers Local 807 v. Bohack Corp., 541 F.2d 312, 317 (2d Cir. 1976). The *Petrusch* court also relied on this pre-1978 decision to evaluate the conflict between the Bankruptcy Code and the Norris-LaGuardia Act. *Petrusch,* 667 F.2d at 299; *see supra* note 39.

[42] 107 F.2d 127 (6th Cir. 1939).

[43] *Id.* at 131.

[44] *Id.*

[45] *See id.* The reasoning of the court is further faulted because the Norris-LaGuardia Act specifically excludes any requirement that "the disputants stand in the proximate relation of employer and employee." 29 U.S.C. § 113(c) (1982).

[46] 680 F.2d 979 (5th Cir. 1982) (en banc), *rev'd on other grounds sub nom.* Local 610, United Bhd. of Carpenters v. Scott, 463 U.S. 825, 830 (1983).

[47] 680 F.2d at 985–86.

organizational activities, even if they involve otherwise illegal conduct, can nevertheless give rise to a labor dispute for purposes of the Norris-LaGuardia Act.[48] Although *Moore* did not involve any bankruptcy-law issues, it is a significant decision, and in the Fifth Circuit, at least, it should pave the way for injunctive relief under section 105(a) when the bankrupt employer's nonunion status is the object of the union's strike or picketing.

Another early case that seemingly used the alleged lack of a labor dispute to avoid the apparent conflict between bankruptcy and labor law is *In re Cleveland & Sandusky Brewing Co.*[49] This case arose when a union's mass-picketing and violence forcibly prevented a debtor-employer from removing 12,000 barrels of beer from a struck plant to preserve this asset for its creditors in the reorganization proceedings as a result of an ongoing jurisdictional dispute.[50] The Special Master found that this activity did not involve a labor dispute and enjoined the union's interference.[51] The district court, perhaps recognizing that in a broad sense a labor dispute did exist, nevertheless issued an injunction after concluding that "the relief sought by the debtor is not upon the basis of *rights* arising in respect of a labor dispute."[52] The court, however, gave no clue as to what that verbal formulation might mean or how to distinguish the relief or rights asserted in *Sandusky* from those that might exist whenever a bankrupt estate tries to protect its assets from predatory union conduct.

Ultimately, the court suggested a somewhat broader basis for its decision. It stated: "[I]f Congress intended to curtail the bankruptcy power where the threatened destruction of property within its jurisdiction was related to a labor dispute, it would have said so, because the enactment of . . . the Bankruptcy Act came more than two years after the enactment of the labor disputes [Norris-LaGuardia] act."[53] Congress did not say so, and the court therefore exercised its power to enjoin the union's activities. In the last analysis, the *Sandusky* decision is not so much an attempt to avoid the conflict through a narrow construction of the term "labor dispute," as it is a resolution of that conflict in favor of the Bankruptcy Code.

---

[48] *Id.* at 1007.

[49] 11 F. Supp. 198 (N.D. Ohio 1935).

[50] *Id.* at 205.

[51] *Id.* at 203.

[52] *Id.* at 205 (emphasis added).

[53] *Id.* at 207. The court's reference to the Bankruptcy Act was directed to a group of amendments to the 1898 Bankruptcy Act, which were passed in 1934. Act of June 7, 1934, ch. 424, 48 Stat. 912, 912 (current version at 11 U.S.C.A. §§ 101-151326 (West Supp. 1985)).

Finally, in *In re The Ryan Company,*[54] a bankruptcy court judge used a theory about the meaning of labor dispute that, if universally adopted, would virtually eliminate any conflict between the Bankruptcy Code and the Norris-LaGuardia Act. As in *Petrusch,* an employer defaulted on his obligations to make payments into a union's pension plan. He filed an involuntary petition in bankruptcy and applied for permission to reject the collective bargaining agreement. The court granted this permission and the union went on strike. The judge enjoined the strike, even in the face of the Norris-LaGuardia Act's prohibitions, holding that although a labor dispute might exist between the union and the debtor who incurred the obligation, the debtor-in-possession was a separate entity and between it and the union no such dispute existed.[55] The Supreme Court's recent rejection of the "new entity" theory in *NLRB v. Bildisco & Bildisco*[56] would, however, now seem to foreclose this particular approach for avoiding the conflict.

The Alleged "Unlawfulness" of the Strike

As stated earlier, the Norris-LaGuardia Act allows injunctions in certain limited circumstances provided, among other things, that the conduct to be enjoined involves "unlawful acts."[57] Because the Bankruptcy Code in essence declares conduct in violation of the automatic stay provisions to be unlawful, such conduct seemingly could be enjoined, provided that the procedural requirements of the Norris-LaGuardia Act were otherwise met.[58] However, the only opinion to seriously consider this argument has rejected it.

---

[54] 83 Lab. Cas. (CCH) ¶ 10,487, at 17,948 (D. Conn. 1978).

[55] *Id.* at 17,950.

[56] 465 U.S. 513, 528 (1984). The "new entity" approach was originally used by the Second Circuit in Shopmen's Local 455 v. Kevin Steel Prods., 519 F.2d 698, 704 (2d Cir. 1975), to avoid the apparent conflict between section 8(d) of the Labor Management Relations (Taft-Hartley) Act, 29 U.S.C. § 158(d) (1982) (prohibiting an employer from repudiating the terms of a collective bargaining agreement) and section 313(1) of the Bankruptcy Code, 11 U.S.C. § 713(1) (1976) (current version at 11 U.S.C. § 365(a) (1982)) (allowing the rejection of executory contracts by a debtor-in-possession, i.e., the "new entity").

In rejecting this approach, the Supreme Court stated: "For our purposes, it is sensible to view the debtor-in-possession as the same 'entity' which existed before the filing of the bankruptcy petition. . . ." 465 U.S. at 528. Presumably, the same would be true when the purpose is to determine whether the person seeking the injunction, the debtor-in-possession, is the same entity as the one with whom the union has a dispute.

[57] 29 U.S. C. § 107(a) (1982); *see supra* notes 16–18 and accompanying text.

[58] *See supra* notes 9–11 and accompanying text.

In *Crowe & Associates v. Local 2, Bricklayers & Masons Union,*[59] the bankruptcy court held that a disagreement between an employer and a union is no longer a labor dispute once the union demands that the employer do something unlawful.[60] Because the union's demand that Crowe pay money into the union pension fund violated the bankruptcy laws, the judge held that a labor dispute did not exist and that an injunction could issue.[61]

This simply represents another approach to defining a labor dispute. In this regard, the court stated: "Norris-LaGuardia was enacted to prevent courts from interfering with union conduct directed to the pursuit of the union's legitimate and lawful goals,"[62] but that "the refusal of the debtor to comply with the unauthorized and unwarranted demands of the union cannot be termed a labor dispute within the meaning of Norris-LaGuardia."[63] This logic provides a reasonable rule for reconciling the two statutes.

Upon appeal, the nature of the bankruptcy court's holding changed. The federal district court inexplicably indicated that the bankruptcy judge had held the Norris-LaGuardia Act inapplicable not only because there was no labor dispute within the statutory meaning of that term, but also because the Norris-LaGuardia Act bars only injunctions against legal strikes.[64] After seemingly bifurcating the issue, the court nevertheless evaluated the bankruptcy judge's actual holding that there was no labor dispute because the strike was for an otherwise illegal purpose.[65] In rejecting this definition, the district court reasoned that most pre-Norris-LaGuardia Act injunctions had been predicated on the unlawfulness of the strike under the federal antitrust laws—an approach Congress specifically repudiated when it passed the Act.[66] From this reasoning, the court concluded that "Congress could not have intended to preclude application of the act in cases in which the union was found to have acted illegally."[67]

The court, however, may have overgeneralized in this regard. The relationship between the Norris-LaGuardia Act and the antitrust

---

[59] 16 Bankr. 271 (Bankr. E.D. Mich. 1981), *rev'd.* 20 Bankr. 225 (E.D. Mich. 1982), *aff'd,* 713 F.2d 211 (6th Cir. 1983).

[60] 16 Bankr. at 274 (citing Lystod v. Local 223, Int'l Bhd. of Teamsters, 135 F. Supp. 337, 341 (D. Or. 1955)).

[61] 16 Bankr. at 274.

[62] *Id.*

[63] *Id.*

[64] Crowe & Assocs. v. Local 2, Bricklayers & Masons Union, 20 Bankr. 225, 226 (E.D. Mich. 1982) *aff'd,* 713 F.2d 211 (6th Cir. 1983) (per curiam).

[65] 20 Bankr. at 227.

[66] *Id.*

[67] *Id.*

laws is unique, and a historical analysis of this relationship indicates that Congress intended the Norris-LaGuardia Act to address union activities, primarily in the context of those activities' alleged illegality under the antitrust laws. Although the Sherman Act of 1890 declared illegal "every contract, combination ... or conspiracy, in restraint of trade or commerce among the several States,"[68] courts usually applied the Sherman Act only to employee activities designed to inhibit competition in the product market or to those activities deemed objectionable for reasons extrinsic to antitrust policy. These categories included both organizational strikes and secondary boycotts.[69] But even this limited application of the Sherman Act to union activities was more than Congress intended. Congress thus passed the Clayton Act in 1914,[70] in part to generally exclude peaceful strikes and picketing from the Sherman Act's substantive prohibitions.[71] Despite the Clayton Act, the Supreme Court held in *Duplex Printing Press Co. v. Deering*[72] that the Sherman Act still applied although there was no direct employment relationship between the defendant employees and the company that was the ultimate object of their boycott. Congress, however, was to have the final word, implementing its intent through the Norris-LaGuardia Act's broad definition of labor dispute, which specifically excludes any requirement that "the disputants stand in the proximate relation of employer and employee."[73]

This history of judicial point and legislative counterpoint demonstrates that Congress intended the Norris-LaGuardia Act to function as a substantive amendment to the Sherman Act. Through its broad definition of labor dispute, Congress overruled the judicial determination that peaceful strikes and picketing were unlawful conspiracies in restraint of trade. Because this conduct no longer violated the Sherman Act, the impropriety of enjoining the conduct followed as a matter of course.

In sum, and contrary to the implications of *Crowe,* Congress's response to injunctions issued under the antitrust laws does not suggest that Congress intended strikes and picketing to be unenjoinable *in spite of* their unlawfulness under the antitrust laws;

---

[68] Sherman Antitrust Act, ch. 647 § 1, 26 Stat. 209 (1890) (current version at 15 U.S.C. § 1 (1982)). If literally construed, the Sherman Act is broad enough to encompass any strike that shuts down a business.

[69] *See, e.g.,* Duplex Printing Press Co. v. Deering, 254 U.S. 443, 478–79 (1921) (upholding injunction against secondary boycott); R. Gorman, Labor Law 3 (1976).

[70] Clayton Act, ch. 323, 38 Stat. 730 (1914) (current version at 15 U.S.C. § 18 (1982)).

[71] *See* 51 Cong. Rec. 14,588 (1914) (statement of Sen. Cummins).

[72] 254 U.S. 443 (1921).

[73] 29 U.S.C. § 113(c) (1982).

rather, it suggests that Congress intended strikes and picketing to be unenjoinable *because of* the absence of statutory prohibition under those laws. Thus, it cannot be concluded that the unlawfulness of strikes under some other, nonantitrust statute, such as the Bankruptcy Code, is necessarily irrelevant to the proper definition of a protected, and thus unenjoinable, labor dispute under the Norris-LaGuardia Act.[74]

Even if the unlawfulness of a strike under the automatic stay provisions of the Bankruptcy Code is somehow analogous to the unlawfulness of strikes under the antitrust decisions, Congress presumably intended to exclude neither from the definition of a labor dispute under Norris-LaGuardia; moreover, the unlawfulness of the conduct addressed by the *Crowe* court was of an entirely different nature.[75] The strike by Crowe's employees did not merely contravene the Code's automatic stay provisions; it also attempted to force the debtor-employer to violate a specific Bankruptcy Code provision prohibiting him from making payments to a pension fund in derogation of the other creditors' rights.[76] If injunctive relief is unavailable in that situation, the debtor-in-possession is placed in an untenable position. If he yields to the union's pressure, he will run afoul of the Bankruptcy Code; but if he refuses to make the demanded payments, he risks having the entire reorganizational effort frustrated by a crippling strike. It seems unlikely that Congress sought such a result by intending to include, under the rubric of a protected labor dispute, a union's attempts to force a debtor to do something that Congress itself has prohibited.

Upon appeal to the Sixth Circuit, the debtor-in-possession, unfortunately, reemphasized the lower court's allegedly bifurcated holding by arguing that a labor dispute did not exist but, if it did, the strike was still unlawful and thus enjoinable under section 107(a) of the Norris-LaGuardia Act.[77] The Sixth Circuit, without

---

[74] Although unlawful conduct under the Sherman Act does not preclude application of the Norris-LaGuardia Act, the Supreme Court has held that when conduct is illegal under another labor statute, the Norris-LaGuardia Act is superseded and such conduct can thus be enjoined. Railroad Trainmen v. Chicago River & Ind. R.R., 353 U.S. 30, 42 (1957) (reading Norris-LaGuardia in conjunction with the Railway Labor Act, 45 U.S.C. § 151 (1982)). Later, in Railroad Telegraphers v. Chicago & N.W.R.R., 362 U.S. 330 (1960), the Court addressed the *Chicago River* decision: "The [*Chicago River* Court] ... regarded as inapposite those cases in which it was held that the Norris-LaGuardia Act's ban on federal injunctions is not lifted because the conduct of the union is unlawful under some other, nonlabor statute." *Id.* at 339 (footnote omitted).

[75] *See supra* text accompanying notes 60–64.

[76] *See* Crowe & Assocs. v. Local 2, Bricklayers & Masons Union, 713 F.2d 211, 214 (6th Cir. 1983) (per curiam).

[77] *Id.* at 213.

specifically focusing on "unlawfulness" as part of the definition of labor dispute, nevertheless accorded the term a typically broad construction and held that a controversy over pension fund payments fell within its parameters.[78] Addressing unlawfulness as a separate issue, the court concluded, again by analogy to antitrust law, that Congress did not intend the ban on injunctions to be lifted merely because the conduct in question was unlawful under some other federal law.[79] The appellate court's reasoning on that point is, however, no more convincing than that of the district court. The court also concluded that the employer's reliance on section 107(a) of the Norris-LaGuardia Act, which allows injunctive relief when "unlawful acts have been threatened . . . or have been committed,"[80] was misplaced. This, the court stated, refers only to acts of violence. Given the logical structure of the Act, as well as the precedent that has construed that section, the court probably decided this narrow issue correctly.[81]

Union Strikes and Picketing Do Not Violate the Automatic Stay Provisions

Unions generally are subject to the automatic stay provisions.[82] However, a third way to avoid the apparent conflict between the labor laws and the bankruptcy laws is to hold that these laws simply

---

[78] *Id.*

[79] *Id.* at 214.

[80] 29 U.S.C. § 107(a) (1982).

[81] The unlawful acts referred to in section 107(a) are simply acts not fully protected by section 104—acts involving "fraud or violence" or which are other than peaceful. *See* 29 U.S.C. §§ 104(e), (f), (i), 107(a) (1982); Local 721, Bhd. of R.R. Trainmen v. Central of Ga. Ry., 229 F.2d 901, 903–05 (5th Cir. 1956), *cert. dismissed for mootness,* 352 U.S. 995 (1957). Courts can enjoin unlawful acts of this variety if they occur within the context of a labor dispute, but only if the procedural and proof requirements of section 107 are satisfied. *E.g.,* Bonanno Linen Serv. v. McCarthy, 532 F.2d 189, 191 (1st Cir. 1976) (finding the identification of perpetrators and credible oral testimony adequate proof). *See generally* Thieblot & Haggard, *supra* note 22, at 212–18; (discussing the elements of proof required under section 107); Haggard, *Private Injunctive Relief Against Labor Union Violence,* 71 Ky. L. J. 509 (1983) (complainant must show unlawful conduct, substantial and irreparable injury, procedural compliance, and necessity of injunction). Although this necessarily suggests that a labor dispute may exist under the Norris-LaGuardia Act even though unlawful and otherwise enjoinable violence has occurred, the fundamental question is whether such a dispute exists when the objective of the union's violent or nonviolent conduct is to force the employer to do something Congress has expressly prohibited in another statute.

[82] The automatic stay provisions apply to "all entities." 11 U.S.C. § 362 (1982), including persons. *Id.* § 101(14). The Code's definition of persons includes a corporation, *id.* § 101(30), as well as an unincorporated company or association. *Id.* § 101(8)(A)(iv). Congress regarded labor unions as falling within this classification. S. Rep. No. 989, 95th Cong., 2d Sess. 22 (1978), *reprinted in* 1978 U.S. Code Cong.

do not encompass union-sponsored strikes and picketing. The district court in *Crowe* recognized that the automatic stay against attempts to collect pre-bankruptcy debts primarily addressed the problem of unscrupulous creditors who harass unwary consumers into paying their debts after filing a bankruptcy petition.[83] The court concluded, however, that Congress did not intend to limit the stay against collection of pre-petition debts to consumer bankruptcy situations,[84] and that the union's strike to compel payments into the pension fund fell within the stay's prohibitions.[85] On the other hand, a strike to compel agreement to a new labor contract is not clearly an attempt to "obtain possession of property"[86] of the debtor,[87] and an unfair-labor-practice strike also does not appear to fit into any of the automatic stay provision's categories. Finally, the Clayton Act not only limits the federal court's power to grant equitable relief against strikes; it also specifies acts that shall not "be considered or held to be violations of any law of the United States."[88] If construed literally, the Clayton Act could prevent strikes and picketing from violating the automatic stay provisions of the Bankruptcy Code. The Clayton Act's language, however, like that of the Norris-LaGuardia Act, should be construed in the context of its substantive purpose. Congress intended the Clayton Act to exclude peaceful, concerted activity by employees from the definition of "illegal combinations or conspiracies in restraint of trade"[89]—a purpose that is not frustrated by including strikes within the ambit of the Bankruptcy Code's prohibitions.

In any event, courts have had no difficulty in ruling that conduct such as striking, picketing, and other forms of union pressure[90] is proscribed by the automatic stay provisions.

& Ad. News 5963, 6266; H.R. Rep. No. 595, 95th Cong., 1st Sess. 309 (1977), *reprinted in* 1978 U.S. Code Cong. & Ad. News 5963, 6266; *see In re* Schatz Fed. Bearing Co., 5 Bankr. 543, 546 (Bankr. S.D.N.Y. 1980), *appeal precluded,* 11 Bankr. 363 (Bankr. S.D.N.Y. 1981).

[83] 20 Bankr. at 228.

[84] *Id.*

[85] *Id.* at 229. Even if a particular strike is not proscribed by the automatic stay provisions of section 362, section 105(a) still gives the bankruptcy court broad equitable power to do whatever is necessary to preserve the debtor's assets and to ensure the success of a Chapter 11 reorganization. 11 U.S.C. § 105(a) (1982).

[86] *See supra* note 22.

[87] *See In re* Warren-Ehret-Linck, 52 B.R., 47 (Bankr. E.D. Pa. 1985).

[88] 29 U.S.C. § 52 (1982).

[89] 15 U.S.C. § 17 (1982).

[90] A court has held union pressure to include an attempt to force a debtor-employer to arbitrate a grievance. Local 692, United Food & Commercial Workers v. Pantry Pride, 522 F. Supp. 1009, 1012–13 (D. Md. 1981). However, the court ultimately lifted the stay to permit arbitration, albeit with some limits on the remedies that the arbitrator could grant. *Id.* at 1014.

The Self-Enforcing Aspect of the Automatic Stay Provisions

On its face, the Norris-LaGuardia Act is primarily a limitation on the power of the federal courts to issue injunctions in the context of a labor dispute. Technically, most conflicts between that Act and the Bankruptcy Code would thus arise only if the debtor-in-possession filed a complaint for affirmative injunctive relief under section 105(a). Enforcement of the automatic stay provisions by means other than the issuance of an injunction thus would not appear to fall within the Norris-LaGuardia Act's prohibitions.

Because the automatic stay provisions of section 362 are self-enforcing, a debtor does not need to proceed by way of complaint.[91] The bankruptcy court in *Crowe* recognized the self-enforcing nature of section 362 and stated that a debtor need only move for an order compelling a union to show cause why the union should not be held in contempt for violating a section 362 stay.[92]

This suggests that the Bankruptcy Code can provide some degree of relief to the debtor against the effects of union strikes and picketing without the debtor formally resorting to the section 105(a) powers of the bankruptcy court. The automatic stay provisions are self-enforcing, and the bankruptcy court has both express and implied power to award monetary damages to the debtor-in-possession for union conduct that derogates from these provisions.[93] Consequently, the limits of the Norris-LaGuardia Act are never even brought into play.

Although at first blush this may appear to be a somewhat artificial, if not overly clever, distinction, closer analysis suggests that it may effect a minimally adequate accommodation of the two statutes. Of the several congressional concerns that led to the passage of the Norris-LaGuardia Act, two are particularly relevant for analyzing this accommodation. First, before 1932, the judiciary, not the

---

[91] *See Re* See Re Crowe & Assocs., 16 Bankr. 271, 272 n.1 (Bankr. E.D. Mich. 1981).

[92] *Id.; see also In re* Tom Powell & Son, Inc., 22 Bankr. 657, 660 (Bankr. W.D. Mo. 1982) (distinguishing *Petrusch* and *Crowe* on the narrow ground that court-ordered injunctions issued, and focusing on the impact of a purely statutory stay, effective upon filing). The *Tom Powell* court declined to hold the union in contempt because it did not knowingly or willfully violate the automatic stay. *Id.* at 661.

The Bankruptcy Amendments and Federal Judgeship Act of 1984, Pub. L. No. 98-353, 98 Stat. 333, added section 362(h) to clarify the power of the bankruptcy court to impose sanctions for willful violations of the automatic stay. Section 362(h) provides: "An individual injured by any willful violation of a stay provided by this section shall recover actual damages, including costs and attorneys' fees, and, in appropriate circumstances, may recover punitive damages." 11 U.S.C.A. § 362(h) (West Supp. 1985).

[93] Miller v. Savings Bank of Baltimore, 22 Bankr. 479, 481–82 (D. Md. 1982); *In re* Eisenberg, 7 Bankr. 683, 686 (Bankr. E.D.N.Y. 1980). *But see* Stoops, *supra* note 11, at 439.

legislature, had the initiative in defining the substance of the law governing unions' collective activity; Congress designed the Norris-LaGuardia Act to bring this situation to an end.[94] Additionally, Congress was concerned with the often *ex parte* and uniquely preemptive qualities of an injunction; Congress believed that even if after a hearing an improvidently granted injunction was ultimately vacated, the injunction would have effectively "killed" the strike.[95]

The self-enforcing aspects of the automatic stay provisions encroach upon neither of these concerns. Congress, not the courts, has defined the specific scope of the conduct prohibited by the Bankruptcy Code. Further, a "show cause" hearing to determine the legality of a union's past conduct is neither *ex parte* nor a "prior constraint." To be sure, this is not the optimal approach, but it is better than providing no relief to a debtor suffering economic harm because of a union's illegal harassment.

Avoiding the Conflict by Reference to the Underlying Purposes of the Two Statutes

Another approach for avoiding the apparent conflict between the Norris-LaGuardia Act and the Bankruptcy Code goes beyond the literal wording of the statutes and focuses instead on their underlying purposes; this focus demonstrates that the conflict is more cosmetic than real.

The Supreme Court established this approach in *Boys Markets, Inc. v. Local 770, Retail Clerks Union,*[96] a decision that seemingly presented the Court with a fundamental and troublesome statutory inconsistency between the Norris-LaGuardia Act and section 301(a)

---

[94] *See* 75 CONG. REC. 4930 (1932) (statement of Sen. Norris); *id.* at 4932 (statement of Sen. Bratton). Congress believed the legislative prerogative to establish social policy was being usurped by federal judges, who, by issuing injunctions hostile to labor, in accordance with their own political views, were in effect creating a "government by injunction." *See* THIEBLOT & HAGGARD, *supra* note 22, at 198; *see also* Jacksonville Bulk Terminals v. International Longshoremen's Ass'n. 457 U.S. 702, 715–16 (1982) (rendering the anti-injunction provisions of the Norris-LaGuardia Act applicable despite the political motivations of work stoppage).

[95] *See* 75 CONG. REC. 4929 (1932) (statement of Sen. Norris) ("The harm of an injunction ninety-nine times out of one hundred is done and the injustice is completed within a few days after the restraining order is given.... The only way to correct such an order is take an appeal. But by the time [the appeal is heard the] organizations [are] practically destroyed."); Brotherhood of R.R. Trainmen v. Toledo, P. & W.R.R., 321 U.S. 50, 65–66 (1944); *see also* Wimberly, *supra* note 13, at 690 (effect of temporary injunction was to break a strike's momentum and end it); Winter, *supra* note 13, at 73 (infrequency of seeking permanent injunctions attests to the finality of temporary injunction).

[96] 398 U.S. 235 (1970).

of the NLRA.[97] That section of the Act provides that suits for breach of a collective bargaining agreement may be brought in federal district court.[98] Notwithstanding the apparent limitations of the Norris-LaGuardia Act, the Supreme Court previously held in *Textile Workers Union v. Lincoln Mills*[99] that this section "authorizes federal courts to fashion a body of federal law for the enforcement of these collective bargaining agreements and includes within that federal law specific performance of promises to arbitrate grievances under collective bargaining agreements."[100] But despite the ready availability of arbitration as a means of resolving industrial disputes, and even when contracts contained express "no-strike" clauses, unions often found it more expedient to go on strike—a course of action that undermined both the sanctity of the collective bargaining agreement and the federal policy favoring arbitration. When employers attempted to have such strikes enjoined, they were confronted with the prohibitions of the Norris-LaGuardia Act—prohibitions that the Supreme Court upheld in *Sinclair Refining Co. v. Atkinson*[101] after an exhaustive review of the legislative history of both the Norris-LaGuardia Act and the NLRA.[102] A scant eight years later, in *Boys Markets, Inc. v. Local 770, Retail Clerks Union*[103] the Court overruled *Sinclair Refining.* Although the Court again purported to justify its conclusion by reference to legislative intent and the so-called plain meaning of the two statutes, a more realistic reading of the opinion suggests that the Court was adopting an entirely new approach to the problem.[104] The Court took the Taft-Hartley Act's policy favoring arbitration, stood it beside the original purposes of the Norris-LaGuardia Act, and concluded that the two were not in conflict; this conclusion thus justified the issuance of an injunction that advanced the policies of the one statute and did not frustrate the purposes of the other.

---

[97] 29 U.S.C. § 185(a) (1982).

[98] *Id.*

[99] 353 U.S. 448 (1957).

[100] *Id.* at 451. Subsequently, in the famous *Steelworkers Trilogy,* the Court further enshrined arbitration as the linchpin of federal labor policy by broadly construing an employer's duty to arbitrate and by narrowly limiting the scope of judicial review of arbitral decisions. *See* United Steelworkers v. American Mfg. Co., 363 U.S. 564, 567–69 (1960); United Steelworkers v. Warrior & Gulf Navigation Co., 363 U.S. 574, 581–82 (1960); United Steelworkers v. Enterprise Wheel & Car Corp., 363 U.S. 593, 599 (1960).

[101] 370 U.S. 195 (1962), *overruled,* Boys Mkts., Inc. v. Local 770, Retail Clerks Union, 398 U.S. 235, 238 (1970).

[102] 370 U.S. at 205–09.

[103] 398 U.S. 235 (1970).

[104] *See* Wellington & Albert, *Statutory Interpretation and the Political Process: A Comment Upon* Sinclair v. Atkinson, 72 YALE L.J. 1547, 1548–49 (1963).

A similar approach could be followed in accommodating the Bankruptcy Act and the Norris-LaGuardia Act. Two of Congress's primary purposes in enacting the Norris-LaGuardia Act were to stop the issuance of injunctions against unions' concerted activity that courts deemed unlawful (and thus enjoinable) based only upon preconceived notions of social utility or the lingering influence of the criminal-conspiracy doctrine in antitrust law, and to correct the procedural abuses associated with the labor injunctions of the early 1900s.[105] Even if these purposes continued to be matters of concern in the 1980s, enforcing the automatic stay provisions of the Bankruptcy Code would not run afoul of these particular objectives of the Norris-LaGuardia Act. Congress, not a court acting on a personal predilection, has established the policy that the debtor-in-possession should be protected against the self-help remedies of creditors, even though the creditors' conduct would, in other circumstances, be perfectly legal. In short, issuing these injunctions does not engender the problem of judicial usurpation of legislative prerogatives in setting social policy. Procedurally, a petition in bankruptcy is "a *caveat* to all the world,"[106] and the Bankruptcy Code gives advance notice of prohibited conduct. No court will impose a sanction upon a union until the union has had an opportunity for a hearing. Further, a union will not be in contempt of the automatic stay provisions unless it has actual knowledge that the employer has filed for bankruptcy or reorganization.[107] And finally, the Code provides procedures for obtaining relief from an automatic stay if it can be shown that the creditor's interest would be irreparably harmed by the stay's continued effect.[108] This would seem to counteract any unusual situation in which the automatic stay provisions would hinder a union's right to use concerted activity to protect the legitimate interests of its members.

Moreover, even if the bankruptcy court is acting only under its broad section 105 powers, it is still unlikely that the perceived abuses that led to the passage of the Norris-LaGuardia Act would suddenly spring up anew, like some jurisprudential phoenix. The Bankruptcy Rules provide fair and adequate procedures for the issuance of all injunctions.[109] Further, because the bankruptcy court is a court of equity, it can be expected to account for the constitutional and other statutory interests that are at stake, to balance

---

[105] *See supra* text accompanying notes 12–18.

[106] Mueller v. Nugent, 184 U.S. 1, 14 (1902) (emphasis in original).

[107] *In re* Tom Powell & Son, Inc., 22 Bankr. 657, 661 (Bankr. W.D. Mo. 1982).

[108] 11 U.S.C. § 362(d) (1982).

[109] Bankruptcy Rule 7065 substantially incorporates the provisions of Rule 65 of the Federal Rules of Civil Procedure. *See* BANKR. R. 7065; FED. R. CIV. P. 65.

those interests against the hardship a strike would impose on the debtor-in-possession and the other creditors, and to enjoin the strike only if equitable.[110]

The *Boys Markets* approach[111] thus seems reasonable. Indeed, two factors suggest that the conflict between the Bankruptcy Code and the Norris-LaGuardia Act presents an even better context in which to apply that approach than did the conflict in *Boys Markets.* First, the NLRA's policy of encouraging arbitration, which the *Boys Markets* Court had to reconcile with Norris-LaGuardia, was itself mainly a judicial creation, a gloss that the Supreme Court had placed upon the otherwise general language of section 301(a) of that Act.[112] In contrast, the Bankruptcy Code's policy of protecting the debtor-in-possession and other creditors from the predatory acts of one creditor is a policy that Congress expressly mandated. In *Jacksonville Bulk Terminals v. International Longshoremen's Association*[113] the Court stated: "In the past, we have consistently declined to constrict Norris-LaGuardia's broad prohibitions except in narrowly defined situations where accommodation of the Act to specific congressional policy is necessary."[114] It would seem that the automatic stay provisions of the Bankruptcy Code represent such a "specific congressional policy."

Further, Congress actually considered creating exceptions to the Norris-LaGuardia Act, to accommodate the apparent implications of section 301, but decided against it.[115] Yet in *Boys Markets* the Court found such an exception by considering the underlying policies of the Norris-LaGuardia and Taft-Hartley Acts.[116] A court could adopt a similar construction of the Bankruptcy Code to accommodate the Norris-LaGuardia Act, but without having to overcome an inconsistent legislative history. The lack of any reference to the Norris-LaGuardia Act in the Bankruptcy Code legislative history suggests that Congress was simply unaware of the potential conflict. Congress's silence thus opens the door to the kind of "creative"

[110] NLRB v. Bildisco & Bildisco, 465 U.S. 513, 527 (1984). A balancing approach would presumably also satisfy the constitutional test for an injunction. *See* United Fed'n of Postal Clerks v. Blount, 325 F. Supp. 879, 885 (D.D.C.), *aff'd,* 404 U.S. 802 (1971) (Wright, J., concurring) ("[R]ight to strike is, at least within constitutional concern, and should not be discriminatorily abridged without substantial or 'compelling' justification."); R. Gorman, *supra* note 69, at 211.

[111] *See supra* note 96 and accompanying text.

[112] *See* Textile Workers Union v. Lincoln Mills, 353 U.S. 448, 455–56 (1957).

[113] 457 U.S. 702 (1982).

[114] *Id.* at 720; *see id.* at 708, 717 n.17.

[115] S. 2830, 89th Cong., 1st Sess., 111 Cong. Rec. 13,435 (1965); H.R. 5315, 89th Cong., 1st Sess., 111 Cong. Rec. 13,767 (1965); *see* Boys Mkts., Inc. v. Local 770, Retail Clerks Union, 398 U.S. 235, 259 (1970) (Black, J., dissenting).

[116] 398 U.S. at 253.

statutory interpretation represented by *Boys Markets.* If a judicial limitation on the scope of the Norris-LaGuardia Act was appropriate in *Boys Markets,* it would seem doubly appropriate as a means of resolving the apparent conflict between the literal wording of that Act and the automatic stay provisions of the Bankruptcy Code.

Courts, however, have not adopted the *Boys Markets* argument. The Sixth Circuit in *Crowe* seemed to conclude that the *Boys Markets* decision was limited to its specific facts.[117] To be sure, the Supreme Court itself has narrowly construed the *Boys Markets* decision, even within the context of its origin.[118] But the Court has never intimated that the underlying rational of *Boys Markets* is necessarily limited to injunctions against strikes over arbitrable disputes. Instead, the Court's test is simply whether a judicial construction of the Norris-LaGuardia Act's broad prohibition is necessary to accommodate another specific congressional policy.[119] The need to accommodate the Norris-LaGuardia Act with the automatic stay provisions of the Bankruptcy Code would seem to satisfy this test.

Courts have, however, rejected the *Boys Markets* approach for other reasons. In *NLRB v. Brada Miller Freight System,*[120] the district court relied on language from *Boys Markets* to conclude that "the central purpose of the Norris-LaGuardia Act [is] to foster the growth and viability of labor organizations,"[121] a purpose that the court thought a *Boys Markets* injunction was intended to advance.[122] The court thus rejected the *Boys Markets* approach because "[i]n stark contrast to the considerations present in *Boys Market,* [sic] the issuance of an injunction by the Bankruptcy Court under the facts of this case effectively eviscerates the central purpose of and

117 *Crowe & Assocs.,* 713 F.2d at 215; *see* Briggs Transp. Co. v. Local 710, Int'l Bhd. of Teamsters, 40 Bankr. 972, 975 (D. Minn.), *aff'd,* 739 F.2d 341 (8th Cir. 1984), *cert. denied,* 105 S. Ct. 295 (1984). *But see In re* Tucker Freight Lines, 115 L.R.R.M. (BNA) 2202, 2204–05 (Bankr. W.D. Mich. 1983) (finding *Boys Markets* exception where the purposes of the Norris-LaGuardia Act would not be frustrated by the issuance of an injunction requiring a debtor-in-possession to comply with the terms of a collective bargaining contract between the union and the bankrupt employer). Of course, the bankruptcy court can certainly grant an injunction if the strike falls literally within the *Boys Markets* exception. *In re* Elsinore Shore Associates, 66 Bankr. 743 (Bankr. D. N.J. 1986).

118 *See* Jacksonville Bulk Terminals v. International Longshoremen's Ass'n, 457 U.S. 702, 724 (1982) (recognizing exception where underlying dispute arbitrable); Buffalo Forge Co. v. United Steelworkers, 428 U.S. 397, 410–11 (1976) (limiting exception to cases where injunction necessary to enforce promises to arbitrate).

119 *Jacksonville Bulk Terminals,* 457 U.S. at 720.

120 16 Bankr. 1002 (N.D. Ala. 1981), *vacated and remanded on other grounds,* 702 F.2d 890 (11th Cir. 1983).

121 16 Bankr. at 1011 (quoting *Boys Mkts.,* 398 U.S. at 252–53).

122 16 Bankr. at 1011.

the public policy embodied in Norris-LaGuardia."[123] That, however, represents an unduly narrow, if not strained, reading of the *Boys Markets* rationale.[124]

Just as the Norris-LaGuardia Act yielded to the NLRA in *Boys Markets,* so also did the Taft-Hartley Act yield to the Bankruptcy Code in *NLRB v. Bildisco & Bildisco*[125]—in both instances because the Supreme Court concluded that the underlying purposes of the yielding statutes were not frustrated, while the purposes of the prevailing statutes were significantly enhanced. Although the Supreme Court's decision in *Bildisco* has been superseded by provisions of the Bankruptcy Amendments and Federal Judgeship Act of 1984,[126] the *Bildisco* Court's approach toward the reconciliation of bankruptcy and labor law issues continues, insofar as the lower federal courts are concerned, to control. Indeed, the approach that the Court took in *Bildisco* is very similar to the Court's approach in *Boys Markets.* In resolving the apparent conflict between the Bankruptcy Code's suspension of executory contracts and the NLRA's requirement of adherence to collective bargaining agreements, the Court focused on the underlying purpose of section 8(d) of the NLRA and found that giving precedence to the Bankruptcy Code would not frustrate section 8(d)'s purpose of limiting an employer's power to unilaterally modify the terms of an otherwise enforceable collective bargaining agreement.[127] The Court concluded that "[i]n a Chapter 11 case, . . . the 'modification' in the agreement has been accomplished not by the employer's unilateral action, but rather by operation of law . . .,"[128] and reasoned that because the filing of a petition in bankruptcy makes the collective bargaining

---

[123] *Id.*

[124] The Supreme Court in *Boys Markets* never unequivocally stated that the issuance of an injunction would advance the Norris-LaGuardia Act's alleged goal of promoting unionism. The Court certainly did not make such advancement the *sine qua non* of an exception of the literal words of that Act. Rather, the Court stated: "[*I*]*f anything,* this goal [of fostering labor organizations] is advanced[ ] by a remedial device that merely enforces the obligation that the union freely undertook under a specifically enforceable agreement to submit disputes to arbitration." *Boys Mkts.,* 398 U.S. at 252–53 (emphasis added). How that remedial device does this is far from clear, especially from the union's perspective. In any event, the *Boys Markets* Court emphasized that the original purposes of the Norris-LaGuardia Act were not inconsistent with, and had indeed been superseded by, the congressional policies implicit in section 301(a) of the NLRA. *Id.* at 249–53. In this regard, section 301(a) of the NLRA stands on the same footing as to the automatic stay provisions. 11 U.S.C. § 105 (1982); 11 U.S.C.A. § 1113 (West Supp. 1985).

[125] 465 U.S. 513, 516–17 (1984).

[126] Pub. L. No. 98-353, 98 Stat 333, 390–91 (codified at 11 U.S.C.A. § 1113 (West Supp. 1985)).

[127] *Bildisco,* 465 U.S. at 532–33.

[128] *Id.*

agreement an unenforceable contract within the meaning of section 8(d), the failure of a debtor-in-possession to adhere to its terms in no way violates section 8(d).[129]

Although a broad reading of *Bildisco* suggests that the Norris-LaGuardia Act should now yield to the Bankruptcy Code, the Eighth Circuit, in *Briggs Transportation Co. v. Local 710, International Brotherhood of Teamsters,*[130] more or less limited *Bildisco* to its specific holding.[131] In *Briggs,* the Eighth Circuit considered "whether the logic of the Supreme Court's decision in *Bildisco* requires injunctive relief from legitimate strike activities and peaceful picketing by union members who do not wish to accept the abrogation of their contracts and fail to negotiate new agreements with employers attempting Chapter 11 reorganization," and concluded that "*Bildisco* does not stretch this far, nor should it."[132] The Eighth Circuit instead adopted the reasoning of the district court: "[W]hile *Bildisco* may have authorized Briggs to cut its employees' wages ..., it does not prohibit the employees from complaining."[133]

In any event, the court in *Briggs* refused to accommodate the Norris-LaGuardia Act and the Bankruptcy Code; instead, the two statutes were left in conflict.

RESOLVING THE CONFLICT IN FAVOR OF ONE STATUTE OR THE OTHER

Because courts have not been particularly responsive to the arguments for avoiding the apparent conflict between the Norris-LaGuardia Act and the Bankruptcy Code, they necessarily have had to concede the existence of that conflict, and resolve it in favor of one statute or the other.

Most courts that have confronted this choice have opted in favor of the Norris-LaGuardia Act. Although these courts advance a plethora of seemingly objective reasons for their choice, an underlying

---

[129] *Id.* at 1199.

[130] 739 F.2d 341 (8th Cir.), *cert. denied,* 105 S. Ct. 295 (1984).

[131] *Id.* at 344.

[132] *Id.* at 343.

[133] *Id.* (quoting Briggs Transp. Co. v. Local 710, Int'l Bhd. of Teamsters, 40 Bankr. 972, 975 (D. Minn. 1984)). In blithe disregard of historical sequence, the court further stated:

> The Norris-LaGuardia Act [enacted in 1932] was designed in large measure to prevent federal courts from enjoining the legitimate exercise of the rights of American workers created and protected by the National Labor Relations Act [enacted in 1935]. We would unnecessarily limit those rights by easing the jurisdictional restrictions of the Norris-LaGuardia Act in the present case.

739 F.2d at 344.

emotional bias in favor of the Norris-LaGuardia Act is also evident in these decisions. The courts treat the Bankruptcy Code like any other business or regulatory statute serving ordinary commercial interests, but regard the purposes of the Norris-LaGuardia Act as almost sacrosanct. The Second Circuit called the Act "historic."[134] The district court in *Crowe* stated that eliminating the right to strike, even if the strike is for otherwise illegal purposes, would be such a "devastating step"[135] that the court simply could not believe Congress would have done so without notice and hearing.[136] The *Petrusch* court exhibited a similar degree of incredulity in its oft-quoted statement that omission of any reference to the Norris-LaGuardia Act in the legislative history of the Bankruptcy Code is "self-evident proof that Congress never intended to supersede or transcend it, since we cannot believe the Norris-LaGuardia Act was to be superseded, *sub silentio.*[137]

Reinforcing this near presumption in favor of the preeminence of the Norris-LaGuardia Act is some courts' emphasis on Congress's decision to couch the Act in terms of a denial of jurisdiction to the federal courts.[138] In the hierarchy of statutory commands, this apparently outranks ordinary substantive and procedural provisions, such as those contained in the Bankruptcy Code.

The jurisdictional nature of the Norris-LaGuardia Act is, however, a makeweight in the current conflict. To be sure, the Act's original purpose may have been to send a clear and emphatic message to the courts to stop their allegedly biased interference in labor-management matters, something Congress had been unable to accomplish through the Clayton Act. But like the other original objectives of the Norris-LaGuardia Act, this objective is no longer germane to the current industrial relations scene. Moreover, the ostensibly jurisdictional nature of the Norris-LaGuardia Act has never really been taken literally, even in situations in which it could make a significant difference, such as when a defendant union attempts to remove an injunction case from state to federal court.[139]

---

[134] Petrusch v. Teamsters Local 317, 667 F.2d 297, 298 (2d Cir.), *cert. denied,* 456 U.S. 974 (1981).

[135] *Crowe & Assocs.,* 20 Bankr. at 228.

[136] *Id.*

[137] *Petrusch,* 667 F.2d at 300; *see also* Briggs Transp. Co. v. Local 710, Int'l Bhd. of Teamsters, 40 Bankr. 972, 975 (D. Minn.) (refusing to believe that Congress would silently repeal the Norris-LaGuardia Act), *aff'd,* 439 F.2d 341 (8th Cir.), *cert. denied,* 105 S. Ct. 295 (1984).

[138] *See, e.g.,* Truck Drivers Local 807 v. Bohack Corp., 541 F.2d 312, 317 (2d Cir. 1976); Third Ave. Transit Corp. v. Quill, 192 F.2d 971, 973 (2d Cir. 1951).

[139] *See* Avco Corp. v. Aero Lodge No. 735, Int'l Ass'n of Machinists, 390 U.S. 557, 560, *reh'g denied,* 391 U.S. 929 (1968): *cf.* Bethlehem Mines Corp. v. United Mine

The conflict must be resolved on a more substantive basis than the allegedly jurisdictional nature of the Norris-LaGuardia Act's prohibitions. The district court in *Petrusch* suggested one such basis, and other courts have implicitly followed this approach. The *Petrusch* court reasoned from the "fundamental tenet of statutory construction that a statute dealing with a narrow, precise, and specific subject is not submerged by a later enacted statute covering a more generalized spectrum. . . ."[140] The court further found that this presumption can be overcome only by compelling evidence that Congress was aware of the conflict and expressly intended for the broader statute to supersede the more specific one.[141] Applying this tenet of statutory construction, the court concluded that "the specific jurisdictional dictates of the Norris-LaGuardia Act must take precedence over the general power of the Bankruptcy Court."[142]

It is, however, difficult to see how the Norris-LaGuardia Act was, even at the time of the district court's decision in *Petrusch,* necessarily the more specific of the two statutes. Rather, the Second Circuit in *Petrusch* stated that the Norris-LaGuardia Act is a "broad" prohibition against the issuance of injunctions in labor disputes, except in conformity with the statute.[143] The statute's broad language is followed by some specific instances in which an injunction can never issue. On the other hand, although section 105 of the Bankruptcy Code is an admittedly broad and indefinite grant of equitable powers to the bankruptcy court, which standing alone might fall to the more specific provisions of the Norris-LaGuardia Act, section 105 is further elaborated by the automatic stay provisions of section 362. These provisions and the Norris-LaGuardia Act are equally specific with regard to defining acts prohibited to creditors and guaranteed to unions, respectively.[144] But whatever the statutes' ratios of specificity to generality were at the time of the *Petrusch* decision, the new Code provisions have definitely altered these ratios, at least with respect to the role unions are ex-

---

Workers, 476 F.2d 860, 862–63 (3d Cir. 1973) (finding that the Norris-LaGuardia Act only limits the court's injunction powers and does not remove federal jurisdiction); *In re* Rath Packing Co., 116 L.R.R.M. (BNA) 2039, 2043 n.4 (Bankr. N.D. Iowa 1984) (finding the issue to be one of power to issue injunctions, not one of jurisdiction).

[140] *Petrusch,* 14 Bankr. at 829.

[141] *Id.*

[142] *Id.*

[143] *Petrusch,* 667 F.2d at 299.

[144] *Compare* 11 U.S.C.A. § 105 (West Supp. 1985) (granting courts broad power to make orders and issue process) *and* 11 U.S.C.A. § 362 (West Supp. 1985) (providing automatic stays which stop collection-efforts harassment and foreclosure actions) *with* 29 U.S.C. §§ 101–115 (1982) (preventing injunctive interference in labor relations).

pected to play vis-à-vis a debtor-employer's continuing obligation to honor a collective bargaining agreement.

In any event, having concluded that the Norris-LaGuardia Act was the more specific statute, the district court in *Petrusch* concluded that nothing in the legislative history of the Bankruptcy Code suggests that Congress expressly intended to supersede the anti-injunction provisions of the Norris-LaGuardia Act.[145] It is difficult to quarrel with that conclusion. A court can avoid this issue, however, if it rejects the *Petrusch* court's premise and refuses to consider the Bankruptcy Code to be the broader, rather than the more specific, of the two statutes. In this situation, there is no requirement for an express congressional intent to supersede the Act, and, according to an equally venerable canon of statutory construction, a reasonable argument can be advanced for the implied pro tanto repeal of the earlier statute by the contrary commands of the latter.[146]

Some courts have indeed granted supremacy to the Bankruptcy Code over the Norris-LaGuardia Act. For example, in *In re Cleveland & Sandusky Brewing Co.*,[147] a district court held that the provisions of the Bankruptcy Code prevailed over those of the Norris-LaGuardia Act, primarily because the court could not believe that Congress would have intended anything else.[148] Beyond that, the court based its predilection primarily on a 1934 amendment to the Bankruptcy Act of 1898, in which Congress specifically guaranteed employees the right to join the labor union of their choice, free from coercion by a judge, debtor-in-possession, or trustee acting under the authority of the Bankruptcy Code.[149] From this, the court concluded that Congress considered the effect of the bankruptcy amendments on the rights of labor unions,[150] and stated: "[I]f Congress intended to curtail the bankruptcy power where the threatened destruction of property within its jurisdiction was related to

---

[145] 14 Bankr. at 829.

[146] Although even pro tanto repeals are certainly not favored, a clear repugnancy between an old statute and a newer one requires the former to yield. *See* Georgia v. Pennsylvania R.R., 324 U.S. 439, 456–57 (1945); Walling v. Patton-Tulley Transp. Co., 134 F.2d 945, 948 (6th Cir. 1943).

[147] 11 F. Supp. 198 (N.D. Ohio 1935).

[148] *Id.* at 206. The court stated: "It is not to be supposed that Congress intended that the bankruptcy court should be impotent to preserve and administer property within its jurisdiction, in conformity to the express provisions of the act." *Id.* This logic represents an equally unconvincing reversal of the incredulity displayed by most courts.

[149] Chandler Act, ch. 575 § 1, 52 Stat. 840 (1938) (*repealed by* Bankruptcy Act of 1978, Pub. L. No. 96-598, 92 Stat. 2544 (codified as amended at 11 U.S.C.A. §§ 101-151326 (West Supp. 1985)).

[150] 11 F. Supp. at 206–07.

a labor dispute, it would have said so. . . ."[151] Congress did not say so; therefore, the court was empowered to enjoin the employees' strike, notwithstanding the provisions of the Norris-LaGuardia Act.

A similar argument has been made, but without the same degree of success, with respect to the 1978 Bankruptcy Code.[152] There are many enumerated exceptions to the automatic stay provisions,[153] and one commentator has, with some degree of cogency, suggested "if Congress had intended such a broad, blanket exception to the automatic stay provision—which 'labor dispute' activities would be—surely Congress would have included this exception in the list of exceptions to the automatic stay in section 362(b)."[154] The Supreme Court in *Bildisco* was certainly receptive to this kind of argument. The *Bildisco* Court observed that the Bankruptcy Code enumerates several express limits on a debtor-in-possession's power to reject executory contracts. Although the Code exempts collective bargaining agreements under the Railway Labor Act from rejection,[155] agreements under the NLRA are not similarly mentioned. The Court therefore concluded that Congress intended agreements under the NLRA to be subject to rejection,[156] essentially a conclusion that the Bankruptcy Code prevails over the apparently inconsistent provisions of the NLRA. Presumably, the Supreme Court would draw the same inference from Congress's enumeration of several specific exceptions to the automatic stay provisions that lacks any mention of a "labor dispute."

THE EFFECT OF THE NEW SECTION 1113 OF THE BANKRUPTCY CODE ON THE BANKRUPTCY COURT'S POWER TO ENJOIN STRIKES

How does section 1113 affect the apparent conflict between the automatic stay provisions (and section 105) of the Bankruptcy Code and the anti-injunction provisions of the Norris-LaGuardia Act? Although neither *Bildisco* nor the new Code provisions refer to this conflict, these authorities certainly suggest a controlling principle and several attendant corollaries. The general or controlling prin-

---

[151] *Id.* at 207; *see also* Anderson v. Bigelow, 130 F.2d 460, 464–65 (9th Cir. 1942) (finding power to issue injunction against threatened interference with the conduct of a business within its control) (Mathews, J., dissenting).

[152] Note, *The Automatic Stay of the 1978 Bankruptcy Code Versus the Norris-LaGuardia Act: A Bankruptcy Court's Dilemma,* 61 Tex. L. Rev. 321 (1982).

[153] 11 U.S.C. § 362(b) (1982).

[154] Note, *supra* note 152, at 325.

[155] 45 U.S.C. § 152 (1982).

[156] 465 U.S. at 521–22.

ciple is this: once a business finds it necessary to file in bankruptcy, the rights and duties of the debtor-employer and the union should be determined almost exclusively by bankruptcy rather than labor law. By enacting section 1113, Congress has shown that it can accommodate the special needs of employees and unions to the bankruptcy process; the necessary accommodation is made through the Bankruptcy Code. The first corollary of this principle is that the express provisions of the Code, and even the broader exigencies of the bankruptcy process itself, should nearly always prevail over any patently inconsistent labor law provision. A second corollary is that labor law provisions that merely duplicate or add to Code provisions should also be deemed preempted, but only to the extent that their enforcement would interfere with the bankruptcy process.

Applying this policy to the bankruptcy court's power to enjoin strikes is fairly straightforward. In a Chapter 11 proceeding, a union might strike for four different reasons: to protest the debtor-employer's proposed modifications of an old contract;[157] to compel continued adherence to a collective bargaining agreement that the bankruptcy court has allowed the debtor-employer to reject;[158] to compel the debtor-employer to agree to certain terms in a new collective bargaining agreement;[159] or to protest an alleged unfair labor practice by the debtor-employer.[160]

First, the union might find modifications that a debtor-employer must make under section 1113 unacceptable and strike to elicit more favorable terms. The debtor-employer, however, is under an affirmative duty to propose a modification that "assures that all creditors, the debtor and all of the affected parties are treated fairly and equitably. . . ."[161] A proposed modification that meets those requirements may not comport with what the union wants or what the employer might be willing to agree to under other circumstances. A strike under such circumstances thus may pose a direct conflict with the duties imposed on an employer by the Bankruptcy Code. Moreover, such a strike would substantially interfere with the reorganizational effort and could easily drive the debtor-employer into an otherwise unnecessary liquidation,[162] thus defeating the very purpose of the bankruptcy provisions.

---

[157] *See infra* notes 161–164.
[158] *See infra* notes 165–168.
[159] *See infra* notes 169–170.
[160] *See infra* notes 171–175.
[161] 11 U.S.C.A. § 1113(b)(1)(A) (West Supp. 1985).
[162] "[T]he argument that [the debtor-employer] may go out of business absent the requested injunction is no more than a recognition that one of the unfortunate side effects of labor-management strife is economic loss to the employers and employees."

Unions have a remedy for unacceptable debtor-employer proposals.[163] If a union convinces the bankruptcy court that it had good cause for rejecting the debtor-employer's proposal, the court will deny the petition for rejection, thus keeping the old agreement in full force and effect.[164] This, however, should be the exclusive remedy: a strike would undermine the entire reorganizational effort.

If the bankruptcy court approves the rejection of the old collective bargaining agreement, the union might nevertheless strike to compel continued adherence to the terms of the old contract.[165] Of all the reasons why a union may strike, this one does the greatest amount of violence to the integrity of the bankruptcy process. In deciding *Bildisco* and in enacting section 1113 of the Code, neither the Supreme Court nor Congress doubted that once the bankruptcy court has approved the rejection of the old agreement, the debtor-employer's refusal to continue to follow that contract can in no sense be considered an unfair labor practice under the NLRA.[166] It would be highly ironic if another labor law, the Norris-LaGuardia Act, were allowed to impose an indirect but equally effective prohibition against repudiation, by depriving the bankruptcy court of the power to enjoin such strikes.[167]

In *Bildisco,* the Supreme Court said that a debtor-employer remains subject to the NLRA's duty to bargain with the union over the terms of the new contract, and nothing in the new Code provision relieves the debtor-employer of that obligation. The Court has also observed, however, that "[t]he presence of economic weapons [,i.e., strikes,] in reserve, and their actual exercise on occasion by the parties, is part and parcel of the system [of collective bargaining] that the Wagner and Taft-Hartley Acts have recognized."[168]

Briggs Transp. Co. v. Local 710, Int'l Bhd. of Teamsters, 40 Bankr. 972, 975 (D. Minn.), *aff'd,* 739 F.2d 341 (8th Cir.), *cert. denied,* 105 S. Ct. 295 (1984). Other courts have similarly acknowledged the devastating effect a strike can have on a Chapter 11 reorganization. *See* Crowe & Assocs. v. Local 2, Bricklayers & Masons Union, 713 F.2d 211, 216 (6th Cir. 1983) (per curiam); Petrusch v. Teamsters Local 317, 14 Bankr. 825, 830 (N.D.N.Y.), *aff'd,* 667 F.2d 297 (2d Cir. 1981), *cert. denied,* 456 U.S. 974 (1982); Truck Drivers Local 807 v. Bohack Corp., 541 F.2d 312, 318 (2d Cir. 1976), *cert. denied,* 439 U.S. 825 (1978).

[163] *See, e.g.,* NLRB v. Bildisco & Bildisco, 465 U.S. 513, 526 (1984).

[164] *E.g., In re* Pesce Baking Co., 43 Bankr. 949, 959–60 (Bankr. N.D. Ohio 1984).

[165] Indeed, this is what the union apparently threatened to do in Briggs Transp. Co. v. Local 710, Int'l Bhd. of Teamsters, 739 F.2d at 342–43.

[166] *Bildisco,* 465 U.S. at 532.

[167] *Accord* Letterman v. Carpenters 46 N. Cal. Conference Bd., 29 Bankr. 351, 353 (Bankr. E.D. Cal 1983) (when a creditor ignores the discharge of a bankrupt, an injunction may properly be issued to protect the fresh start of a bankrupt from being whipsawed in abortive attempts at collecting the discharged debt).

[168] NLRB v. Insurance Agents' Int'l Union, 361 U.S. 477, 489 (1960). In *In re* Gray Truck Line, 34 Bankr. 174 (Bankr. M.D. Fla. 1983), which was decided after *Bildisco*

Unlike the two former varieties of strikes, strikes to compel negotiations for new contractual terms are not inconsistent with any express provision of the Bankruptcy Code. On the other hand, the court and the official creditors' committee have a legitimate interest in both the terms of this new contract and in the overall success of the corporate reorganization. In some situations, a strike could seriously jeopardize these interests. To the extent that this is so, the labor statute that seemingly provides affirmative protection to such strikes should be subordinated. Thus, the bankruptcy court, in the exercise of its discretion and pursuant to its powers as a court of equity, should be empowered to enjoin a strike that threatens the success of a Chapter 11 reorganization, free from the unrealistic and Draconian restraints of the Norris-LaGuardia Act.[169]

Again, the union is not totally helpless. The new collective bargaining agreement generally will be subject to the prior review of the creditors' committee and the ultimate approval of the bankruptcy court. As a party in interest, the union has the right to be heard on the merits of any reorganization plan that incorporates the collective bargaining agreement as a part of its solution to the debtor's financial problems.[170] The union should press its case in this forum, rather than on the picket line.

Finally, a union may strike to protest the debtor-in-possession's alleged violation of the NLRA's unfair labor practice provisions, including the good-faith-bargaining duty, to the extent that it applies, or the multifaceted duties to refrain from any "discrimination"[171] or interference with the employees' "concerted activities."[172] Normally, the Taft-Hartley Act affords a strike in protest of an alleged unfair labor practice greater protection than it affords a mere "economic strike."[173] Nevertheless, in the bank-

---

but before the enactment of section 1113, the bankruptcy judge opined that the corollary of the debtor-employer's duty to bargain over the terms of a new contract was that "the employees also retain their right to strike should negotiations fail." *Id.* at 179. However, this view is not clearly correct.

[169] This would merely require that the Norris-LaGuardia Act be superseded, thus freeing the debtor-employer to obtain an injunction. However, this resolution need not affect striking employees' rights under the NLRA. The debtor-employer, thus, could not discharge striking employees or deny them the reinstatement rights guaranteed by the NLRA. *See* C. Morris, *supra* note 27, at 1011–15.

[170] *See* 11 U.S.C. § 1109(b) (1982); Bankr. R. 2018(d); Soble, Eggersten & Bernstein, *Pension Related Claims in Bankruptcy,* 56 Am. Bankr. L. J. 155, 174 (1982).

[171] 29 U.S.C. § 158(a)(3) (1982).

[172] *Id.* §§ 157, 158(a)(1).

[173] Although economic strikers may be permanently replaced, NLRB v. Mackay Radio & Tel. Co., 304 U.S. 333, 345–46 (1938), unfair-labor-practice strikers are entitled to reinstatement after the strike, regardless of whether the employer has hired replacements. Collins & Aikman Corp., 165 N.L.R.B. 678, 679 (1967). Moreover,

ruptcy context, although such strikes may not directly conflict with any specific Code provision, they can destroy the entire reorganizational effort, by driving the debtor into an unnecessary liquidation. In such a case, the bankruptcy court should have the discretion and power to enjoin the strike, free from the restraints of the Norris-LaGuardia Act.

Again, the labor laws afford a remedy to the union and the striking employees; if the debtor-employer has committed an unfair labor practice, the processes of the NLRA can vindicate the rights of the union and the injured employees.[174] Indeed, the purpose of these procedures is to provide an alternative to the coercive, self-help measure of a protest strike.[175] Thus, a bankruptcy court's injunction against an unfair-labor-practice strike, if necessary to protect the debtor's estate, would not encroach upon the NLRA's interest in curing unfair labor practices and vindicating employees' rights.

In sum, although they disagree over certain specific details, both the Supreme Court and Congress seem willing to let bankruptcy law regulate the employer-employee-union relationship. To the extent federal labor laws dictate a contrary result, they must yield. This should be as true of the anti-injunction provisions of the Norris-LaGuardia Act as it is of the NLRA.

---

although a mid-term strike to modify or terminate a collective bargaining agreement is subject to the notice and loss-of-status provisions of the NLRA, 29 U.S.C. § 158(d) (1982), the Supreme Court exempted unfair-labor-practice strikes from section 158(d) and held that such strikes are not covered by most "no strike" clauses. Mastro Plastics Corp. v. NLRB, 350 U.S. 270, 284 (1956).

[174] This resolution would also leave in effect the NLRA's prohibitions against discharge, *see supra* note 173, as well as other protections that the NLRA affords to unfair-labor-practice strikers. *See* C. Morris, *supra* note 27, at 1007–11.

[175] *See* 29 U.S.C. § 141(b) (1982). Indeed, given the NLRA's policy of encouraging the use of legal processes as a substitute for economic warfare, it is somewhat ironic that strikes against unfair labor practices, for which the act provides an alternative legal remedy, are given greater protection against an employer's response than are strikes over economic issues, which the act attempts to resolve only by requiring good faith bargaining.

CHAPTER X

Bankruptcy Status of Claims for Employee Compensation and Benefits

Bankruptcy laws exist for the benefit of debtors, not creditors. When a company files a petition for reorganization under Chapter 11 of the Code, its creditors' claims are assigned statutory priorities depending on when and how they arose. Claims designated as administrative expenses are paid first. If anything remains of the debtor's estate after these first priority claims are paid, specified unsecured claims are paid second. After all second priority claims have been paid, third priority claims are allowed, and so forth, until either all creditors have been satisfied or, more typically, the assets of the estate have been exhausted.

Debtors in Chapter 11 proceedings are usually also employers. Whether or not the debtor's employees are covered by a collective bargaining agreement, the employees may have claims as creditors against the debtor's estate, for various types of unpaid wages or benefits. The 1841 Bankruptcy Act[1] established a third priority for claims by workmen against a bankrupt's estate for the "full amount of wages due" on account of "any labor as an operative in the service of any bankrupt." Ever since then, Congress has conferred priority status on claims for wages owed by a debtor to its employees. However, as the Supreme Court noted in *United States v. Embassy Restaurant, Inc.*,[2] "not all types of obligations due employees from their employers are regarded by Congress as being within the concept of wages, even though having some relation to employment."

This chapter provides an overview of the bankruptcy status of employment-related claims for wages, various fringe benefits, severance pay, retirement or pension benefits, pension contributions, and withdrawal liability under the Code, the Employee Retirement Income Security Act of 1974 (ERISA),[3] and the Multiemployer Pension Plan Amendments Act of 1980 (MPPAA).[4]

---

[1] Act of August 19, 1841, ch. 9, 5 Stat. 445. The priority was limited to $25.
[2] 359 U.S. 29, 32 (1959).
[3] Pub. L. No. 93-406, 88 Stat. 829, codified at 29 U.S.C. §§ 1001 *et seq.*
[4] Pub. L. No. 96-364, 94 Stat. 1208, codified at 29 U.S.C. §§ 1001a, *et seq.*

WAGES AND RELATED BENEFITS

The Code expressly covers the allowance and priority of many types of employee compensation and benefits. The bankruptcy status of these claims depends in large part on whether they arose before or after the filing of the bankruptcy petition.

Claims Arising Pre-Petition

Under section 507(a)(3) of the Code, claims for "wages, salaries, or commissions, including vacation, severance, and sick pay earned by an individual" within 90 days prior to the filing of the petition or the cessation of the debtor's business, whichever occurred first, are entitled to a third priority as unsecured claims, subject to a maximum of $2,000 per employee.[5] "The wage provision [in § 507(a)(3)] is established to protect workers who may not have received their checks at the time the petition is filed although they have provided services prior to that time."[6] Wages are "earned" within the meaning of section 507(a)(3) if they are owing at the time of the filing of the petition or if they have accrued at that point.[7] Claims by employees[8] for wages and benefits earned for services rendered *more* than 90 days prior to the employer's filing for bankruptcy or cessation of operations, whichever occurred first, are generally unsecured claims which have no statutory priority.

Claims Arising Post-Petition

Under sections 365(g)(1) and 502(g), claims for unpaid wages and benefits arising from post-petition rejection of a collective bargaining agreement are allowed or disallowed "as if such claim had arisen before the date of the filing of the petition."[9] Some courts have held that section 502(g) claims are not entitled to priority under section

---

[5] 11 U.S.C. § 507(a)(3). "The Code thus eliminates the inequitable situation resulting under the old Act whereby employees were deprived of all or part of their priority merely because the employer ceased doing business before filing the bankruptcy petition." 2 ABA Section of Labor and Employment Law, The Developing Labor Law 1587 (C. Morris, ed. 1983).

[6] *In re* Crouthamel Potato Chip Co., 52 Bankr. 960, 967 n.5 (E.D. Pa. 1985), *rev'd on other grounds,* 786 F.2d 141 (3d Cir. 1986).

[7] 52 Bankr. at 965.

[8] The employees' collective bargaining representative may have standing as a creditor to assert claims for unpaid wages and benefits. *See In re* Altair Airlines, Inc., 727 F.2d 88 (3d Cir. 1984). *But see* In re Continental Airlines Corp., 64 Bankr. 874, 878 (Bankr. S.D. Tex. 1986) (at least under Railway Labor Act, contract damage claims are "minor disputes," in which the union has no authority to act on behalf of the affected employee(s) absent independent authorization by the employee(s)).

[9] 11 U.S.C. § 502(g).

507(a)(3), reasoning that sections 365(g) and 502(g) were designed only "to assure that [such] claims . . . are included among the group of unsecured prepetition creditors whose rights are to be determined by the Bankruptcy Court and not as post-petition creditors."[10] The Supreme Court noted in *Bildisco* that

> [d]amages on the contract that result from the rejection of an executory contract ... must be administered through bankruptcy and receive the priority provided general unsecured creditors. . . .
>
> Section 502(c) provides that any contingent or unliquidated claim shall be estimated for purposes of settling a bankrupt estate. Under this provision losses occasioned by the rejection of a collective-bargaining agreement must be estimated, including unliquidated losses attributable to fringe benefits or security provisions like seniority rights.[11]

Because a damages claim arising from the debtor's rejection of a collective-bargaining agreement pursuant to section 502(g) is not a claim for "wages" within the meaning of section 507(a)(3), and because in any event section 502(g) only deems such claims to have "arisen"—*not* to have been *earned*—pre-petition, damage claims arising from rejection will be unsecured claims entitled to no priority under section 507.[12] Accordingly, a debtor should always seek rejection of the collective bargaining agreement, even if operations have been discontinued indefinitely, in order to convert any wage or benefit delinquencies into unsecured claims.

Wages and benefits earned *after* filing are deemed to be administrative expenses, which are given first priority.[13] Section 503(b)(1)(A) expressly covers "the actual, necessary costs and expenses of preserving the estate, including wages, salaries, or commissions for services rendered after the commencement of the case."[14]

---

[10] *In re* Crouthamel Potato Chip Co., *supra,* 52 Bankr. at 966 n.4. *Cf. In re* Robinson Truck Lines, Inc., 47 Bankr. 631, 636 (Bankr. N.D. Miss. 1985) (claim for debtor's rejection of, and possibly for debtor's post-petition failure to make contributions to health and welfare plan, governed by section 507(a)(4)).

[11] NLRB v. Bildisco & Bildisco, 465 U.S. 513, 531 & n.12 (1984). The valuation of claims under sections 365(g)(1) and 502(g) can be difficult. In *In re* Continental Airlines, Inc., 64 Bankr. 865, 871–73 (Bankr. S.D. Tex. 1986), the bankruptcy court disallowed entirely ALPA's claim for over $408 million, and ruled that such claims are subject to all applicable contract defenses under section 502(b)(1); are limited by the expiration date of the rejected contract; and are further limited to a maximum of one year's compensation under section 502(b)(7). Moreover, the court ruled that if the alternative to rejection was the debtor's liquidation, employees suffer no recoverable damages unless the contract expressly guaranteed future employment.

[12] *In re* Crouthamel Potato Chip Co., *supra,* 52 Bankr. at 966 n.4.

[13] 11 U.S.C. §§ 503(b)(1)(A), 507(a)(1).

[14] 11 U.S.C. § 503(b)(1)(A). "The administrative expense provision [in §507(a)(1)] assures that the debtor-in-possession or the trustee will be able to contract for goods

For non-union employees, claims for post-petition compensation are valuated by reference to the applicable wage rate, salary structure, or commission formula established by the debtor. For employees covered by collective bargaining agreements, rejection of the contract post-petition complicates the matter of valuation because the claim will be determined by the reasonable value of the services rendered. Wages and benefits earned for services performed prior to rejection will generally be calculated in quantum meruit at the former contract rate, and after rejection at the modified rate, if any.

The Supreme Court in *Bildisco* summarized the applicable principles as follows:

> If the debtor-in-possession elects to continue to receive benefits from the other party to an executory contract pending a decision to reject or assume the contract, the debtor-in-possession is obligated to pay for the reasonable value of those services, ... which, depending on the circumstances of a particular contract, may be what is specified in the contract.... Should the debtor-in-possession elect to assume the executory contract, however, it assumes the contract *cum onere,* ... and the expenses and liabilities incurred may be treated as administrative expenses, which are afforded the highest priority on the debtor's estate, 11 U.S.C. § 503(b)(1)(A).[15]

In *In re Tucson Yellow Cab Co.,*[16] the Ninth Circuit applied the contract rate to compute the "fair value" of the services rendered by unionized employees during the period following rejection of the union contract until their termination. The court concluded that the employees were entitled to two weeks' pay in lieu of notice because this amount—specified in the rejected contract—was "the fair value of the employees' services" that were rendered after rejection.[17] The court's decision to award full contractual severance pay appeared to be influenced by the following factors: (1) the contract remained in effect for over 14 months after the Chapter 11 petition was filed; (2) the contract was formally rejected just 11 days prior the termination of all bargaining unit employees; and (3) "the work done by the employees after [rejection] was necessary to the preservation of the estate. Although they knew that their discharge was inevitable, they did not know the date it would take

---

and services necessary to maintenance of the value of the estate." *In re* Crouthamel Potato Chip Co., *supra,* 52 Bankr. at 967 n.5.

[15] NLRB v. Bildisco & Bildisco, 465 U.S. 513, 531–32 (1984) (citations omitted) *See In re* Pulaski Highway Express, Inc., 57 Bankr. 502, 510 (Bankr. M.D. Tenn. 1986) (reasonable value of post-petition services determined by reference to collective bargaining agreement that was never rejected).

[16] 789 F.2d 701 (9th Cir. 1986).

[17] *Id.* at 704.

effect. *They continued to work in the reasonable belief that their wages had been unchanged.*"[18]

Under the reasoning of *Tucson Yellow Cab,* the contract rate will represent the ceiling of quantum meruit valuation for services rendered post-rejection because one can assume that "the debtor would [not] have paid its employees greater wages than what their work was worth."[19] However, depending on the circumstances, the quantum meruit valuation of services rendered post-rejection could be less than the contract rate, particularly if the contract was rejected promptly, the contract compensation rates were in excess of market, and the modified terms were clearly communicated to the employees.

There is a conflict among the courts of appeals as to the scope of post-petition compensation entitled to administrative priority status. The consequences of this status are significant. "Administrative expenses" is the highest bankruptcy priority; "it is paid ahead of tax claims and other debts owed to the U.S. Government. The claims are paid in full, without any dollar limitation, before other unsecured claimants (including prepetition wage claimants) are paid anything on their claims."[20] As if to illustrate this principle, the U.S. Court of Appeals for the Ninth Circuit recently held that union employees' claim for post-petition compensation qualified for treatment as "administrative expenses" and thereby would be paid out of the debtor's assets before a judgment creditor—the plaintiff in a personal injury case who had lost part of one leg—could attempt to satisfy her claim.[21]

The issue of whether wages and benefits are "earned" after filing and therefore entitled to treatment as administrative expenses sometimes raises difficult questions. Wages allocable to work performed after filing are earned post-petition. Courts have taken varying approaches to benefits such as vacation pay and severance pay.

In *In re Public Ledger, Inc.,*[22] the U.S. Court of Appeals for the Third Circuit reasoned that benefits such as vacation and severance pay are "earned" over a long period of time. Accordingly, the court in *Public Ledger* held that only the portion of vacation pay accrued pro rata by employees post-petition was entitled to administrative priority; vacation pay accrued pro rata within the priority period pre-petition (90 days under the Code) was entitled to a lesser prior-

---

[18] *Id.* at 705–05 (emphasis added).

[19] *Id.* at 704.

[20] Developing Labor Law, *supra* note 5, at 1589.

[21] *See In re* Tucson Yellow Cab Co., 789 F.2d 701 (9th Cir. 1986).

[22] 161 F.2d 762 (3d Cir. 1947).

ity.[23] The court in *Public Ledger* also held that the *entire amount* of severance pay required by a collective bargaining agreement for all employee layoffs without two days' prior notice was entitled to administrative priority if the layoffs occurred post-petition.[24] The court reasoned that the pay-in-lieu-of-notice provision

> protects against a sudden, unexpected and unprepared for stoppage of wages. It provides that knowledge of a break in the continuity of work and the consequent lack of pay shall be given the employee and it is the employer's duty to give it. If he does not give it, the wage continues unaffected for the term of the required notice.[25]

Severance pay under a different agreement, which required specified payments upon termination based on the employees' length of service regardless of notice, was, in contrast, entitled to administrative priority only to the extent that it was "earned" post-petition.[26] Hence, the court in *Public Ledger* distinguished between two types of severance pay: pay-in-lieu-of-notice, which is "earned" in a lump sum if the requisite notice is not given; and longevity-based severance, which is "earned" over a long period of time, similar to vacation pay.

In *Straus-Duparquet, Inc. v. Local Union No. 3, IBEW,*[27] the Second Circuit departed from this analysis of severance pay[28] and held that

> [s]everance pay is not earned day to day and does not "accrue" so that a proportionate part is payable under any circumstances. After the period of eligibility is served, *the full severance pay is due whenever termination of employment occurs*. . . .
>
> Since severance pay is compensation for termination of employment and since employment of these claimants was terminated as an incident of the administration of the bankrupt's estate, severance pay was an expense of administration and is entitled to priority as such an expense.[29]

---

[23] *Id.* at 767–69. Vacation pay earned prior to this period is entitled to no priority.

[24] *Id.* at 769–71.

[25] *Id.* at 770.

[26] *Id.* at 771–73.

[27] 386 F.2d 649 (2d Cir. 1967).

[28] The court agreed with the Third Circuit in *In re* Public Ledger that "claimants are entitled to priority for vacation pay as an expense of administration only to the extent of the proportionate part of total vacation pay earned during the period from the beginning of the bankruptcy administration to the date of termination of employment." 386 F.2d at 650–51. *See also In re* Schatz Federal Bearings Co., 5 Bankr. 543, 549 (Bankr. S.D.N.Y. 1980).

[29] 386 F.2d at 651 (emphasis added).

The Second Circuit has adhered to this approach,[30] while the First and Ninth Circuits have followed the *In re Public Ledger* reasoning.[31] In *In re Pacific Far East Line, Inc.*, the Ninth Circuit explained its rationale:

> Our severance pay rule divides severance pay into two general types: pay at termination in lieu of notice, and pay at termination based on length of employment. . . . Pay in lieu of notice is considered an administrative expense; but pay based upon length of employment is not, because the latter is actually a form of remuneration for work performed before the filing date.[32]

The practical effect of the courts' differing approaches is that only a small part of seniority-based severance pay will be entitled to administrative priority under the *In re Public Ledger* analysis followed by the First, Third, and Ninth Circuits. In contrast, the Second Circuit treats *all* severance pay for post-petition terminations as administrative expenses. In 1980 the Supreme Court declined to settle this conflict when it denied certiorari in *In re W.T. Grant.*[33]

PENSION CLAIMS

Pension claims can be divided into claims for unpaid *contributions* and claims for pension plan *withdrawal liability.* Each of these categories can be further divided into single-employer and multi-employer pension plans. Multi-employer plans,[34] are subject to special rules regarding withdrawal, contained in Subtitle E of Employee Retirement Income Security Act (ERISA).[35] Certain types of single-employer plans are also subject to the ERISA requirements of termination insurance, which is provided by the Pension Benefit Guaranty Corporation (PBGC). Single-employer plans cover employees of a single-employer or group of employers related through common ownership. Most plans covering non-union employees and some

---

[30] *See In re* W.T. Grant Co., 474 F. Supp. 788 (S.D.N.Y. 1979), *aff'd,* 620 F.2d 319, 321 (2d Cir.) (per curiam) ("The entire portion of the employees' severance pay claims is entitled to first priority as costs and expenses of administration"), *cert. denied,* 446 U.S. 983 (1980).

[31] *See In re* Mammoth Mart, Inc., 536 F.2d 950, 953 (1st Cir. 1976); *In re* Health Maintenance Foundation, 680 F.2d 619, 621 (9th Cir. 1982); *In re* Pacific Far East Line, Inc., 713 F.2d 476 (9th Cir. 1983); *In re* Tucson Yellow Cab Co., 789 F.2d 701 (9th Cir. 1986).

[32] 713 F.2d at 478.

[33] *See* note 30 *supra.* "It is well settled that a claim for wages or benefits earned post-petition is only recoverable as an administrative expense if the payment conferred some benefit on the debtor-in-possession or trustee." *In re* Crouthamel Potato Chip Co., *supra,* 52 Bankr. at 966.

[34] *See* 29 U.S.C. § 1002(37).

[35] *See* 29 U.S.C. §§ 1381 *et seq.*

plans covering union employees are single-employer plans. Multi-employer plans are plans to which more than one employer or group of related employers are required to contribute pursuant to one or more collective bargaining agreements.

Unpaid Contributions

An employer's failure to make timely contributions to multi-employer or single-employer pension or health and welfare plans pursuant to collective bargaining agreements is a violation of ERISA.[36] Claims against a Chapter 11 debtor for delinquent contributions under ERISA are within the jurisdiction of the bankruptcy court.[37] The allowance and priority of such claims, however, are controlled by the Code:

> Pension and health plan claims against a Chapter 11 debtor-in-possession, whether based on judgments or otherwise, are nonetheless subject to the provision of the Bankruptcy Code. ERISA does not impair the bankruptcy court's fundamental authority to administer a debtor's reorganization.... The Bankruptcy Code controls the allowance of claims including those arising under ERISA.[38]

The Code assigns a specific priority to such claims. "Immediately below the priority status accorded to wages is a priority for contributions to employee benefit plans."[39] This provision of the Code, which legislatively overrules the holding in *United States v. Embassy Restaurant, Inc.* that fringe benefits were not entitled to wage priority status, is limited to claims for contributions to employee benefit plans arising from services rendered within 180 days prior to the earlier of either the filing of the petition or cessation of the debtor's business.[40] Such claims are entitled to a fourth priority up

---

[36] 29 U.S.C. § 1145.

[37] *See* Cott Corp. v. New England Teamsters and Trucking Industry Pension Fund, 26 Bankr. 332 (Bankr. D. Conn. 1982); *In re* Braniff Airways, Inc. 24 Bankr. 466 (Bankr. N.D. Tex. 1982). This includes delinquent contributions to single-employer pension plans. *See In re* J.L. Thomson Rivet Corp., 19 Bankr. 385 (Bankr. D. Mass. 1982).

[38] *In re* Columbia Motor Express., Inc., 33 Bankr. 389, 393–94 (M.D. Tenn. 1983). *See also In re* Baptist Medical Center of New York, Inc., 52 Bankr. 417 (E.D.N.Y. 1985) (bankruptcy court has jurisdiction to stay execution of judgment against a Chapter 11 debtor for unpaid post-petition contributions to multi-employer employee benefit plans), *aff'd per curiam,* 781 F.2d 973 (2d Cir. 1986).

[39] Developing Labor Law, *supra* note 5, at 1587; 11 U.S.C. § 507(a)(4).

[40] 11 U.S.C. § 507(a)(4). "Employee benefit plans" include pension plans, health and welfare plans, life insurance plans, and all other forms of employee compensation that is not in the form of wages. *See* H.R. Rep. No. 595, 95th Cong., 1st Sess. 187 (1977); S. Rep. 989, 95th Cong., 2d Sess. 69 (1978); *In re* Shearon, 10 Bankr. 626, 627–28 (Bankr. D. Neb. 1981) (indirect compensation covered by § 507(a)(4)). Although § 507(a)(4) does not distinguish between single-employer and multi-employer

to a maximum of $2,000 for each covered employee, minus the amounts paid to such employees under the wage priority provisions and "the aggregate amount paid by the estate on behalf of such employees to any other employee benefit plan."[41] Thus, the $2,000 per employee limitation is "placed on the total of the wage priority and all contributions payable under the benefits priority provision."[42] Claims for unpaid contributions arising post-petition are entitled to first priority as administrative expenses.[43] Administrative claims must be paid in full as a prerequisite to confirmation of a plan for reorganization under Chapter 11.[44]

Withdrawal Liability

The Multiemployer Pension Plan Amendments Act of 1980 (MPPAA) was designed to strengthen multi-employer pension plans financially by discouraging employers from withdrawing from such plans and leaving behind unfunded, vested liabilities.[45] Underfunding of vested benefits is generally possible only with respect to "defined benefit plans," and not to "individual account plans" or "defined contribution plans." An "individual account plan" or "defined contribution plan" is a pension plan which provides for an individual account for each participant and for benefits based solely upon the amount contributed to that account.[46] In general, such plans are not covered by the termination insurance provisions of ERISA,[47] unless the plan is a "plan under which a fixed benefit is promised if the employer or his representative participated in the determination of that benefit."[48] In this case, the "defined contribution plan" would more closely resemble a "defined benefit plan."

---

plans, as a practical matter this priority will operate only in the context of multi-employer plans, in which benefit contributions are made on behalf of covered employees based on the number of hours worked, and not in single-employer, defined benefit plans, in which benefit contributions are made without regard to particular hours worked or "services rendered."

[41] 11 U.S.C. § 507(a)(4)(B). *See In re* Columbia Packing Co., 47 Bankr. 126, 131–32 (Bankr. D. Mass. 1985).

[42] Developing Labor Law, *supra* note 5, at 1588. "In other words, the sum total of employee claims given priority under [11 U.S.C. § 507(a)(3) and (a)(4)] cannot exceed $2,000 per employee, and the claims of multiple employee benefit plans are to be prorated to keep within that limit." Labor and ERISA Law In and Out of the Bankruptcy Courts 48 (H. Miller & R. Ordin, eds. 1984).

[43] *See* 11 U.S.C. §§ 503(b)(1)(A), 507(a)(1); *In re* Pacific Far East Lines, Inc., 713 F.2d 476, 478–80 (9th Cir. 1983). There is no express limit on the amount of an employee claim under 11 U.S.C. § 507(a)(1).

[44] *See* 11 U.S.C. § 1129(a)(9).

[45] 29 U.S.C. §§ 1001a, 1381, *et seq.*

[46] *See* 29 U.S.C. § 1002(34).

[47] *See* 29 U.S.C. § 1321(b)(1).

[48] 29 U.S.C. § 1321(c)(1).

"Defined benefit plans," defined as any plan other than an individual account or defined contribution plan,[49] are covered by the termination insurance provisions of ERISA. The critical difference between these two types of pension plans is that a participant's benefit in an individual account or defined contribution plan is based solely on the amount of his account.[50] Therefore, in theory individual account or defined contribution plans "can never be underfunded"[51] and are excluded for this reason from ERISA's funding rules and termination insurance coverage.[52]

MPPAA accomplishes its goal of discouraging the underfunding of vested benefits in multi-employer pension plans by requiring a withdrawing employer to pay its share of the shortfall, known as the "withdrawal liability."[53] As the Second Circuit noted in *Trustees of Amalgamated Insurance Fund v. McFarlin's, Inc.*,[54] "[t]he withdrawal payment is not made by the withdrawing employer to his own employees but to the [multi-employer plan] in order to help defray the total unfunded vested liability of the pension plan to which he had been contributing."[55] Withdrawal liability may be triggered by the employer's cessation of covered operations, which can result from either curtailment or elimination of the business in which the covered employees were engaged.[56] The employer's rejection of a collective bargaining agreement pursuant to which the employer was obligated to contribute to a pension plan may also trigger withdrawal liability.[57]

In the Chapter 7 liquidation context,[58] a debtor's maximum withdrawal liability is reduced by 50 percent.[59] The maximum withdrawal liability for asset sales prescribed by MPPAA section 4225(a) specifically excludes "an employer undergoing reorganization under Title 11."[60] MPPAA section 4225(a) governs "an insolvent em-

---

[49] *See* 29 U.S.C. § 1002(35).

[50] *See* 29 U.S.C. § 1002(23)(B).

[51] Connolly v. PBGC, 581 F.2d 729, 733 (9th Cir. 1978), *cert. denied*, 440 U.S. 935 (1979).

[52] *See* 26 U.S.C. § 412(h); Connolly v. PBGC, *supra*. Technically, certain types of defined contribution plans, such as money purchase pension plans, *can* be underfunded.

[53] *See generally* Granada Wines, Inc. v. New England Teamsters and Trucking Industry Pension Fund, 748 F.2d 42, 44 (1st Cir. 1984); 29 U.S.C. §§ 1381–1391. In addition, the PBGC will guarantee basic benefits and provide financial assistance to an *insolvent* multi-employer plan. *See* 29 U.S.C. §§ 1322a, 1361.

[54] 789 F.2d 98 (2d Cir. 1986).

[55] *Id.* at 100.

[56] 29 U.S.C. §§ 1383(a) (complete withdrawal), 1385(a) (partial withdrawal).

[57] 29 U.S.C. §§ 1383(a)(1) (withdrawal triggered by cessation of "obligation to contribute under the plan"), 1385(a)(2), (b)(2)(A).

[58] 11 U.S.C. §§ 701 *et seq.*

[59] *See* MPPAA § 4225(b), 29 U.S.C. § 1405(b).

[60] 29 U.S.C. § 1405(a).

ployer undergoing liquidation or dissolution."[61] What limitation, if any, applies in a Chapter 11 reorganization? In *Granada Wines, Inc. v. New England Teamsters and Trucking Industry Pension Fund,*[62] the court of appeals held that "Congress equated reorganization with asset sales, rather than liquidations, and decided that that type of asset sale needed no withdrawal liability limitation."[63] Still, the withdrawal liability "should be treated like any other unsecured claim under Chapter 11."[64]

MPPAA pension withdrawal liability triggered by the debtor's rejection of a collective bargaining agreement or cessation of covered operations during a Chapter 11 reorganization constitutes a general unsecured claim against the estate.[65] Withdrawal liability claims are *not* entitled to administrative priority under section 507(a)(1) of the Code.[66] The reason for this treatment of withdrawal liability is that

> [t]he amount of the claim for withdrawal liability ... is based upon employees' services rendered prior to the commencement of the bankruptcy proceedings.... While the cessation of [the debtor's] business operations and termination of its employees may serve to preserve the estate for the benefit of all creditors, no actual value is received by the estate such as would warrant administrative status.[67]

The bankruptcy court in *In re Kessler* rejected the union's argument that withdrawal liability should be treated like severance pay under the Second Circuit's *Straus-Deparquet* analysis:[68]

---

[61] 29 U.S.C. § 1405(b).

[62] 748 F.2d 42 (1st Cir. 1984).

[63] *Id.* at 45. The court reasoned that "Congress evidently drafted the MPPAA with the Bankruptcy Court in mind, since § 4225(a) includes an express reference to Title 11. Thus, the MPPAA must be viewed as Congress' effort to balance the policies of the Bankruptcy Code with the goal of shoring up multi-employer pension plans, and any inconsistencies should be addressed to Congress, and not the Courts." *Id.*

[64] *Id.* at 47.

[65] *See In re* Kessler, 23 Bankr. 722, 724–26 (Bankr. S.D.N.Y. 1982), *aff'd sub nom.* Amalgamated Insurance Fund v. William B. Kessler, Inc., 55 Bankr. 735 (S.D.N.Y. 1985); *see also In re* Pulaski Highway Express, Inc., 41 Bankr. 305, 311 (Bankr. M.D. Tenn. 1984) (dicta), *cf. In re* Pulaski Highway Express, Inc., 57 Bankr. 502, 509 (Bankr. M.D. Tenn. 1986) (when union contract is neither rejected nor assumed, but withdrawal results from cessation of operations post-petition, portion of withdrawal liability arising from post-petition labor may be entitled to administrative priority).

[66] *In re* Kessler, *supra; accord, In re* McFarlin's Inc., 46 Bankr. 88, 90 (Bankr. W.D.N.Y. 1985) *aff'd sub nom.* Trustees of Amalgamated Ins. Fund v. McFarlin's, Inc., 789 F.2d 98 (2d Cir. 1986); *In re* Cott Corp., Bank L. Rep. (CCH) ¶ 70,034 (Bankr. D. Conn. 1984); *In re* Concrete Pipe Machinery Co., 28 Bankr. 837 (Bankr. N.D. Iowa 1983).

[67] *In re* Kessler, *supra,* 23 Bankr. at 724–25.

[68] As a bankruptcy court in the Southern District of New York, Judge Ryan was bound by the holding of *Straus-Duparquet.*

The Union herein argues that withdrawal liability, like severance pay, is compensation to the employees for the termination of the employment relationship and, as post-petition compensation, is entitled to administrative status.

However, the Union misses the obvious distinction between severance pay and withdrawal liability. Severance pay is direct compensation to an employee who works post petition and whose employment is nevertheless terminated. Such an employee has contributed to the preservation of the estate by working post petition. He is therefore entitled to the full benefits flowing directly from his employment. One such direct benefit which comes due upon termination of employment is severance pay.

Withdrawal liability, however, is not direct compensation to an employee for termination of his post petition employment relationship with the debtor in possession. . . . Therefore, withdrawal liability, unlike severance, is not entitled to administrative status.[69]

The United States District Court for the Southern District of New York affirmed Bankruptcy Judge Ryan's decision in *In re Kessler.*[70] Noting that "[t]here appears to be no judicial holding directly on point,"[71] the court applied the "well established" rules governing administrative expenses.[72] Guided by the Second Circuit's opinions in *Straus-Duparquet* and *W.T. Grant,* the Court analogized MPPAA pension withdrawal liability to vacation pay accrued pro rata prior to the debtor's entry into Chapter 11:[73]

[W]ithdrawal liability is merely a substitute for the continuing contributions a withdrawing employer would otherwise make toward fully funding vested benefits. Kessler's liability for its share of Amalgamated's unfunded vested benefits existed long before the start of the Chapter 11 proceeding. Thus, withdrawal liability is not a cost of business activity occurring during the Chapter 11 proceeding.

Withdrawal liability is not analogous to the severance pay in *Straus-Duparquet,* as is so strongly argued by Amalgamated. Severance pay is "compensation for termination of employment." *Straus-Duparquet,* 386 F.2d at 651. When termination occurs during the bankruptcy proceeding, claims for severance pay are entitled to administrative expense status because severance pay is compensation for losses terminated employees will bear after the bankruptcy proceeding commenced. Withdrawal liability, on the other hand, is imposed on employers withdrawing from multiemployer pension plans to make up for past failures by employers to fund fully pension plan benefits.

---

[69] *In re* Kessler, *supra,* 23 Bankr. at 726. *In re Kessler* was followed in *In re* Blue Ribbon Delivery Service, Inc., 31 Bankr. 292 (Bankr. W.D. Ky. 1983) and was cited with approval in *In re* Pacific Far East Line, Inc., 713 F.2d 476, 479 (9th Cir. 1983).

[70] *See* Amalgamated Insurance Fund v. William B. Kessler, Inc., 55 Bankr. 735 (S.D.N.Y. 1985).

[71] *Id.* at 739.

[72] *Id.*

[73] *Id.*

> Essentially, withdrawal liability is belated compensation for services provided before the start of bankruptcy proceeding. As such, a claim for withdrawal liability is not entitled to administrative expense status.[74]

In the first court of appeals decision on this issue, the Second Circuit recently validated the reasoning and holding of *In re Kessler.* Judge Mansfield's opinion in *Amalgamated Insurance Fund v. McFarlin's, Inc.*[75] rejected the analogy between withdrawal liability and severance pay because withdrawal liability is determined by reference to the withdrawing employer's contributions to the multi-employer pension plan prior to withdrawal,[76] not to services rendered by particular employees post-petition.

> An employer's withdrawal liability payment . . . is the means by which the employer funds benefits that his employees have "earned" by their past service and that he would normally finance through continuing contributions to his employees' pension plan. Indeed, it appears to be the general rule that when severance pay, like vacation pay, represents compensation for the employee's past services it is not an administrative expense entitled to priority. . . . The "severance pay" decisions, therefore, lend no support to the [pension plan's] contention in the present case.[77]

It is important to note that the Code's assignment of priorities for pension-related claims is applicable only to claims that arose prior to and during the debtor's reorganization under Chapter 11. Counsel for debtors who wish to reject labor contracts and pension plans maintained pursuant thereto[78] should therefore be careful to do so prior to confirmation of the Chapter 11 plan of reorganiza-

---

[74] *Id.* at 740.

[75] 789 F.2d 98 (2d Cir. 1986).

[76] *Id.* at 104; *see* 29 U.S.C. § 1391.

[77] 789 F.2d at 104 (citations omitted). The court also rejected the pension plan's argument that at least 50 percent of an insolvent employer's withdrawal liability is entitled to priority treatment under MPPAA § 4225(b), 29 U.S.C. § 1405(b). The court concluded that

> "[n]either the language nor the purpose of § 1405(b)(1) suggests that the first 50% of an employer's withdrawal liability is entitled to priority over other debts. It establishes only the extent or amount by which a fund claiming withdrawal liability against an insolvent employer will receive full creditor treatment."

789 F.2d at 105.

[78] Multi-employer plans may be terminated by rejection of the collective bargaining agreement pursuant to which they are maintained, under section 365 for Chapter 11 petitions filed from October 1, 1979, until July 9, 1984, and under section 1113 for Chapter 11 petitions filed on or after July 10, 1984. *See generally In re* Robinson Truck Line, Inc., 47 Bankr. 631, 635 (Bankr. N.D. Miss. 1985).

tion.[79] In *In re Computerized Steel Fabricators, Inc.*[80] the employer terminated its collective bargaining relationship with the union and permanently ceased all covered operations seven months *after* confirmation of a plan of arrangement under Chapter 11 of the Act, triggering a withdrawal liability claim of over $200,000. The bankruptcy court rejected the employer's argument that the withdrawal liability was extinguished by the bankruptcy court's order of confirmation:

> [A]n executory contract may be rejected in a Chapter XI case under Section 313(1) only by affirmative action and . . . unless it is so rejected, the contract continues in effect. . . . Accordingly there can be no discharge or extinguishment of the Pension Fund's claim by the order of confirmation because the Pension Fund did not have a provable claim while the union contract continued during the Chapter XI case and while the debtor continued to make contributions in accordance with MPPAA. . . . Manifestly, post-confirmation claims are not affected by the discharge.[81]

In the event of a debtor's withdrawal from the multi-employer pension plan(s) to which it was required to contribute, the trustees of the plan(s) may hold substantial claims against the estate for withdrawal liability. The size of these claims is potentially enormous, and could conceivably constitute the largest unsecured claims against the debtor. Ironically, the withdrawal liability is significantly lower if the debtor is being liquidated under Chapter 7 rather than reorganized under Chapter 11. It has been suggested that

> [i]n Chapter 11 cases in which the withdrawal liability is significant, this fact may enter into the dynamics of the debtor-creditor negotiations and may, in marginal situations, have the effect of encouraging

---

[79] *See* 11 U.S.C. § 1129. *See generally In re* U.S. Truck Co., Inc., 800 F.2d 581 (6th Cir. 1986). In *In re U.S. Truck Co.,* the union objected to a "cram down" plan of reorganization under section 1129(b) because the debtor had excluded the union's contract breach claims from a class of similar impaired claims in order to gain acceptance of the plan by the debtor's other creditors. The court upheld the debtor's segregation of the dissenting union creditors because the interests of the union differed substantially from those of the other creditors: "The Teamsters Committee's claim is connected with the collective bargaining process.

. . . [T]he Teamsters Committee has a noncreditor interest—*e.g.,* rejection will benefit its members in the ongoing employment relationship." 800 F.2d at 587.

[80] 40 Bankr. 344 (Bankr. S.D.N.Y. 1984).

[81] *Id.* at 348–49. Similarly, under both section 365 and section 1113, a debtor may reject only executory contracts. In order to convert any wage and benefit delinquencies into unsecured claims, the debtor must reject the contract, or any benefit plans maintained thereunder, prior to their expiration. *See* note 12 *supra* & accompanying text. *See also In re* The Bastian Co., 66 Bankr. 92 (Bankr. W.D.N.Y. 1986) (debtor's application to reject expired union contract and pension plan denied).

a liquidation even though a reorganization might otherwise be possible.[82]

Termination of Single-Employer Pension Plans

Under Title IV of ERISA,[83] the Pension Benefit Guaranty Corporation (PBGC) guarantees that upon termination of a single-employer plan, the PBGC will pay certain vested benefits under the plan to the extent the plan's assets are insufficient to pay those benefits.[84] The sponsoring employer is liable to the PBGC for any such insufficiency, up to 30 percent of the employer's net worth.[85] Prior to the passage of Title XI of the Consolidated Omnibus Budget Reconciliation Act of 1986 (COBRA),[86] the relevant provisions of which became effective January 1, 1986, a Chapter 11 debtor could terminate an under-funded single-employer pension plan and possibly avoid even 30 percent liability to the PBGC.[87]

Prior to COBRA, single-employer pension plans covering nonunion employees were subject to rejection under section 365(a) of the Code.[88] Single-employer plans covering union employees were subject to rejection on the same basis as multi-employer plans.[89] Employers could, and with increasing frequency did, terminate under-funded single-employer plans in Chapter 11 and transfer the pension liabilities to the PBGC. The PBGC insurance program, which is funded by premiums paid by each insured plan, reportedly had a $1.3 billion deficit as of February 1986.[90] Title XI of COBRA, entitled the Single-Employer Pension Plan Amendment Act of 1986 (SEPPAA), reflects Congress' determination that "the current termination insurance system in some instances encourages employers to terminate pension plans, evade their obligations to pay benefits,

---

[82] Novikoff & Polebaum, *Pension-Related Claims in Bankruptcy Code Cases,* 40 Bus. Law. 373, 415 (1985).

[83] 29 U.S.C. §§ 1361 *et seq.*

[84] *See* 29 U.S.C. § 1322.

[85] 29 U.S.C. § 1362.

[86] Pub. L. No. 99-272, 100 Stat. 82.

[87] *See* PBGC v. Ouimet Corp., 711 F.2d 1085, 1091–92 (1st Cir.) ("The thirty percent of net worth limitation clearly appears to eliminate the bankruptcy estates as a source of payment to PBGC because the estates have zero, actually negative, net worth. . . . There is simply no provision [in Title IV of ERISA] which authorizes PBGC to impose termination liability on an insolvent entity."), *cert. denied,* 104 S. Ct. 393 (1983). *Cf.* 29 U.S.C. § 1362(d)(1) (successor entity will be liable if reorganization "involves a mere change in identity, form, or place of organization").

[88] *See* 11 U.S.C. § 365(a); *In re* Bastian, Inc., 45 Bankr. 717, 720–22 (Bankr. W.D.N.Y. 1985).

[89] *See* note 78 *supra.*

[90] *See Pension Welfare,* Wall St. J. (Feb. 3, 1986), at p. 18 (editorial).

and shift unfunded pension liabilities onto the termination insurance system and other premium-payers."[91]

As a result of SEPPAA, after January 1, 1986 an employer may terminate an under-funded single-employer plan only if the plan sponsor (including corporate parents and many affiliated entities under a broadly defined "controlled group" standard) qualifies under one of the three specified "distress" tests at the time of termination: (1) the sponsor is in a pending liquidation proceeding in bankruptcy; (2) the sponsor is in a pending reorganization proceeding in bankruptcy *and* the bankruptcy court approves the termination; or (3) the sponsor proves to the PBGC's satisfaction either that the sponsor is unable to pay its debts when due and will be unable to continue in business, or that pension costs "have become unreasonably burdensome," solely as a result of a decline in the sponsor's workforce.[92] SEPPAA states that a plan sponsor may not terminate a plan if "termination would violate the terms and conditions of an existing collective bargaining agreement,"[93] but does not specify who is to make this determination, or whether a debtor's prior rejection of the union contract would satisfy this requirement.

Even if a plan sponsor qualifies for a distress termination, it will no longer be able to shift its unfunded liability to the PBGC. The controlled group of a plan sponsor that has terminated a plan is jointly and severally liable to the PBGC, to the plan, and to a new "post-termination trust" established to pay additional benefits to plan participants.[94] Under SEPPAA the plan sponsor is liable to the PBGC for unfunded guaranteed benefits up to 30 percent of the combined positive net worths of all entities within the sponsor's controlled group, plus 75 percent of the amount of guaranteed benefits in excess of 30 percent of net worth, plus interest from the date of termination.[95]

SEPPAA purports to make its provisions the exclusive means of terminating under-funded single-employer plans,[96] but the statute as passed and the legislative history are not clear on this point.[97] In any event, SEPPAA requires the plan administrator to provide

---

[91] SEPPAA § 11002(4), 100 Stat. 237.

[92] SEPPAA § 11009, 100 Stat. 248–50.

[93] SEPPAA § 11007, 100 Stat. 244.

[94] Kershaw, *COBRA Puts New Bite Into Pension Terminations,* Nat'l L.J. (May 5, 1986), at p.15; SEPPAA § 11011.

[95] Kershaw, *supra* note 94, at 15; SEPPAA § 11011.

[96] SEPPAA § 11007.

[97] *See* Kershaw, *supra* note 94, at 15; 131 Cong. Rec. H13252 (daily ed. Dec. 19, 1985) ("The distress termination criteria are not intended to make any substantive changes in the bankruptcy laws. The conferees take no position on when or whether a pension plan is an executory contract.").

60 days' notice of termination to each affected party, including all plan participants and beneficiaries, the employees' union representative, if any, and the PBGC.[98] Any person adversely affected by the termination, or any union that represents an adversely affected person, may sue the sponsor in federal district court for injunctive or other appropriate equitable relief. The PBGC has the right to intervene in any such action.[99]

Many of SEPPAA's complex provisions will undoubtedly have to be clarified through judicial interpretation.

Of all the areas in which bankruptcy law intersects with other fields of law, the bankruptcy treatment of pension-related claims under ERISA is the most complex. This chapter is intended as an overview of the bankruptcy status of claims for employee compensation and benefits, and obviously does not analyze all aspects of issues arising from termination of multi-employer and single-employer pension plans.[100] Debtors and their bankruptcy counsel would be well-advised to consult with pension specialists during reorganization in Chapter 11.

---

[98] SEPPAA § 11007, 100 Stat. 244.

[99] Kershaw, *supra* note 94, at 18; SEPPAA § 11014.

[100] For a comprehensive discussion of pension claims in bankruptcy, *see* Labor and ERISA Law, *supra* note 42; Dowdle & Morgan, *Employee Benefit Claims in Bankruptcy*—Gulliver's Travels *Revisited,* in 2 Pension, Profit-Sharing, and Other Deferred Compensation Plans (ALI-ABA, ed. 1985); Novikoff & Polebaum, *supra* note 82; Soble, Eggertsen & Bernstein, *Pension-Related Claims in Bankruptcy,* 56 Am. Bankr. L. J. 155 (1982); Soble, *Bankruptcy Claims of Multiemployer Pension Plans,* 33 Labor L. J. 57 (1982); and Perkins, *Pension Claims in Bankruptcy,* 32 Labor L. J. 343 (1981). For a discussion of the implications of ERISA to an individual-debtor under Chapter 7, *see* Wohl, *Pension and Bankruptcy Laws: A Clash of Social Policies,* 64 N.C. L. Rev. 3 (1985).

CHAPTER XI

The Appointment of Union Representatives to Chapter 11 Creditors' Committees[1]

When a company files for reorganization under Chapter 11 of the Bankruptcy Code,[2] the financial interests of its business creditors are suddenly and dramatically affected. When, how, and whether the debts owed creditors will be paid are no longer determined by the free play of market forces and the law of contracts, but rather by a "reorganization plan" that is subject to the approval of the bankruptcy court.

The interests of the debtor's employees and of any union representing them are also significantly affected by a Chapter 11 proceeding, albeit in a slightly different way. Although employees have interests like any other creditor with respect to back wages, accrued fringe benefits, and the like, they have an even more compelling interest in the Chapter 11 proceeding's effect upon their present and future relationship with the debtor-employer. While the Bankruptcy Code provides some degree of priority to wage and pension claims,[3] individual employees are essentially left to the mercy of the process. On the other hand, unions representing organized employees have made more vigorous attempts to vindicate employee and union interests in Chapter 11 reorganizations. Such interests, moreover, almost always derive, directly or indirectly, from a collective bargaining agreement between the union and the debtor-employer. The contract-rejection procedures of section 1113 of the Bankruptcy Code provide some degree of protection for those interests, and even if the contract is rejected the NLRA still requires the debtor-employer to continue to bargain with the union over the terms of a new collective agreement.

[1] Portions of this chapter originally appeared in Haggard, *The Appointment of Union Representatives to Creditors' Committees Under Chapter 11 of the Bankruptcy Code*, 35 S.C.L. Rev. 517 (1984).

[2] 11 U.S.C. §§ 101–151326 (1984).

[3] 11 U.S.C. § 507(a)(3), (4) (1984); *see generally* Chapter X *supra*.

It is still unclear exactly how, as a practical matter, these contract rejection procedures and bargaining duties will mesh with the normal Chapter 11 reorganization process or how they will affect the negotiations that the debtor conducts with an official committee of its unsecured creditors, a group whose role in the reorganization process is substantial. The matter is complicated further by the fact that unions are increasingly seeking additional protection of their interests by claiming "creditor" status and then petitioning for an appointment to the committee of creditors.[4]

Although such an appointment was affirmed by the Third Circuit in *In re Altair Airlines,*[5] the matter is not entirely free of doubt. This chapter will explore the parameters of the problem, with particular emphasis on the effect of the new legislation upon the union's role in a Chapter 11 reorganization.

CREDITORS' COMMITTEES IN GENERAL

Under Chapter 11, the court must appoint a committee of creditors, "as soon as practicable,"[6] to represent the interests of the general, unsecured creditors.[7] This committee consists of the persons who hold the seven largest claims of this type, provided they are willing to serve in that capacity.[8] It is not necessary that these seven largest claimholders be representative of *all* of the different kinds of general, unsecured creditors, *i.e.* represent institutional and trade creditors in the exact proportion of those types of claims asserted

---

[4] *See generally A Louder Union Voice in Settling Bankruptcies,* Bus. Wk., Dec. 8, 1980, at 87, 90.

[5] 727 F.2d 88 (3d Cir. 1984). The court of appeals cited several other instances in which labor organizations had been appointed to creditors' committees. *Id.* at 89 n. 2. However, as the bankruptcy court in *Altair* earlier pointed out, "in those cases, the issue of the [union's] right to serve on the committees does not appear to have been considered by the courts. Certainly, there was no objection raised by the debtors as in the case at bench." *In re* Altair Airlines, Inc., 25 B.R. 223, 225 (Bankr. E.D. Pa. 1982). *See also In re* Northeast Dairy Coop. Fed'n, 59 Bankr. 531 (Bankr. N.D. N.Y. 1986) (appointed a representative of the union and a representative of the pension fund); *In re* Enduro Stainless, Inc., 59 Bankr. N.D. Ohio, 1986); *In re* Salant Corp., 53 Bankr. 158 (Bankr. S.D. N.Y. 1985) (court refused to appoint a separate employees' creditors' committee, but ordered that a representative of each of the two unions and a representative of the nonunionized employees be added to the official creditors' committee). *But see, In re* Allied Delivery Sys., Bankr. 85 (Bankr. N.D. Ohio, 1985) (union failed to prove that the existing committee was unrepresentative).

[6] 11 U.S.C. § 1102(a)(1) (1984); *see also* 11 U.S.C. § 151102(a) (1984).

[7] At the request of a "party in interest," the court may also appoint additional committees of creditors or equity security holders if necessary to assure adequate representation of their interest. 11 U.S.C. § 1102(a)(2) (1984).

[8] 11 U.S.C. § 1102(b)(1) (1984).

against the debtor,[9] but some degree of balance is obviously desirable. Alternatively, members of the unofficial committee organized by the creditors before the order for relief may be appointed to the official committee if they were fairly chosen and are representative of the different kinds of claims against the debtor.[10]

The functions of a Chapter 11 creditors' committee are broad and varied. Section 1103(c) provides, first, that the committee may "consult with the trustee or debtor in possession concerning the administration of the case."[11] Presumably, that ability will now include a right of consultation over the debtor-employer's prerejection proposal to the union. Normally, a debtor submits orders to the committee prior to submitting them to the court, and thus allows the committee to review the proposed actions and make its own determinations.[12] The legitimate purview of the committee would therefore extend to evaluating and commenting upon the debtor-employer's formal application to the bankruptcy court for permission to reject the contract.

The investigatory function of a creditors' committee is also very important in a Chapter 11 proceeding, particularly when the reorganization is large and complex. The Code provides that a committee may "investigate the acts, conduct, assets, liabilities, and financial condition of the debtor, the operation of the debtor's business, and the desirability of the continuance of such business, and any other matter relevant to the case or to the formulation of a plan."[13] This would seem to give the committee virtually carte blanche access to the debtor's financial records, a right considerably broader than that of the union under the recent Code's provision for "such relevant information as is necessary to evaluate the [employer's] proposal."[14]

Finally, the committee is authorized to participate in the formulation of the debtor's reorganization plan and to solicit acceptances or rejections of that plan from various creditors.[15] If the debtor should lose its exclusive right to file a plan, the committee, or any other "interested party," may file one.[16] As a practical matter, the

---

[9] *See* DeNatale, *The Creditors' Committee Under the Bankruptcy Code—A Primer,* 55 AM. BANKR. L.J. 43, 50 (1981).
[10] 11 U.S.C. § 1102(b)(1) (1984).
[11] 11 U.S.C. § 1103(c)(1) (1984).
[12] *See* DeNatale, *supra* note 9, at 52.
[13] 11 U.S.C. § 1103(c)(2) (1984).
[14] 11 U.S.C. § 1113(b)(1)(B) (1984).
[15] 11 U.S.C. § 1103(c)(3) (1984).
[16] 11 U.S.C. § 1121(c) (1984).

negotiation of a reorganization plan is often the most important and complicated function the committee performs.

It is apparent, therefore, that the creditors' committee plays an important role in a Chapter 11 reorganization proceeding.[17] Accordingly, it is not surprising that unions representing a debtor's employees seek to participate in the reorganization process through membership on such a committee.

PROBLEMS ASSOCIATED WITH THE APPOINTMENT OF UNION REPRESENTATIVES TO CREDITORS' COMMITTEES

In many respects, labor unions are unique institutions, in large part because of their unique relationship with both the employees they represent and with the employers with which they negotiate collective bargaining agreements. Most labor unions are, in a legal sense, "unincorporated associations";[18] membership in these employee associations is voluntary and is a matter of contract.[19] One of the usual terms of the membership contract is that the employee-member appoints the union as his or her agent to negotiate and agree upon the terms and conditions of the employee-member's employment with a particular employer.[20]

A union's power to represent employees is, however, considerably broader than its ability to bargain on behalf of its actual members. Under federal law, once a union is selected as bargaining representative by a majority of employees in a particular employment unit, that union becomes the exclusive bargaining representative of *all* the employees in that unit, whether or not they are members of the union or individually consent to such representation.[21] At that point, the union has not only that *power,* but also the *duty* to provide "fair representation" to each employee for whom it is a statutory agent.[22] Unlike other business entities with which an employer might possibly contract, a union has the power under

[17] *See In re* Johns-Manville, 26 B.R. 919, 925 (Bankr. S.D.N.Y. 1983).

[18] At common law unions could neither sue nor be sued in their own name. *See, e.g.,* Baskins v. UMWA, 150 Ark. 398, 234 S.W. 464 (1921); Pickett v. Walsh, 192 Mass. 572, 78 N.E. 753 (1906). Section 301 of the Labor Management Relations (Taft-Hartley) Act, 29 U.S.C. § 185(b) (1982), changed that as a matter of federal law, and most states have also recognized the "standing" of such associations. *See* A. Thieblot & T. Haggard, Union Violence—The Record and the Response by Courts, Legislatures, and The NLRB (1983) 473 nn. 63 & 64.

[19] NLRB v. Allis-Chalmers Mfg. Co., 388 U.S. 175, 192 (1967).

[20] For an example of an authorization form used by a union, see J. Swann, NLRB Elections: A Guidebook for Employers (1980) 114–15.

[21] 29 U.S.C. § 159(a) (1982); *see generally* R. Gorman, Labor Law (1976) 374–81.

[22] Steele v. Louisville & N.R.R., 323 U.S. 192 (1944); *see generally* R. Gorman, *supra* note 21, at 695–728.

federal law to compel an employer to deal with it. Additionally, federal law dictates the subject matter and method of the bargaining process.[23] The result of the heavily regulated bargaining process, a so-called "collective bargaining agreement," is itself something of an anomaly. Under the common law, there was serious doubt whether a collective bargaining agreement was an enforceable "contract," and if so, of what sort it was.[24] Section 301 of the National Labor Relations Act (NLRA)[25] ultimately resolved the issue in favor of enforceability. Section 8(d)[26] of the NLRA also makes an employer's mid-term repudiation of a collective bargaining agreement an unfair labor practice.

The Supreme Court in *Bildisco* held that collective bargaining agreements were subject to mid-term rejection under the Bankruptcy Code and that a Chapter 11 debtor-employer's unilateral suspension of performance, pending court approval of that rejection, was not an unfair labor practice. However, the Court also stated that federal labor laws otherwise continue to apply during the reorganization process, so that the debtor-in-possession remains legally "obligated to bargain collectively with the employees' certified representative over the terms of a new contract pending rejection of the existing contract or following formal approval of rejection by the bankruptcy court."[27]

In sum, it is apparent that the nature and function of a labor union, and the statutory rights it has vis-à-vis the debtor, are radically different from those of other business entities that have an interest in Chapter 11 reorganizations. Further, the source of a union's purported interest in Chapter 11 proceedings, a collective bargaining agreement, materially differs from an ordinary commercial contract. It is therefore understandable that the appointment of labor union representatives to creditors' committees poses rather complex legal problems.

The Union as a "Creditor"

To be eligible for appointment to a creditors' committee, a union must first qualify as a "creditor." Unions generally base their argument for creditor status on one of the following four types of

[23] 29 U.S.C. § 158(a)(5), (d) (1982); *see generally* R. GORMAN, *supra* note 21, at 399–531.

[24] *See, e.g.*, Gregory, *The Collective Bargaining Agreement: Its Nature and Scope*, 1949 WASH. U.L.Q. 3, 11–13. Another leading author has noted that "[t]he collective agreement differs as much from a common contract as Humpty Dumpty differs from a common egg." Summers, *Judicial Review of Labor Arbitration or Alice Through the Looking Glass*, 2 BUFF. L. REV. 1, 17 (1952).

[25] 29 U.S.C. § 185(a) (1982).

[26] 29 U.S.C. § 158(d) (1982).

[27] 104 S. Ct. at 1201.

claims: (1) claims for withheld union dues which the debtor-employer has not forwarded to the union; (2) claims for unpaid contributions to union pension and welfare plans; (3) claims for unpaid wages and other accrued benefits; and (4) claims for damages flowing from the debtor-employer's rejection of the collective bargaining agreement.

Section 101(9) defines a "creditor" as an "entity that has a claim against the debtor that arose at the time of or before the order for relief"[28] or which the law treats as having arisen at that time. A union can easily maintain that it is an "entity." Under section 101(14),[29] an "entity" includes a "person"; under section 101(33),[30] "person" includes a "corporation"; under section 101(3),[31] "corporation" includes an "unincorporated company or association"; and the legislative history clearly indicates that Congress intended for "unincorporated associations" to include labor organizations.[32]

A labor union may have more difficulty, however, establishing that it has a "claim" against the debtor. Section 101(4) defines "claim" in terms of a "right to payment."[33] Certainly a labor union has a "right to payment" of the union dues which the employer is obligated to forward under an agreement. The other payments which the employer is obligated to make are actually owed to the individual employees (in the case of wages), to a pension fund administrator or plan (in the case of employer pension fund contributions), to an insurance carrier (in the case of insurance premiums), or to some other third party, and not to the union as an entity in its own right. With respect to these obligations, it is difficult to see how the union has a "right to payment." Indeed, failure to establish a "right to payment" was one of the reasons why the bankruptcy court in *In re Altair Airlines*[34] declined to appoint a representative of the Air Line Pilots Association to the creditors' committee of Altair Airlines. Although the debtor airline owed the pilots, in the aggregate, $676,120 in unpaid wages and fringe benefits, which was the second largest claim against it, the bankruptcy court concluded that the "right to payment" for these claims lay in the individual employees, and as a result, the Pilots

[28] 11 U.S.C. § 101(9) (1984).

[29] 11 U.S.C. § 101(14) (1984).

[30] 11 U.S.C. § 101(33) (1984).

[31] 11 U.S.C. § 101(3) (1984).

[32] H.R. Rep. No. 595, 95th Cong., 1st Sess. 309, *reprinted in* 1978 U.S. Code Cong. & Ad. News 5787, 6266; S. Rep. No. 989, 95th Cong., 2nd Sess. 22, *reprinted in* 1978 U.S. Code Cong. & Ad. News 5787. *See also In re* Schatz Federal Bearings Co., 5 B.R. 543, 546 (Bankr. S.D.N.Y. 1980).

[33] 11 U.S.C. § 101(4) (1984).

[34] 25 B.R. 223 (Bankr. E.D. Pa. 1982).

Association did not qualify for membership on the creditors' committee.[35]

The court also concluded that the Association lacked standing to assert a claim or to serve on the creditors' committee as the agent of the individual employees. While noting that under the old bankruptcy act the definition of "creditor" specifically included a "duly authorized agent, attorney, or proxy," the court observed that this language was omitted from the new Code. The court construed this omission as a clear manifestation of congressional intent to preclude the appointment of representatives to creditors' committees.[36] In this regard, the court apparently believed that the Supreme Court's decision in *Nathanson v. NLRB*[37] was implicitly superceded by certain provisions of the new Code.

The *Nathanson* Court, citing the statutory definition of "creditor" which then included the "agent" of anyone to whom a debt was owed,[38] held that the National Labor Relations Board had standing to file proof of a claim for the back wages that the Board had ordered the bankrupt to pay its employees as a result of unfair labor practices. The Court noted that

> [t]he Board is the public agent chosen by Congress to enforce the National Labor Relations Act.... A back pay order is a reparation order designed to vindicate the public policy of the statute by making the employees whole for losses suffered on account of an unfair labor practice.... Congress has made the Board the only party entitled to enforce the Act.[39]

It is unclear whether the new Code overruled *Nathanson* on this narrow question; even if it did not, its facts are easily distinguished from a situation involving a labor union's claims of "creditor" status vis-à-vis debts that have accrued to employees under a collective bargaining agreement. The latter situation does not involve the enforcement of a federal statute; failure to pay wages under a collective bargaining agreement is merely the breach of a contract,

---

[35] *Id.* at 225. In *In re* Northeast Dairy Coop. Fed'n, 59 Bankr. 351 (Bankr. N.D.N.Y. 1986), the debtor allegedly owed employees $180,000 in accrued vacation and sick leave pay, notice and severance pay, and holiday and personal pay. The court appointed the union to the creditors' committee without ever discussing the union's technical status as a creditor with respect to these claims. The court in *In re* Salant Corp., 53 Bankr. 158, 161 (Bankr. S.D. N.Y. 1985), also recognized that claims for various accrued benefits belonged to each individual non-management employee, but nevertheless ordered that group representatives be appointed to the creditors' committee.

[36] *Id.* at 224–25.

[37] 344 U.S. 25 (1952).

[38] Current version codified at 11 U.S.C. § 101(9) (1984).

[39] *Id.* at 27.

not an unfair labor practice. A breach-of-contract award for back pay, although certainly consistent with federal labor policy, is essentially a matter of private relief and not the vindication of public rights. Unlike an NLRB back pay order, which can be enforced only by the Board, debts owed under a collective bargaining agreement may be enforced by individual employees.[40]

The district court affirmed the bankruptcy court's decision in *Altair.* Although its order is unreported,[41] the district court apparently relied on language in *In re Schatz Federal Bearings Co.*[42] to support the conclusion that a union is not a creditor with respect to unpaid wage claims.[43] In *Schatz,* the union sought appointment to a creditors' committee by virtue of its claim to $462,843 in unpaid pension fund contributions. The court recognized the union as the "creditor" with respect to these monies, noting that "*unlike wages,* which are owed to and enforceable by the debtor's employees, the pension plan payments are funding contributions under a collectively bargained labor agreement."[44] The court in *Altair* interpreted this language as implying that a union would *not* qualify as a "creditor" with respect to unpaid wages, and as a result the court rejected the union's claim. On appeal, the debtor-employer in *Altair* thus characterized the test in terms of a union's right to actually "collect" the debt, in contrast to serving merely as a conduit through which the payment is made. The Third Circuit Court of

---

[40] Smith v. Evening News Ass'n, 371 U.S. 195; *In re* Cortland Container Corp., 30 B.R. 715 (Bankr. N.D. Ohio 1983). *Contra In re* Braniff Airways, Inc., 33 B.R. 1 (Bankr. N.D. Tex. 1983), where the court unequivocally stated, in connection with a suit over alleged improperties in the administration of a collective bargaining agreement pension plan, that "[t]he individual workers have no standing to assert claims based on alleged violations of a collective bargaining agreement." *Id.* at 3. The court, however, was undoubtedly mistaken. The authority cited by the court, Ramsey v. Signal Delivery Serv., Inc., 631 F.2d 1210, 1212 (5th Cir. 1980), stands for the proposition that individual employees cannot be sued for *their* breaches of the collective bargaining agreement, a correct conclusion. *See* Atkinson v. Sinclair Ref. Co., 370 U.S. 238 (1962). The court in *Braniff* erred in assuming that the converse of that is also true.

[41] *See In re* Altair Airlines, Inc., 727 F.2d 88, 88 (3d Cir. 1984).

[42] 5 B.R. 543 (Bankr. S.D.N.Y. 1980).

[43] 727 F.2d at 89 (the court of appeals indicated that the district court had relied on *Schatz*).

[44] 5 B.R. at 545 (emphasis added). The distinction drawn by the court in *Schatz* is unconvincing. First, unpaid wages are usually no less an obligation "under a collective bargaining agreement" than are unpaid pension contributions. Second, the wage provisions of a collective bargaining agreement are as "enforceable" by a union as they are by individual employees. Finally, pension payments are not usually paid to the union any more than are wage payments. Indeed, in *Schatz,* the pension payments were to be made to a specific insurance company, a company which the debtor had correctly listed as a "creditor" in the case. *But cf.* Johnson v. England, 356 F.2d 44, 51 (9th Cir. 1966), *cert. denied,* 384 U.S. 961 (1966) (identifying the employees as "creditors" with respect to unpaid pension fund contributions).

Appeals found this distinction "entirely too metaphysical."[45] The court noted that the Bankruptcy Code recognizes estates and trusts as entities capable of having claims against debtors, and that "[t]he representative capacity of such fiduciaries is essentially no different for purposes of participation in a creditors' committee, than the representative capacity, under federal common law, of a labor organization."[46]

The court of appeals in *Altair* adopted a different test for determining whether an entity like a labor union has a "right to payment," and is therefore a "creditor" with a "claim" against the debtor, thus making the union eligible to serve on a creditors' committee, by focusing on the entity's standing to bring the claim. Under the *Altair* analysis, an entity with standing to sue on a claim is necessarily a "creditor" with respect to that claim. Noting that federal law permits a labor union to enforce the terms of a collective bargaining agreement in the federal courts, including suits for unpaid wages and vacation pay, the court apparently concluded that, as a matter of logic, a union is a "creditor" with respect to those wage claims.[47] The notion that having the right to sue to enforce the contract under which a debt arises makes one a "creditor" in the statutory sense was explored more fully by the bankruptcy court in *Schatz. Schatz,* in fact, adopted the standing test as controlling with respect to unpaid pension fund contributions.[48] This standing-equals-creditor analysis, however, is flawed. Under federal law, many entities, including the Secretary of Labor,[49] have authority to enforce an employer's contractual obligation to fund a pension plan. Not all of these entities, however, have a "claim" against the debtor in the sense that they have a "right to payment."[50] Addi-

---

[45] 727 F.2d at 90.

[46] *Id.* The court's analogy, however, ignores certain distinctions. Trusts and estates *are* entitled to "collect" debts owed the beneficiary or deceased, and payment to the trust or estate discharges the debt. P. HASKELL, PREFACE TO THE LAW OF TRUSTS 107 (1975); RESTATEMENT (SECOND) OF TRUSTS, § 177 (1959). In contrast, a union has no right to collect or to receive the wages due an employee, and any such payment would certainly not discharge the employer's debt to the employee.

[47] 727 F.2d at 90. *But see In re* Continental Airlines Corp., 64 Bankr. 874, 878–80 (Bankr. S.D. Tex. 1986) (applying Railway Labor Act rather than NLRA law, the court concluded that a union has no standing to enforce employee wage claims in the absence of clear and specific authorization from the individual).

[48] 5 B.R. at 547–48. The court concluded that although the union had no right to sue under the Employee Retirement Income Security Act of 1974 (ERISA), 29 U.S.C. §§ 1001–1461 (1982), it could sue under § 301 of the Labor Management Relations (Taft-Hartley) Act, 29 U.S.C. § 185(a) (1982), because the employer's funding obligation under the pension plan had been incorporated by reference into the terms of the collective bargaining agreement.

[49] 29 U.S.C. § 1132(a)(5) (1982).

[50] *See* Soble, Eggerstsen & Bernstein, *Pension Related Claims in Bankruptcy,* 56 AM. BANKR. L.J. 155, 174 (1982).

tionally, the *Schatz/Altair* approach fails to account for the difference between a "right to payment" and a "right to compel payment." Although the triangular employer/union/employee relationship and the collective bargaining agreement regulating it are unique in many respects, the closest common law analogy is to a third party beneficiary arrangement. In the simplest example of a third party beneficiary arrangement, A, for adequate consideration, makes a promise to B to pay C $100. If A fails to perform and C's rights under the contract have vested, then C may sue to recover the $100. C, in other words, has a "right to payment" of $100; C has a "claim" against A; and C is thus a "creditor" under the Code. B, of course, would also have a cause of action, because A has breached the contract. B could thus sue to compel A to make payment to C. B's suit, however, would have to be in the form of an equitable action for specific performance; under the Bankruptcy Code, a right to an equitable remedy does not give rise to a "claim" unless the breach could also be translated into monetary damages.[51] Certainly the original obligee of a third party beneficiary contract may suffer monetary damages when the obligor fails to make payment to the beneficiary. However, the measure of those damages is not the amount the obligor promised to pay to the beneficiary; it is the economic injury that the original obligee suffered as a consequence of the breach. With respect to those damages, the obligee B clearly has a "right to payment" or a "claim" against the obligor A in that amount, and is thus a "creditor" who, if the amount of that claim is among the top seven claims, is entitled to sit on the creditors' committee.

The right of the union representative to be a member of the creditors' committee should be evaluated in a similar fashion. If a debtor-employer has breached its duty under the collective bargaining agreement to pay its employees' wages or to contribute to a pension or welfare fund, then the union which has suffered a breach of contract is certainly a "creditor" under the Bankruptcy Code with respect to any damages that flow to it from that breach. The ranking that the union enjoys as a creditor must be determined, however, not by reference to the total amount of payments owed to third parties (*i.e.,* payments owed to employees, pension fund administrators and others), but rather by reference to whatever incidental damages the union suffers as a result of the breach.[52]

---

[51] 11 U.S.C. § 101(4)(b) (1984); *see* 2 Collier on Bankruptcy ¶ 101.04 at 101–16.2 (15th ed. 1983).

[52] *See* Soble, Eggerstsen & Bernstein, *supra* note 50, at 174.

A union's status as the statutory "agent" of the employees does not improve its position as a would-be "creditor." This lack of creditor status does not result because agents necessarily lack standing under the Code, notwithstanding the contrary implications of *Altair*. The omission of any reference to "agents" in the Code's definition of "creditors" is more readily explained by the redundancy of any such inclusion: if a person is qualified to file a claim, then that person's agent is necessarily similarly qualified. The agent's status does not necessarily result in creditor status because being the agent of 100 creditors who each have a $100 'claim" against a debtor does not make that agent a $10,000 "creditor" under the Bankruptcy Code, whether the individual creditors are small businesses and tradesmen, or individual employees.

In sum, if the term "creditor" is given its ordinary and intended meaning, then it would be a rare case indeed in which a labor union would be legally entitled to sit on a creditors' committee. Moreover, even if the right to bring a lawsuit is sufficient to qualify the union as a creditor, there are still other reasons why an entity of this nature should not be appointed to a creditors' committee.

The "Conflict of Interest" Problem

Under the old bankruptcy act, the most common disqualification of a creditor from membership on the creditors' committee was the existence of conflicts of interest between that creditor and others.[53] Because of the increased importance of the creditors' committee under the Bankruptcy Code, it is believed that the pre-Code conflict-of-interest rules will continue to apply, perhaps even more strictly.[54] Assuming that under a broad definition of the term, a labor union somehow qualifies as a "creditor" whose claim is of sufficient size to make it otherwise eligible for membership on the creditors' committee, considerable conflict-of-interest problems remain.

The most obvious conflict arises from the fact that the union's primary interest in representing the employees often will not be the collection of the debt which qualified the union as a "creditor," but rather the immediate preservation of jobs. This interest, however, may conflict with the interests of the other creditors in re-

---

[53] Meir & Brown, *Representing Creditors' Committees Under Chapter 11 of the Bankruptcy Code,* 56 AM. BANKR. L.J. 217, 219 (1982).

[54] *Id.* The House Report referred to creditors' committees as "*representative* bodies which must speak for groups of creditors *with similar interests.*" H. R. REP. No. 595, 95th Cong., 2nd Sess. 235 (1977), *reprinted in* 1978 U.S. CODE CONG. & AD. NEWS 5963 (emphasis added). *See also In re* Johns-Manville Corp., 26 B.R. 919, 924–25 (Bankr. S.D.N.Y. 1983).

ducing the workforce or liquidating the business in order to preserve the debtor's estate.[55]

The conflict-of-interest argument has not been well received by the courts. The court in *Altair* responded that "[s]uch conflicts of interest are not unusual in reorganizations. Materialman creditors, for example, may sometimes prefer to forego full payment for past sales in hopes of preserving a customer, while lenders may prefer liquidation and prompt payment."[56] Moreover, one of the functions of the creditors' committee is to study the debtor's business and "the desirability of the continuance of such business."[57] The court further reasoned that if the voice of the creditor most interested in continuance is not heard, the committee cannot make a fair and reasoned decision on that issue.[58] The *Altair* court's reasoning is unpersuasive. First, it simply assumes that materialman creditors would likewise not be subject to disqualification due to divergency of their interests from those of other creditors.[59] Indeed, in such a situation, two committees might be appropriate.[60] Further, the union's interest in being heard can be served in other ways. If the union qualifies as a "creditor," it must approve the plan, or, if it is a "cram down," it can defeat the plan by showing that it is not "fair and equitable."[61] And even if the union is not a "creditor," the Code itself contemplates the right of a "party in interest" to be heard on the merits of a reorganization plan.[62] More specifically, Bankruptcy Rule 2018(d) provides:

---

[55] *See* Soble, Eggerstsen & Bernstein, *supra* note 50, at 174. *Accord, In re* U.S. Trucking Co. 800 F.2d 581 (union interest in ongoing employment relationship justifies putting it in a separate creditor classification for plan-confirmation purposes). Court in *In re* Salant Corp., 53 Bankr. 158 (Bankr. S.D.N.Y. 1985) *seemed* to recognize that the employees' primary interest was in continued employment, since their individual claims were relatively small; the court, however, failed to recognize the potential for conflict of interest.

[56] 727 F.2d at 90. *See also* 5 B.R. at 548.

[57] 727 F.2d at 90 (quoting 11 U.S.C. § 1103(c)(2)).

[58] *Id.* at 90–91. In should be noted that as soon as the bankruptcy court in *Schatz* approved the sale of the debtor's business to a third party, with whom the union then negotiated a new labor contract, the union sought and obtained the court's permission to withdraw from the committee. Such a course of conduct may be taken as evidence of the narrowness of the union's interest in these matters. *In re* Schatz Federal Bearings Co., 11 B.R. 363 (S.D.N.Y. 1981).

[59] *See generally* 5 Collier Bankruptcy Practice Guide ¶ 83.03[2] (1984) (the existence of possible adverse interests should not automatically bar an unsecured creditor from serving on a creditors' committee).

[60] *See* 5 Collier on Bankruptcy ¶ 1102.02 at 1102–14 (15th ed. 1983) ("where there are significant groups of creditors or equity security holders with conflicting claims which are likely to be affected by the plan of reorganization, the court should authorize the appointment of additional committees").

[61] 11 U.S.C. § 1129(b)(1) (1984).

[62] 11 U.S.C. § 1109(b) (1984); *see* Soble, Eggerstsen & Bernstein, *supra* note 50, at 174 n. 113.

> In a Chapter 9 or 11 case, a labor union or employees' association, representative of employees of the debtor, shall have the right to be heard on the economic soundness of a plan affecting the interests of the employees but it may not appeal from any judgment, order, or decree in the case unless otherwise permitted by law.[63]

Alternatively, it has been suggested that a union representative be appointed as an ex officio, nonvoting member of the creditors[64] or otherwise asked to participate informally in some of the committee's functions.[65] Either approach would allow due recognition to the union's primary interest in the preservation of jobs, while preventing that recognition from conflicting with the other creditors' primary interests in collecting their debts.

There are, however, additional conflict-of-interest problems. One problem arises when the union's status as a "creditor" is allegedly based on the debtor-employer's unpaid contributions to a pension plan. As the surrogate creditor, the union would be expected to represent all of the intended beneficiaries of the plan, including active employees *and* retirees. The two groups, however, do not have concurrent interests. Active employees are usually more interested in preserving their jobs than they are in providing full funding to the pension plan, while pensioners have the opposite interest.[66] Moreover, the union is not free to compromise or accommodate these two interests. Under the NLRA, the union has a combined right/duty (with the emphasis here upon the element of "duty") to represent the interests of *active* employees within a collective bargaining unit.[67] In *Allied Chemical & Alkali Workers v. Pittsburgh Plate Glass Co.,*[68] the Supreme Court, in an analogous situation, held that this duty of representation precluded the union from attempting to bargain on behalf of the retired employees over certain changes the employer had made to health benefits. Similarly, if a union attempts to serve as the "representative creditor" of the beneficiaries of a pension plan, it would seem that there is a high probability of its violating one of two different fiduciary duties, either that owed under the Bankruptcy Code to all beneficiaries, including retirees, or that owed under the NLRA only to active employees within the bargaining unit.[69]

---

[63] Bankr. Rule 2018(d).

[64] DeNatale, *supra* note 9, at 57 n. 71. The union requested that in *In re* Salant Corp., 53 Bankr. 158 (Bankr. S.D.N.Y. 1985) but was turned down by the committee.

[65] 5 Collier Bankruptcy Practice Guide ¶ 83.04[1] (1984).

[66] Soble, Eggerstsen & Bernstein, *supra* note 50, at 175; DeNatale, *supra* note 9, at 57–58.

[67] *See supra* note 22.

[68] 404 U.S. 157 (1971).

[69] *Accord, In re* Century Brass Prod., Inc. 795 F.2d 265 (2d Cir. 1986) (union cannot

This conflict would not, however, preclude a union representative from serving on a creditors' committee in the capacity of a union-appointed trustee of a jointly administered Taft-Hartley Act trust.[70] In such a capacity, the union representative's real interests may still lie in favor of active employees, but the conflict of interest has already been resolved: the labor-law duty of fair representation is subordinated *by federal statute* to the duties of the plan trustee. The Employee Retirement Income Security Act (ERISA)[71] dictates that the union-appointed representatives serve the interests of all plan participants.[72] The courts have held that this fiduciary duty is breached when the exclusive interests of the union or of its active members are given priority.[73] Similar statutory protection of all plan participants is lacking, however, when a union attempts to gain creditor status in its own right rather than as a plan trustee.

The union's duty, under federal labor law, to represent vigorously the interests of bargaining unit employees may conflict with its duties as a member of the creditors' committee in yet another way. Under the recently enacted Code provisions, the debtor-employer is required to propose contract modifications that "assure that *all creditors,* the debtor and all of the affected parties are treated fairly and equitably."[74] Presumably, if the proposal meets that requirement, the members of the creditors' committee must view it favorably. As a member of that committee, a union representative would have the duty to support such a proposal or, at least, to refrain from active, partisan opposition. A proposal that is fair to "all creditors" and to other "affected parties," including equity stockholders, is not necessarily a proposal that is in the best interests of the employees as a separate class. Yet, in its capacity as the statutory bargaining representative of these employees, the union is compelled by federal law to represent only the employee's special interests, even at the expense of the interests of other creditors.[75]

---

represent retirees in the bargaining that must occur prior to a section 1113 contract rejection).

[70] *See generally* Soble, Eggerstsen & Bernstein, *supra* note 50, at 175–77 (discussing the priority that plan trustees must place upon the interests of the plan participants, as required by ERISA).

[71] 29 U.S.C. §§ 1001–1461 (1982).

[72] 29 U.S.C. § 1104(a) (1982).

[73] *See, e.g.,* Blankenship v. Boyle, 329 F. Suppl. 1089, 1094–95 (D.D.C. 1971).

[74] 11 U.S.C. § 1113(b)(1)(A) (1984).

[75] Presumably, a union's refusal to accept proposed modifications that are fair to all of the creditors as a class would be deemed "without good cause," thus freeing the court to approve the debtor-employer's rejection of the contract. That, however, is not the end of the union's influence, as it can still use economic power to prevent the debtor-employer from putting the rejection into effect. *See infra* notes 76–79 and accompanying text.

In short, the union's duties as a member of the creditors' committee are inherently inconsistent with its duties as a bargaining representative.

Moreover, while bargaining over the debtor-employer's proposed modifications, the union *apparently* retains the right to strike. The new Code provision certainly does not prohibit it. Although the bankruptcy court, under its broad section 105 equity powers,[76] would otherwise have the power to enjoin such an egregious interference with the reorganization process, in analogous contexts the courts have held that the anti-injunction provisions of the Norris-LaGuardia Act control. For example, unions have been allowed to strike to compel continued adherence to the terms of a contract even after a bankruptcy court has approved its rejection[77] and to strike in support of its demands for a new contract.[78] Although such conduct may not be affirmatively illegal under the Bankruptcy Code, it is certainly inconsistent with the fiduciary duties of a member of the creditors' committee. Such a strike not only puts the union at an unfair advantage vis-à-vis the other creditors, but, more importantly, it may frustrate the entire reorganization process, driving the debtor into an otherwise unnecessary liquidation.[79]

This conflict between a union's duty under the federal labor laws to represent vigorously the special interests of the debtor's employees and its fiduciary duties as a member of a creditors' committee is somewhat analogous to the conflict that arose in *In re Johns-Manville Corp.*[80] There, an attorney for an asbestos claimant continued a state court legal action even after Manville had filed under Chapter 11 and the automatic stay against such actions had come into effect. The attorney apparently acted on the theory that the bankruptcy court lacked jurisdiction. The court not only found the attorney in contempt, but also disqualified him from further membership on the creditors' committee. The court noted the critical role of the members of a creditors' committee in negotiating a

---

[76] 11 U.S.C. § 105(a) (1984).

[77] *See, e.g.,* Crowe & Assocs. v. Bricklayers Local 2, 713 F.2d 211 (6th Cir. 1983); Petrusch v. Teamsters Local 317, 667 F.2d 297 (2d Cir. 1981), *cert. denied,* 456 U.S. 974 (1982); Briggs Transp. Co. v. International Bhd. of Teamsters, 116 L.R.R.M. (BNA) 2241 (D. Minn. 1984).

[78] *See In re* Gray Truck Line Co., 34 B.R. 174, 179 (Bankr. M.D. Fla. 1983) (dicta).

[79] "The argument that [the debtor-employer] may go out of business absent the requested injunction is no more than a recognition that one of the unfortunate side effects of labor-management strife is economic loss to the employers and employees." *Briggs Transp. Co.,* 116 L.R.R.M. (BNA) at 2244. *See also* Crowe & Assocs., 713 F.2d at 216; Truck Drivers Local 807 v. Bohack Corp., 541 F.2d 312, 318 (2d Cir. 1976); Petrusch v. Teamsters Local 317, 14 B.R. 825, 830 (Bankr. N.D.N.Y. 1981).

[80] 26 B.R. 919 (Bankr. S.D.N.Y. 1983).

plan of reorganization, in supervising the debtor, and in protecting their constituents' interests:

> Accordingly, the individuals constituting a committee should be honest, loyal, trustworthy, and without conflicting interests, and with undivided loyalty and allegiance to their constituents.... Conflicts of interest on the part of representative persons or committees are thus not [to] be tolerated.... Thus, where a committee representative or agent seeks to represent or advance the interest of an individual member of a competing class of creditors or various interests or groups whose purposes and desires are dissimilar, this fiduciary is in breach of his duty of loyal and disinterested service.[81]

The court then found that in at least three ways the attorney's functions on the committee and his larger fiduciary duty to the estate were in conflict with his actions and duties on behalf of a single claimant. First, the court noted that in the state court proceeding the attorney was contesting the very jurisdiction of the bankruptcy court, while as a committee member he was sanctioning the bankruptcy court's jurisdiction by working within its framework to foster his constituents' interests in the context of a reorganization plan.[82] A union which strikes over the proposed rejection of a collective bargaining agreement and then contests the bankruptcy court's jurisdiction to enjoin that strike would be in a similar position.[83]

Second, the court in *Manville* noted that the attorney's actions in independently prosecuting a law suit in state court were "designed to benefit his client ... and/or his own private interests in particular as opposed to benefitting [sic] all members of the asbestos claimants class which he represents as a committee member and fiduciary."[84] The court pointed out that because the interests of a single asbestos litigant may differ substantially from the interests of all asbestos claimants, one of these interests is bound to suffer as a result of the attorney's dual representation.[85] A union's action in making interim wage and benefit demands, in going on strike to

---

[81] *Id.* at 925.

[82] *Id.* at 926.

[83] Although several lower courts have held that the Norris-LaGuardia Act deprives the bankruptcy court of jurisdiction to enjoin such a strike, see cases cited *supra* at notes 77–78; the Supreme Court has never addressed the question. Thus, the correctness of those decisions may certainly be questioned. *See generally* Note, *The Automatic Stay of the 1978 Bankruptcy Code Versus the Norris-LaGuardia Act: A Bankruptcy Court's Dilemma,* 61 Tex. L. Rev. 321 (1982). Because the issue is still unsettled, it is quite probable that a union might pursue the dual strategy of striking over a collective bargaining agreement and contesting the jurisdiction of the bankruptcy court to enjoin the strike.

[84] 26 B.R. at 926.

[85] *Id.*

enforce them, or even in filing unfair labor practice charges would similarly be expected to benefit the special interests of the union and of the employees it represents, rather than the creditors as a class, who may indeed be positively harmed by such conduct.

Third, the court noted that as a member of the committee the attorney had access to confidential information regarding Manville's reorganization plans and operations, "which information is not intended to be used in fostering the rights of private litigants outside the context of protecting these creditors as a group in these bankruptcy proceedings."[86] In *Schatz,* a similar objection was made to the appointment of the union to the creditors' committee, but the court discounted it. There, the court reasoned that because of the employer's status as a Chapter 11 debtor, much of the information revealed to the creditors' committee could be obtained by the union through alternative channels.[87] It is not clear exactly what the court had in mind. The new labor provisions of the Bankruptcy Code would, of course, have entitled the union to whatever information it needed in order to evaluate the debtor-employer's proposed modifications.[88] Also, to the extent that it applies to bargaining at that stage,[89] the LMRA would impose a similar duty.[90] However, the quantum and nature of information that the union may obtain as a member of the creditors' committee is considerably broader. Apparently recognizing the inherent danger of granting a union free access to the debtor-employer's business files and records, the court in *Schatz* also noted that it had the power to issue protective orders.[91]

The *Johns-Mansville* type of conflict of interest was arguably present in *In re Enduro Stainless, Inc.*[92] There, the debtor-employer argued

[86] *Id. See also In re* Wilson Foods Corp., 31 B.R. 272 (Bankr. W.D. Okla. 1983) (disqualification of a creditor who also happened to be a substantial competitor).

[87] 5 B.R. at 548.

[88] 11 U.S.C. § 1113(b)(1)(B) (1984). The court may also enter a protective order where further disclosure by the union "would compromise the position of the debtor with respect to its competitors in the industry in which it is engaged." 11 U.S.C. § 1113(d)(3) (1984).

[89] *See* Chapter IV, nn. 261–263 and accompanying text.

[90] Under the Labor Management Relations (Taft-Hartley) Act, 29 U.S.C. § 158(a)(5) (1982), a union has a right to obtain from the employer information that is directly relevant to the union's collective bargaining duties. *See generally* C. Morris, The Developing Labor Law 606–29 (2d ed. 1983). In particular, when an employer claims an "inability to pay," as would the debtor in the context of bankruptcy, then it must be possible to substantiate that claim with relevant financial data. NLRB v. Truitt Mfg. Co., 351 U.S. 149 (1956).

[91] 104 Bankr. at 548. *See also, In re* Enduro Stainless, Inc., 59 Bankr. 603, 605 (Bankr. N.D. Ohio, 1986).

[92] 59 Bankr. 603 (Bankr. N.D. Ohio, 1986).

> [T]he fact that the Union has been unavailable for negotiations with management, has met with a competitor regarding an employee buyout of the plant, has indicated that it is considering requesting appointment of a trustee, presumably will oppose any rejection of the labor contract and is involved in pending NLRB litigation against Enduro, all support denial of the USWA's appoint.[93]

The court, however, held that until "such actions are taken indicative of some breach or conflict, the court should not deny a creditor a position on a creditors' committee based upon 'speculation.' "[94]

There may be other reasons why the appointment of a union representative to the creditors' committee would be inappropriate. For example, in *In re Allied Delivery Sys.,*[95] the court noted that the priority claimants represented by the union were different from the other general unsecured claimants, that an adversarial relationship existed between the union and the debtor-employer because of the breakdown in negotiations and the filing of an unfair labor practice charge, and that the insurance fund that the union sought to represent had been appointed to the committee but declined to serve.

Certainly, the employees of a Chapter 11 debtor-employer, and the union representing them, have a legitimate interest in an attempted reorganization. It is not an interest, however, that warrants membership on the official unsecured creditors' committee. A union qualifies as a major "creditor" only in a loose and figurative sense of the word. Even if the prevailing definition of that term is correct, the union's real or primary interest will often lie not in the collection of the funds owed it or its members, already afforded some degree of priority, but in insuring the continuation of the business. Thus, a union would obtain membership on the creditors' committee by reference to one interest, but then use that membership to promote quite a different interest.[96]

Moreover, a union's duties as the employees' exclusive bargaining agent under the federal labor laws potentially conflict with the duties that a union would have as a member of the committee. Indeed, to the extent that the union through the negotiation of high wages and restrictive work rules, may have contributed significantly to the very financial condition that the Chapter 11 debtor and its

---

[93] *Id.* at 605.

[94] *Id.*

[95] 52 Bankr. 85 (Bankr. N.D. Ohio, 1985).

[96] The court in *In re* Salant Corp., 53 Bankr. 158, 161 (Bankr. S.D.N.Y. 1985) recognized that while the desire for continued employment was understandable, eligibility for membership on a creditors' committee was predicated on an entirely different basis.

committee of creditors attempt to resolve, the union could be deemed to be in an "adversarial" position with respect to the other creditors.

The exclusion of union representatives from the official creditors' committee does not leave union and employee interests unprotected. The new Code provisions give a union rights concerning the rejection of existing collective bargaining agreements enjoyed by no other party to an executory contract with the debtor. Moreover, under the NLRA, the debtor-employer remains obliged to continue to recognize the union as the exclusive representative of its employees and to bargain with it in good faith over the terms of any new agreements that are reached. It would seem that these rights, coupled with the union's status as a "party in interest" with standing to be heard on the reorganization plan, give more than adequate protection to the interests of the employees. The presence of a union representative on the creditors' committee adds nothing to these rights and only creates unnecessary conflict and confusion in the statutory scheme.

CHAPTER XII

Conclusion

The areas of bankruptcy and labor law are extremely complex, in both theory and practice. When these two vast bodies of law cross paths, the complexity multiplies fourfold. This study has attempted to explore the details of that relationship and to suggest solutions to the many problems of reconciliation that still remain. In a broader vein, however, certain conclusions and observations emerge from this study.

First, this area of law may be *unnecessarily* complex, a condition for which Congress and the courts are equally to blame. When Congress did a major overhaul of the bankruptcy law in 1978, it seemingly ignored that most debtors are also employers subject to a multitude of federal labor and employment laws. Rather than define specifically the relationship between labor law and the new bankruptcy law, Congress chose to remain silent, thus leaving it to the courts to resolve the conflicts on a piecemeal basis. Although it is unrealistic to expect a legislature to anticipate every possible statutory conflict, congressional action in this instance borders on a dereliction of responsibility.

On the other hand, even if Congress had attended to the problem, there is no guarantee that the results would have been any more satisfactory. If the enactment of section 1113 is an example of current legislative craftsmanship and deliberation, perhaps piecemeal judicial interpretation is preferable. The congressional response to the *Bildisco* decision shows the legislative process in its poorest light. Except for the fact that labor unions felt wounded by the Supreme Court's apparent change in attitude toward them and thus frantically demanded some measure of reassurance from a more sympathetic branch of government, Congress probably would not have been inclined to alter a Supreme Court decision as unexceptional as *Bildisco.*

Section 1113 may have provided that reassurance, but it neither changed the law materially nor clarified its substance. Indeed, the section provides many fresh ambiguities and uncertainties, and the trail of current litigation seems to be heading again to the Supreme Court. Section 1113 not only deals poorly with the contract rejection issue, it also deals with it incompletely. A debtor's use of the section 1113 procedures potentially implicates several major NLRA rules and doctrines; yet, the section is silent as to the consequences of this. In sum, by omission and commission Congress has contributed appreciably to the confusion, complexity, and conflict that currently exist with respect to bankruptcy and labor law.

Although the courts have been left with the task of hauling the congressional chestnuts out of the fire, they, too, have sometimes contributed to the problem. For example, because they perceived a conflict when one arguably did not exist, the courts took the contract rejection issue down a trail of accommodation and balancing that was fraught with ambiguity and uncertainty. In other instances, the courts have dealt questionably with precedent and interpreted the statutes in an often result-oriented way, which has given the law in this area a certain bizarre, surrealist glaze.

The contract rejection issue also warrants several subsidiary observations. Although this issue has been the center of attention, its importance has probably been overestimated. Regardless of the standard for allowing or disallowing rejection, it is unlikely that many otherwise solvent employers would subject themselves to the radical procedures of bankruptcy merely to rid themselves of an unwanted collective bargaining agreement. Bankruptcy is not an expedient strategy for employers wishing to avoid the obligations of a union contract. Filing for bankruptcy entails enormous economic and operating costs. One commentator observes that "[f]iling a Chapter 11 petition to get rid of a collective bargaining agreement is like treating a headache by taking a drug with side effects known to be protracted, often fatal."[1] Moreover, it does not appear that the standard is as important as its application; the number of agreements that are successfully rejected would probably not vary appreciably regardless of which standard the courts were applying. This is because most employers seeking relief in bankruptcy *need* relief, and also because bankruptcy law (and bankruptcy courts) are sympathetic to debtors.

The most significant feature of the rejection controversy, however, is the premise that collective bargaining agreements should be treated differently from other commercial contracts. This is a dubious premise. Labor unions are mature, self-sufficient economic organizations that are as able (if not more so) to protect their interests vis-à-vis the debtor as other commercial entities. The spe-

---

[1] Kennedy, *Creative Bankruptcy? Use and Abuse of the Bankruptcy Law—Reflections on Some Recent Cases,* 71 Iowa L. Rev. 199, 213 (1985).

cial status accorded to labor unions as creditors impairs the bankruptcy policy of equality of treatment. Indeed, to the extent that the inflated wage structure of a collective bargaining agreement has contributed to the need for bankruptcy reorganization, it would seem that a more relaxed, rather than a more rigorous, standard for rejection would be more appropriate. Professor James J. White observes that

> [a]ll creditors suffer in bankruptcy. Without exception non-unionized employees find their terms of employment changed upon the filing of a petition in bankruptcy. Indeed, if it could be proven that the very inefficiencies that brought the business to its knees had been imposed by the union demands in collective bargaining, one could argue that the union contract should receive worse, not better treatment in bankruptcy. Why should union employees receive more favorable treatment?[2]

The increasingly intense international competition and domestic deregulation which American companies face sometimes make refuge in Chapter 11 an unfortunate but necessary reality. "It can hardly be doubted that some collective bargaining contracts are too burdensome to permit some employers to survive in a competitive economy."[3] The ultimate question is whether, when a company becomes financially distressed, its employees and the union which represents them should be treated differently from the company's other creditors.

With respect to other bankruptcy / labor issues, it is the thesis of this study that in achieving an accommodation between the two areas of law, if that is possible, or in holding that one statute preempts the other, if accommodation is not possible, the courts should give preeminence to the bankruptcy law interests. There are several reasons for this.

Although the current Bankruptcy Code may be poorly drafted and perhaps even misguided in its approach, it is nevertheless based on the *current* business and economic climate—a climate which includes a significant unionized segment. The bankruptcy laws implicitly take the labor element into account. The federal labor laws, on the other hand, were drafted in response to problems of an entirely different era. This is particularly true of the 1932 Norris-LaGuardia Act, the need for which has been long since totally eclipsed by a changing legal and political environment. Many commentators are also questioning the continued relevance of the

---

[2] White, *The Bildisco Case and the Congressional Response,* 30 WAYNE L. REV. 1169, 1203–04 (1984) (footnote omitted).

[3] Kennedy, *supra* note 1, at 213.

NLRA, which was passed in 1935 and substantially amended in 1947 and 1959. Even if the labor laws still properly reflect federal labor policy in the abstract, they certainly do not take into account the current federal bankruptcy policies with respect to rehabilitation of financially distressed businesses.

Moreover, bankruptcy was designed as a comprehensive solution for *all* the problems that a financially distressed company has with its creditors and the others with whom it does business. In this respect bankruptcy law is more neutral than labor law. Not all employers are debtors, and not all debtors are employers. Likewise, unions are not always the creditors in bankruptcy cases. In fact, some unions have filed for bankruptcy to discharge burdensome liabilities. In *In re American Federation of Television & Radio Artists,*[4] for instance, a union filed for reorganization under Chapter 11 to avoid paying an antitrust judgment in excess of $10 million.

Although the comprehensive nature of bankruptcy jurisdiction entails an almost impossible level of expertise in the Bankruptcy Code itself and many other state and federal statutes, bankruptcy jurisdiction is predicated on the need for such a unified approach. The labor laws, on the other hand, were designed to deal with one specific kind of problem, and the National Labor Relations Board is expected to deal only with the statutory issues that lie within its specialized expertise. In the words of Professor Frank Kennedy, "[t]he resolution of disputes between organized employees and a debtor-employer seems no less appropriately assigned to the bankruptcy court than disputes involving tax claims, securities law violations, the antitrust laws, or transportation statutes and regulations."[5] In sum, while bankruptcy can take labor law into effect, the converse is not necessarily true. The most comprehensive statute should thus generally prevail.

The final conclusion that emerges from this study—and it is one which renders the former conclusion moot to some extent—is that bankruptcy and labor law, properly construed, are largely complementary. This is evident, for example, in the symbiotic relationship that exists between arbitration and bankruptcy. Similarly, bankruptcy is not more tolerant of the employer who attempts to use Chapter 11 as a "union busting" technique than is labor law. Federal policy with respect to the other bargaining and contract issues

---

[4] 32 Bankr. 672 (Bankr. S.D.N.Y. 1982).

[5] Kennedy, *supra* note 1, at 213–14.

that can arise in a business reorganization seems to be about the same, regardless of which statutory device is applied.

Thus, while the relationship between bankruptcy and labor law is still uncertain and troubled, and will require the careful attention of the entire legal community, the problem is not insoluble. Hopefully, this study will contribute to that solution.

Index of Cases